BIRDS OF THE ISLE OF MAN

Birds of the Isle of Man

by J. P. Cullen and P. P. Jennings

Illustrated by Alan Harris

© 1986 J. P. Cullen and P. P. Jennings

ISBN 0 9511499 0 3

First published in 1986 by Bridgeen Publications,
Troutbeck, Tromode Road, Douglas, Isle of Man.

All rights reserved. No part of this book may be
reproduced, stored in a retrieval system, or
transmitted in any form or by any means, electronic,
mechanical, photocopying or otherwise, without the
permission of the publisher.

Printed in Great Britain at The Bath Press, Avon

Contents

Preface	vii
The Isle of Man	1
The Calf of Man	25
History of Manx ornithology	39
The breeding distribution maps	47
Systematic list of the birds of the Isle of Man	51
Appendix. 1. Category D species	339
Appendix. 2. Plant species mentioned in the text	340
Appendix. 3. List of Manx mammals	342
Appendix. 4. Fishes mentioned in the text	343
Gazetteer	345
Bibliography	351
Index of English and scientific names of birds	359

Preface

For over eighty years the standard work on Manx ornithology has been P. G. Ralfe's *The Birds of the Isle of Man*. This beautifully written book is almost unobtainable on the second-hand market and very few people have access to a copy. Ralfe produced a short supplement in 1924, while in 1934 H. W. Madoc's very personal *Bird-Life in the Isle of Man* was published although this could in no way be used as a comprehensive reference work. In 1956 the Manx Museum and National Trust produced a short check-list of the Island's birds which was revised in 1962 and then considerably extended in the 3rd and 4th editions of 1975 and 1983. Our own *Birds of the Isle of Man* is a summary of all that has been published about the Island's avifauna, concentrating especially on the changes which have taken place during the present century. There is a special pleasure in reading Ralfe's descriptions of this beautiful island, and in particular its coast, so we make no apology for including a number of pictorial essays from his book which we would in any case be quite incapable of matching.

In writing this book we have referred constantly to the Manx Bird Reports and the Calf of Man Bird Observatory Annual Reports and we are very grateful to all contributors to the former and to the several Calf wardens and their assistants. Additional much appreciated ringing details were produced by G. D. Craine, R. Cripps and B. Karran, while H. S. Collister, J. C. and R. Q. Crellin, K. Johnson, E. D. Kerruish, J. and M. Kneen, E. F. Ladds, P. R. Marshall, A. S. Moore, R. Watson, T. Whipp and F. Wilkinson have all provided valuable information which has never been published. We would also like to thank Mrs Anderson, P. N. Bates, H. Briggs, J. Q. Cannell, G. K. Crowe, K. Kerruish, Mrs F. Kinvig, Mrs W. Kirkpatrick, Mrs M. Moore and A. D. Radcliffe for their information regarding Corncrakes and Barn Owls and C. J. Bennett, G. Hull, the Earl of Northesk and C. K. Spittall for their help over game birds.

A very valuable source of information was the collection of diaries of Will Cowin which his brother Sidney very kindly made available to us.

We received early advice and encouragement from Dr J. T. R. Sharrock who introduced us to J. G. Dony whose advice on D.I.Y. publishing has been invaluable.

At the Manx Museum Dr L. S. Garrad was a most valuable friend, while Miss A. M. Harrison and the library staff were unfailingly helpful.

We are grateful to Dr J. W. Birch and the Cambridge University Press for permission to reproduce the map on land usage in the Isle of Man, to the British Library for permission to reproduce Daniel King's drawing of the Great Auk and to the Manx Museum for providing the photographs of the same Great Auk drawing and of Sandulf's and Thorwald's crosses.

Six other photographs were kindly taken for this publication by T. W. B. Cullen.

More than anybody we must thank Alan Harris for his illustrations, all of which were produced specially for this book and Mrs Pat McRuvie for typing (and all too often patiently retyping) the manuscript.

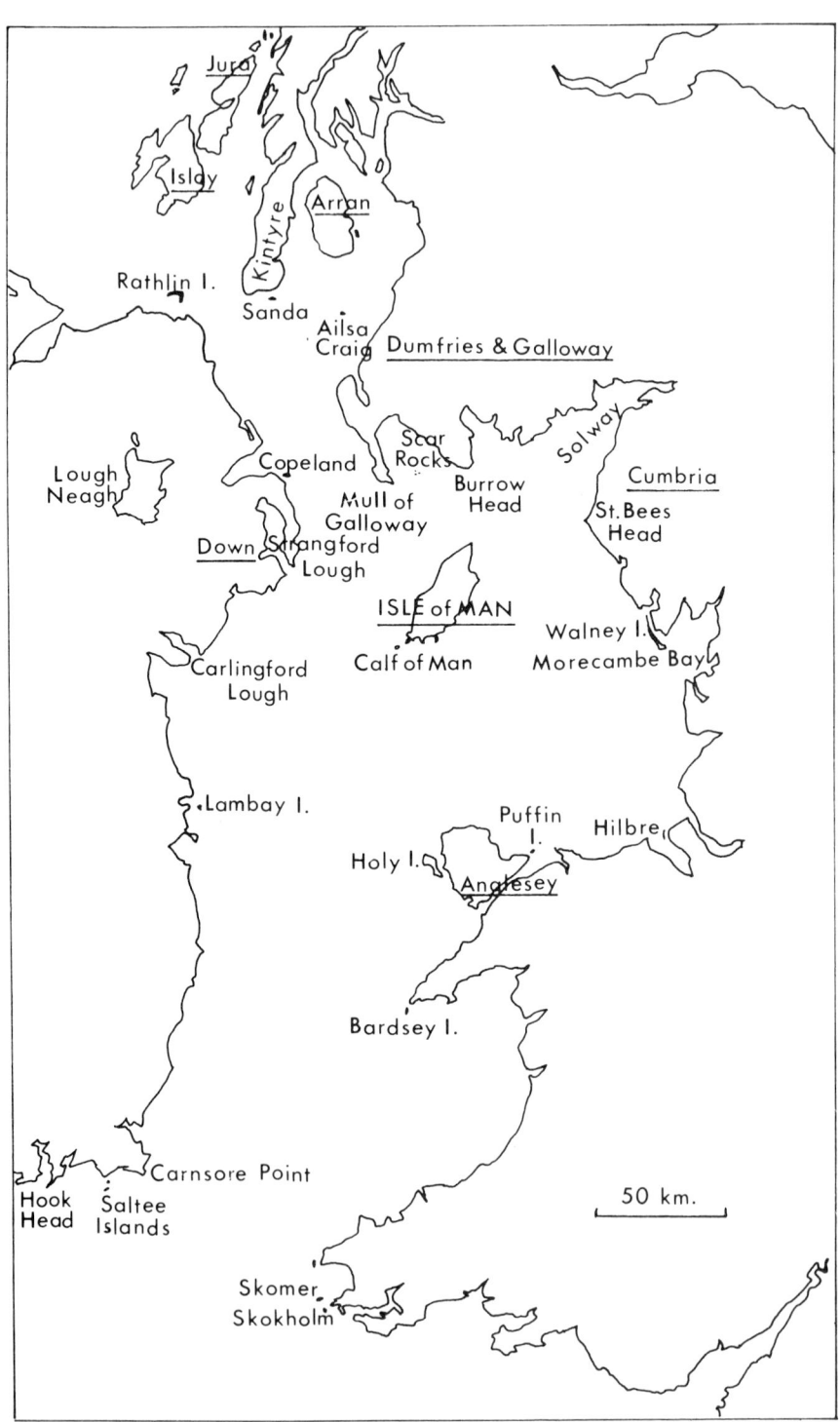

The Irish Sea

The Isle of Man

The Isle of Man lies in the northern part of the Irish Sea being roughly equidistant from the coasts of Cumbria and County Down and rather closer to the Galloway coast. It is situated between latitude 54°4′N and 54°22′N and longitude 4°20′W and 4°50′W. It is 51 km long, has a maximum breadth of 21 km, covers an area of 588 sq. km and has a coastline circumference of about 120 km. The nearest point on the adjacent islands is Burrow Head, lying just 29 km north of the Point of Ayre, while St Bees Head is 48 km to the east. The entrance to Strangford Lough is 53 km from Contrary Head on the Island's west coast and the northern most point of Anglesey is 70 km due south of Langness. Sulby village occupies the mid-point of a straight line joining Land's End and John O'Groat's.

On clear days the proximity of southern Scotland can be quite startling when seen from the roads which descend from the northern hills. The different colours of the coastal landscape from the Mull of Galloway to the Solway can be amazingly clear, backed by the sharply defined outlines of Cairnsmore of Fleet, Cairnharrow, Screel Hill and Criffel away to the east. Nowadays the most prominent features of the Cumbrian coast are the chimneys of Seascale, and beyond, dominating a mass of great hills are the tops of Great Gable, Great End, Scafell Pike and Scafell – to the south the outline of Black Combe is unmistakable. Slieve Donard dominates the Mountains of Mourne, which can often be seen from the southern hills, while Snowdonia and Anglesey are frequently visible from the Calf.

Topography of the Isle of Man

The Island consists of a main central mass of highland starting at Maughold Head and continuing in a south-westerly direction to Bradda Head. This hill mass is made up of three parts – the northern most and largest rises via North Barrule and Clagh Ouyr to the highest point – Snaefell summit (621 m), and then falls away over a number of substantial hills to the central valley. In all there are 19 peaks in excess of 400 m grouped in several ranges separated by the valleys of the Sulby, Glen Auldyn, Cornaa, Laxey, Glass and Rhenass rivers. The central valley is formed by the Rivers Dhoo and Neb which flow into the sea at Douglas and Peel respectively.

Slieau Whallian is the first feature of the smaller southern hill mass which is dominated by South Barrule (483 m) and Cronk ny iree laa (437 m) whose steep western slopes, together with those of the humbler Lhiattee ny Beinnee, fall away impressively into the sea. The Carnanes slope gently down to the little Fleshwick valley, beyond which is the third and smallest piece of high ground – Bradda Hill. Although rising to only 233 m Bradda possesses some

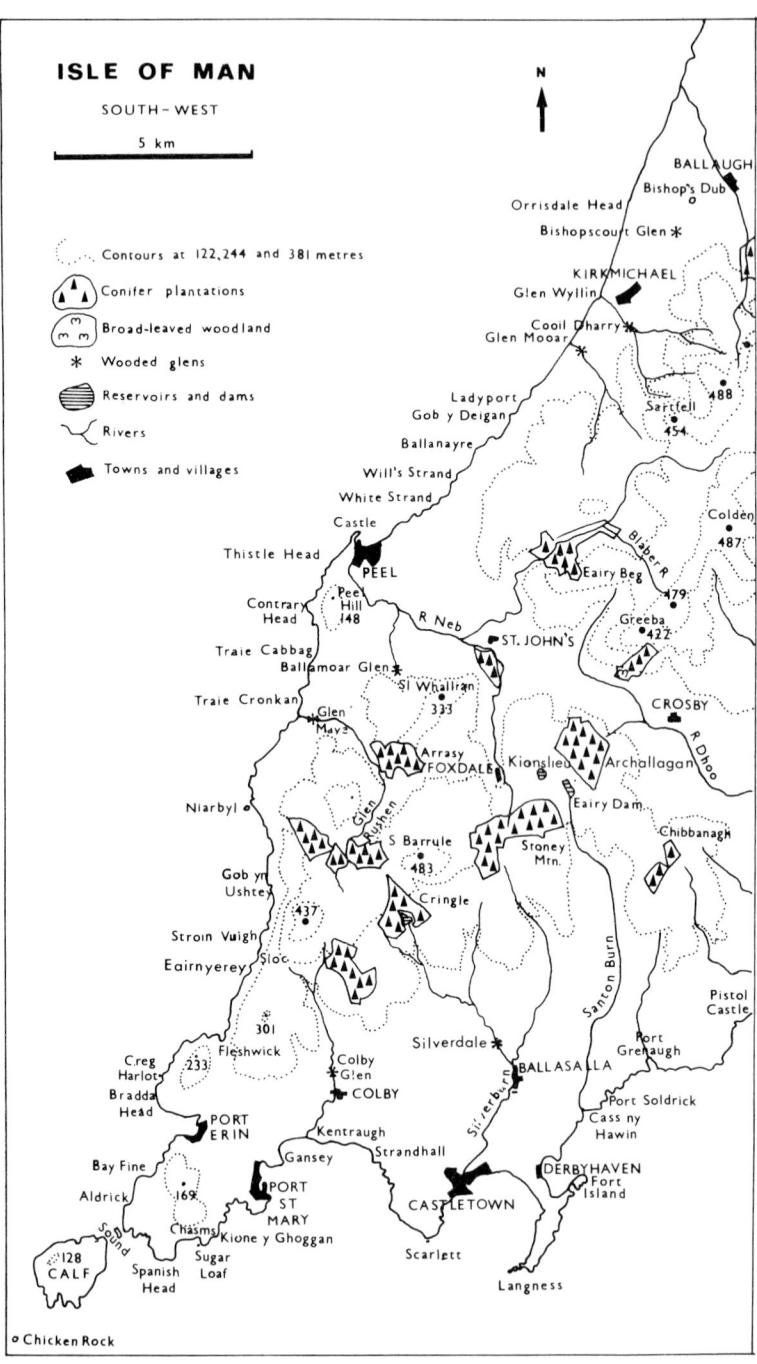

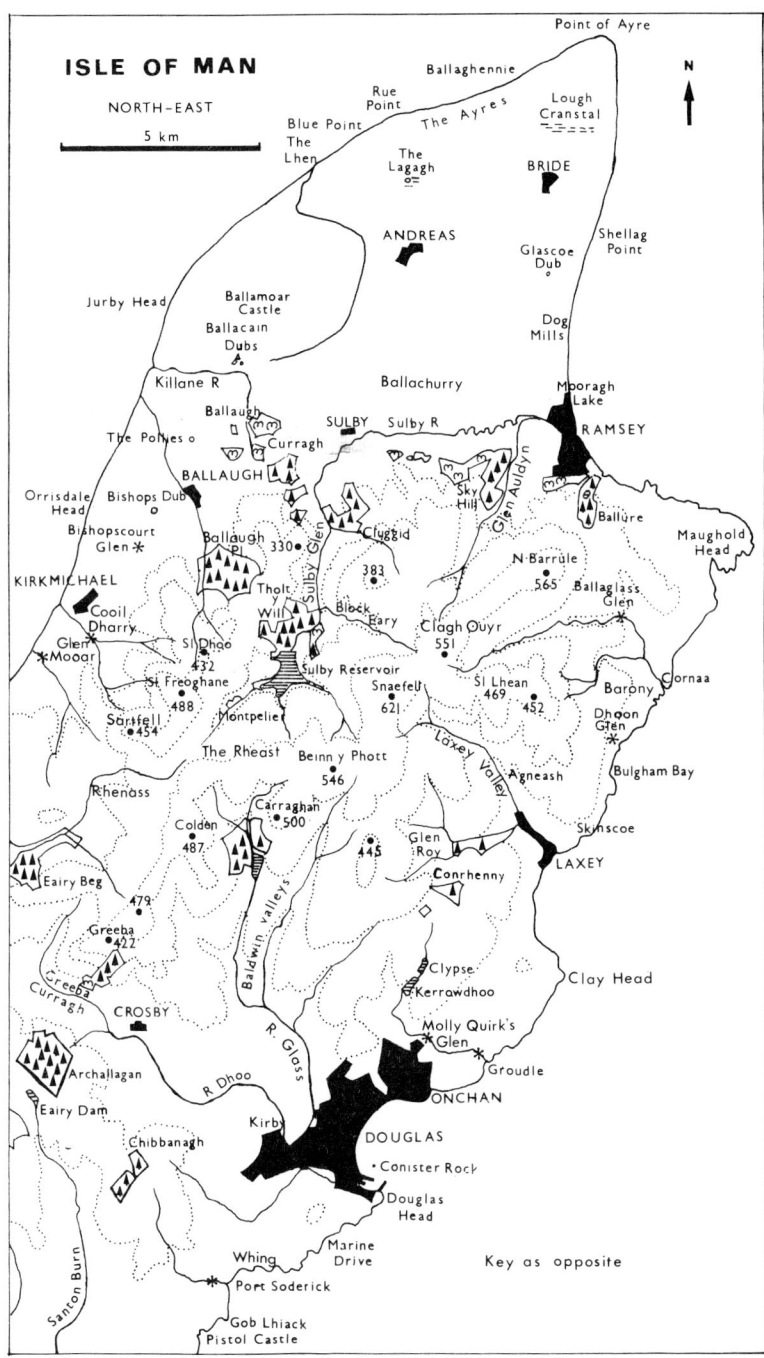

dramatic cliff scenery as does the coast from Port Erin round to Port St Mary. Separated from the main island by the Sound is the Calf of Man a hilly islet of 2½ sq. km which rises to 128 m. Finally 1 km away to the south west is the Chicken Rock surmounted by its lighthouse.

Occupying the entire northern one sixth of the Isle of Man and a much smaller area in the south east are flat lowlands of considerable ornithological importance.

Geology

Most of the Island's rocks are hard slates and grits originating from the Primary period, and it is these slates (about 650 m in thickness) which form the hills and give the Isle of Man its magnificent coastal scenery. Earth movements have twisted the strata into numerous undulations seen at their best at Whing between Douglas and Port Soderick. At the Chasms huge fissures have formed and elsewhere cracks in the coastal slate cliffs provide nesting sites for the Chough, while slate ledges accommodate Ravens and auks.

As in parts of Galloway and Cumbria the overlying rock has been eroded in a few places laying bare the igneous rocks of Stoney Mountain, Dhoon (Lonan) and Oatlands (Santon). At each of these sites the granite has been quarried and is often incorporated in local buildings. In the south east, around Castletown, a shallow alluvial drift covers an area of limestone. Again the stone has been quarried and can be seen to its best advantage at the Scarlett quarry. To the north of Peel is an area of red sandstone, which is probably of similar antiquity to the carboniferous limestone. It is visible on the coastal brooghs and just as Castle Rushen is built of limestone, so Peel Castle, the Cathedral of St German and many of the city's buildings are of red sandstone. Also from the carboniferous period is the basement conglomerate or pudding stone well represented on Langness where it forms several arches.

The Isle of Man was subjected to three successive periods of glaciation over many thousands of years and ending about 20,000 years ago. During the first period the upper slopes of the hills were covered with ice, then followed a period of climatic amelioration before the second glaciation wherein the ice rose to about 400 m. The resultant smooth layer of drift now covers the hills up to perhaps 300 m, while their tops are almost devoid of soil. In the wake of this cold period another ice-front advanced southward over the Island covering the lowlands. The ice age produced the rounded Bride Hills which end abruptly at their eastern end in an imposing drift cliff at Shellag. Boulders were borne by the ice sheets from Ulster, Galloway and Cumbria and deposited in the northern plain and pieces of granite have similarly drifted from Stoney Mountain towards the south-western extremity of the Island. Some of the northern dubs may result from large pieces of residual ice melting and leaving a depression in which water collected. After the ice age the land of the extreme north of the Island underwent an uplift resulting in the raised beach of the Ayres. Formerly this would have been below high water mark, but it now lies a few metres above it.

Following the retreat of the ice Mann remained connected to mainland

Britain for a period before the ultimate severance of the land bridge made it into an island. Even now the sea between the Isle of Man and Cumbria is quite shallow and does not exceed 40 m in depth. To the west however a deep channel in excess of 100 m separates the Isle of Man from Ireland. It was by the land bridge that the Island acquired most if not all of its mammals, although this link was probably of minor importance in the establishment of our avifauna.

Climate

The Isle of Man, lying close to the Gulf Stream, enjoys a western climate characterised by relatively cool summers but mild winters. The average maximum July temperature is about 17.5°C and the minimum January temperature about 3.5°C allowing palm and eucalyptus, and fuchsia and escallonia to thrive. The average annual rainfall is 94 cm but differs markedly between the hills, where considerably higher levels occur, and the coast. The prevailing wind is south westerly.

The Isle of Man showing the six sheadings and seventeen parishes

Manx habitats

1. WOODLAND

It seems that in post glacial times there was a minor readvance of the ice around 8500 BC producing a cold period in Britain, but the climate then became warmer reaching its peak about 5000 BC. By now the Isle of Man was probably clothed in a forest in which oak was the dominant species, but lime, pine and, in the wetter areas, alder were all well represented and hazel formed the dominant shrub layer. The hill peat up to about 330 m has yielded stumps of oak and pine as well as birch catkins and hazel nuts.

Neolithic man, and with him the axe, reached the Island about 1500 BC and much of this woodland was slowly cleared for agriculture. By the 11th century AD trees must have been very sparse, for while Godred Crovan was able to hide 300 men in the woods and ambush the Manx at Sky Hill in 1079, a few years later the Norwegian King Magnus Barefoot had to import timber for building.

It is very likely that such species as Great Spotted Woodpecker, Jay and Bullfinch were Manx residents in the well wooded era but were lost through the period of treelessness which was to continue until the middle 17th century when the first attempts at planting began. From about 1750 a good variety of trees was planted at Bishopscourt, to be followed in due course by plantings around other country mansions such as Ballamoar (Patrick), Ballachurry (Andreas) and Injebreck. These together with Billown Mooar, the Nunnery, Kirby, Milntown, Ballakillingan and Ballamoar (Jurby) have fine parkland together with areas of denser woodland with a fair shrub layer and all have at some time held large rookeries.

Elsewhere the Island's most extensive broad-leaved woods occupy the slopes of the Lezayre hills around Glentramman and Lezayre Church and overlook the lower reaches of the Sulby River and the northern plain. They contain a good scatter of oaks and one of the Island's few birch woods and deserve more study than they have received. East of Glen Auldyn, Claghbane is a most interesting and varied plantation containing an attractive oak wood. It is continuous with the steep-sided Elfin Glen and Lhergy Frissel which hold a mixture of beech, sycamore, ash, oak, birch and rowan. These woods were for a while the regular breeding haunt of the Wood Warbler.

All over the Island there are small shelter belts, usually consisting of sycamore or ash, around farm buildings. Many accommodate rookeries.

Most of the streams are associated with narrow fillets of mixed woodland over much of their lowland courses. Hardwoods dominate and there is often a well developed field layer. Many wooded glens are made easily accessible by the Forestry Board's maintenance of paths and bridges and although much frequented by visitors it is one of these – Silverdale, which with its notable diversity of habitat, has the richest avifauna. Glenmaye, Groudle, Port Soderick, Cooil Dharry (a reserve of the Manx Nature Conservation Trust) and the several woods of the Cornaa system are other important sites; most are tenanted by Sparrowhawks and several have tree-nesting Ravens.

Surrounded by moorland near the head of the Sulby River is Montpelier, a small and rather uniform beech plantation. It is the site of the Island's highest rookery, in which from time to time Ravens have also nested.

The Island has several areas of willow carr or *curragh* of which the most extensive and best known is to the north west of Ballaugh village. Although dense tracts of willow form the dominant tree species there are also numerous birches and the Ballaugh Curragh holds most of the breeding population of the Island's Redpolls.

The first major conifer plantation was started in 1883 at Archallagan, soon to be followed by South Barrule, Greeba, and in 1906 Slieau Whallian. Two world wars saw extensive felling in the older plantations, but fresh plantings have taken place in these, while some forty other plantations have been established. The total area of conifer plantation is now a little over 2,000 hectares – about $3\frac{1}{2}$% of the Island's area. The principal tree species are Sitka spruce, lodge pole pine and Japanese larch.

Manx conifer plantations provide a good variety of habitat, both through the age range of their trees and because physical factors have resulted in failure of some planted areas. South Barrule (128 ha.) has been cleared patchily and restocked over a long period and now possesses an attractive mixture of tree species of many different ages. Goldcrest, Coal Tit, Woodcock, Long-eared Owl and Sparrowhawk are the typical inhabitants of the mature plantations, while cleared areas, especially where some trees are left standing, and young plantations have a greater variety. Glen Rushen (46 ha.) is a good example of how large parts may fail due to poor drainage and heather check. The result was an extensive area of long heather scattered with struggling conifers, a habitat which attracted the Island's first breeding Hen Harriers. At Archallagan (nominally still the largest plantation at 154 ha.) about 25% of the replanted area has failed creating similar conditions. At present the most extensive tract of uninterrupted coniferous woodland is the Ballaugh Plantation with 140 ha.; Tholt y Will, Cringle and Arrasy are all about 100 ha. in area and other notable plantations are Eary Beg (85 ha.) Colden (71 ha.), Conrhenny (66 ha.) and Greeba (63 ha.). (Some of the older plantations have a peripheral fringe of hard woods which at Greeba has been extended to provide quite a broad band of birch wood.) Occupying the Fern Glen, an arm of Glen Auldyn, the substantial Brookdale Plantation is still in its infancy and the three plantations of the Glen Rushen watershed have very recently been augmented by intensive planting along the eastern slopes of Dalby Mountain.

2. UPLANDS

In the Isle of Man cultivated land ceases for the most part at about 200 m above sea level. The highest working farm is Druidale at 230 m and in its vicinity ploughing has taken place up to perhaps 290 m. The ruins of Park Llewellyn below North Barrule are at 300 m and all of the many deserted crofts, whose ruins are known as *tholtans* and are such a feature of the upper parts of Sulby Glen and Glen Rushen, are below this altitude.

Grass heath characterises most of the central hills while the more peripheral Michael range in the west, Slieau Lhean and Slieau Ouyr in the east and especially the southern hills are covered largely with ling and bell heather. Often the transition zone with farmland is marked by bracken, which occurs up to about 300 m. In spring the young green shoots are overshadowed by the masses of bluebells which grow among them, but in autumn bracken forms a red/brown blanket over the slopes of Sulby Glen and other valleys of the central hills and blots out the green grass as it spreads in from the edges of the enclosed upland pastures. Bilberry occupies some small areas of hillside (e.g. on the north west slopes of Slieau Ree), but grows much more luxuriantly along the upland roadside hedges and within plantations such as South Barrule.

The Manx hills are smooth and rounded in outline and the few rocky crags are found mainly on North Barrule and Clagh Ouyr and in Sulby Glen. Conifer plantations have taken away rather more than 2,000 ha. of moorland and now surround fine rocky outcrops at Ballakerka, Sharragh Vane and Greeba. The best rock faces are found in the numerous slate quarries, many of which have nesting Ravens. While the hills support a dwindling population of Red Grouse, the Golden Plover is absent as a breeding bird. Short-eared Owls, Kestrels and, to an increasing extent, Hen Harriers hunt over the moors, the Curlew is widely distributed (its call one of the most evocative sounds of the hills), while Snipe are found in the many boggy areas of grassy moorland and provide an alternative, albeit elusive, target to the frustrated grouse hunter. The commonest small birds are the Meadow Pipit and the Skylark – Wheatears are plentiful along the stone walls on passage, but very few breed in the hills. The northern slopes of the Laxey valley, covered with a luxuriant growth of bracken, support a growing population of breeding Whinchats. The Michael hills now have a population of some 200 pairs of Herring Gulls, which nest from 370–400 m above sea level.

Sheep graze the moors up to the highest hill tops and their occasional corpses, together with those of the abundant hares, rabbits and not infrequent polecat-ferrets which can usually be found along the Snaefell Mountain road, provide valuable carrion for the all too common Hooded Crows and other corvids.

Apart from the *tholtans*, the uplands still possess relics of the mining industry which was in its heyday during the 19th century. Fine remnants of Beckwith's and Cross's mine between Glen Rushen and Foxdale still exist, the latter (better known as Snuff-the-Wind) is one of the Island's most familiar landmarks. Others exist in the Laxey and upper Cornaa valleys and their wheelcases, engine houses and shafts have often provided nest sites for the Chough, indeed Choughs and Ravens both nested one year in the wheelcase below Beinn y Phott.

3. FARMLAND

The topography of the Isle of Man dictates the distribution of improved farmland which is found particularly in the northern plain and the south eastern lowlands. Mixed farming is practised, but since 1945 an increasing proportion of the land has been devoted to grass and hay at the expense of grain, potatoes and green crops. Cattle and to a lesser extent sheep have increased considerably, while increasing mechanisation has seen the Island's horse population fall from 3,700 in 1939 to under 500 in 1968.

Use of Farmland 1939–85 expressed as a percentage of the total area of the Isle of Man based on the Annual Reports on the Agricultural Returns.

	1939	1945	1955	1965	1975	1985
Grain	10.45	12.22	10.17	8.39	7.32	8.19
Potatoes	1.00	1.78	0.96	1.09	0.52	0.50
Green Crops	4.69	4.69	4.29	3.65	2.42	1.64
Non-grassland arable	16.14	18.69	15.42	13.13	10.26	11.33
Hay and grassland	36.33	33.23	36.72	39.82	42.67	43.95
Rough grazing	28.02	29.64	31.57	30.68	29.66	27.02
Total	80.49	81.56	83.71	83.63	82.59	82.30

The amount of farmland lost to the building developments of the 1970s is negligible.

Total Livestock in the Isle of Man 1939–85 from the Annual Reports on the Agricultural Returns.

	1939	1945	1955	1965	1975	1985
Cattle	20,072	23,885	25,665	31,307	43,159	34,558
Sheep	98,704	74,522	87,843	118,332	109,047	138,107
Horses	3,707	2,665	1,060	499	695	1,015

Little farms have long been typical of the Isle of Man and over one quarter are still small holdings of less than 20 acres. Nevertheless the total number of farm holdings has fallen from 1,035 in 1964 to 778 in 1984 due to larger properties engulfing those particularly in the 50–100 acre range. Outwardly farmland has changed little, fields remain small and hedges unspoilt. Indeed the typical Manx hedge, a great bank of stones and sods, 2 metres or more thick at its base, clothed in grass and overgrown with brambles, bracken or gorse is our farmland's greatest asset. Often surmounted by ash, hawthorn and, particularly around Ballamodha and Dalby, fuchsia, this is a valuable nesting habitat for Robin, Pied Wagtail, Yellowhammer and Whitethroat.

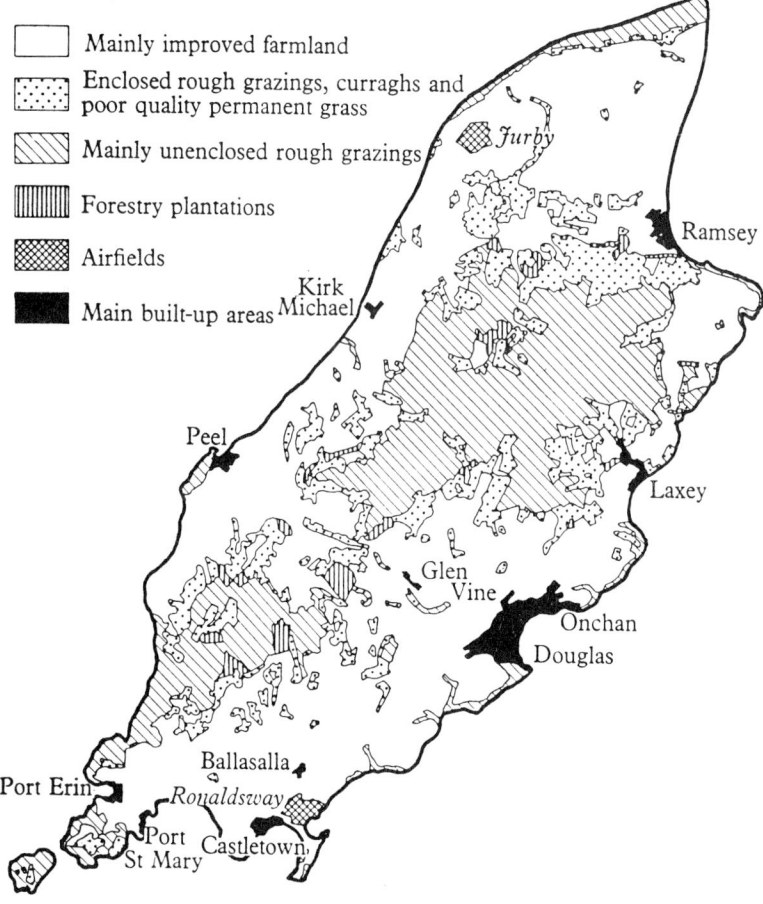

Land use distribution 1957 (after Birch)

Several farmland species have declined drastically during the last fifty years. The Corn Bunting has been lost, only the odd pair of Corncrakes may still breed and the Barn Owl population is greatly reduced. There is a strange contrast between the Yellowhammer's continuing abundance all over the northern plain and its near extinction from the lowlands of Malew.

In winter the upland fields and hawthorn hedges play host to large numbers of Fieldfares and Redwings and seed eaters gather on stubble and turnip fields. The airfields at Ronaldsway, Jurby and Braust provide quite extensive flat grasslands, which together with neighbouring fields of grass and stubble attract considerable flocks of Lapwing, Golden Plover and Curlew.

The Grey Partridge population is vulnerable to the fickle Manx spring weather, but overall numbers seem to be maintained, while the Pheasant, aided by regular introductions, prospers as never before.

4. MARSHLAND

Two words *curragh* and *garey* are used to describe marshland in the Isle of Man. According to Garrad the term *curragh* is used to describe willow carr, while *garey* refers to boggy land containing willow scrub and usable for rough grazing.

Ballaugh Curragh, the Island's most extensive wetland, is a relic of Lake Andreas which arose on the northern plain at the end of the Ice Age. The first human intrusion must have been the cutting of peat for fuel and from the early sixteenth century marginal Curragh lands were drained and reclaimed for grazing, but this was balanced by mills on both the Killane and Lhen rivers which required the maintenance of a good water level in the Curragh for their operation. It was not until the mills closed down during the last century that this balance was lost and much more extensive drainage took place, presumably altering significantly the avifauna of the area. Although considerably reduced there are still quite extensive areas of bog and a few small pieces of open water. There is a dense growth of willow and birch is plentiful over much of the Curragh, but some areas are dominated by low shrubs such as creeping willow and the aromatic bog myrtle. Although traversed by a few narrow lanes, much of the area is hard to penetrate and little disturbed. Over 40 species have bred in the Curragh during the last decade and include Little Grebe, Shoveler, Water Rail, Long-eared Owl, Grasshopper and Sedge Warbler and Redpoll. The wet rushy meadows hold breeding populations of Snipe, Curlew and Lapwing. A good variety of wildfowl occur in winter, when Hen Harriers quarter the marshes and the Bittern is very occasionally seen.

Other wetlands in the north are Lough Cranstal, which has some open water with marginal *curragh*, the Dog Mills Lough with its dense reed beds and the Lagagh where Shoveler and Teal nest and whose hummocky marsh supports a colony of Black-headed Gulls.

At Greeba in the central valley *curragh* is associated with the upper waters of the River Dhoo. There is some dense willow thicket and some damp overgrown areas but no open water. There is a particularly good population of breeding Woodcock and Corncrakes probably still nest here.

Patches of *garey* are widely distributed particularly across the gently sloping upper parts of Arbory, Malew and Santon (Tosaby and Ballacorris are good examples), at Congary near Peel, Cronk y Voddy and Ballacoine (Michael) and Ballacreetch (Onchan). Reed Bunting and Sedge Warbler are the most typical breeding birds and roding Woodcock are often seen at dusk.

5. STILLWATERS

Of the several larger artificial lakes of the Isle of Man, the shallow Foxdale Dams – Eairy and Kionslieu – are of much greater interest than the reservoirs created for the supply of drinking water. The two dams are separated by an area of *garey* which is continuous with the head of the Eairy (1.2 ha.) with its rich growth of water horsetail. Kionslieu (1.6 ha.) is bordered along its north shore by a conifer plantation from which it is separated by a fringe of rushes. They are the best inland waters for wildfowl with autumn flocks of Mallard and Teal well in excess of 100 and small but regular wintering populations of Pochard, Goldeneye and Tufted Duck. Long-tailed Duck and Scaup occur most years and for half a century a small party of Whooper Swans wintered annually.

Of the reservoirs, the Clypse and Kerrowdhoo system with its intervening settling pool is the oldest (1876–1893) and attracts the same common wildfowl as the Foxdale Dams. Baldwin (17 ha. 1904) and Cringle (1.6 ha. 1940) are of little interest and the same is likely to be true of the new Sulby Reservoir, which at 22 ha. is the Island's largest and reaches a depth of over 60 m.

Unusual wildfowl sometimes appear briefly on the Mooragh Park's pleasure lake in winter and when it is drained early in the year its muddy floor is attractive to waders.

Scattered over the northern plain are numerous dubs which are either naturally occurring kettle holes of flooded marl or clay pits. Glascoe Dub, effectively the duck pond of the farm, attracts over 100 Mallard in winter, and flooding in neighbouring fields brings in good flocks of Wigeon; there are nearly always several Shoveler and wild geese and swans are occasional visitors. Other dubs attractive to Whooper Swans are those at Ballacain and the Bishop's Dub. Little Grebes have bred recently at the latter and at the Dollagh, a delightful pond with rich surrounding vegetation and a luxuriant growth of bog bean.

On the landward side of the Ayres heath, along the foot of the line of fixed dunes which separate it from the adjacent farmland, is a number of shallow pools, most of which dry off to a greater or lesser degree in summer. These are the 'Back Slacks', the first Manx breeding station of Shoveler, Redshank and Black-headed Gull and still often tenanted by all three species.

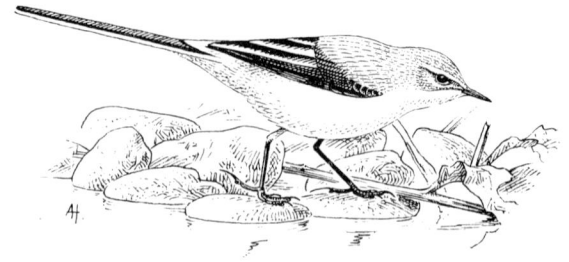

6. RIVERS

Most of the Island's rivers are small streams which hurry over a stony bed, often cutting through rocky gorges and pouring over relatively quite majestic falls. Their sources are in bare grassy moorland, but in their lower reaches alders usually grow along their banks and their courses will often pass through sheltered glens of mixed woodland. The largest river, the Sulby, rises on the boggy moor of the Rheast and its peaty waters remain tea coloured until they reach the sea 19 km away at Ramsey. During the last century mining resulted in severe pollution of the waters of the Glenmaye, Foxdale and Laxey Rivers and only recently have they shown signs of recovery with the ubiquitous brown trout thriving again. Unlike most of the streams, which have little aquatic vegetation, the Dhoo and the Lhen, whose courses are more leisurely, are rich in weed. Often the rivers are reduced to a mere trickle, joining up apparently lifeless pools in summer, more especially if their headwaters are interrupted by a reservoir, but autumn spates can be quite dramatic and allow a fair run of salmon and sea trout. Eels are plentiful but sticklebacks are scarce and Kerrowdhoo may be the only place where minnows exist. Grey Wagtails and Moorhens are the typical birds, but Dippers, which once bred in the tributary streams of the Laxey and Sulby Rivers are strangely absent. Kingfishers have also bred occasionally but most of the streams, except perhaps the lower Sulby, are poorly suited to their requirements.

7. THE COAST

Most of the Manx coastline is rocky, but within the sheadings of Michael and Ayre it is composed of sand cliffs and dunes.

The rocky coast is made up mostly of slate cliffs interrupted by the large bays of Laxey, Douglas, Port Erin and Peel and by a number of small shingle-bordered coves. North of Peel the slate is replaced by red sandstone and between Cass ny Hawin and Port St Mary there is a succession of low lying promontories and bays.

The magic of the lonely coast between Dalby and Fleshwick was beautifully captured by P. G. Ralfe with prose which is no less valid eighty years later. 'The western cliffs . . . with their flowery swards of squill, thrift and campion, their ivied and fern-decorated recesses, their dark caves filled with clear green water, their white pebbled strands and pinnacled stacks, are unequalled in the island for beauty and interest, backed as they often are by the steep and lofty slopes (clad with heather, gorse and bracken, and broken by crags and stony screes) of the western end of the mountain-range. An extent of high sheer cliff, however is not common, the craggy scarps constantly alternating with slopes of grass and boulders, stony debris, and little damp clefts full of profuse vegetation.' Beyond Fleshwick, Bradda and the south west peninsula possess the Island's barest and sheerest cliffs, but there are also imposing precipices on Peel Hill and on the east coast between Santon and Maughold. All around the coast the farmland is limited by substantial hedges or stone walls, beyond which there is an uncultivated zone of variable width which merges into the rocky seaboard. In places it is covered with heather and gorse, in others there is a dense tangle of blackthorn thicket, brambles and bracken. Closely associated with the bracken, bluebells grow in marvellous profusion in spring. Elsewhere short maritime turf is decorated with thyme and vernal squill and the rocks with English stonecrop. Although outnumbered by Robin, Dunnock and Wren, *the* bird of the coastal margins is the Stonechat. Ravens and Choughs are well distributed, the Peregrine is no longer the rarity of the 1960s and there are a few small colonies of cliff-nesting House Martins. The Herring Gull is the dominant seabird, amongst whose colonies the odd Lesser Black-back may be found. The ever increasing Fulmars occupy earthy ledges, there is a good scatter of Shags and Razorbills and in addition to colonies at Peel and Maughold, Black Guillemots can be found at Clay Head, Bay Fine and in the Fleshwick area.

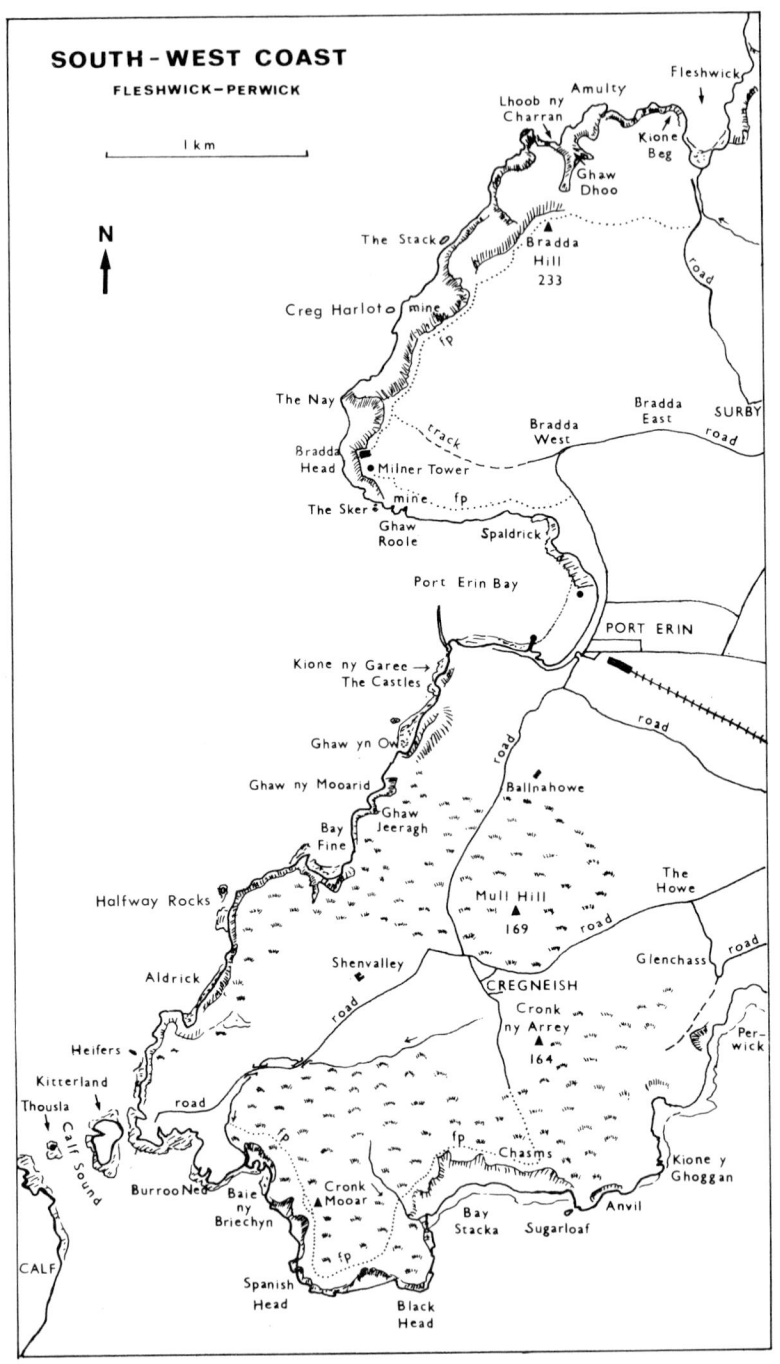

Apart from the Calf which is considered in the next chapter, three other sites – the Chasms, Peel Hill and Maughold Head stand out for the diversity of nesting sea birds. The Chasms, approached from either Fistard or Cregneish, are vertical rifts presumably arising from major earth movements. Some are narrow and treacherously overgrown with heather, others are broad and many descend 60 m to sea level. On their seaward side, the calls of young Choughs may echo from a cave, but the dominant features are the Sugar Loaf rock and its adjacent cliffs whose ledges are crowded with Guillemots and Kittiwakes. Further east towards the Anvil and Kione y Ghoggan are more colonies and a few Puffins can be found. Peel Hill is well served by footpaths and boasts similar seabird colonies, with the important addition of the Black Guillemot. In winter the Castle rocks are a favourite resort of the Purple Sandpiper. At Maughold Head there is a considerable Kittiwake colony and all four auks breed, while a little to the north is a picturesque Cormorant colony, which can be studied in comfort and safety from the grassy brooghs above.

From Santon Gorge south and then west the rocky coast is low lying until the cliffs start again after Port St Mary. Derbyhaven is a shallow bay protected to seaward by a detached breakwater. It possesses a good expanse of intertidal mud and extensive weed-covered rocks and attracts a good variety of waders. The southern part of the bay is formed by the Langness peninsula which is joined to the rocky St Michael's Isle (Fort Island) by a causeway. Oystercatchers have nested on the causeway wall and Kestrels have bred in the walls of the fort. The narrow isthmus by which Langness is joined to the 'mainland' is crossed by a sandy track which connects Derbyhaven with that part of Castletown Bay, known as Sandwick where the broad sandy shore gives way to weed covered rocks which are much favoured by duck and by considerable flocks of Curlew and Golden Plover. The Sandwick shore is rarely without interest during the winter months – a few Bar-tailed Godwits are always present dwarfing at passage times the scurrying Sanderlings, Ringed Plover and Dunlin, among which one may pick out an occasional Curlew Sandpiper. The sandy track follows the shore southward between low dunes and a foreshore, regularly frequented by a good flock of Choughs in winter, to rejoin the Lighthouse road. Soon one reaches Poyll Breinn, known simply as the Pool, a little basin of stinking mud, covered at high tide and surrounded by a mixture of bare shingle and long tussocky grass. Ringed Plover, Oystercatcher, Lapwing and Redshank all breed here. Beyond the gate the road climbs up to the ruins of Langness farm (the Haunted House) and the memorial to Col. Madoc which overlook a 'garden', whose stone walls are overgrown by brambles, and a small area of saltmarsh where Wigeon graze and Snipe are plentiful. There follows a flat grassy area with an abundance of gorse, merging to seaward into grass on shingle, shingle and low rock. The rocks become steeper as the Lighthouse and Point are approached and the entire south east side of the peninsula is made up of steep rocks of slate. Here, on a far too accessible ledge, Ravens have nested for 60 or more years. The broader northern part holds a busy golf course, rough pasture near the farmhouse is regularly grazed by cattle or sheep and

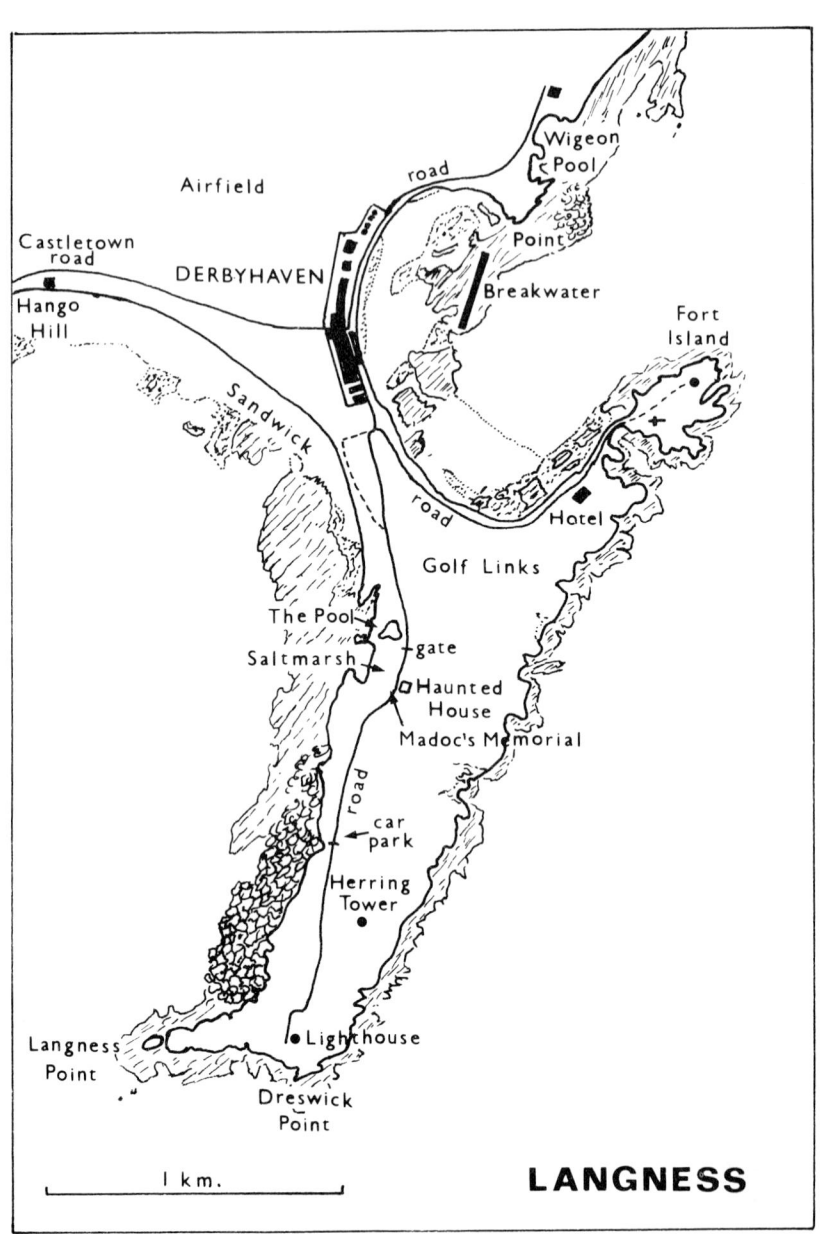

Mixed woodland at Cornaa – breeding place of Woodcock and Sparrowhawk. (J. P. Cullen)

Parkland at Kirby. (J. P. Cullen)

The edge of the long established South Barrule plantation. (J. P. Cullen)

A clearing in South Barrule plantation. (J. P. Cullen)

Glen Rushen plantation – first Manx nesting place of the Hen Harrier. (T. W. B. Cullen)

Typical Manx moorland above Block Eary. (J. P. Cullen)

The Cluggid – Raven country. (T. W. B. Cullen)

The upper Laxey valley where Whinchats breed. (J. P. Cullen)

Upland pastures at Glen Roy. (J. P. Cullen)

The upper limit of cultivated land above Rhenass with a narrow fillet of woodland tracing the river's course.
(J. P. Cullen)

An overgrown lane above Foxdale. (J. P. Cullen)

Typical hedges in Marown parish. (J. P. Cullen)

Ballaugh Curragh – the Killane River in high summer. (T. W. B. Cullen)

Ballaugh Curragh where there is a good population of breeding Redpolls. (J. P. Cullen)

Eairy Dam. (J. P. Cullen)

Ballacain – a typical northern dub. (J. P. Cullen)

River Neb near Ballamoar. (J. P. Cullen)

River Neb above the Raggatt. (J. P. Cullen)

Sulby Glen. (J. P. Cullen)

Sulby Glen – the river reduced to a trickle in high summer. (T. W. B. Cullen)

The west coast from Traie Vane. (J. P. Cullen)

Eairnerey – former eyrie of the White-tailed Eagle. (J. P. Cullen)

The coast north of Glenmaye. (J. P. Cullen)

The Black Guillemots' coast at Peel. (J. P. Cullen)

Seabird ledges at the Sugar Loaf Rock. (T. W. B. Cullen)

The House Martins' sea cave at Port Soldrick. (T. W. B. Cullen)

The Santon coast. (J. P. Cullen)

The Groudle coast where Chough and Raven both nest. (J. P. Cullen)

Intertidal mud at Derbyhaven. (J. P. Cullen)

The Sandwick shore. (J. P. Cullen)

Langness Pool. (J. P. Cullen)

Langness Pool with the ruined farm (Haunted House) and the Herring Tower. (J. P. Cullen)

The Shellag sand cliffs. (J. P. Cullen)

Little Tern breeding ground between Blue Point and Rue Point. (J. P. Cullen)

The Ayres heath. (J. P. Cullen)

Point of Ayre gravel pit. (J. P. Cullen)

Cabbage palms in Woodbourne Square, Douglas. (J. P. Cullen)

Douglas Bay, becoming an attractive site for Goldeneye. Cormorants, Grey Heron and waders roost on the Conister rock. (J. P. Cullen)

Ramsey Harbour. (J. P. Cullen)

The Calf seen across the Sound. (J. P. Cullen)

Calf Sound and Kitterland. (J. P. Cullen)

The west coast of the Calf. (J. P. Cullen)

The Calf of Man Bird Observatory. (J. P. Cullen)

Sandulf's cross (Kirk Andreas) – Woodpigeon faces a cockerel.

Thorwald's cross (Kirk Andreas) – Raven perched on Odin's shoulder.

(Photographs by courtesy of the Manx Museum and National Trust.)

The earliest definite figure of the Great Auk, drawn in the Isle of Man by Daniel King about 1652.
(Reproduced by permission of the British Library. MS. Add. 27362)

beyond this the highest area, surmounted by the Herring Tower, is of moorland quality with gorse, heather and rough grassland peppered with rocky outcrops of slate.

The remaining part of Castletown Bay attracts all the commoner waders and Goldeneye regularly collect in some numbers just to the west of the town, while, in Carrick Bay, Strandhall is reminiscent of Sandwick and its adjacent littoral and has a similar though smaller winter population of waders and duck.

North of Gob ny Creggan Glassey on the Michael coast the rocks give way to steep sandy brooghs which continue for about 12 km to beyond Jurby Head before giving way to dunes. Ornithologically this is the dullest part of the Manx coast, although Oystercatchers and Ringed Plover are plentiful along the shingle beaches and to the north of Orrisdale Head there is an extensive sandy cliff top warren where Wheatears breed. On the east coast there are sand cliffs from Port Cranstal to south of the Dog Mills where there is a good Sand Martin colony. The Bride Hills terminate abruptly in the Island's highest sand cliffs at Shellag, a favourite Raven nest site, and further north Herring Gulls and Fulmars also breed in these heavily eroded cliffs.

Stretching for nearly 8 km from the mouth of the Lhen to the Point of Ayre are the Ayres, a considerable tract of heath adjacent to the coast and backed by fixed dunes densely overgrown with bracken, gorse and brambles. At its western end the Ayres shore has relatively few pebbles and there is an intertidal zone of sand up to 120 m broad as far as Rue Point – it then gradually narrows as the pebbles increase and culminates in the imposing curve of the storm beach. About Rue Point the upper part of the beach is in places separated from the line of marram-covered dunes by a shallow depression which at its western end has a sparse covering of sessile plants, while to the east it fills with water forming a lagoon. Behind the dunes the heathland is very narrow near the Lhen, but from the Rue Point road to the Point of Ayre is between 1 km and 1,300 m broad. The heath has developed on a raised shingle beach now covered with blown sand – at its western end it is covered mainly by grass or a mat of burnet rose, but further east heather dominates and dwarf gorse takes over as the lighthouse is approached. Throughout its length the sandy heath is riddled with rabbit burrows. On either side of the road from Bride to the Point of Ayre are pits from which sand and gravel are extracted.

About 50 pairs of Little Terns now nest along the beach, while smaller numbers of Arctic as well as a few pairs of Common Terns breed here and in the gravel pits. Amongst the other breeding birds Oystercatcher and Ringed Plover are abundant and Curlew plentiful especially in the marram grass. The gravel pits now regularly accommodate a thriving colony of Black-headed Gulls and have very recently provided the first Manx breeding records of Common Gull and Red-breasted Merganser. Sandwich Terns do not breed, but variable numbers are normally present throughout the summer and in August they far outnumber the other terns. From late July good numbers of small waders appear along the beaches and a few Arctic Skuas come to harry the terns. A recent development, no doubt resulting from the use of one gravel pit as a refuse tip, is the regular presence of a flock of over 40 Ravens during the winter.

8. VILLAGES, TOWNS AND INDUSTRIAL DEVELOPMENTS

In 1727 the population of the Isle of Man was estimated at 14,400 people. At that time only 17% of the total lived in the four main towns, whose populations ranged between 460 and 810. The first official census in 1821 showed that 28% of the 40,000 inhabitants now lived in towns and 150 years later 73% of a population in excess of 56,000 were now town dwellers. The twenty year period 1961–81 saw a population increase of 16,500 and this expansion was associated with peripheral building around the main towns and smaller communities such as Onchan, Port Erin, Port St Mary, Ballasalla, Glen Vine and Andreas. Yet in spite of this the loss of farmland has been remarkably small. The new housing estates have proved irresistable to nesting House Martins and Collared Doves are now present in many of the older residential areas. Town houses which have retained large gardens usually have a rookery and both Magpies and Hooded Crows now penetrate the town centres to a greater degree. The mild climate allows the cabbage palm to prosper and it can be found not only in town parks and squares, but in many suburban gardens and sometimes provides an unusual nest site. In winter Oystercatchers, Black-headed and Common Gulls, and at times Redwings, collect in good numbers on playing fields, while strangers such as Grey Wagtail and Meadow Pipit appear in the streets of Douglas.

The Isle of Man's traditional industries were formerly agriculture and fishing, but from the middle of the 18th century mining was of increasing importance up to its decline 150 years later. The economic losses resulting from this decline were balanced by the establishment of the Isle of Man as a major tourist resort. As early as the 1830s the number of visitors to the Island compared favourably with those holidaying in the fashionable south coast resorts, but it was the late Victorian era which saw the building of promenades and their attendant boarding houses and hotels and the development of a small network of railways linking the major towns and providing access to rural attractions such as Glen Wyllin and Laxey Glen. A notable engineering feat was the building of an electric tramway along the coast from Douglas to Port Soderick and although this closed in 1939 it was later replaced by the Marine Drive which still provides easy access to one of the finer stretches of coast. The tourist industry was at its peak immediately prior to the First World War, was well sustained between the wars and enjoyed a brief resurgence in the period 1947–9 since which it has steadily declined. A number of small factories have been established but these have resulted in minimal environmental change.

The herring fishery has existed since the Middle Ages and although its economical contribution, together with that of farming, is now very small, the presence of fishing boats in the harbours of Peel, Port St Mary and Douglas remains one of the Island's most characteristic sights. Ramsey and Castletown also have well protected harbours used by small coasters and there are small piers and quays at Port Erin and Laxey. The port of Douglas has of course been considerably extended with piers and breakwaters for the passenger services and the increasing container traffic. All the harbours provide temporary shelter for a variety of species and gulls and waders feed on their muddy floors at low tide. Mute Swans regularly nest close to the harbours of Castletown, Douglas and Ramsey and outside the breeding season the principal Manx herd usually assembles in Castletown before moving up to Ramsey.

The Calf of Man

In 1937 The Calf of Man was given to the National Trust of England and Wales by F. J. Dickens 'to preserve its nature and beauty', and the administration of the islet was taken over by the Manx National Trust on its establishment in 1951. Attempts at farming failed due in part to poor soil, a huge rabbit population and the weather, so in 1959 a warden was appointed to look after the islet and carry out birdwork rather than farming. A warden and his assistant have been present (except for an annual winter break) every year since.

In the late 1930s Ken Williamson first suggested that the Calf would be an ideal site for a bird observatory to join other stations such as Skokholm and the Isle of May. The war years intervened and then Ken became warden of Fair Isle Bird Observatory. However his papers in *Peregrine* and the *Proceedings* of I.O.M.N.H. and A.S. on the ornithology of the Calf were important contributions leading eventually to The Calf of Man Bird Observatory being recognised by the British Trust for Ornithology in 1962.

Since then over 100,000 birds of 138 different species have been ringed on the islet and more than 1,300 recoveries reported. The list of species seen has grown from about 120 to 248 and includes no fewer than 40 'firsts' for the Isle of Man in the period 1959–85.

Much of the Isle of Man, including the Calf, was once clad in forests of oak and hazel but the ravages of the Celts for homesteads and clearance for agriculture resulted in their almost total destruction by the middle of the 16th century. Legislation did exist to protect remaining woods during the 18th century and a man was fined for destroying a wood on the Calf.

A refuge from time to time of monks and hermits, the Calf was farmed intermittently for several centuries. Farming was always dominated by sheep and during the 18th and 19th centuries there were several hundred animals together with five or six resident families including lighthouse keepers. Much overgrazing resulted and doubtless contributed to the failures of the 1950s.

There has been a steady increase in woody vegetation on the islet since farming ceased although the few Loaghtan sheep which were introduced in

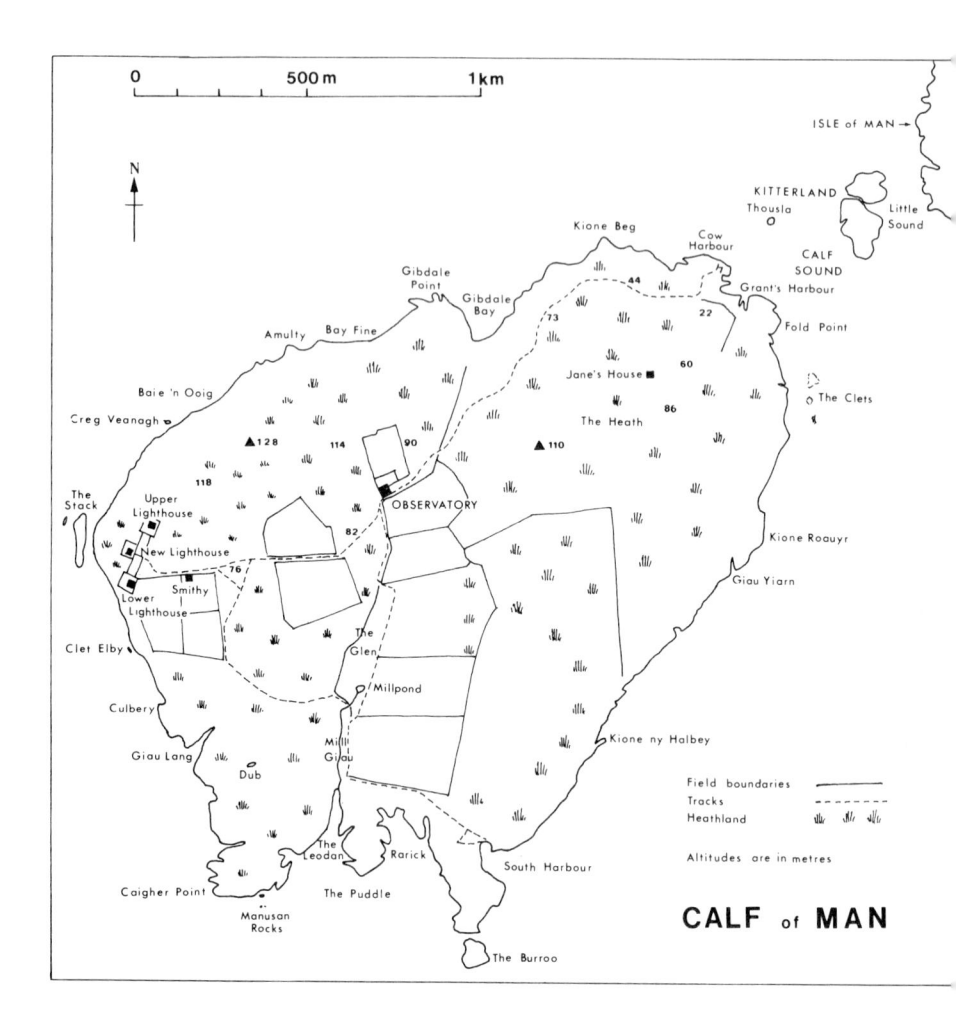

1969 have been allowed to increase to the extent that there are now up to 200 old sheep and lambs present in mid-summer and they adversely affect the growth of perennial plant species so important as cover for both migrant and breeding birds. Much of the heath is tall and rank providing excellent habitat for Meadow Pipit, Wren, Reed Bunting and Stonechat. A few years ago Short-eared Owl and Mallard nested in the main Heath but ill-considered burning may well prevent the return of the former as a regular breeding bird. Patches of bramble grow in the Glen area and along the dry-stone walls providing nest sites for Magpie, Blackbird and Dunnock as well as feeding and cover for migrants. The majority of trees are around the Observatory at the head of the Glen. Sycamore, fuchsia and Sitka spruce flourish making this the most attractive area for migrant birds. A single large ash grows at the head of the Mill Giau where several Yellow-browed and *Hippolais*

Warblers have been spotted over the years. Patches of basket weaving willows have existed to the east of the Observatory and below the Mill pond for many years and in the late seventies the margins of the pond and an area in front of a new Heligoland trap in the middle of the Glen were planted. Much of the Glen is very wet with extensive *Juncus* so the willows grow quickly and are very attractive to warblers. Unfortunately the mill-pond is rapidly silting up and becoming choked with weed. A hundred years ago it was far more extensive stretching up the Glen and a Bewick's Swan was shot there from a flock of 14 as well as Barnacle and other geese. There is even an old print showing a sailing dinghy on the water! A few years ago it still attracted ducks including a Goldeneye which fed on the numerous eels. A Ferruginous Duck spent a short time on the mill-pond and a Long-billed Dowitcher an even briefer period before departing to more suitable habitat at Langness.

Much of the rest of the islet is covered with heath and the ever increasing bracken. The bracken is a great nuisance, not only because it requires constant checking from invading the pastures, but also because it yields a small green caterpillar which in some autumns attracts many warblers away from the trapping areas. More than one rarity has disappeared amongst the dense fronds never to be seen again. There is a marshy area in the centre of the main Heath and a wet flush above Jane's Cottage in which grow some dwarf willows. These and the brambles around Jane's can sometimes shelter many migrants.

A total of 46 species of 'landbirds' have been found nesting on the Calf although only about 24 do so regularly. Several have been lost during the last decade having previously bred annually. Grey Partridge were common until the late seventies with up to 50–100 present in autumn. A succession of wet breeding seasons, many eggs being sucked by crows and Magpies and a great increase in Hen Harriers resulted in none breeding in 1979 and there have only been a handful of records since. Hen Harriers were also responsible for the loss of Moorhens in 1979, at least one pair having bred on the mill-pond for as long as anyone could remember. A pair reappeared in 1984 and bred the following year but without success. The waders have always suffered from the attentions of the crows and gulls. Lapwings bred regularly from the late 1960s but although up to ten pairs attempted very few young were reared and numbers have now dwindled to zero following several years of total failure at the egg stage. Similarly a pair of Curlew have gone in the last few years. About 25 pairs of Oystercatchers nest, mainly near the coast, but also in certain of the old pastures and on grassy patches amongst the bracken and heath. They are much more pugnacious than the Lapwing and vigorously chase off any crow or Raven that passes within a hundred yards. They certainly hatch plenty of young, but few survive, and some years are a total failure.

One or two pairs of Short-eared Owls nested in the tall heath for many years until 1981 but much of their favourite area has been damaged by fire recently. Barn Owls seem to have bred in the past, at least in 1943, but definitely not since the early 50s. Rock Doves were once abundant around the Calf and the main Island but shooting and netting in the 19th century led to their extinction. A pair of Stock Doves bred in the Mill Giau in the 1970s and Woodpigeons have nested in the ash tree there and on the ground, on a ledge, in the back garden of the Observatory. Pairs of Shelduck frequent Fold Point and the Rarick areas but many ducklings fall prey to the usual enemies. Several pairs of Mallard nested high up on the heath until recently. Invariably they did so close to the Short-eared Owls as protection from the Hoodies and Magpies. Broods of up to 15 would walk to the mill-pond but few ever fledged although one female managed to raise 9 out of 10 one year by being particularly vigilant and with the help of the wardens who provided grain and bread.

Several pairs of Skylarks have always nested, it seems, mainly in the rough grassy areas on Caigher Point and in the fields at the south end of the Glen. Meadow Pipits are easily the commonest passerine breeding birds with 60–100 pairs censused annually. They collect much of their food in the pastures but nest often several hundred yards away on the heath. Forty to fifty pairs of Rock Pipits occupy the entire coastline with a few 'overspill' pairs nesting some way inland in stone walls and under heather.

Since the late 1970s a few pairs of Pied Wagtails have nested, not only in expected places such as the lighthouses and around the observatory but also in Rock Pipit-like sites around the harbours and on the west coast. They do well and there seems to be room for several more pairs on the islet. Wrens and Dunnocks are almost entirely resident, especially the former for which there has been just the one ringing recovery from over 2,000 trapped – and that to Port Erin just over the Sound. Calf Wrens are rather unusual in several respects. Many of them spend a considerable amount of time down rabbit holes during the winter months, collecting food as far down as light permits, including many rabbit fleas. They are particularly wriggly when handled for ringing and their plumage seems especially dark and rusty when compared with those from the mainland. Their flight seems noticeably weak, probably because they have little need for sustained travel, remaining largely in one area, be it on the highest heath or down amongst the Shags on the north west cliffs.

Perhaps the Calf, or the Isle of Man as a whole, can lay claim to a new sub-species for *Troglodytes troglodytes* to add to the 37 so far described. The Wren population does suffer in some winters and has been halved from the usual 40–50 pairs by some cold spells. However, either side of the 1962–63 winter the number remained unchanged at about 18 pairs. Since then it may well be that the species has spread to occupy more vulnerable sites away from the sheltered Glen and buildings.

Wrens are not the only small birds which are sometimes found scurrying amongst the Shag colonies as a few Dunnocks also frequent these rather foul areas particularly on the south-side. Many flies are of course attracted to the mess in the sea-bird colonies but Dunnocks have also been seen taking pieces of partly digested, regurgitated sand-eel that have gone astray during the feeding of the young Shags. Most Dunnocks nest in the Glen and around some of the bramble patches along the stone-walls but a few do so in tall heather and dead bracken where they are very inconspicuous. They do not start breeding until comparatively late, due to the lack of cover, and it is sometimes mid-May or later before some pairs commence nest-building. Clutches are small with 3 or 4 eggs being the norm. The Blackbirds too are usually late and lay few eggs except for one or two about the observatory. About 20 pairs are usually present, mainly in the Glen and old pasture area, but a few are found high up on the heath, around Jane's Cottage and there is occasionally a pair down the north cliffs. Their song used to be very poorly developed but from 1979, following a sharp increase in numbers, it became much more complex and typical of mainland birds, especially around the observatory where there can be quite a dawn chorus.

Only one or two pairs of Robins stay to breed on the Calf, usually occupying sites around the observatory, in the Mill Giau or, sometimes, by Jane's Cottage. They sing very little and once settled are very inconspicuous. The calls of recently fledged nestlings or the occasional glimpse of an adult are often all that give away their presence. From late June onwards juveniles from the main island come over and confuse the breeding picture. The Stonechat was lost as a breeding species after the 1962–63 winter and it was some years before the number of pairs reached double figures once more. Nowadays 5–10 pairs breed annually with some birds resident and others going as far south as the Mediterranean for the winter. Resident birds have the advantage of early choice of territory whilst the migratory ones escape the rigours of November to February on the Calf. They have two or three broods and nestlings are quite frequent in August. They nest in the heather and under bracken and bluebells, sometimes out of sight several inches along a tunnel through the vegetation.

The Stonechat's close relative, the Whinchat, frequently sings in spring but has only bred twice on the islet, in 1943 and 1957. Wheatears have probably long suffered from rats as they usually nest down rabbit holes. Six pairs bred in 1984, the most for many years, and with the rat population now very low hopefully they will become well established. Song Thrush and Mistle Thrush have both bred from time to time, the former on the ground under bracken on one occasion. Of the four species of warbler that have bred the only one to do so regularly has been the Whitethroat with up to 4 pairs. The odd Grasshopper and Sedge Warbler has nested in the Glen or by the mill-pond and a Willow Warbler once did so under bracken to the east of the observatory some way from the nearest tree.

Earlier this century Spotted Flycatchers were said to have bred regularly about the farmhouse (now the observatory) and, although the truth of this has been questioned, birds have sung in many recent springs and established temporary territories. The environs appear quite suitable even though the summers are a little unreliable for flying insects. The only breeding since the establishment of the observatory was in 1971 when a pair nested on the cliff face of the Mill Giau about 150 metres from the nearest tree. There is also just one breeding record of the Blue Tit – a pair overwintered after the big irruption of 1957 and then occupied a nest box in the back garden.

There seems to be no positive evidence of Jackdaws nesting on the Calf although they were undoubtedly more frequent in the days of farming, and in the 1960s many used to frequent the sea-bird colonies feeding on fish remains, eggs and dead young. These were visitors from across the Sound where many breed in the cliffs. A few have been seen about the cliffs of the Calf early in the season in recent years, but these have been given a hostile reception by the Choughs who chivvy them constantly when they come anywhere near their traditional nesting crevices. All suitable sites are taken by Choughs and indeed there are few to attract the very colonial Jackdaws. Up to ten pairs of Choughs have bred on the Calf since the late 1970s, the densest population recorded anywhere in north-west Europe. Also 10–20 non-breeding birds often feed on the Calf but usually frequent the southern end of the main island. The old pastures are without doubt responsible for the high density as, together with the short turf of the cliff tops, they provide important feeding areas. The short grass of most of the pastures is due to the now constantly high population of rabbits – over 1,000 were counted above ground on a July evening in 1981 in just four fields in the Glen. It has been stated recently that the introduction of Loaghtan sheep has been responsible but they were kept out of the fields in the growing season for some years because of mist-netting operations. Indeed at other times the sheep much prefer to browse the heather or the grassy cliff slopes. When myxomatosis decimated the rabbit population on several occasions from the late 1950s to the early '70s the grass in the fields grew unchecked with tall species such as Yorkshire fog becoming dominant. Resistance to myxomatosis was very noticeable from the late 1970s with many animals seen to recover from a fairly advanced state of infection and others appearing not to contract the virus at all. Although large numbers still succumb the fields never become overgrown and are therefore suitable for the Choughs to feed in and for the crane-flies to lay their eggs. The Chough will continue to thrive on the Calf so long as the rabbit population is high, bracken is prevented from taking over the fields and extreme winters are infrequent.

There are not many suitable nest sites for Choughs on the Calf and some of these are often accessible to rats, while the dampness of others results in the young developing respiratory problems. There is a very poor site close to the tide line near Cow Harbour – adaptation of the chimney in the harbour store or the attic at Jane's Cottage would create an infinitely safer nest site. Birds frequently inspect these places but as yet they are not suitable. Another pair has nested on the Burroo often in a crevice behind a Shag which guards the entrance – a rather exposed site – smelly, but safe. A site on Caigher Point has been used but is very wet while the one at the top of a cave on the north-west side is rather cold and exposed to gales. Far and away the most successful nest sites have been in the staircase recess of the old lower lighthouse and in the firegrate of the upper lighthouse. As there seemed to be room for an extra pair in the area a large nest box was placed in a recess in the old grain silo by the observatory in 1978. The box was occupied by a roosting Kestrel for a while but was regularly inspected by Choughs who later took it over to roost. Eventually in 1981 a pair built a nest and successful breeding has taken place each year since. The Choughs often form into flocks especially in spring and autumn. Breeding birds gather together especially before nest re-lining starts, during egg laying and on hatching. They form an excited flock coming together from all parts of the islet attracted by much calling. A period of calling and aerobatics lasts several minutes at least, before the birds divide to return to their nests. The significance is presumably connected with their loose colonial nature, young birds 'learning' from old as to the timing of the breeding cycle. In autumn and winter flocks are more permanent but much of the time is spent over on the main island. The flocks consist of several family parties in the early autumn and, in a ritualised form, the young follow the older birds both in the air and on the ground where a 'parade' may take place. The flock lands and walks about with an exaggerated gait, there is much wing-flicking and calling by the adults which take up position at the front of a rough V formation.

The Chough's food on the Calf consists mainly of crane-fly larvae (leatherjackets) with some agrotid moth caterpillars, earwigs, worms and beetles. Ants' nests are unearthed for the eggs and stones of up to 300 grammes turned over for woodlice and other invertebrates. One bird on the Calf used to walk along the mill-pond dam in the summer picking off emerging damsel flies from the rushes, whilst another was seen to drop off a stone wall and catch a lizard. Several pellets collected from this bird's roost site afterwards showed that it had eaten several of these in the previous week. The crane-fly larvae are, however, easily the most important prey item and these do best in damp fields. Dry springs and summers result in very few young being reared. Choughs have been persecuted in the past usually because they are sometimes seen around sheep carcases pecking at the body. They are, however, only feeding on blow flies and their maggots or, in the spring, gathering wool to line their nests. They may also sometimes take wool from a living animal – this often looks a bit vigorous and may well be responsible for the few tales of the species attacking sheep.

Numbers of Magpies on the islet have dropped markedly, since a peak of 14 pairs in 1979, to only three in 1984. They nest mainly in brambles along the stone walls, but occasionally on the cliffs. The nests are sometimes roofless and predation from rats and Hooded Crows may be high. The crows on the Calf are mainly Hoodies but increasingly they are showing hybrid characteristics and there are one or two Carrions present. Eight to ten pairs nest around the coast and, until recently, in the Sitka in the observatory garden and in a gorse bush in the Glen. A single pair of Ravens nest annually in the Amulty/Baie 'n Ooig area whilst a second pair occupied a site at Kione Roauyr one year.

House Sparrows bred until farming stopped, and in one year since, but Starlings are now found breeding only in cliff sites. These birds which occupy the archetypal habitat for the species have very worn claws due to their rocky nesting areas and totally ignore bread and crumbs put out in the garden. They tread on it in their probings for leather jackets, even in winter. Chaffinches bred in 1939 and 1969 and one or two pairs have done so each year since 1979. Greenfinch and Goldfinch have also nested in recent years but the only finch to do so regularly is the Linnet, 15 to 30 pairs breeding in loose colonies spread over the island, but it is a difficult species to census accurately. As elsewhere Reed Buntings have expanded considerably on the Calf in their choice of habitat. They now nest in dry areas high on the heath as well as in the Glen and areas of bracken. Up to 19 pairs have been found but it is another difficult species when it comes to censusing breeding numbers. They show some loose colonial habits and fly some way to feed and drink; there is also some polygyny.

Seabird breeding numbers fluctuate greatly from year to year on the Calf but since the observatory has been manned there have been between three and four thousand pairs of 8 to 10 species. Until the end of the 18th century it seems that there were probably at least 30,000 pairs of Manx Shearwaters on the Calf judging by the numbers collected for eating. Shipwrecked rats wiped them out however and there has been no positive proof of breeding since. A large population of Puffins may also have been lost and the thirty or so pairs which still breed tend to occupy very inaccessible areas. Auks in general were described as being very numerous about the Calf in the last century but suitable nesting places for Razorbill and Guillemot are limited and there is no reason to believe that there have ever been more than 150

to 250 pairs of each. Kittiwakes have gone from zero to 720 pairs and back to zero in the past 25 years. At present the trend is upwards again with over 60 pairs occupying ledges at Kione Roauyr and Caigher Point. One thousand to two thousand pairs of Herring Gulls nest all round the coast with large unaccountable fluctuations. Lesser black-backed Gulls have always been present in small numbers mainly above South Harbour but have had little success in recent times. A hundred or more pairs of Great black-backs nest especially on Caigher Point, and there are many more on Kitterland.

Cormorants once nested at Kione Roauyr but abandoned the area in the early 1970s probably because of a great increase in the number of Fulmars. There are still several large Shag colonies around the Calf but numbers have fallen from about 400 to around 250 pairs recently and their main area shifted to the north side. They are still very successful and large fishing flocks of several hundred birds may be seen in the Sound in autumn, although the main feeding banks are a few miles south-east of the Calf. Storm Petrels may well breed, as they very probably did in large numbers before the rats came. There have been many retraps from ringing and birds have been caught with muddy feet – regular churring was heard from Gibdale Point in 1981. Black Guillemots nest not far away over the Sound and are a frequent sight around the Calf. There have been suspicious goings on for many years with calling and birds seen ashore now and then on the north side.

Although the Calf is usually only observed from mid-March to mid-November each year migration takes place in all months and often Blackbirds and winter thrushes do not reach their peak numbers until December due to mild weather and/or abundant food in Scandinavia. It is a pity that bird records cannot be kept throughout the year but the wardens need at least a couple of months break to renew contact with civilisation. Hardy types have returned in February in some years and witnessed northwards passage of Curlew, Skylark and Gannet as well as numbers of thrushes in cold weather. Early March continues much as February, but from the middle of the month the first Chiffchaffs and Goldcrest appear. The male Goldcrests precede the females by several days in the overall passage with the peak for the species in late March and early April. Northwards passage does however continue surprisingly late, into early May. Up to 400 have been recorded during a single spring day. Chiffchaffs usually number 50–100 on a few days in mid-April but there can be a strong late movement with, on one occasion, a fall of 200 on 4th May. In March and early April large numbers of thrushes and Starlings can be grounded by fog and rain. Two thousand Blackbirds were logged on 4th April 1960, 2,000 Redwing on 7th March 1965, 500 Fieldfare on 1st April 1981, 150 Song Thrush on 6th March 1965 and 1,000 Starlings on 22nd March 1976. These are unusual totals and in many years triple figure day totals for any of these are rare. The second half of March also brings a strong northwards movement of Meadow Pipits with a few hundred off-passage birds scattered in the fields. Seven hundred and fifty were counted on the last day of March 1979.

Wheatears, particularly males, are daily arrivals, though usually less than 50 in a day of British breeding types. The first Willow Warbler often arrives in the last few days of March as do a few Ring Ousels. A small passage of *alba* wagtails, finches and Sand Martins is also usually seen.

Throughout April Willow Warblers, Chiffchaffs and Wheatears dominate the arrivals but from the middle of the month a far greater variety begin to arrive. Sedge and Grasshopper Warblers, Redstarts, Whitethroats and Common Sandpipers all appear in small numbers. Nowadays a good day total for Whitethroats in April or May is 20–30 but previously numbers were much greater and passage considerably earlier. One thousand were present on 11th May 1965 and it was the commonest warbler in those days before the droughts in the former scrub areas of the southern edges of the Sahara. Redstarts too have become later arrivals and there has been a definite increase in the species' winglength since the 1960s, at least as far as birds trapped on the Calf are concerned. Sedge Warblers are also less plentiful – 50 is now a big day for them on the Calf. 32 Grasshopper Warblers were trapped one May day in 1970 out of an estimated presence of 75 and there could well have been a lot more as the species seems quite happy in the heath and bracken where many can sometimes be found.

All the common spring migrants continue to pass through during the first half of May and this is the period when most large falls occur. Up to 500 Willow Warblers may be grounded, 2–300 Wheatears and smaller numbers of a dozen other species. Most of the later Wheatears are of the large, bright Greenland type which often spend a period off passage in western Britain on their two-legged trip from north Africa to Greenland and the extreme north-east of Canada. Many establish temporary territories and sing and display. On average they are much larger than British breeders. The longest winged bird trapped on the Calf had a maximum chord of 114 mm whilst a bird of 111 mm first trapped at 29.5 g was recaught 13 days later when it weighed 46.9 g ready for its long flight over the north Atlantic. Spotted Flycatchers are the latest migrants to arrive, usually a few days after the first Swift. In some years the first bird isn't seen until mid-May but they continue to pass through until mid-June. Up to 50 in a day have been counted with a dozen or more in the observatory garden flycatching from the walls and sycamores. A few Pied Flycatchers also pass through as well as good numbers of Whinchats, Swallows and House Martins. By the end of May a ringing total of 2,000 is hoped for given plenty of winds in the easterly half and light winds for netting. May and June usually produce the odd rarity. Four Subalpine Warblers have been caught in recent springs and there are often a few Lesser Whitethroats or Turtle Dove – both rarities this far

north west. A few Bluethroats have been drifted westwards in the last few springs, Woodchat and Red-backed Shrike recorded and even a Yellow-rumped Warbler from across the Atlantic. A Rustic Bunting was caught around the mill-pond, Scarlet Rosefinch has sung in the withy for a few days and Golden Oriole in the garden for a few minutes. A Cory's Shearwater alighted on the Puddle one calm day and a fine male Red-footed Falcon dashed by Gibdale Point on a June morning. June is also favourite for other raptors with Hobby, Honey Buzzard and two Black Kites recorded. There have been several records of Greenish Warbler in June and July on the Calf, reflecting the line of advancement of the species' breeding range into northwest Europe in recent times. A few have been singing in the garden or withy. Most of these rare birds have turned up during or after a period of anticyclonic weather with east or south-east winds.

Some notable spring days:

16th April 1982	450 Willow Warbler, 70 Chiffchaff, 65 Goldcrest, 47 Fieldfare, 2 Ring Ousel, 200 Meadow Pipit.
2nd May 1981	400 Willow Warbler, 200 Wheatear, 15 Redstart, 15 Chiffchaff, 60 Swallow.
6th May 1970	300 Willow Warbler, 150 Whitethroat, 25 Whinchat, 100 Sedge Warbler, 75 Grasshopper Warbler, Corncrake.
8th May 1983	1,000 Swallow, 250 Sand Martin, 45 House Martin.
11th May 1965	1,000 Whitethroat, 400 Sedge Warbler, 200 Willow Warbler, 36 Grasshopper Warbler, 30 Chiffchaff, 15 Blackcap, 12 Garden Warbler. (451 birds were ringed including 215 Whitethroat, 134 Sedge Warbler and 10 Grasshopper Warbler.)

The time gap between spring and autumn passage through the Calf is very small. No sooner has the last Spotted Flycatcher gone north than the first Curlews are going in the opposite direction. They continue, especially at night, through July and August along with a few other waders such as Common and Green Sandpiper, Greenshank and Whimbrel. Unfortunately there is no sandy beach on the Calf, nor is the mill-pond very attractive to waders, so records are few and many are of birds heard flying over at night. Redshanks do frequent rocky shores and are therefore often recorded. Their numbers on the Calf have dropped markedly since the 1960s reflecting the decreases noted in breeding numbers in Britain as a whole through drainage and loss of habitat. Turnstones and Purple Sandpipers are frequent, particularly at Cow Harbour, in the winter months when stormy weather can concentrate up to 50 of either species there. Curlews also come in to roost there from the main island.

A few Willow Warblers start to arrive from mid-July, usually in single figures, although 50 have been recorded in a day. A few Sedge Warblers and Wheatears pass through as well as one or two Cuckoos. Willow Warblers dominate August with 50–150 usually recorded on several days in the month. Wheatears continue through the month and into October but there are rarely more than 50 in a day. Chiffchaffs and Whitethroats turn up in small numbers from about mid-August onwards and Redstarts and Whinchats usually start in the last week. All these species continue into September and are soon joined by many Meadow Pipits, Grey Wagtails, Robins and Goldcrests in the daily log.

> 6th September 1980 20 Golden Plover, Green Sandpiper, Greenshank, Turtle Dove, 2 Wryneck, 100 Meadow Pipit, 10 Tree Pipit, 30 Grey and 60 White Wagtail, 100 Robin 15 Redstart, 25 Wheatear, 2 Ring Ousel, 20 Garden Warbler, 15 Whitethroat, 80 Chiffchaff, 70 Willow Warbler, 100 Goldcrest and 7 Spotted Flycatcher.

The early Goldcrests come from Northern Ireland, the main island and probably south-west Scotland whilst later ones in October are associated with large arrivals on the east coast of Britain and are doubtless of continental origin. Later in September passage becomes dominated by diurnal movements with birds flying west and south-west over the Glen and, particularly, the observatory. Meadow Pipits, finches and Skylarks often pass through in hundreds and even the Tree Pipit (such a rarity in Ireland) has reached three figures. Hirundines rarely reach the hundreds although a thousand Swallows once gathered in the Glen. More than 50 Grey Wagtails have been counted in a morning as they cross the Sound from the main island coming in at Cow Harbour and Fold Point. White Wagtails tend to feed in the old fields from about mid-August sometimes numbering 1–200. Pieds dominate from mid-September but in much smaller numbers.

At this time of year the wardens often have to do the ringing outside so that they can keep some count of what is flying over. Even so, many are missed which are either flying down the line of the cliffs or high over the Glen only coming into sight from the lighthouse area. Half a dozen birdwatchers, not to mention several ringers, can be kept very busy on the Calf on a day of strong dirunal movement. Unfortunately both are extreme rarities on the Calf and it usually all depends on the warden and his assistant.

October is the busiest month of the year when the total number of migrants is considered. Blackbirds can arrive in large numbers from mid-month especially with strong south-easterlies, rain and fog – up to 500 have been grounded in such conditions. Diurnal thrush movements, especially of Fieldfare and Redwings, are frequent right through to December and after their main movement in September or early October there is usually a late passage of Song Thrushes of continental origin in November. Fieldfares have reached 3,000 and Redwings 1,000 on big thrush days although 1–300 are more usual. Starlings too move south and west in large numbers across the island; 500 to 1,000 in a day are fairly regular whilst 6,000 were counted on 24th October 1971. Thrushes, Starlings, Skylarks and Goldcrests usually dominate any attractions at the lighthouse which, fortunately, with its modern design and 2.5 million candle power, results in very few deaths. The attractions can be impressive with the occasional Short-eared Owl chasing birds in the beam. Most birds do not spend long around the light but land in the heath nearby or depart to the north and east. Many hundreds of thrushes may be grounded but once the weather clears they depart. In the space of an hour or so the whole attraction may be over and the following morning hardly a migrant is to be found anywhere on the islet.

Finches are very numerous in October with several hundred Chaffinches passing over on some days, perhaps alighting briefly in the tops of the sycamores or diving into the fuchsia hedge to avoid a Merlin. Two thousand five hundred Chaffinches were logged in one day in late October 1972 but counts of more than 1,000 are rare. Redpoll, Siskin, Brambling, Greenfinch and Linnet all pass through in numbers although, (apart from the Linnet, which has reached 500 in a day more than once) day totals of 50 for any of these species are uncommon.

There are usually at least a few rarities from August to October especially with winds between south-east and north-east. Although many have turned up with the wind from the west half, Red-breasted Flycatcher, Great Grey Shrike, Yellow-browed Warbler and Barred Warbler have all arrived in north-westerlies more than once. The Pallas's Warbler arrived in a stiff westerly after a period of easterlies. On average one or two *Hippolais* warblers turn up each year usually in August or early September with the odd Wryneck and Barred Warbler about the same time. Red-breasted Flycatchers have appeared from early September to the end of November and there have also been several spring records. Yellow-browed Warblers and Firecrests are mainly recorded from mid-September through October.

Sea-watching from the Calf can be excellent in autumn especially from Cow Harbour looking north with a north-west gale blowing. With the wind in that quarter visibility and light conditions are invariably excellent and birds pass very close by on their way down the north coast or through the Sound. Divers generally fly high over to the south whilst Leach's Petrels may come over the rocks within feet of the observer. Skuas, including the occasional Long-tailed, are common but numbered often in thousands are auks, Gannets and Kittiwakes. If winds are not very strong then more can often be seen from the Stack area or from the hide at Culbery. Looking south from Caigher Point towards the Chickens has produced several good shearwater records in recent years including Balearic and Great, as well as Sooty. Here Gannets can also be observed extremely closely on occasions.

12th September 1980 800 Fulmar, 1 Sooty Shearwater, 650 Manx Shearwater, 2,000 Gannet, 2 Pomarine Skua, 15 Arctic Skua, 23 Great Skua, 700 Kittiwake, 2 Black Tern, Long-tailed Skua and Little Gull.

20th September 1981 8 Red-throated Diver, 400 Fulmar, 30 Sooty Shearwater, 130 Manx Shearwater, 1,500 auks, 900 Gannet, 7 Great Skua.

16th October 1983 4,000 Gannet, 13 Storm Petrel, 5 Leach's Petrel, 8,000 Guillemot, 1,200 Razorbill, 9,000 auk sp., 2 Little Gulls, 5 Pomarine Skua, 40 Arctic Skua, 45 Great Skua, 2 Great Shearwater, 3 Black Tern and a Glaucous Gull.

Unfortunately observatories and migration points are increasingly judged by the number of rarities they receive. Although the Calf produces several each year it gets fewer than stations to the south and east. As an island recording bird migration in the British Isles, however, it is second to none. It lies on major migration routes in both spring and autumn and at the crossroads for birds crossing the Irish Sea. The topography and size of the islet allow for much more accurate recording than can be carried out elsewhere and the level of recording has been steady for more than 25 years continually with the vast majority of coverage carried out by just the warden and his assistant. There is no seasonal or week-end bias as elsewhere and so collected data is extremely useful for comparative purposes. Fortunately the Calf has a stable administration in the form of the Manx Museum and National Trust and hopefully the high standard of birdwork will continue there for many years to come.

History of Manx Ornithology

The early descriptions

Although in the works of Thorwald and Sandulf, the Scandinavian crosses of the 10th century depict the Raven and the Woodpigeon, the Peregrine is the first bird to appear in extant Manx literature. In 1406 Henry IV granted the Kingdom of Man to Sir John Stanley on the condition of doing homage and giving two falcons to him and to succeeding monarchs on their coronation day. The first evidence of bird protection followed a few years later when a law passed in 1422 laid down fines for taking any *Hawke* or *Hyron*. This law was repeated in 1577 and in 1601 we learn that a falconer was regularly employed to warden the Peregrines' nests and to provide doves for them as food.

William Camden (1551–1623) in his *Britannia* of 1586 described great numbers of *Bernacles*, *Clakes* or *Soland Geese* occurring on the Calf – almost certainly referring to the Gannets. He was also the first person to write, albeit briefly, of the *Puffin* (Manx Shearwater), but the earliest descriptive writings about Manx seabirds were those of James Chaloner and Francis Willughby. Born in London, the son of Sir Thomas Chaloner of Guisborough, Yorkshire, James Chaloner (1603–1660) had sat as a judge during the early part of the trial of Charles I and was later a member of the Commission appointed by his wife's cousin Lord Fairfax, the Lord of Mann, to visit the Island in 1651–2. He was a noted antiquarian and an astute observer of wild life, writing a vivid description of the *Puffin* in his *Short Treatise of the Isle of Man* which was published as an appendix to Daniel King's *Vale-Royall of England* or *The County Palatine of Chester Illustrated*. He also wrote of 'some Ayries of mettled *Faulcons*, that build in the Rocks' and of how 'in the Summer time there arrive here out of Ireland and the western parts of Scotland, many of those small Hawks, called *Merlins*' suggesting a discerning appreciation of migratory movement. It was at Chaloner's instigation that Daniel King executed drawings of the Gannet and the Great Auk on the Isle of Man in 1652. Not only does this provide evidence that the Great Auk occurred in the Manx waters during the 17th century, but it is also the earliest recognisable representation of the species known to exist. Chaloner returned to the Island in 1658 as Governor, was imprisoned for a while in Peel Castle for trying to secure the Island for the Parliamentary Party and took poison shortly after his release in 1660.

John Ray (1627–1705) was the son of an Essex blacksmith and a versatile scholar who, during his sojourn at Trinity College, Cambridge was successively Lecturer in Greek and Mathematics and Reader in Humanity. He was ordained in 1660, but is remembered principally as a botanist and as the author of *The Ornithology of Francis Willughby* which was published in 1676.

Francis Willughby (1635–72) came from an aristocratic Warwick family and was a pupil of Ray at Cambridge. In 1662 the two men agreed to attempt a systematic description of the whole organic world and that summer they visited the midland counties, the Isle of Man and Wales. During 1663 and 1664 they travelled widely in Europe and during the summer of 1667 visited south-west England. Willughby died in 1672 and entrusted to his friend the writing up of his ornithological observations and the upbringing of his sons. Willughby is justly regarded as the first scientific naturalist. Ray's book gives a detailed description of the *Puffin of the Isle of Man*, which they found on the Calf and clearly differentiated from *Fratercula arctica*, which they also found breeding in great numbers. He also mentions the nesting of the Guillemot and Razorbill in the Island giving an attractive description of the nesting ledges.

Towards the end of the 17th century the Castle Rushen papers contained notes about the introduction of Partridges and details of payments for killing vermin, notably Kites, Magpies, Ravens and Crows.

During the first half of the 18th century the Island's dominant figure was Bishop Wilson. Thomas Wilson (1663–1755) was born in Cheshire and educated at King's School, Chester and Trinity College, Dublin – he was Bishop of Sodor and Man from 1698 until his death 57 years later. He was a great ecclesiastical reformer and a remarkably generous man. He rebuilt Bishopscourt, was responsible for much tree-planting and wrote an excellent *History of the Isle of Man*, which was included in the second (1722) edition of Bishop Gibson's revision of Camden's *Britannia*, and mentions the absence of the Woodpecker, the Jay and the *Maup* (Bullfinch). He alludes to an *airy* of Eagles and the recent introduction of the Magpie.

Most other references to birds in 18th century writings relate to game, thus Sacheverell (1701) was able to describe how well the Partridges introduced by the Earl of Derby were thriving and Waldron (1731) commented on the excellence of the Teal and Woodcock. Grouse are mentioned in an enactment of 1748 and John Christian, vicar of Marown in 1776 included Grouse and Woodcock among the birds of his parish, although in the same year John Quayle wrote that efforts to introduce Grouse onto the Calf had failed.

Richard Townley spent nearly a year on the Island in 1789–90 and kept a detailed diary. *A Journal kept in the Isle of Man* is the work of an accurate observer with a particular appreciation of natural history. Like other writers he marvelled at the abundance of seabirds on the Calf and also at Fort Island and Douglas Head. He wrote of the very shy wild pigeons which were so plentiful between Peel and the Calf, of Shelduck at Douglas Head, of *Cranes* frequenting the rocks and (with distaste) of the Cormorant. He was impressed by the numbers of small birds – Blackbirds, Thrushes and Linnets in July, Yellowhammers (a flock of over 100), Sparrows (innumerable), Chaffinches and *Tit-larks* (Meadow Pipits) in December. He found Swifts in the Douglas area and also mentions Redbreasts and (Sky) lark – Woodlarks and Nightingales being absent. Strangely he fails to mention the Chough or the Raven although he did find the Grey Crow and the Jackdaw and was told of a small rookery which had existed at the Nunnery. Another visitor John Feltham, writing a few years later repeated a number of Townley's observations but also noted the abundance of Grouse, Golden Plovers, Corncrakes and *Night-larks*. He seems to have been the first to list the Cuckoo (on the Calf).

In 1827 the Island was visited by Sir William Jardine (1800–74), a Scottish baronet who had read both literature and medicine at Edinburgh University. Like many of the naturalists of this era he was also a keen fisherman and a ruthless shot. Between 1833 and 1845 he produced 14 volumes of the *Naturalists' Library* which included many notes on the birds of the Isle of Man. He was the first person to describe the occurrence of the Chough in the Isle of Man, where it was more abundant than anywhere else in his experience. He gives a detailed description of this species and of the great Shag colony on the Calf and also mentions the Storm Petrel, Cormorant and Black Guillemot.

The first half of the 19th century was the age of the naturalist/collector of which Jardine was a typical example. In the Isle of Man J. R. Wallace, a Douglas printer and Dr J. F. Crellin (1816–86) of Orrisdale (Ballaugh) both built up fine collections of birds and contributed respectively to William Yarrell's *British Birds* (1843) and A. G. More's 'Distribution of Birds in Great Britain during the Nesting Season' which appeared in *Ibis* in 1865. Contemporary with Crellin at King William's College and as a long serving Member of the House of Keys was the advocate J. M. Jeffcott (1817–92) an enthusiastic naturalist, archaeologist and geologist who, in his old age, was a frequent source of information to P. G. Ralfe. Dr Crellin's son J. C. was the leading Manx ornithologist of his day making regular contributions to *Yn Lioar Manninagh* and now a century later members of this same family are among the leading authorities on the Island's bird life.

P. G. Ralfe and his contemporaries

The first attempt at a list of Manx species was that of Kermode, originally compiled in 1880 but eventually appearing in 1888 in a much revised form in the *Transactions of the Isle of Man Natural History and Antiquarian Society*. A parson's son, P. M. C. Kermode (1855–1932) was born in Ramsey into an intellectually stimulating family and was much influenced by the example of the great Manx naturalist Edward Forbes (1815–54). In 1879 he founded the Isle of Man Natural History and Antiquarian Society, a title appropriately embodying his two great interests. His first list in 1880 contained 142 species, but this had been trimmed to 127 in the published form. After this the Society's *Transactions* contained frequent ornithological notes and in 1901 he published another list in *Yn Lioar Manninagh*, now extended to 175 species and with quite lengthy notes. By now archaeology was becoming his dominant interest, but he had provided the foundation for P. G. Ralfe's great work *The Birds of the Isle of Man*.

Pilcher George Ralfe (1861–1936) was born in Lezayre, where his father farmed Ellanbane, and worked from the age of 17 in the Isle of Man Bank. A bachelor, he was an indefatigable walker, an intrepid sailor, a keen continental traveller, a capable linguist and for over 40 years the dominant figure of Manx Ornithology. His *Birds of the Isle of Man* published in 1905 is a work of great scholarship and reflects meticulous research. His endearing descriptions of the Manx coastal scenery will never be bettered and many of them have been reproduced in our own *Birds of the Isle of Man*. His book introduced the Island's bird-life to a widespread audience and this was continued with the increasingly regular publication of 'Manx Ornithological Notes' in *British Birds*. For the years 1905–27 these dealt only with the more unusual observations, but between 1925 and 1927 a much more comprehensive *Report on Bird Migration* was published by the Manx Museum. The Notes for 1928 were even more detailed and after their publication in *British Birds* they continued in the same format as 'Ornithology of the Isle of Man' in *The North Western Naturalist*. In 1924 Ralfe's *Supplement to the Birds of the Isle of Man* had been published and his last report was that of 1934.

Ralfe's debt to Kermode has already been mentioned, but he also received much help in compiling *The Birds of the Isle of Man* from F. S. Graves. Frank Graves (1863–1935) was born in Peel into a family which had been prominent in the city for 200 years. Although a partner in a firm of Manchester architects for 40 years he was a frequent visitor to the Island and retired to Peel in 1921. He was an astute observer and the first person to prove the breeding of a mixed Carrion/Hooded Crow pair on the Isle of Man.

1911 saw the arrival of Lt Col. Madoc to take up his appointment as Chief Constable. Henry William Madoc (1870–1936) was a Worcestershire man who had taken part in the Siege of Kimberley when serving with the Cape Mounted Rifles. After the Boer War he had joined the South African Constabulary, eventually retiring as Assistant Inspector General. Soon after his arrival the Isle of Man Constabulary began to feel his infectious enthusiasm for birds. The long arm of the law gave him a useful network of observers and it has often been suggested that the prompt report of some unusual migrant might enhance a young p.c.'s prospects of promotion. His *Bird-Life in the Isle of Man* was published by Witherby in 1934. It does not attempt to provide a complete description of the Manx avifauna, but is very much a personal account of his own observations. It has a style particularly appealing to the bird-lover rather than the serious ornithologist, but nevertheless contains much valuable information. It must however be said that his supporting evidence for a number of rarities was flimsy in the extreme. Shortly before his death he wrote the 'Manx Ornithological Notes' for 1935. A small memorial overlooking the Langness saltmarsh recalls a kindly and much-loved man.

James Bell and Fred Craine were two Ramsey men who made important contributions to Manx ornithology during this period. Bell, who was for many years the Town Clerk, was a keen oologist, whose collection of Manx eggs is now preserved in the Manx Museum. Craine, a dentist, was the pioneer of bird-ringing in the Isle of Man, marking six Herring Gulls in 1926. In those days, when nearly all birds ringed were nestlings, Bell's skill at nest finding made him an obvious partner and the two worked together from 1928 to 1934 ringing over 1,100 birds. Craine compiled 'Ornithology of the

Isle of Man' in 1937 and 1938 and was the first to find a Manx Quail's nest in 1940, not long before he died.

Rogers, Cowin and Williamson

Another of the early Manx ringers was Henry Montague Rogers (1885–1951), whose activities in this field spanned the period 1931 to 1947. He was a patient observer and the first to find the Redshank and the Black-headed Gull breeding in the Isle of Man. Together with A. H. Karran and K. Williamson he founded the Manx Field Club in 1938 and he edited 'Ornithology of the Isle of Man' in 1936 and from 1939 to 1948. Before he died he compiled a check-list entitled *Birds of the Isle of Man*, which was published by the Manx Museum in 1956 – for almost 20 years this was the only contemporary guide to the status of Manx birds.

Will Cowin (1908–58) was an all-round naturalist with a particular interest in ornithology and entomology. He lived and worked (as a banker) in the Island throughout his life, but his best birding was done with his great friend Ken Williamson (1914–77), who in 1937 came to the Manx Museum as librarian. A Lancastrian by birth, Williamson's sojourn at the Museum was cut short by the war and he was obliged to spend 4 years on service in the Faeroe Islands, returning to the Isle of Man for leave. His contribution to Manx ornithology was considerable. As already mentioned he was a founder member of the Manx Field Club and with Cowin he initiated the annual census of rookeries in 1938 and organised the census of breeding Ravens in 1941. Thanks largely to his initiative the ringing effort increased hugely in 1938 and was sustained throughout the war when ringing elsewhere in Britain was of necessity severely limited. He was a meticulous field observer, took copious notes and contributed many papers on Manx ornithology in lucid and effortless prose. His interest in history and folklore produced fascinating articles on the Manx Shearwater, Great Auk, Gannet and Peregrine. His love of islands had its origin in the Isle of Man and was further strengthened while serving on the Faeroes. After a brief period at the York Museum where he pursued his interest in avian taxonomy, he became in 1948 the first warden of the Fair Isle Observatory where he developed his theories on various aspects of migration. Before the war he had with others considered the feasibility of a Bird Observatory on the Calf of Man and had published a valuable hand list of the islet's birds in the *Proceedings* of I.O.M.N.H. and A.S. Soon after his arrival on Fair Isle he wrote an important paper for *Peregrine* which provided the inspiration for the eventual establishment of the Observatory ten years later. In 1957 he spent a season as warden on the remote islands of St Kilda and was then appointed Migration Research Officer of the British Trust for Ornithology. In 1963 he became that body's Population Research Officer, establishing the Common Birds Census scheme and later becoming Chairman of the International Bird Census Committee. The Christmas of 1941 had seen the publication of *Yn Shirragh ny Ree* under the joint editorship of Williamson and Cowin. This awkward title was replaced in future numbers by its English equivalent *Peregrine* which soon became firmly established as the journal of the Manx Field Club. Williamson gave up the editorship in 1948, but characteristically resumed together with E. F. Ladds after Cowin's death in 1958, continuing in this role until 1965. Will Cowin deserves the credit for reviving *Peregrine* in 1952 when it could so easily have died and under his editorship the 'Manx Ornithological Notes' for 1948 and subsequent years appeared in the journal. Cowin's most important contribution to Manx natural history was probably in the field of entomology when in 1944 he discovered a large new Asilid robber-fly at several Manx localities. It has been given the name *Epitriptus cowini*.

Modern times

In the late 1950s D. J. Slinn and A. G. Bourne published important articles on the distribution and population of seabirds heralding the modern era of Manx ornithology of which the Calf of Man Bird Observatory has been the dominant feature.

Einar Brun (1936–76) was born at Sandefjord in Norway and in 1959 was appointed by the Manx Museum and National Trust to be the first warden on the Calf of Man. He and his wife Dido were present from 9th April to 25th September ringing 3,282 birds and making a census of all breeding species. The following year they returned with their baby daughter for a further three months and through their efforts showed that a fully operational observatory should be established on the islet. After obtaining a Ph.D. at Liverpool University's Marine Biological Station at Port Erin in 1969 he was appointed Professor of Marine Biology at Tromsö in 1972. Sadly he was killed when the plane he was piloting crashed into the sea when approaching Bardufoss Airport. W. R. P. Bourne wrote of him in *British Birds*: 'He was a pleasant, stocky, determined character ... of vast energy, knowledge, ability and daring, concealed behind a quiet modest demeanour, with whom it was a pleasure and privilege to deal. ... Whilst he did not take foolish risks, he fearlessly explored the boundaries of human achievement, and it is a tragedy that his luck has failed.'

Since 1962 the Calf observatory has been manned for all but the winter months and has established its place in the network of British bird observatories. Forty-two of the 56 species added to the Manx list since 1959 have been first recorded on the Calf while over 100,000 birds have been ringed there. Malcolm Wright, warden from 1968–74, has vividly described the work of the observatory in *Birdwatchers' Year* (1973).

This same period has seen the emergence of the Manx Bird Club, now called the Manx Ornithological Society. Its membership of around 100 has contributed to a number of national projects and has carried out important studies on the breeding populations of Fulmar, the three species of tern, Chough, Rook and Raven.

Bird ringing

Although the first modest attempts at bird-ringing had taken place in Britain in 1890, it was in Denmark that systematic large scale ringing was started by Christian Mortensen of Viborg in 1899. Other schemes were started in Germany in 1903, Hungary in 1908 and Britain in 1909 in which year over 2,000 birds were ringed. The first ringed bird to be recovered on the Isle of Man was a Starling found at Andreas in late May 1914, having been ringed three months previously at the lighthouse of the Mull of Galloway. By the time Fred Craine ringed his first Herring Gulls in 1926, more than 175,000 birds had been ringed in Britain and while he had two insular Blackbird recoveries in 1927, the first recovery away from the Island was a Woodcock shot in Wigtownshire in January 1931, having been ringed at Ballaugh 8 months previously. Between 120 and 200 birds were ringed on the Island annually until 1938 when the total jumped to 586 and almost doubled to 1,140 the following year when over 55,000 were ringed in Britain as a whole.

The majority of birds ringed in the early years were nestlings (pulli), but trapping increased in importance (especially for passerines) so that in 1939 totals of pulli and trapped birds ringed in Britain were almost indentical, although in the Island pulli still made up 88% of the total.

In Britain as a whole the War drastically restricted the activities of ringers, more especially with regard to trapping, but on the Island restrictions were much less marked. The relative Manx contribution to the national effort increased to over 15% of all birds ringed in 1943. In each year from 1942 to 1945 the group led by Will Cowin ringed more than any other individual or group in Britain. Even as late as 1948 this group was 4th in the national league table.

Trapping gained in importance after the war and especially after the introduction of the almost invisible mist net in 1956. By 1959 pulli only constituted 23% of birds ringed in Britain and although this proportion had sunk as low as 15% in 1976 the 1959 figure was repeated in both 1983 and 1984.

Bird-ringing on the Island had declined during the 1950's but revived with the establishment of the Calf Observatory in 1959. Over 30% of birds ringed by the Bruns were pulli but trapping has dominated the Calf ringing effort and in recent years has accounted for 81–93% of the annual total. Calf wardens have been able to assist in the training of local ringers and in 1969 a small ringing station was set up in an overgrown Port Erin garden by Brian Karran. Here regular mist-netting has recently provided about 1,000 birds per annum for ringing. Over 5,000 birds were ringed on the Calf of Man in 1970, but it was another ten years before this figure was achieved again. In 1981 a Calf total of 6,155 together with 2,250 from the main Island gave a record Manx figure of 8,405.

Until 1958 Swallows were consistently ringed in much greater numbers than any other species, followed by Blackbirds and Herring Gulls, Song Thrushes and Robins, Chaffinches and then Yellowhammers. Willow Warblers, Goldcrests and Blackbirds are now the most ringed species owing to the use of mist nets, with Meadow Pipits almost rivalling Blackbirds in the moorland habitat of the Calf.

The Perwick cave midden deposit

In 1969 F. J. Radcliffe excavated a cave at Perwick Bay which had, he suspected, been used for human habitation. Sealed under slate slabs which had fallen from the roof, and overlying a beach deposit, he found a midden deposit. The following year he and L. S. Garrad obtained carbonised wood from the deposit and subsequent radiocarbon dating suggested an original date of approximately AD 90.

The deposit consisted mainly of limpet shells and the bones of wild and domestic animals and wild birds. The avian skeletal remains identified by D. Bramwell (represented by single individuals unless otherwise stated) were as follows:

Cormorant, Shag, Goose (possibly domestic), Buzzard, Kestrel, Razorbill, Great Auk, Guillemot (several), Puffin, Rock Dove, Meadow Pipit (or similar species), Jackdaw, Chough (several), Blackbird (or Song Thrush) and Robin.

The Great Auk was represented by a furcula which was almost identical with a specimen in the zoological department of Manchester University and a femur identifiable by virtue of its auk features and size.

The Breeding Distribution Maps

Field work for *The Atlas of Breeding Birds in Britain and Ireland* (Sharrock 1976) was carried out between 1968 and 1972 and in the published maps the Isle of Man was represented by 14 ten kilometre squares. Like many counties on the adjacent islands we were soon prompted to try and produce a more detailed survey, and much as we would have liked to use the tetrad (2 sq. km) as our unit area it would have been quite impossible for our small band of 23 recorders to adequately survey 186 squares. The Isle of Man's 39 five kilometre squares were therefore surveyed during the period 1977–1981.

Each ten kilometre square was divided into four, the resultant five kilometre squares being identified by the addition of NW, NE, SW, or SE to the two letter and two number label of the larger square. Each five kilometre square was also named after a geographical feature exclusive to that square.

The degrees of evidence of breeding were represented by the following code:

Possible Breeding (shown as a small dot on the maps)
  Bird recorded in breeding season in possible nesting habitat, but no other indication of breeding noted.

Probable Breeding (shown as a medium sized dot on the maps)
S Singing male present (or breeding calls heard) on more than one date in same place.
T Bird (or pair) apparently holding territory.
D Courtship and display; or agitated behaviour or anxiety calls from adults, suggesting probable presence of nest or young nearby; or brood patch on trapped female.
N Visiting probable nest site.
B Nest-building (including excavating nest-hole).

Confirmed Breeding (shown as a large dot on the maps)
DD Distraction-display or injury feigning.
UN Used nest found.
FL Recently fledged young.
FS Adult carrying faecal sac.
FY Adult(s) with food for young.
ON Adult(s) entering or leaving nest-site in circumstances indicating occupied nest (including colonies).
NE Nest and eggs, or bird sitting and not disturbed, or egg shells found away from nest.

NY   Nest with young or *downy* young of ducks, game birds, waders etc.

The map illustrates the quality of cover achieved.
High small dot totals in a few squares reveal the deficiencies.

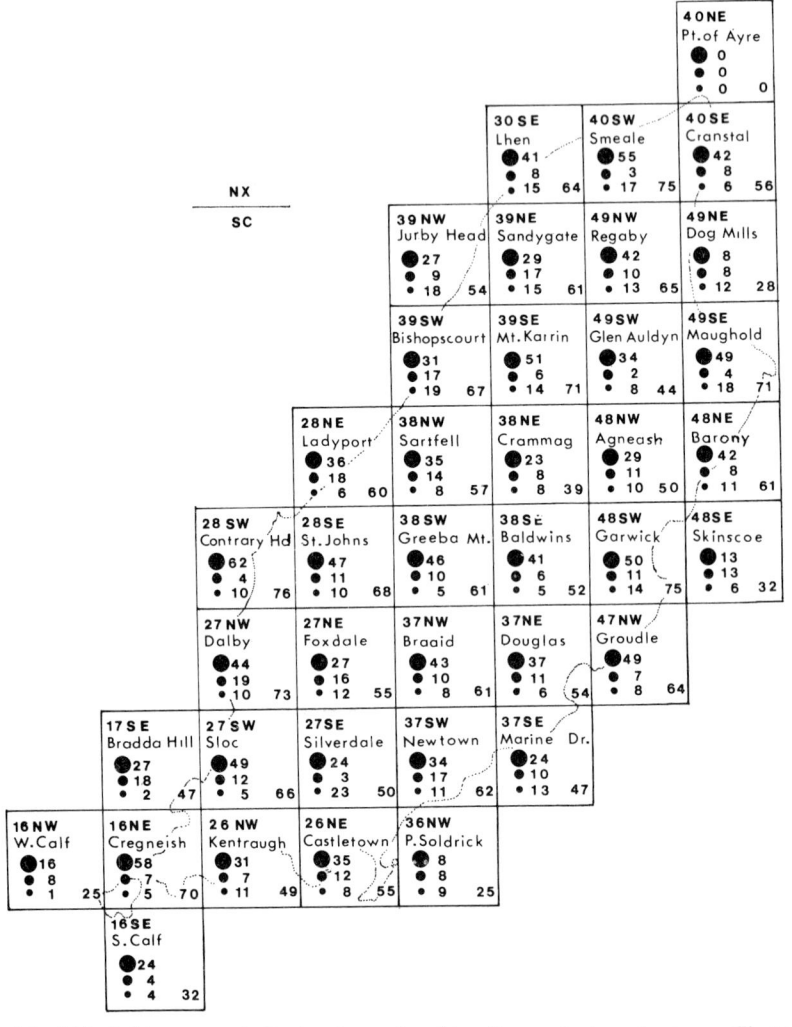

						40NE Pt.of Ayre ●0 ●0 ●0 0	
				30SE Lhen ●41 ●8 •15 64	40SW Smeale ●55 ●3 •17 75	40SE Cranstal ●42 ●8 •6 56	
			NX SC	39NW Jurby Head ●27 ●9 •18 /54	39NE Sandygate ●29 ●17 •15 61	49NW Regaby ●42 ●10 •13 65	49NE Dog Mills ●8 ●8 •12 28
				39SW Bishopscourt ●31 ●17 •19 67	39SE Mt.Karrin ●51 ●2 •14 71	49SW Glen Auldyn ●34 ●4 •8 44	49SE Maughold ●49 ●4 •18 71
			28NE Ladyport ●36 ●18 •6 60	38NW Sartfell ●35 ●14 •8 57	38NE Crammag ●23 ●8 •8 39	48NW Agneash ●29 ●11 •10 50	48NE Barony ●42 ●8 •11 61
		28SW Contrary Hd ●62 ●4 •10 /76	28SE St.Johns ●47 ●11 •10 68	38SE Greeba Mt. ●46 ●10 •5 61	38SE Baldwins ●41 ●6 •5 52	48SW Garwick ●50 ●11 •14 75	48SE Skinscoe ●13 ●13 •6 32
		27NW Dalby ●44 ●19 •10 73	27NE Foxdale ●27 ●16 •12 55	37NW Braaid ●43 ●10 •8 61	37NE Douglas ●37 ●11 •6 54	47NW Groudle ●49 ●7 •8 64	
	17SE Bradda Hill ●27 ●18 •2 47	27SW Sloc ●49 ●12 •5 66	27SE Silverdale ●24 ●3 •23 50	37SW Newtown ●34 ●17 •11 62	37SE Marine Dr. ●24 ●10 •13 47		
16NW W.Calf ●16 ●8 •1 25	16NE Cregneish ●58 ●7 •5 70	26NW Kentraugh ●31 ●7 •11 49	26NE Castletown ●35 ●12 •8 55	36NW P.Soldrick ●8 ●8 •9 25			
	16SE S.Calf ●24 ●4 •4 32						

The Isle of Man's 5 km squares indicating the number of breeding species in each category. The total (all categories) is given for each square.

Ninety-six species were proved to breed in the Isle of Man, 6 more were graded as *probable* breeders and 11 *possible*. In the second category the Stock Dove can be assumed to breed regularly, Redstart, Garden Warbler and Wood Warbler probably nest sporadically, while Quail and Nightjar are unlikely to have bred – all are former breeding species. Possible breeding birds were Storm Petrel, Pochard, Goldeneye, Merlin, Water Rail, Common Gull, Roseate Tern, Sandwich Tern, Turtle Dove, Kingfisher and Tree Pipit. Of these it can be assumed that the Water Rail is a regular breeder and the Common Gull was to nest after 1981. The Red-breasted Merganser, unrecorded during the survey period, was found nesting in 1985.

Recorders:
J. A. Burn, H. S. Collister, J. P. Cullen, B. Denner, A. Harris, R. J. Haycock, C. Howland, P. P. Jennings, K. Johnson, M. S. Keig, E. D. Kerruish, C. J. Lowe, P. R. Marshall, D. J. Milne, A. S. Moore, F. B. Moore, J. Nuttall, A. J. Sayle, J. D. Stigant, J. Thomas, J. D. Tinkler, M. M. Williams and M. Woodworth.

A Systematic List of the Birds of the Isle of Man

This list follows the sequence and scientific nomenclature of *List of Recent Holarctic Bird Species* by K. H. Voous (1977). It is based on data available at the end of 1982, but additional important records for the period 1983–5 have been included.

Unless otherwise stated the histograms illustrating passage on the Calf of Man are based on analysis of records for the period 1959–81. The maps illustrating ringing recoveries include all known movements involving the Isle of Man up to the end of 1982. Circular symbols are shown at recovery site where a bird has been ringed on the Isle of Man. Oval symbols are shown at the ringing site where a bird has been recovered on the Isle of Man. Marks on the symbols indicate months as on a clock face (e.g., 4 o'clock = 4th month = April). Month of ringing is shown inside the symbol and month of recovery is shown outside.

The Common Birds Census (C.B.C.)

The text contains frequent references to the Common Birds Census. This was started by the British Trust for Ornithology in 1962 and was at first confined to farmland but later embraced woodland as well. Census work involves the mapping of territorial males of each species within the observer's plot over a series of visits during the breeding season. At present over 300 plots are censused in Britain annually, farmland plots averaging 70 ha. in area and woodland about 23 ha. Using data from all plots surveyed in successive years fluctuations in population can be quite accurately assessed. In the C.B.C. the annual index is the population level of a species relative to 100 in 1966.

Red-throated Diver
Gavia stellata

Red-throated Diver   Great Northern Diver

Regular passage migrant and rather scarce winter visitor to coastal waters.

Ralfe regarded the Red-throated Diver as a regular winter visitor and described several wintering in Douglas Bay in 1891.

Only recorded in 10 of the 30 years up to 1960, but since then has occurred annually and with increasing frequency.

First autumn birds usually appear in mid September, but 1 was seen at Fleshwick on 26th July 1972 and there have been occasional August records. Autumn movement is seen principally off the Ayres coast, and to a lesser extent around the intensively watched waters of the Calf, up to the end of November, though the frequent December records are also probably of southbound birds. Not often seen between January and March, there is modest passage during April extending into the first week of May. A very late bird was seen from the Calf on 28th May 1970.

Recently there have been several reports of small parties off the Ayres and around the Calf. The exceptional autumn of 1980 produced no less than 5 records of 5–10 birds and there were 30 off the Ayres coast on 22nd April 1984. Calf records of the Red-throated Diver are nearly all of birds flying past – only very rarely have birds been seen fishing offshore.

Manx: *Lhargey Mooar*

Black-throated Diver

Gavia arctica

Scarce passage migrant and winter visitor to coastal waters.

As in Ralfe's time this is easily the rarest of the three divers on the Manx list. Of a number of mid-September records the earliest was 1 off the Calf, on 8th September 1981. Records have been fairly evenly distributed through the winter to early April with late birds on 11th May in 1973 and 1979. From September to early November and during March and April the Ayres account for the greatest number of records. Although there have been 16 autumn records from the Calf, only 1 has been seen there in Spring. In the remaining winter months the sheltered bay of Peel is favoured particularly. Nearly always seen singly, there were 3 at Blue Point on 5th November 1948 and off the Calf on 15th September 1985.

Manx: *Lhargey*

Great Northern Diver

Gavia immer

Regular winter visitor and passage migrant.

Ralfe considered the Great Northern Diver to be 'far from rare during the winter months' and its present status is similar. To the Isle of Man it is essentially a winter visitor often spending many weeks in the bay of its choice. Peel Bay is favoured to a quite remarkable degree – Derbyhaven, though infinitely less popular, is definitely preferred to Port St Mary, Port Erin and Ramsey. Wintering birds are usually seen singly, although in January

1928 rough seas brought 13 into Peel Bay and the following year 14 were seen there during a south-westerly gale in early December. Such numbers were exceptional and have not been approached during the last 30 years – 5 in Port Erin Bay in late December 1973 being the most notable winter gathering.

Migrants are considerably less common than Red-throated Divers and are seen principally from the Calf and off the north coast. Spring passage is notably thin and irregular, occurring from early March to late May. There have been 4 June records, the latest being 1 at Port e Vullen on 10th June 1945. There are only 2 spring records for the Calf of Man.

The earliest autumn record for the Manx coast was an immature bird seen by Ken Williamson at Derbyhaven on 24th July 1938. There has been one August record, but from about 10th September reports become increasingly frequent and passage continues strongly until mid-November.

There are no inland records for any of the divers.

According to J. R. Bruce the Great Northern Diver was known as Harry Preston to Port Erin fishermen (Ralfe 1930).

Manx: *Arrag Vooar* = Big Pullet. *Thummeyder*.

Little Grebe

Tachybaptus ruficollis

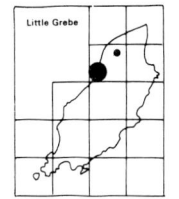

Scarce and irregular breeder. Regular winter visitor.

It seems likely that Little Grebes bred annually in the north of the island during the first half of this century. The Bishop's Dub, Ballaugh Curraghs and Ballacain Dubs were particularly favoured and there were also breeding records from Lough Cranstal and Gat y Wing. Sporadic nesting also took place at the Eairy Dam. At least 3 pairs bred on the island in 1928. During the last 30 years breeding records have been very infrequent although it is possible that nesting has occurred unnoticed as there is an abundance of suitable habitats in the north. First clutches are usually laid in April, although laying has occasionally started on the last few days of March. In 1938 young hatched from successive clutches at Ballacain on 24th April and 5th June. Four eggs appear to be the usual clutch size.

Little Grebes can regularly be found around the Manx coast from November to March, the extreme dates being 9th October and 7th April. They also occur every winter on the reservoirs, the dams at Foxdale and Tromode and on the more sluggish streams such as the Dhoo at Kirby, the lower Sulby and the Killane River. Two to three birds may be seen together and there were 5 in Ramsey Harbour in mid December 1975. One on 24th September 1980 was the first Calf record, to be followed by single birds from 12th to 15th April and on 10th November 1981.

Manx: *Eean Kereen Beg*

Great Crested Grebe

Podiceps cristatus

Scarce but regular winter visitor.

One or two Great Crested Grebes are reported annually from coastal sites between October and March, Derbyhaven Bay being far and away the most favoured location. There have been 5 records for the Calf of Man all within the period 2nd September to 15th October. Inland a male was shot at Kerrowdhoo in May 1938, 1 was seen at Ballacain on 25th April 1962 and 1 was at Ballamoar Reserve during the winter of 1973/74. One was seen at Langness on 29th June 1984, an adult female was found dying in a tidal pool at Castletown on 15th July 1910 and 2 were seen off Fort Island on 17th August 1923. Wintering birds are nearly always single, but during passage periods 2 together have been seen on a number of occasions and there were 4 off Fort Island on 22nd March 1928.

Manx: *Eean Kereen*

Red-necked Grebe

Podiceps grisegena

Uncommon winter visitor.

Ralfe's assertion that this was the most frequently recorded of the larger grebes is no longer true as the Red-necked shares with the Black-necked the distinction of being the rarest of the grebes on the Manx list.

With the exception of 1 shot at Ramsey in 1894 and 1 at the Eairy in February 1934, records (7 in the last 30 years) have been confined to the south east corner of the Island, and then almost exclusively Derbyhaven Bay. Although 1 was seen at Derbyhaven on 17th April 1889, it has been exclusively a winter visitor during the present century with records evenly spread between 13th October and 26th March. Usually seen singly, there are a few records of 2 together and there were 3 in Castletown Bay on 21st November 1949.

Manx: *Eean Kereen Jiarg*

Slavonian Grebe

Podiceps auritus

Irregular winter visitor.

To the Isle of Man the Slavonian Grebe is almost exclusively a maritime winter visitor, occurring with a frequency comparable to that of the Great Crested Grebe with some 15 records during the 30 years up to 1983.

Records are spread fairly evenly from mid November to the end of February. Of a handful of records outside this period the earliest was 1 on 9th October 1928 and the latest 1 off Langness on 28th March 1939. Nearly all records are from Derbyhaven Bay and recently single birds only have been reported, but 2 have occurred on a number of occasions and Derbyhaven Bay held 6 on 9th March 1939.

The only inland record was of one shot on a dub at Andreas in February 1924.

Manx: *Eean Kereen Cleayshagh*

Black-necked Grebe
Podiceps nigricollis

Occasional winter visitor.

Rarest of the grebes, the Black-necked has been recorded 7 times in the last 30 years, mostly in January and early February. Overall, Derbyhaven accounts for the large majority of records, although it has not been seen there since 1960. The 3 most recent occurrences have been single birds at the Eairy on 2nd October 1964 (the only inland record), Port St Mary on 17th December 1967 and Ramsey Harbour on 7th and 8th February 1974.

Madoc had a number of records from as early as 24th August and through March to 6th April in the late 20s and early 30s, suggesting that the Black-necked Grebe was perhaps a more regular passage migrant then.

Fulmar
Fulmarus glacialis

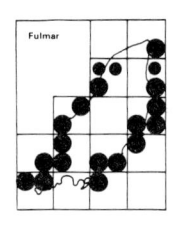

Common resident.

According to Fisher Fulmars first bred in Co. Donegal in 1912, spreading to Rathlin Island in 1921 from which the Isle of Man was subsequently colonised perhaps via the Antrim coast. The first Manx record was in the winter of 1927 and in June 1931 one was seen off Peel Hill. During the next few years prospecting on the west cliffs of the Calf took place and 6 pairs were finally found nesting below the Old Lower Light in 1936. Colonisation of the Isle of Man was thus 4 years behind that of the Mull of Galloway where breeding first occurred in 1932 but preceded Lambay Island (Dublin), St Bee's Head and the Great Orme (North Wales) where prospecting began in the late 1930s. On the main island the cliffs eastwards to the Chasms, Aldrick, Clay Head and Maughold were all prospected from 1938, with breeding finally proved at Kione y Ghoggan and Kione ny Garee in 1941. By 1949 eggs had been laid at Aldrick, 5 sites on the west coast and at Shellag. Ten years later breeding had been confirmed at 10 more sites, 8 of these being on the east coast between Maughold and Port Soderick (Slinn 1962). In 1959 the Isle of Man held about 250 occupied sites.

By 1969 3 new colonies had appeared between Niarbyl and Contrary Head, 2 between Port Moar and Dhoon, and 4 more between Port Soderick and Port Soldrick. There was also a new colony at Perwick (Slinn 1971). Occupied sites now numbered close to 600.

Since then the overall population has continued to expand with 900–1,000 occupied sites in 1980, a minimum of 1,860 in 1984 and over 2,200 in 1985 (Moore 1985). Since 1969 the population has increased at a rate of 8% per annum. In the period 1949–70 the rate for Britain as a whole (excluding St Kilda) was 7% per annum (Cramp et al. 1974), but although still increasing this rate has slowed considerably since. On the Calf a peak of 125 sites was achieved in 1981, since which there has been a slight decline and there is some evidence that other colonies in the south west are also less prosperous. In contrast there has been huge expansion between Glen Maye and Peel and between Will's Strand and Glen Wyllin.

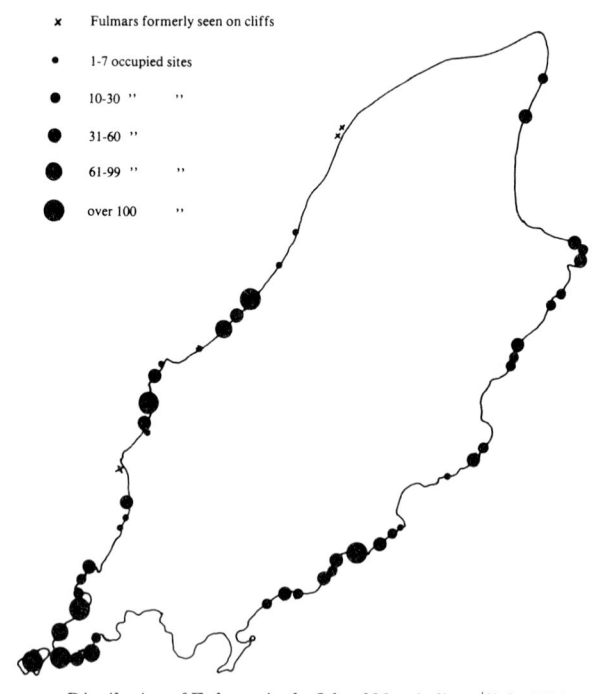

Distribution of Fulmars in the Isle of Man in June/July 1984

Occupied Fulmar sites at selected parts of the coast.

	1959	1969	1973	1975	1977	1979	1980	1981	1984
Calf	41	40	60	124	99	114	110	125	105
Glen Maye to Peel	12	55	?	50	84	90	135	177	215
Will's Strand to Glen Wyllin	?	32	?	?	?	95	140	148	244

Slinn has studied the Kione ny Garee colony at Port Erin very thoroughly. Here there is a rapid increase in numbers during December after which numbers may vary quite markedly during the winter. In early May the colony is virtually deserted but after about 2 weeks numbers again increase and laying takes place in late May and early June. Numbers decline again in July. At the Calf southward movement is seen during August and September with a peak towards the middle of the latter month. One hundred to five hundred birds per day are often seen with a maximum of 800 flying south on 12th September 1980. All around the Island Fulmars are very scarce or absent from late September to the first week in November, during which month some of the breeding colonies become tenanted once more.

An example of the rare dark phase occupied the same ledge at Kione ny Garee between 1959 and 1961 and other individuals have been seen at Wood's Strand in 1981 and 1982, the southern end of Bulgham Bay in 1982 and 1983 and Keristal in 1983.

Slinn describes how in 1962 a Fulmar took over a nest at Kione ny Garee on which a Herring Gull had been sitting until 3 days previously, the Fulmar subsequently laying an egg in the gull's nest and in 1984 Moore found Fulmars occupying two gulls' nests in the Peel area.

At 14 localities Fulmars have occupied Ravens' nests, although there is no evidence that they actually ejected the Ravens. At the Chasms a Raven sat on a nest 5 metres away. On at least two occasions Fulmars have used the nests of Hooded Crows.

Three Fulmars ringed on the Calf have been recovered, from the Galloway and Cumbrian coasts in September and from St Abb's, Berwickshire in June. In addition a bird ringed at Shellag in August 1946 was recovered inland in Lincolnshire 3 weeks later.

Manx: *Eean Croymmagh*

Cory's Shearwater
Calonectris diomedea

The only accepted record is of one off the Calf on 7th May 1979 (Jennings 1981).

Great Shearwater
Puffinus gravis

One was seen off the Calf on 23rd June 1966 and 2 more between the Chicken Rock and the Calf on 16th October 1983.

Sooty Shearwater
Puffinus griseus

First recorded in Carrick Bay in August 1955, southbound Sooty Shearwaters now regularly pass the Island in autumn. Although there are records from 16th July to 16th October, mostly from the Calf, the great majority have been in September. There have been two particularly noteworthy days for Calf passage. On 9th September 1978 12 flew south past the west coast, 13 having passed Machrihanish (Kintyre) 170 km NNW the previous day. On 20th September 1981 30 flew south past the Calf. Three birds seen from the Calf on 7th October 1981 were the lastest Manx records by 2 weeks.

Manx Shearwater
Puffinus puffinus

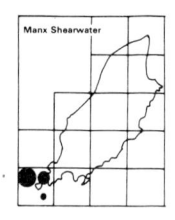

Abundant summer visitor. Probably breeds in small numbers.

'The Manx Shearwater colony of the Calf, probably in its hey-day the largest the world has ever known,' (Williamson 1940) is first mentioned in Njál's Saga which describes how the ships of the two chieftains Ospak and Brodir spent 3 nights near the Calf prior to the battle of Clontarf which took place outside Dublin on Good Friday 1014. Ospak's ships were anchored in the Sound, while those of Brodir were immediately outside it. Each night a terrible clamour was heard by Brodir and his men and there seems no doubt that they were listening to the nocturnal chorus of a large breeding colony of Manx Shearwaters (Williamson 1973).

James Chaloner, writing in 1656, was the first to describe the Manx Shearwater in any detail. 'Of Fowl, this Island hath plenty and great variety especially in the Isle of the Calf, where there is a sort of Sea-Fowl, called Puffines, of a very unctuous constitution, which breeds in the coney holes (the conies leave their burrows for that time) are never seen with their young but either very early in the morning or late in the evening, nourishing (as is conceived) their Young with Oyl; which drawn from their own Constitution, is dropped into their mouths; for that being open there is found in their Crops no other sustenance but a single Sorrel leaf, which the Old give their Young, for digestion's sake, as is conjectured; the flesh of these birds is nothing pleasant fresh, because of their rank and Fish-like taste; but pickled or salted, they may be ranked with Anchoves, Caviare, or the like; but profitable they are in their feathers, and Oyl, of which they make great use about their Wooll.'

Much was written about the Manx Shearwater during the 17th and 18th centuries, although nearly all related to their annual harvest on the Calf. The earliest such references appear in the Books of Charge contained in the Castle Rushen papers which are held in the Manx Museum. An entry in 1599 revealed that oil extracted from the young birds was used in both the treatment of wool and for cleaning firearms. There are also entries relating to payment to a man for dressing puffins, to another for making firkins for puffins and to others for carriage of puffins by fishing boat to Douglas and to England. The young birds were taken from their burrows using an iron hook (Quayle 1812) and 'that they may the more readily know and keep an account of the number they take, they cut off one foot and reserve it, which gave occasion to the fable that the puffins are single-footed' (Ray 1678). Several 17th century authors state that the harvest took place in late July and early August, the birds were potted or pickled and would last up to a year and while some were exported the majority were eaten on the Isle of Man.

Writers during this period persisted in calling the Manx Shearwater the Puffin and undoubtedly this led to some confusion with *Fratercula arctica* towards the end of the 18th century. This was not so of Willughby who accurately described both species and gives a detailed account of the family life of the shearwater. He related how the Earl of Derby allowed certain people to take the birds from their burrows to sell 'for about nine pence the dozen, a very cheap rate.' In some years the sale of young shearwaters could realise as much as thirty pounds. As that is equivalent to 9,600 young birds the breeding population was clearly enormous. As the flesh tasted of fish the Roman Catholic Church allowed it to be eaten during Lent (Ray 1678).

From various sources it has been calculated that subsequent harvests were 1674 – 2,524 birds, 1708 – 3,186 birds, 1711 – 6,270 birds and 1716 – 3,174 birds (Megaw 1941), but in 1789 Townley does not appear to have seen any shearwaters and wrote of a decline 'since the rats have got such a footing in the place'. It is popularly supposed that the rats reached the Calf from a Russian merchant ship which was wrecked in the Sound a year or two before Townley's visit. In 1812 Quayle wrote 'not an individual is now bred in the island' and when Jardine visited the Calf in 1827 he was 'much disappointed in scarcely being able to trace even the recollection of their former abundance'.

There is no evidence that Manx Shearwaters bred on the main island – a point specifically made by Sacheverell in 1702 and Robertson in 1794.

Although no longer breeding, Manx Shearwaters remained common around the coast during the summer months. In late June 1938 Williamson et al. explored the west cliffs of the Calf at night without success although next morning 'there were literally hundreds of the birds skimming the waves close inshore below the upper lighthouse and all along the north west coast'. Although birds were heard calling all night on 29th April 1944 it was not until the appointment of a Calf warden in 1959 that it was possible to properly reassess the status of the Manx Shearwater on the islet and the following year birds were heard calling regularly on dark nights from 20th June. Although breeding was not proved 3 birds were ringed and one was heard calling inside a burrow near Kione ny Halbey.

From then onwards shearwaters were assumed to breed on the Calf in small numbers, perhaps 10–12 pairs. Birds were also heard in the central part of the island and below the upper lighthouse where in 1967 a bird still with down was found on 22nd August. While this may have been Calf-bred, some down can often be seen on immature birds after they have left their natal colony.

Although there has been no further proof of breeding, birds have been recorded ashore on summer nights each year on the Calf, the two most favoured areas being Creg Veanagh and Kione ny Halbey. Using a continual loop tape lure in 1982 del Nevo obtained responses from adult birds at over 30 burrows, some of which contained 2 birds simultaneously. This work was carried out at Kione ny Halbey and near the Burroo.

It seems probable that the majority of birds heard in July and August are immature birds prospecting, on the other hand the few birds heard at night in spring are almost certainly breeding adults and the same can be said of a bird ringed in July 1967 and retrapped in the same area in the same month 10 years later. Rats remain serious predators and it will be interesting to see if the major poisoning project initiated in 1979 will be of benefit to the shearwaters.

Manx Shearwaters are most often seen off the coast between July and September, the majority of movement being southerly along the west coast. Large movements in spring are rare, 2,000 moving south off the Calf in 4 hours on 30th May 1972 being quite exceptional. On 14th August 1979 4,000 flew south past the Calf in $4\frac{1}{2}$ hours. Recent extreme dates have been on 1st March 1979 and 21st November 1972.

Adults ringed at Skokholm (1) and Copeland (5) have been recovered on the Isle of Man, while a Calf ringed bird was found dead at Newcastle, Co. Down a month later. One Copeland bird was found dead 11 years and 1 month after ringing, while a bird ringed on the Calf in July 1967 was retrapped there 10 years later.

Nineteen examples of the Balearic race *P.p. mauretanicus* have been recorded – 2 in August, 12 in September, 4 in October and 1 in November – almost always associated with large movements of the nominate race.

Manx: *Scraayl*

Storm Petrel
Hydrobates pelagicus

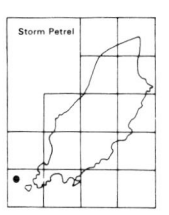

Common summer visitor which probably breeds on the Calf.

The earliest record of the Storm Petrel was by Jardine who saw small parties off Douglas Harbour in June 1829 although he failed to find any evidence of breeding. Train described how Storm Petrels were among the thousands of seabirds wrecked off the south coast after the memorable tempest of 6th and 7th January 1839 and in 1863 Thwaites wrote that the species was still found on the Calf. Williamson (1940) considered that this was another lost breeding species.

The first record of birds coming to land came in 1967 when two birds were netted at night near the Upper Lighthouse on the Calf in mid July. In the late 1970s it was established that Storm Petrels are present on the Calf most nights from late June to mid September. They occur in the vicinity of the cliffs all around the islet, but are most numerous on the north side. Exact numbers are impossible to determine but 50 were caught using a tape-lure and one 40 foot mist net on 28th/29th August 1979 suggesting a presence into triple figures.

The evidence for breeding is as follows. Chasing display flight and singing were recorded in 1978. Five birds that were first ringed in 1978 were retrapped in 1979 and two of these were caught together with fresh soil adhering to their feet and rings. Retraps in subsequent years of birds ringed at non-breeding colonies are very rare or unknown and the adhering soil indicates that the birds concerned had been below ground very near by and were probably a pair. Singing and calling was heard on many nights during the summer of 1981 from a site on the north coast which was both suitable for breeding and inaccessible to rats.

Storm Petrels are seen infrequently off the Manx coast during daylight between July and September, a notable movement was however observed from Peel on 18th July 1976 when 383 flew south between 1920 and 2120. There are 3 records of exhausted birds being picked up in Peel in November and December.

From 1978 to 1982 a total of 662 birds were mist-netted aided by tape lure. Seventy-two of these birds carried rings from other sites and 75 recoveries resulted from ringing the remainder. Birds trapped on the Calf were trapped at other sites as follows – Ailsa Craig 3, Turnberry (Ayrshire), Portencross

(Ayrshire) 2, Mull of Kintyre, Sanda Island (Kintyre) 89, Island Davaar (Kintyre) 5, Treshnish Isles (Mull) 2, Longa Island (Wester Ross), Bottle Island (Wester Ross), Priest Island (Wester Ross) 6, Glas-leac Mor (Wester Ross), Shiant Islands (off Lewis), Hirta (St. Kilda) 2, Stromness (Orkney), Fair Isle 2, Roaninish (Donegal), Inishvickilane (Kerry), Cape Clear (Cork), Great Saltee (Wexford) 2 and Bardsey Island 5.

Over 60 birds were trapped on the Calf and at another location during the same year. The time difference was up to 45 days and involved Sanda in 38 instances, Copeland in 12, Davaar in 3, Ailsa Craig in 2 and Turnberry, Longa, Glas-leac Mor, Shiant Islands, Fair Isle, Bardsey and Great Saltee on one occasion each. Two birds were trapped at 3 different sites during the same summer viz. Calf 10th August – Sanda 20th August – Copeland 26th August and Sanda 13th July – Calf 5th August – Copeland 22nd August. One bird ringed on the Calf was recovered at Sanda the following night and another at Turnberry the following night. Two individuals ringed at Ailsa Craig were controlled on the Calf one night later. Sixty per cent of all movements have been to or from Sanda off the Kintyre peninsula. The remaining recovery was a bird caught aboard a trawler off Cape Town in January 1981, having been ringed on the Calf in August 1978. The food-rich area along the continental shelf in the region is the main wintering place for adults of this species.

Manx: *Kitty Varrey* = Sea Kitty i.e., Wren.

Leach's Petrel

Oceanodroma leucorhoa

Regular on autumn passage.

Until the great wreck of 1952, Leach's Petrel had only been recorded on 4 occasions and 3 of these were obviously storm driven birds such as the one which flew into a woman's face on a wild winter night in Lake Lane, Peel. She caught it and had it stuffed!

The period 21st October–8th November 1952 saw a huge wreck wherein at least 7,000 died in Britain and Ireland. Corpses were found at Ramsey (3) and Port St Mary (1) between 28th October and 3rd November, 30 or 40 were reported off the Calf during the first week of November and there were hundreds in Peel Bay on 6th November.

In 1961 severe storms produced a rare east coast record when 5 were seen circling over Douglas Promenade on 26th October and 2 years later, coinciding with a wreck along the coasts of Lancashire and Cheshire, 174 birds were seen making in a south-westerly direction past the Calf on 27th and 29th September. On the night of 25th/26th September storm force 10 winds had followed 2 days of gale force south-westerlies.

During the last 15 years west to north-westerly gales have regularly brought

Calf records between early September and mid November. 22nd September 1974 was notable because a 4-hour morning watch at Peel yielded 57 southbound birds and a 6-hour watch from the Calf produced 41 flying south. On 11th September 1978 41 were seen from the Calf, while on the same day over 40 were noted at 2 places on the north Derry/Antrim coast (Preston 1979 & 1980) and 20 flew south west past Corsewell Point, Wigtownshire (Dennis 1979). In 1984 22nd September was the best day at Peel and the Calf with 17 and 24 birds and on 15th September 1985 59 flew south past Peel in 3 hours and a record 92 were seen from the Calf. Exceptionally early records have come from Peel with 1 there on 27th June 1976 and 3 on 5th July the following year. The latest Manx record was also the first – 1 off the Chicken Rock on 21st November 1887.

Tape luring on the Calf during the summer months has so far produced no birds.

Manx: *Gollan Varrey*

Gannet
Sula bassana

Common passage migrant. Feed in good numbers in Manx coastal waters during the summer.

There are some grounds for believing that a gannetry once existed on the Calf. The evidence was presented by Williamson (1941) who drew attention to the confusion which existed among early writers between the Barnacle and the Soland Goose. He quotes from Holland's translation of Camden's Britannia (1586). 'Before the south point, there lieth a pretty island called the *Calfe of Man*, wherein are exceeding great store ... of those ducks and drakes which (breeding of rotten wood as they say) the Englishmen call them *Bernacles*, the Scots *Clakes*, and *Soland Geese*.' Several 17th and 18th century authors wrote similarly although they probably copied from Camden. This observation could not possibly apply to the Barnacle Goose, but could quite reasonably refer to the Gannet. Chaloner (1656) did not mention these birds but Williamson believed that he intended to do so as Daniel King made a very accurate drawing of a pair of Gannets on the Isle of Man in 1652 with the intention of illustrating Chaloner's description of the Island. This 'the finest of early drawings of the Gannet' is held in the British Museum and carries the legend 'A Landskip with Gaunts being birds that mount like faulcons i'th Aire and when they see their Prey strike into the water.' Williamson thought that this caption was in Chaloner's hand writing.

Good numbers are seen feeding off the west coast and more especially off the Ayres throughout the summer and the main autumn passage south occurs from late August to mid October. Day counts of up to 3,000 have been recorded from the Calf in the second half of September. Thereafter

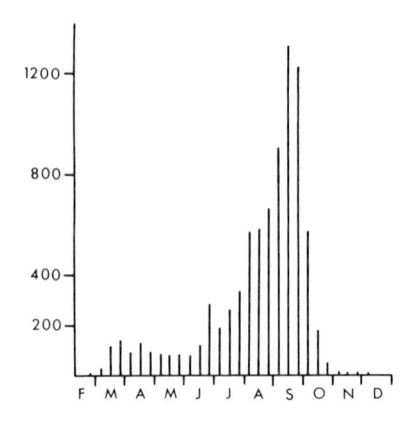

Gannet. Average number of bird days per ten day period. (Calf).

numbers fall away rapidly and the species is only rarely seen from November to February. Immature birds of all ages are seldom seen until June.

Two birds ringed on Grassholm, South Wales have been found dead. A full grown bird ringed in May was recovered in April of the following year at Port Erin and a pullus ringed in July was found at Port St Mary in September. Another bird ringed as a pullus on the Scar Rocks (Dumfries and Galloway) was found injured at Port St Mary 11 years later, while a fourth bird ringed on Ailsa Craig, also as a nestling, was found dead at Jurby Head 16 years 1 month later.

Manx: *Gant*

Cormorant

Phalacrocorax carbo

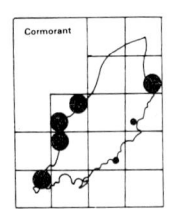

Common resident and summer visitor.

Cormorant bones have been identified from the Perwick cave midden deposit dated AD 90 (Garrad 1972). Jardine (1838–43) mentions several breeding places on very broad ledges of rock on the Isle of Man while Kermode (1901) considered that they bred around the coast in small numbers.

Ralfe regarded the Cormorant as a common bird at most seasons, far better distributed than the Shag. The Conister was a favourite roost where up to 20 birds might be seen and as a result of predation on trout in inland waters the Manx Fishery Board offered half a crown for its head. Ralfe knew of 2 breeding colonies – on the Calf and on the west coast, both having about 12 pairs.

Over the last 90 years the breeding population has varied between 25 and 50 pairs, the highest number being in the late 1950s. At present there are again about 50 breeding pairs.

A colony near the Sloc was first noted in 1895 and had moved to the rocks above Eairnerey cave in 1899. This colony was still thriving in 1923 and held 8 nests in 1955. By 1959 there were only 4 nests, in 1969 1 and there have been no records since. Ralfe's Calf colony was at Kione Roauyr and was first noted prior to 1900 and had 10 nests in 1907. It seems likely that the majority of nests on the Calf were always in this area of the north east coast although in 1965 there were 3 nests below the Lower Lighthouse. With only 4–6 nests in 1938–41 Kione Roauyr held 10 in 1955, 13 in 1959 and still 12 in 1962. Thereafter there was a gradual decline to 4 nests in 1974 since which Comorants have failed to breed on the Calf.

For the last 40 years the principal colony has been near Maughold Head, a site first noted to have 5 nests in 1926. Twenty to twenty-four nests are usual but in 1956 Maughold held two colonies of 20 and 26 nests (giving a minimum of 53 nests for the Isle of Man as a whole), in 1969 there were 32 and in 1984 41 nests. At present most of the nests are on a fairly low gently sloping rocky platform with a few more scattered on narrow ledges on the adjacent cliffs. Pairs have nested occasionally at several other coastal

Cormorant (all ringed as pulli). Ringing sites of birds recovered on the Isle of Man – open circles. Recovery sites of birds on the Isle of Man – closed circles.

sites and in 1981 a colony of 5 nests appeared at Ghaw Jeeragh just to the north of Bay Fine – 6 pairs bred here in 1982 and 10 in 1984. Although most eggs are laid during April, a few clutches are not started until mid May. An exceptionally early nest on the Calf held young on 8th April 1961.

Outside the breeding season Cormorants are widely distributed. Flocks of immature birds, presumably Maughold-bred occur off the northern coasts in late July e.g., 48 off Ballaghennie in 1964 and 98 off Maughold in 1973. Up to 20 birds usually winter in Douglas Bay, while inland single birds are often found on the reservoirs and the Foxdale dams. An unusual record was of 5 in a tree top at Kirby on 7th January 1982.

From the Calf small autumn passage is seen in August and September with flocks of 10–20 occasionally flying south and west usually high over the islet.

Ringing recoveries are shown on the map.

Manx-ringed pulli recovered during their first autumn or winter have been found well to the south with the exception of one Maughold bird recovered in Douglas Bay 7 weeks later. The same trend is seen in birds recovered on the Isle of Man. The almost complete absence of local recoveries in this admittedly small sample suggests that our population is considerably more migratory than previously supposed.

An adult of the continental race *P.c. sinensis* was observed at close range off the south of the Calf on 29th February 1980.

Several place names are derived from the old Norse word for Cormorant – Skarfr. Best known is Scarlett, originating from Skarfakluft (Cormorant's Cleft), while from Skarfarip is derived Skeirrip (Cormorant's Crag) on the Lonan coast.

Manx: *Shag. Fannag* or *Feeagh Varrey* = Sea Crow or Raven *Arragh Vooar* (cf. Great Northern Diver).

Shag

Phalacrocorax aristotelis

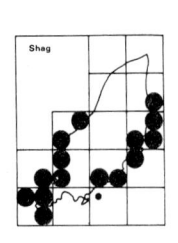

Abundant resident, showing northerly dispersive movement.

Bones have been identified in the Perwick Bay midden deposit dating from AD 90 (Garrad 1972).

Although Kermode described the Shag as breeding all round the rocky coast, Ralfe indicated that nests were largely confined to the coast from Peel south to Bradda, the Calf, where they were numerous and at Spanish Head and the Sugar Loaf. On the west coast there was a recognisable colony at Stroin Vuigh but nests were for the most part scattered irregularly. He also mentioned a few breeding at Maughold Head but had no proof of breeding either between Groudle and Clay Head or at Pistol Castle although Shags could always be seen in good numbers there. There were no nests north of Peel. When Jardine visited the Island in 1821 he found 'the most extensive colony which has ever come under our observation.' This was on the precipitous coast adjacent to the Calf and must have been on Spanish Head, probably at Giau Vooar, where a rich guano find was made (Williamson 1941). Clearly this colony had greatly declined during the 18th century but there are no details for the rest of the Island or for the Calf so that it is impossible to say whether there was an overall diminution or merely a redistribution of a stable population.

Since 1959 the Shag population of the Calf has been counted annually. In 1938 Williamson had found 80–120 nests between Kione Roauyr and Kione ny Halbey, 8–10 nests at Culbery and 'some numbers' below Amulty, Oirr Vooar, the cliffs beneath the old lighthouses and on the Stack. The population then must have approached the 1959 total of 165 pairs. By 1977 there were 400 nests, a total which, despite one or two poor years, has been well maintained since. The only census for the Isle of Man took place in 1969 when the Calf accounted for approximately half of the 550 nest sites located (Slinn 1971). On the main island nesting groups had become established between Bulgham Bay and Skerrip, between Clay Head and Groudle, on the Marine Drive and between Gob Lhiack and Pistol Castle. The actual total was probably in excess of 600 as many nests in rocky crevices and behind boulders must have been missed. Breeding on the coast north of Peel was confirmed at Ballanayre Strand in 1978 and 3 pairs now nest there.

The Shag has a notoriously long breeding season. Three nests were partly completed on Peel Hill on 24th December 1976 and Madoc saw birds brooding on 26th January, although nest contents (if any) were not seen. On the Calf some eggs are laid in February most years, the earliest calculated date being 7th February 1964, while eggs were found on 19th February 1981. Most eggs are laid by mid May and young are not often seen in the nest after the second week of August. In 1965 first young hatched on the Calf in March and 3 more eggs in the same nest site hatched during August. Two to four eggs are usual with clutches in excess of 6 being due to two or more females laying in the same nest. Williamson recorded a clutch of 7 on 1st June 1939 and a nest with 10 eggs was found on the Calf in 1978. Although many nests are in open sites on rocky ledges, most are in caves, deep crevices and behind boulders. There are several instances of Shags taking over the new nests of corvids – this was first reported at a Raven's nest on Peel Hill in 1928 and occurred again the following year, while on the Burroo (Calf) Shags took over the nest of a Chough which then rebuilt a few feet away.

Breeding success varies markedly on the Calf – north and west coast sites are particularly vulnerable to storms from that quarter and predation from Hooded Crows and rats takes a heavy toll at some sites.

Post breeding flocks of 600–1,000 are often recorded in the vicinity of the Calf during August and September, with exceptional numbers in 1967 when 4,000 birds were estimated. The Warts Bank is a particularly favoured site and is known to have huge shoals of sand-eels at this time of the year (Slinn 1969). Good numbers also gather off the Point of Ayre and over 500 have been counted on Peel Hill in early autumn. Shags regularly fly south past Peel in the hour before sunset in the latter part of the year. Notable counts have been 442 on 7th September 1980 and 382 on 14th December 1974.

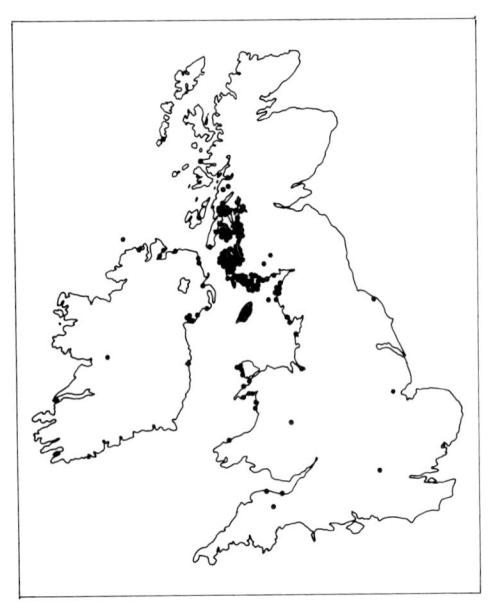

Recoveries of Shags when immature. (Total for Isle of Man = 73.)

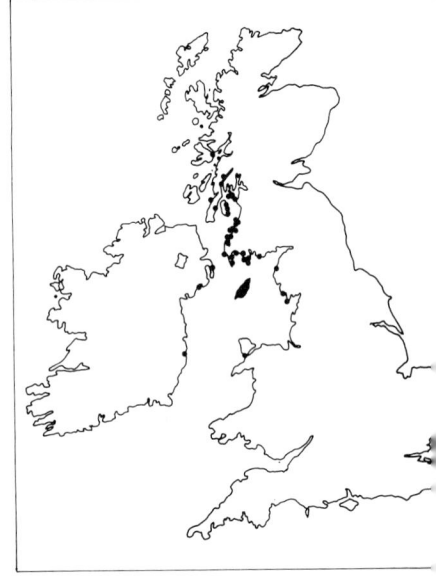

Recoveries of Shags when adult. (Total for Isle of Man = 55.)

Three thousand, four hundred and thirty-nine Shags were ringed on the Calf in the period 1959–82 yielding 273 recoveries. Recoveries are shown on the accompanying maps and illustrate the northerly dispersal of this species. There are 4 interesting longevity records of Calf-ringed Shags – 2 were retrapped 17 years 11 months and 17 years 10 months after being ringed as pulli. One was found dead at Kirkmichael 20 years 7 months after ringing and another was found long dead at Bride 22 years 11 months after ringing.

Manx: as for Cormorant.

Bittern
Botaurus stellaris

Occasional winter visitor.

It is possible that the Bittern formerly bred in the Island when the northern marshland was considerably more extensive than it has been during the last 150 years. Blundell (1656) wrote that Bitterns existed in Man but Ralfe did not regard this as a reliable statement. On the other hand the Bittern does possess a Manx name and tales have been handed down of the bellowing of the *Tarroo ushtey* (water bull), a mythical creature inhabiting pools and swamps. Ralfe was able to list 3 birds shot in the latter half of the 19th century.

Between 1908 and 1951 there were 10 records – 8 of these birds were shot and with the exception of 1 at Bride, all came from Ballaugh Curraghs. There were no further records until 1972 when one was found dead below telegraph wires near Peel, on the late date of 19th April 1973 one was flushed close to the highest point of the Calf and individuals were also seen in the Ballaugh Curraghs in 1974 and near Dalby in 1980. The monthly distribution of all records is January 2, March 1, April 1, September 1, October 1, November 1 and December 7. Six of these 14 records occurred between 28th November and 7th December.

Manx: *Ushag ny boob*

Little Bittern
Ixobrychus minutus

Rare vagrant.

Ralfe did not accept J. C. Crellin's assertion that he shot one near Castletown in the late 19th century and Kermode made a vague statement that he had heard of one or two other instances.

There are two unequivocal records – one was found dying in a Port St Mary garden on 26th April 1947 and another was caught at Port Erin on 21st April 1968.

Little Egret
Egretta garzetta

Vagrant.

A Little Egret was present on the Island from 2nd to 7th July 1985. First seen at Scarlett and Poyllvaaish it spent 4th July on the River Neb at Close Leece and was then seen several times feeding in Derbyhaven Bay and on one occasion in Langness Pool.

Grey Heron
Ardea cinerea

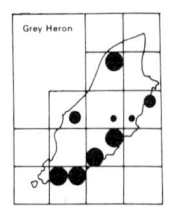

Fairly common breeding bird and partial migrant.

Herons were first protected by law in 1422 and in 1577 an enquiry was set up as to whether anyone was taking old birds, young or eggs out of the nest. This implied that there was a breeding population in the 16th century. Sacheverell (1702) commented that there were 'too many, as being protected by the laws' and Townley (1791) wrote of Cranes on the sands of Douglas Bay. Even now the Heron is often referred to as the Crane in the Isle of Man. There may have been a heronry in the Crofts at Castletown at the beginning of the 19th century.

Ralfe referred to two heronries at coastal sites up to about 1885. One was said to be in willow bushes at the verge of a steep precipice at Coan Shellagh, close to Lag ny Keeilley below Cronk ny iree laa. The other site was in clusters of ivy on a dangerous cliff between Laxey and Dhoon. Isolated nesting was also said to have occurred at Ballamoar (Patrick) in about 1865 and at Greeba in about 1882. In 1905 Ralfe knew of no heronries although he did not discount the possibility of some undiscovered colony. One such may have been the heronry at Ballaskeig (Maughold) which existed about 1910, but was deserted after a fire in the wood, while at least 2 young were seen in a nest at Injebreck in 1912 (not 1902 as stated in Ralfe's supplement).

The recent breeding history of the Grey Heron began in 1931 when 3 pairs nested at Ballamoar (Jurby). In spite of predation by Ravens during this first year (and throughout the 1930s) this colony had increased to 10 nests by 1933 and has been tenanted by 4–8 pairs ever since with peaks of 12 nests in 1948 and 11 in 1975.

As long ago as 1900 Ralfe had noted that Herons frequented conifers by the river at Kirby, but it was not until 1935 that nesting was strongly suspected and 1938 when a single nest was located. Since then the Kirby heronry has been occupied every year with up to 4 nests in the 1940s, 4–8 in the 50s and 60s (with a peak of 11 in 1954) and a notable increase in the early 70s producing 15 nests in 1976. Since then counts have varied between 7 and 12 pairs.

In the period 1946–1948 up to 4 pairs bred in Archallagan plantation, from 1949–1951 and again in 1984 a single nest at Ballachurry (Andreas) was used, and between 1951 and 1954 1–2 pairs nested annually at Greeba Castle (cf., 1882).

In 1952 4 nests were built in hawthorns at Billown Quarries, but all were robbed and the colony was not occupied the following year although there have been 2–4 nests since at least 1972 at Billown Moar 1 km away, and a pair nested at Great Meadow in 1984.

Herons nested at Port Grenaugh in 1964 and 1966 and for a few years up to 1970 4 pairs bred at Ballavale. The present colony is in pines to the east of Ballachrink and since 1972 has held 2–3 nests with a peak of 7 nests in 1982. Nesting took place in the Glen Rushen waterworks plantation in the late 1960s.

Kentraugh was first occupied in 1973 and now holds about 5 nests, while 1–3 pairs have bred at Balladoole since 1975.

There have probably been up to 3 isolated nests in the wooded Cornaa valley annually since about 1964, at Garwick Herons may have nested in a pine under cliffs in 1949 and there have been single nests at Glen Helen in 1952, Close Lake in 1956, Glencrutchery in 1973 and 1974 and possibly at Groudle and East Baldwin in 1973. Ballamoar (Patrick) was last tenanted in 1972 when there were 2 nests (cf. 1865).

There are at present 6 known heronries in the Isle of Man, all but one being in the grounds of a substantial manor house. Since the peak of some 35 breeding pairs in the mid seventies there has been a decline.

In the Isle of Man birds are seen at their nests from the middle of February. First egg shells are usually found during the second week in April, although shells at Kirby on 7th March 1953 suggest laying on the early date of 10th February. Last young have usually flown by the end of July although there is a record of a nest still occupied on 20th August.

As previously mentioned the Ballamoar heronry was persecuted in its early days by Ravens and all Manx heronries are threatened by Hooded Crows. However the major threat is shooting, more so now because of the development of several fish farms on the Island. A large and easy target, the Heron was also shot for the table. Kermode wrote 'I have tried young birds both roast and in soup, and found them very good' and as recently as 1977 a Laxey man reported having had heron for dinner.

Throughout the year Herons frequent the shore line, where the rocky pools of Douglas Bay, Derbyhaven, Langness and Strandhall are particularly favoured, and all the Island's streams. On the coast the biggest gatherings occur in August and September, but while there are records of 30 birds at Langness and Strandhall in the early thirties and an exceptional 35 at Langness on 28th August 1937 there are no counts in excess of 16 during the last 15 years. The Conister rock and Derbyhaven breakwater are popular winter roosting places and at Kirby birds begin to gather in the late autumn with counts of up to 20 from late November onwards.

Movement away from the Island to south and west is sometimes seen from Langness, the Calf and Peel. This is usually between mid-August and mid-September and involves up to 6 birds – exceptionally 20–30 flew west from Langness on 27th August 1929 and single birds have been seen flying south from the Calf up to 4th November.

Four birds ringed as pulli on the Isle of Man have been recovered. Two of these were on the Island in winter, while of the other two one was recovered in Yorkshire 12 weeks after ringing, the other in Lancashire 5 summers later. In addition a Cumberland bird was shot on the Island in January, one from Co. Down was recovered on the Island 4 months after ringing and one ringed in southern Norway turned up at Maughold the following April.

Manx: *Coayr. Coayr ny Hastan* = Crane of the Eel. *Coayr Glass* = Grey Crane.

Spoonbill

Platalea leucorodia

Vagrant.

Recorded once on 8th November 1935 (Ralfe did not accept a report of one repeatedly seen on Langness during 1883, nor one at Gob ny Rona near Ramsey).

Mute Swan

Cygnus olor

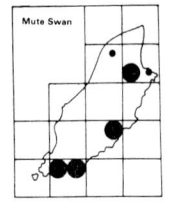

Resident.

The Mute Swan does not appear in Kermode's lists and Ralfe did not recognise it as a wild bird although he did mention birds being kept at Kirby, Bishopscourt and Kentraugh as well as a pair being presented to the Mooragh Park by King Edward VII in 1903. Escapes occurred, and in particular the Kentraugh birds used to use the adjacent bay, straying at times to Castletown Bay.

By 1931 Mute Swans were nesting on the open coast at several places, one of which was Poyllvaaish, where a nest of seaweed continues to be built most years below high water mark and almost invariably falls a victim to the spring tide. At Castletown a pair has bred in the upper harbour or by the Silverburn, usually close to the railway bridge, since 1933 and in spite of vandalism young are often reared. In 1980 a pair attempted several times to build a nest of wrack between the two piers of Castletown outer harbour. The nest was repeatedly washed away, as were the eggs which were eventually laid. There are records of nesting at Ramsey since 1940. Here nests have been built on the north side of the inner harbour, above the stone bridge and, particularly recently, in reeds 2 km upstream. At Douglas there are 3 nesting sites – on the north bank of the river just above the harbour (since 1955), at Tromode Dam (since 1964) and on the island at Kirby (since the 1960s or earlier). All 3 sites have been occupied simultaneously. At the undisturbed Kirby site many young were reared between 1974 and 1978, but full clutches failed to hatch in each of 4 subsequent years. A nest of wrack is built some years at the top of the slipway on Derbyhaven breakwater – a site vulnerable to both the sea and to Great Black-backed Gulls which accounted for the only cygnets which have hatched in recent years.

There are thus 7 nesting sites regularly used, 4 or 5 of which will be occupied in any one year. In addition a pair regularly holds territory at Gansey and there is an old record of nesting on the shore at Maughold. Five to nine eggs are usually laid and cygnets have been seen as early as 17th May. Hatching after mid June is unusual.

During the last decade a herd of up to 17 non-breeding birds has gathered in Castletown Harbour in early July, moving to Ramsey Harbour in September or early October and remaining there until breaking up in January. Paired birds seem to move to the nearest harbour so that a few will winter in Douglas and Castletown, while the harbours of Peel and Port St Mary are occasionally visited in spring. The total Manx population has fluctuated between 20 and 30 birds since about 1940.

While most of the Manx population is presumed to be resident, unusually shy birds are sometimes seen and thought to be migrants and family parties containing immature birds, indisputably bred elsewhere, were seen on the sea at Ballaugh in early June 1978 and at the Bishop's Dub in mid December 1976.

Manx: *Ollay* = Swan.

Bewick's Swan

Cygnus colombianus

Uncommon passage migrant.

Owing to the difficulties in separating Bewick's Swan from the Whooper Ralfe was only able to give 4 records, all of which were corpses obtained during the final decade of the last century. One occurred in December, 2 in January and the 4th bird had reached a Douglas taxidermist by 1st March. At that time Bewick's Swan was very much commoner than the Whooper in Ireland and it was assumed that many unidentified wild swans were of this species.

During the period 1924–75 there were some 30 records, then none until 1984. Most have occurred between 24th October and 26th November and between 27th February and 20th April. Most records have been of single birds but in autumn there have been small parties of 4–6 birds and in spring, especially in late March, several larger herds – notably 66 which flew east over the Calf on 20th March 1972. Unlike those of the Whooper, the visits of Bewick's Swan have been transient with birds rarely lingering more than a day or two. Exceptions were single birds, probably injured, which stayed at Ramsey from 16th April to 7th May 1932 and at Langness from 8th August to 15th September 1960.

Whooper Swan
Cygnus cygnus

Regular passage migrant and winter visitor in small numbers.

Ralfe was able to give a very few late 19th century records and like Kermode thought that the majority of wild swans seen on the Island were Bewick's as at that time this was by far the commoner species in Ireland. A notable scarcity of records continued until 1929 since when Whoopers were reported almost annually until 1952 and every year since, with a notable increase in frequency after 1964.

Many of the wild swans flying over the Island are still not specifically identified, but most are recognised as Whoopers. They are seen principally between 10th October and 10th December. October is easily the richest month and while the majority of birds are flying west or southwest, northbound birds are often seen in autumn. Most records refer to between 2 and 10 birds, but there are several records of 10–20 and one party of 35. The earliest autumn record is of 3 birds which settled briefly on Kionslieu on 2nd October 1977. Whoopers are only rarely seen flying over the Island in the spring although the biggest herds have occurred during March notably 47 at Curragh Beg on 15th March 1964 and 43 at Poyllvaaish on 6th and 7th March 1976. The latest spring record was of 1 at Ramsey on 20th April 1932.

As a winter visitor the Whooper Swan occurs principally at the Eairy Dam and to a lesser degree at the Bishop's Dub. Two other northern dubs – Ballacain and Glascoe are also visited occasionally for a few days by up to 5 birds. The first occurrence of swans at the Eairy Dam was probably in the winter of 1928/29 and between 1938 and 1981 a pair or family party wintered nearly every year. A fairly accurate record of their arrival and departure was kept from 1971/2 to 1980/1: first sightings occurred between 12th October and 16th November with a mean date of 21st October while last dates varied from 5th March to 6th April with a mean of 20th March. Compared with this sojourn of 5 months the visits of up to 7 birds to the Bishop's Dub are brief. Here autumn occurrences are fleeting although in both January and March Whoopers have lingered for up to a month. During January and March they often turn up briefly on other small northern dubs and along the south coast and these birds may well be shifting their winter quarters from Scotland to Ireland.

Manx: *Ollay Chiaullee*

Bean Goose
Anser fabalis

Very rare vagrant.

Ralfe considered that the Bean Goose was a not infrequent visitor to the Isle of Man, a view held at a time when this species was considered to be common and widespread in Ireland. Ruttledge (1966) has cast doubts on this assessment and his 5 Irish records since 1927 are very comparable to the solitary Manx record of 1 on Langness on 16th March 1939.

Manx: *Guiy Poanrey*

Pink-footed Goose
Anser brachyrhynchus

Irregular winter visitor.

The first Manx record was in 1916, when 1 was shot at Ronaldsway on 1st March and between 1930 and 1982 there were 17 records fairly evenly spread between 22nd September and 23rd February. Most records are of 1–6 birds and are largely confined to the Langness and Calf/Cregneish areas of the south. Twenty-eight feeding on stubble at Langness for 2 days in early February 1940 were quite remarkable.

White-fronted Goose
Anser albifrons

Rare winter visitor.

Ralfe listed 4 birds shot in the late 19th century, but the period 1930–82 only yielded 10 records of 1–7 birds between 19th October and 4th March. Half of these records were from Langness and January records predominate.

Two skins in the Manx Museum are of the Greenland race *Anser a. flavirostris* and one which joined farmyard geese at Maughold from November 1956 to February 1957 was of the Russian race *Anser a. albifrons*.

Greylag Goose
Anser anser

Irregular winter visitor.

Ralfe could provide no convincing records of this species, which since 1926 has been easily the most frequently reported of the grey geese. Although there have been a few records in October and November the majority of occurrences have been in December, January and February, the Langness area being the most frequented site. It seems that Greylag, which are seen in groups of up to 8 birds, are more inclined to linger on the Island than are the other grey geese. An exceptional record was of over 200 spending several days on the sea off Port Soderick in November 1948, the only other flock of any size being one of 25 at Castletown in mid January 1947. Three flew north-east over the Calf on 25th May 1981.

The status of the Greylag is a little confused by the presence of a few feral birds. There were 2 or 3 in Ramsey Harbour in the early seventies, and one is still seen with some 20 farm geese; while visits of up to 3 alien Greylags to the Glascoe Dub have no doubt been encouraged by the presence of a resident bird (as well as farm geese) recently.

The earliest record is of 1 over the Calf on 11th August – the latest 21st April.

Grey geese in general are not common on the Isle of Man, the small parties which do settle for a few hours are readily identified but the larger skeins which fly over escape accurate recognition. Clementson (1941) summarised his observations at Peel where he saw a total of 21 skeins in the period 1934–41: the largest skeins, up to 120 birds, were seen flying south in autumn and his extreme dates were 10th September and 20th January. Small west-bound skeins were seen in mid winter and north-bound geese were noted between 19th February and 22nd May.

During the last 50 years the majority of high-flying geese have been seen between 15th October and 9th November, with fair numbers in September, December and March. Although flocks of 120 have been seen once in both September and March most records are of between 5 and 80 birds with an average flock size of 23.

Manx: *Guiy feie* = Wild goose.

Canada Goose

Branta canadensis

Transient, but regular summer visitor.

Ralfe referred to 1 shot on Langness in the late 19th century, but it was not until 1966 that the Canada Goose was to occur again naturally in the Isle of Man. That year one spent a week at the Bishop's Dub in early August and since 1973 there have been almost annual occurrences during May and June. Small parties are usual and the records are as follows: 3 at Baldwin Reservoir for a few hours on 15th May 1973, 2 at Scarlett on 7th May 1974 and 2 at Sulby 13 days later. (Six 'dark geese' flying west over Peel on 23rd July 1976 are likely to have been Canadas.) Three at Port St Mary on 11th June 1977 and 11 flying south over the Calf on 20th June 1977, 1 at Port Cornaa on 17th and 18th June 1978, 9 flying north over the Dog Mills on 15th June 1980 and 13 flying north east over the Calf Stack on 16th June

1983. The situation is becoming complicated by introductions which have taken place at Ballasteen and Glascoe in the north and at Crogga. Prior to these introductions there was just 1 winter record – 4 being seen over the Bride coast on 23rd December 1972.

Barnacle Goose
Branta leucopsis

Occasional passage migrant and winter visitor.

Ralfe could only find one questionable record and between 1929 and 1985 there were just 16 occurrences. The earliest were 1 at Langness on 13th October 1985 and 3 in the vicinity of the Chicken Rock on 16th October 1934 and there is 1 other October record, 3 for November, 4 for December and 3 for January. Of 2 April records, one was of a bird seen often between Langness and Strandhall from 6th to 21st April 1976. The 2 May records are both from the Calf – 3 flying south past the islet on 1st May 1973 and 1 flying east on 6th May 1981.
Manx: *Guiy ny Twoaie*

Brent Goose
Branta bernicla

Irregular passage migrant and winter visitor.

In Ralfe's time small numbers occurred not infrequently and he mentions the storm of 21st December 1894 when Brent Geese 'appeared in great numbers, some being completely beaten by the wind and unable to fly. Some of these birds were caught by the hand, as also were Wild Ducks. Old people say the same thing happened during the storm of 1829.'

During the present century there have been 2 periods wherein the repeated visits of Brent Geese for several weeks have given hope of the establishment of a regular wintering habit. In mid February 1929 a party of 4 arrived at Derbyhaven and from the end of that month there were 8. Although 3 were shot, the remaining 5 stayed on until 16th March. The following year 2 birds were at Derbyhaven again from 3rd February to 16th March, in 1935 1 stayed at Langness from 23rd February to 17th March and in 1938 there was 1 at Langness from 5th to 15th March. The next 35 years saw only 2 transient visits of individuals to this area but in 1975 1 stayed at Derbyhaven from 14th to 26th January and in 1976 1 was present there from 16th October to 7th November. In early March 1979 4 birds settled at Derbyhaven for 10 days and at the end of that year 4–6 were regularly seen for a week at Derbyhaven, Langness and Scarlett, 1 remaining to 20th January. Small parties have lingered for a few days in the south-east in the autumns of 1984 and 1985. Nowhere else have Brent Geese lingered for more than a day although there have been irregular records of 1–8 birds resting at various sites between late September and early May with no bias in favour of any particular month.

Flocks of black geese in flight, nearly always considered to be Brent, have occurred with nothing like the frequency of grey geese. There have been 4 such records in late September, including a small party forming the outer end of a chevron of some 80 grey geese. Flocks of 10–30 have also been seen once in late October, twice in January and once in early April. The extreme dates have been 16th September 1956 and 8th May 1936.

The Dark-bellied Brent Goose *Branta bernicla bernicla* has been identified on two occasions – one was seen in a field near Knock e Dooney on 27th November 1982 and there were 4 at White Strand on 25th October 1985. Otherwise all those occurring since 1963 have been recognised as Light-bellied *Branta bernicla hrota*. One of five present at Poyllvaaish in late September 1985 had been banded on Bathurst Island, Canada in July 1984. It is probable that geese visiting the Isle of Man in autumn have overshot Strangford Lough which is the main early winter stronghold.

Egyptian Goose
Alopochen aegyptiacus

Escape.

Ralfe referred to a flock of 9 having occurred in the Isle of Man in September 1838 (Yarrell 1871) and to 2 having been shot near Castletown in the late 19th century.

Shelduck
Tadorna tadorna

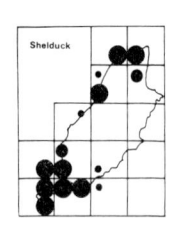

Locally common breeding species and winter visitor.

Although in the late 18th century Townley 'saw several Shell Ducks at the bold point called Douglas Head', Ralfe considered it to be exclusively a bird of the Castletown area. Numbers in spring on Langness were in the order of 10–12 birds with perhaps 3 or 4 breeding pairs. Ralfe also mentioned nesting in the thick gorse cover of the Santon brows. By 1908 they were nesting between Castletown and Poyllvaaish. In May 1922 Shelduck were present in the Sound area and Madoc's remarks suggest that they started to visit the south east of the Island in much greater numbers during the next 10 years. He mentioned over 100 on Langness in March and suggested that some of these birds later bred on the Kitterland. It was probably during the 1930s that Shelduck started to breed in small numbers on the Calf between Fold Point and Cow Harbour and there was also a breeding record for the mainland side of the Sound (Williamson 1940). Nesting took place at Kentraugh in 1933 and possibly at Perwick the same year. Since at least 1955 Strandhall has been regularly tenanted and breeding occurred again at Perwick in 1956, at Port Erin in 1956 and 1959 and at Bay Stacka in 1959. On the Ayres, probably colonised in the 1920s, several pairs were nesting between Knock e Dooney and Ballaghennie by 1946 and in recent years there have been breeding records further west at the Lhen, Jurby Head and Orrisdale Head. During the last decade pairs have been seen in early summer at Glen Moar, Glen Cam, the Chasms, Port Grenaugh and Port Soderick without proof of breeding, while inland pairs have apparently held territory between Regaby and Glascoe in 1973 and 1980, Ballaugh Curragh in 1973 and near the Bishop's Dub since 1979. A family party in a hayfield at Surby in July 1977 suggests that inland breeding has taken place in the south west. At present the breeding population is probably about 15 pairs with 2–3 on the shores of the Calf Sound, 3–4 between Kentraugh and Poyllvaaish, 3–4 at Langness and Derbyhaven, with perhaps another 2 pairs in the Santon Gorge area and at least 3 pairs between Orrisdale and Ballaghennie. First ducklings are usually seen between 20th and 25th May, but eggs had hatched on the Calf by 15th May 1976 and 3 young were seen on Langness on 8th May 1980.

On the Calf Shelduck are not often seen after about 8th June and on Langness breeding birds have usually left on moult migration by mid July with

Mid-month counts of Shelduck at Langness/Derbyhaven

	Nov.	Dec.	Jan.	Feb.	Mar.
1972/73	0	—	16	43	51
1973/74	0	—	26	26	26
1974/75	1	1	15	22	28
1975/76	2	4	9	27	54
1976/77	0	0	11	20	24
1977/78	2	4	9	20	31
1978/79	0	7	27	31	45
1979/80	0	3	10	30	34
1980/81	3	11	9	19	24
1981/82	6	—	9	28	34
1982/83	2	9	9	22	33

up to 5 immatures lingering on into September. Immature birds are occasionally seen singly in October. A few birds begin to arrive after the moult during the last 2 weeks of November and there is a steady build up at Langness and Derbyhaven to a March peak as shown in the accompanying table.

The first record of Shelduck wintering at Strandhall was in 1938. Now numbers there closely parallel those at Langness, the highest combined count of recent years being 75 in March 1975. On the Ayres there may be up to 7 during February and March. There is some dispersal during April when a small party is often seen at Niarbyl in particular. In the south east April numbers are only a little down on those for March and non-breeding flocks of 10–20 birds may be seen until early June. In 1969 up to 60 non-breeders frequented Langness until at least 9th June.

Manx: *Thunnag y Scape*

Wigeon

Anas penelope

Common winter visitor.

Kermode described the Wigeon as occurring in considerable numbers all round the coast and in the curraghs, but Ralfe's observations were more moderate – '... this is one of the commonest winter species of Duck, and fair numbers (taking into account the nature of the country and its coasts) are to be met with. The small ponds and sheets of winter-lying water, which occur especially in the north, are regularly frequented, as well as many localities along the shore, but the Wigeon seldom or never occurs in really large flocks.' To Madoc Derbyhaven and Langness was the Manx stronghold with January flocks in the region of 150 birds.

Langness remains the principal site for Wigeon and although numbers vary from year to year there seems to have been no significant change during the last 50 years. Here the saltmarsh provides good grazing. Just north of Derbyhaven the aptly named Wigeon Pool often has 40–50 birds and up to 30 are often seen at Port Grenaugh. The only other significant coastal site is Strandhall where mid-winter peaks of 40–50 are usual. Inland the flood water which regularly collects to the east of the Glascoe Dub attracts the largest numbers, while the Dub itself often has 20–40 birds. Parties of 2–6 turn up sporadically at some of the other northern dubs and at Kerrowdhoo and the Foxdale dams.

The first Wigeon usually arrive between 25th August and 10th September and, in addition to a winged drake which summered at the Lagagh in 1977, there have been 2 brief visits of individuals to Langness in July – on 6th in 1973 and on 14th in 1978. Winter numbers of Langness are shown on the accompanying graph. The peak is most usually in January although the best recent count of 240 was achieved on 10th February 1974. The biggest count for the Island as a whole was on 27th December 1981 when 128 at Strandhall, over 200 at Langness and 250 on the Glascoe floods gave a total approaching 600. March sees a rapid desertion of Langness and Strandhall, a few stragglers are sometimes seen during the first week of April, the latest dates being on 18th April 1935 and 28th April 1978.

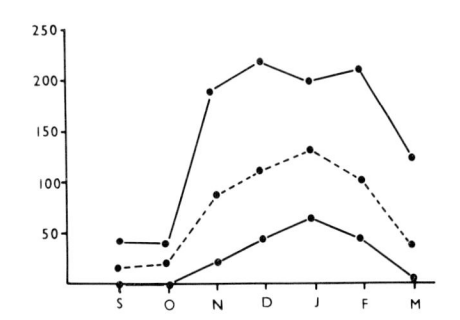

Wigeon: Langness – Derbyhaven. Mid month counts 1972–83. Continuous lines = maximum and minimum, broken line = average.

The only ringing recovery is of one ringed as an adult in Strangford Lough in early October and found dead on Ballaugh beach in November 5 years later.

Manx: *Thunnag veg feie* = Little wild duck.

Gadwall

Anas strepera

Rare winter visitor.

Until 1927 there had only been 3 records of single birds, but during the next 9 years Madoc came to regard the Gadwall as a regular visitor in autumn and winter. He recorded several parties of up to 12 at Langness in late August and early September, with 1–2 occurring frequently through the winter. There were also 2 records of small parties at Langness and the Ayres in April. Between 1936 and 1981 there were just 3 records – 5 at Derbyhaven on 11th December 1952, a duck in Castletown Harbour on 14th January 1963, and a drake at Langness on 21st October 1973. In the 4 years 1982–85 they have been seen annually with two drakes at Langness on 15th January 1982, a duck at the Bishop's Dub on 11th and 13th September 1983, and single drakes at the Clypse Reservoir on 8th August 1984, Knock e Dooney on 17th February 1985 and Strandhall on 9th and 24th March 1985.

Manx: *Laagh ghlass*

Teal

Anas crecca

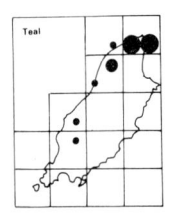

Scarce breeder and common winter visitor

'One of our commoner species,' Ralfe referred particularly to the occurrence of Teal on the pools and stream sides of the Island, breeding in the Curraghs and probably in other similar habitats. He makes no mention of the large numbers which certainly by 1930 were wintering on Langness. Waldron (1744) commented on the excellence of wildfowl in Man, referring in particular to Woodcock and Teal.

Breeding numbers have never been great, perhaps up to 10 pairs during the 1930s and considerably fewer during the last 30 years. Teal still breed in the Ballaugh Curraghs where there is a wealth of suitable nesting habitat neglected by bird watchers. The other traditional site is the line of slack bordering the inland margin of the Ayres; here the only recent record is of a pair present during April and May 1979. Sporadic breeding occurs in the marshy areas scattered over the northern plain and probably at Lough Cranstal, and broods were seen at the Lagagh in 1977 and 1979. Laying usually starts during the last few days in April, the earliest Manx nest containing 9 eggs on 20th April.

Langness is the principal wintering ground with occasional peaks of 300 birds. In recent years numbers varied quite markedly after the high counts of 1971–2. The next 2 winters were poor, but during the following 5 years peaks were between 40 and 90 with just one 3 figure influx in late February. Recent winters have seen a restoration to former numbers with best counts of 330 on 20th December 1980 and 520 on 3rd January 1983. Elsewhere Teal scarcely occur on the coast. Inland parties of 20–30 birds are scattered through the Ballaugh Curraghs, Lough Cranstal and some of the northern dubs and over 100 were seen with Wigeon on the Glascoe flood in January 1983. The Foxdale Dams support a regular winter flock with a peak of 25–40 birds occurring usually in December, although the biggest count of 130 was on Kionslieu on 14th October 1983.

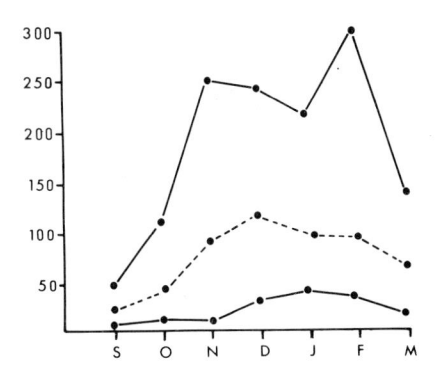

Teal: Langness – Derbyhaven. Mid month counts 1972–83. Continuous lines = maximum and minimum, broken line = average.

The return to Langness of 1 or 2 Teal usually occurs between 3rd and 10th August (13 on 27th July 1980 was exceptional) and small numbers pass through the Calf from early August to late October. Numbers dwindle rapidly in March and Langness is usually deserted during the first week in April. Again, Calf numbers are small but movement shows a peak in April with late birds up to 6th May.

Recoveries of Teal ringed as pulli on the Isle of Man are shown on the map. Three members of one brood were recovered during their first year – from Wexford and Salop in early autumn and from Northern Spain in January while 2 from another brood were recovered in different parts of Holland in the autumn. One ringed as a pullus in Denmark was recovered on the Isle of Man in November.

Manx: *Laagh Laaghag*

Mallard
Anas platyrhynchos

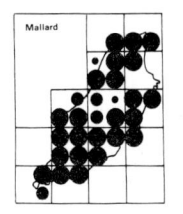

Common on autumn passage, as a winter visitor and as a breeding bird.

Ralfe considered the Mallard to be fairly plentiful in winter. The most important site was on the shingle of the north coast where hundreds of duck collected each year. Elsewhere Mallard were found in remote recesses under the coastal cliffs, while inland small parties occurred in the Curraghs and along lowland streams. Very few bred in the Island, mostly in the marsh lands of Ballaugh and Greeba. Thirty years later Madoc bracketed Langness with the Ayres coast as the principal winter resorts – over 200 occurred in the south-east and about 150 in the north. Breeding by then appears to have been much more widespread.

The Mallard remains a very well distributed breeding bird. Ballaugh and Greeba Curraghs and Lough Cranstal hold good populations and there is scarcely a dub or pond which does not have a nesting pair. They nest along the banks of all the streams, both in their lowland and moorland courses. Mallard nest freely around the coast wherever gorse or heather provide some cover, frequently on brooghs above quite steep rocks. Seven to eight pairs now breed on the Calf where there is a breeding association with Short-eared Owls – one or two nesting within 16 m of owls' nests. First young are usually seen in mid April – the earliest was a clutch of 12 eggs at Ballachurry (Andreas) which were chipping on 29th March 1951 and the latest was a brood of 9 at Ballavarvane (Malew) in mid December 1982.

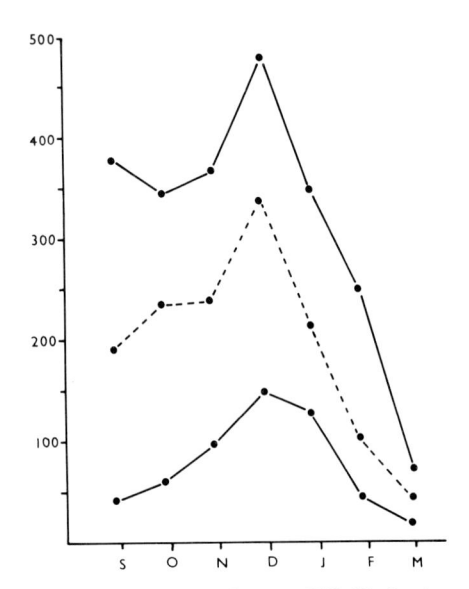

Mallard: Langness – Derbyhaven. Mid month counts 1972–83. Continuous lines = maximum and minimum, broken line = average.

On Langness parties of non-breeding birds number up to 60 in early June and from mid July onwards there is a steady build up with maxima of 120 during that month and 180 in August. Here a September peak of passage birds is sometimes discernible, but more usually numbers gradually increase to a maximum in mid December falling steadily through January and February with just small numbers in March and April. Langness is far and away the most important wintering site and it is doubtful if the Ayres coast is now frequented at all. During September up to 100 may congregate in the Sound and fair numbers are present throughout the winter in Garwick Bay, where there have been three figure counts recently in each month from September to December with a maximum of 172 in mid December 1980. Very similar numbers also winter on the west coast between Ballanayre and White Strand. Inland Mallard are undoubtedly plentiful in Ballaugh Curraghs, but the most important sites are Glascoe Dub, the Foxdale Dams, Kerrowdhoo Reservoir and the secluded little lake at Crogga. At the first two sites autumn influxes are very obvious and the steady winter population starts to dwindle in January.

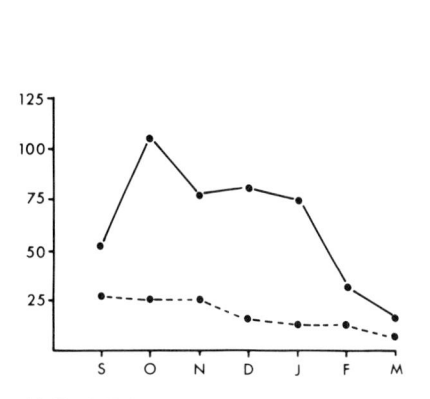

Mallard: Eairy-Kionslieu 1972–83. Upper line = maxima from all counts, lower line = average mid-month counts.

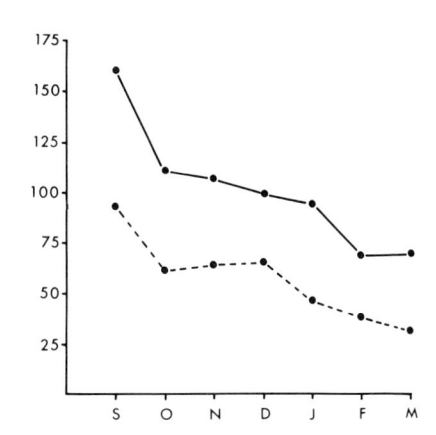

Mallard: Glascoe 1974–83. Upper line = maxima from all counts, lower line = average mid-month counts.

Midwinter counts of over 100 at Crogga are now commonplace, but Baldwin Reservoir which had an early winter population of the same order has been deserted since 1978 in favour of the little lake at Ballachrink 3 km to the south where autumn counts in 1985 reached 180.

There have been just 4 recoveries of Manx-ringed pulli – from Stirlingshire in September, Co. Antrim and north Yorkshire in November and a 12 year old bird from Wexford in mid winter.

Manx: *Thunnag feie* = Wild duck.

Pintail

Anas acuta

Very scarce but regular winter visitor.

It is unlikely that there has been any significant change in the status of the Pintail during the last 100 years although parties of winter visitors were perhaps larger during the 1930s. Then, as now, Langness was the most favoured site and here Madoc saw a party of 12 in 1934. His extreme dates were 3rd August and 6th April. Twenty-five Pintail were seen in flight over Gansey on 2nd November 1937 since which the majority of reports have been of single birds with occasional parties of up to 7. During this period records have been evenly spread from 9th September to 29th March, except for November which has twice as many records as any other month. Two were seen on Langness on 11th and 12th May 1952. Three fifths of all records have come from Langness where birds will often linger for many weeks – the remainder are from the Calf (3) and several inland waters of which Kionslieu with 4 records has been the most frequented.

Manx: *Laagh fammanagh*

Garganey
Anas querquedula

The only definite record is of a drake seen by K. Williamson and H. M. Rogers at Ballacain Dubs on 23rd April 1938.

Shoveler
Anas clypeata

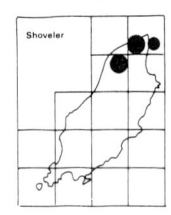

Regular in small numbers as a breeding bird, passage migrant and winter visitor.

Ralfe was only able to quote a handful of winter records, but by 1930 Shoveler were occurring regularly from October to March on Langness. That year a pair was present on the Ayres slacks in mid-April first suggesting the possibility of breeding. Breeding was suspected in 1935 and the next 12 years saw frequent records from several northern sites in April culminating in the finding of 2 nests on the Ayres slacks near Ballaghennie in late June 1947. Since then Shovelers have probably nested in the north most years. Two sites in particular have been favoured – the Lagagh and Ballaugh Curraghs. In addition there have been several records in April and May from the Ballacain Dubs and other marshy pools in that area and nesting has also been occasionally suspected on the Ayres slacks. Since 1947 breeding has only been confirmed on 2 occasions – a duck was seen with 8 young at St Judes in April 1964 and a duck had 5 fluffy young at the Lagagh in early June 1979.

Shoveler have continued to winter on Langness and recently at the Glascoe Dub. Best numbers are usually seen in January and February when these sites may hold up to 10 birds. From October to February records away from Langness and Glascoe are very rare. By March Glascoe is deserted, Langness numbers are low and from the middle of the month, through April Shoveler turn up in two's and threes at a variety of inland sites. Records during May and June are largely confined to probable breeding areas although there is a Calf record for 31st May and Shoveler have twice been seen on Langness in early June. During August and September 1–4 birds have been seen at Langness and the Calf and at several small inland waters.

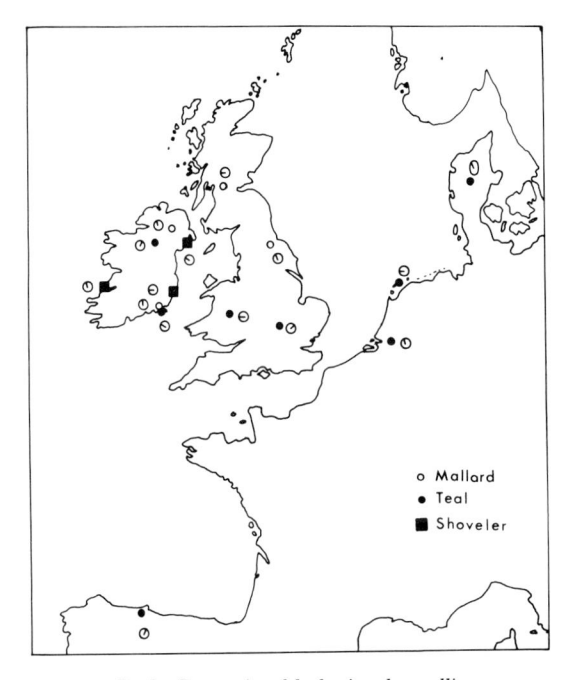

Ducks: Recoveries of ducks ringed as pulli.

There have been just 3 ringing recoveries – all from the same brood ringed in July 1947 and all from Ireland during their first autumn – Wicklow in September, Down in October and Clare in November.

Manx: *Thunnag ny Sleryst*

Pochard

Aythya ferina

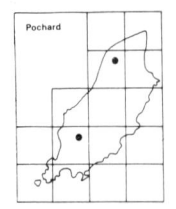

Regular passage migrant and winter visitor.

To Kermode the Pochard was a regular winter visitor in small numbers. By the late 1920s the Foxdale Dams had become established as the most favoured locality as indeed they remain to this day. Up to 5 birds are now seen regularly at Kerrowdhoo during the winter months and they also occur rather less frequently at Glascoe and Billown Quarries, where numbers can approach double figures. One or two are also regular at the Bishop's Dub, both during the winter and on passage and Pochard turn up occasionally at a number of other inland waters. On passage they used to occur with some frequency on the back slacks of the Ayres and at Ballacain Dubs. Coastal records are uncommon.

There are nearly always Pochard on the Foxdale Dams from early October to mid March. Kionslieu is consistently preferred during October, but is used much less in November and December and only occasionally from January to March, while in most years 4–8 birds are present on the Eairy Dam from early November to mid February. Best counts have been 13 on Kionslieu on 28th October 1973 and 12 at the Eairy on 9th November 1974 and 3rd February 1976. One or two Pochard linger on to the first week in April some years and the following late records deserve mention: 12 on the Ayres back slacks on 29th April 1931, one at Kionslieu on 2nd May 1977, a drake at the Bishop's Dub on 5th May 1980 and a pair at Smeale on 20th May 1966. A drake was present at Kionslieu on 20th June 1978 and on 3rd and 4th July 1976, (with a pair on 5th and a drake at the Eairy on 25th July). Four drakes were seen on Kionslieu on 2nd August 1980 and there is a handful of later August records for this dam and the Bishop's Dub. One to three are not infrequently seen for short periods during September at Kionslieu.

Manx: *Kione Mollagh*

Ferruginous Duck

Aythya nyroca

Vagrant.

There are 8 Manx records. First was a drake seen on 13th September in Garwick Bay during the late 1920s. Then in the Derbyhaven – Fort Island area there was a drake on 3rd January 1928, a duck on 16th March 1929 and another drake on 30th November 1930. There were further records on 22nd January and 11th December 1933. These were all seen by Madoc, who knew the species well from Lake Velence near Budapest. The two remaining records were of one on the Eairy Dam on 6th January 1935 and an immature on the Calf Mill Pond on 8th September 1979.

Tufted Duck
Aythya fuligula

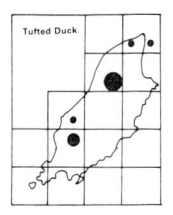

Regular winter visitor in small numbers and prospective breeding bird.

During the late 19th century the Tufted Duck was regarded as an occasional visitor (Jeffcott 1883), but Ralfe could only find one definite record – a drake shot on the Castletown Mill Dam in August 1888. Sporadic occurrences continued during the first quarter of the present century, notably in February 1917 when several were seen, but since 1927 varying numbers have visited the island annually. Nineteen-twenty-nine was notable for the fact that Tufted Duck were present in Peel Harbour from February to April, at Bishopscourt during April and May and at Kionslieau on 9th June leading Madoc to suggest that breeding may have taken place. In fact 45 years were to elapse before the Tufted Duck was again seen in June.

The pattern of occurrences has undoubtedly altered. During the period 1936–62 records of 1–4 birds, and occasionally as many as 6, occurred between December and March with a definite bias in favour of January and February. Twelve were seen in Peel Bay on 18th March 1947. Between 1963 and 1973 there was a marked shift towards the autumn and early winter, October being the peak month. This pattern of winter occurrences has continued but summer records are becoming increasingly common. In 1979 two broods were seen during July in Ballaugh Curraghs (Fitzpatrick 1980) and July records for the Foxdale Dams are now regular. Although not yet proved to breed in the Point of Ayre Gravel Pits birds were present through the summer during 1981–3. There seems little doubt that this prosperous duck is about to colonise the Isle of Man as a breeding bird.

Recent records up to 1983 had mostly been of 1 or 2 birds with occasionally as many as 5, and while autumn visits are often brief, individuals may stay on the same water for many weeks during the winter. The Foxdale Dams had always been the most favoured location, but the Tufted Duck is now a regular winter visitor to Kerrowdhoo (where 12 were present on 27th December 1985) and is not uncommon at the Bishop's and Glascoe Dubs. Coastal records are much less common but the bays of Derbyhaven, Castletown, Port St Mary and Peel each have a handful of records. There have been 5 Calf records – 9 flew south-west past the islet on 7th September 1963 and southbound birds have also been seen on 11th August and 1st and 6th October. One flew north on 15th July 1982.

Manx: *Thunnag Happagh*

Scaup
Aythya marila

Irregular winter visitor.

Ralfe assumed that the Scaup occurred regularly around the Manx coast, but apart from one shot at Sulby in early February 1885, could only record that a number of birds appeared in poulterers' shops in 1891 and 1893. After this there must have been a period of scarcity because no further records appear until 1928. During the next few years Scaup were seen regularly from mid December to early February, favouring Langness/Derbyhaven (7 on 26th January 1930) and the Ramsey area.

Scaup have been recorded in about 25 of the last 50 years. Coastal records predominate but there are records for the Foxdale Dams, Ballasteen, the Bishop's Dub, Billown, Castletown millpond, Block Eary, Baldwin and the Glascoe Dub. Certain sites have enjoyed favour for a year or two viz. Langness/Derbyhaven 1928–31, Port St Mary and Carrick Bay 1954–57 (2–7 birds for several weeks) and Kionslieu 1973–77 – a female wintering there in at least 3 successive years. Cold weather in mid-winter has brought Scaup to Ramsey Harbour and the Mooragh Lake on several occasions recently. The largest gathering was 15 in Peel Bay on 18th March 1947.

Scaup are most often seen during the period October to March – extreme dates being 2 at the Calf on 5th August 1967, a duck on Kionslieu on 12th September 1980, a duck in Peel Harbour on 23rd May 1946 and a drake present in Ramsey Harbour from 19th to 24th May 1962.

Manx: *Thunnag Varrey*

Eider

Somateria mollissima

Irregular and transient visitor occurring more often in winter than summer.

The first Manx record was of a drake off Peel Castle rocks on 2nd December 1928 and there has been a surprisingly meagre score of 21 records since. Several were seen on the sea off Port St Mary during the winter months of 1932, there were up to 6 at Langness from 27th January to 15th March 1934 and as many as 15 were seen together during the following winter. There were 7 in Peel Bay on 26th November 1939 and 4 at Port Erin in mid-November 1975. There have been 7 Calf records. Two of these were in May 1963 when parties of 4 flew south on 2nd and 7th, the remainder have been between 29th August and 13th November – 2 singles, 2 pairs and a group of 5 which flew north on 16th September 1980. On the main island there have been 5–6 summer records – a duck at the Point of Ayre on 8th June 1929 and another at Langness on 26th July 1978. Three flew north past Peel on 29th July 1982, another flew south there on 24th May 1984 and a duck was seen at the Point of Ayre on 6th and 12th August 1984.

Manx: *Laagh Loughlinagh*

Long-tailed Duck
Clangula hyemalis

Irregular winter visitor.

First recorded on the Isle of Man on 1st November 1928, a duck spent 3 weeks in Derbyhaven Bay before being shot. Since then the Long-tailed Duck has occurred with about the same frequency as the Scaup. Although three drakes were seen together in Peel Bay on 7th December 1934, and there have been four other records of pairs, they nearly always occur singly. Derbyhaven Bay has accounted for almost half of the records and there are several for Peel Bay. Apart from 1 on the Mooragh Lake from 10th to 20th November 1959, there has only been 1 inland record – a female present at Kionslieu from 3rd to 13th November 1976 and then moving briefly to the trout farm at St John's. The histogram illustrates the distribution of

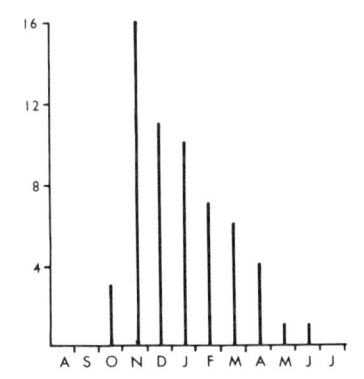

Long-tailed Duck 1928–82. Total individuals per month.

records through the winter. The earliest was seen off the Ayres on 16th October 1981 and the latest was a duck which was present in Derbyhaven Bay from December through to 8th May 1980. It was perhaps the same bird which stayed from December until mid April in both of the following years. There is just one summer record – a drake in breeding plumage off Ladyport on 26th June 1982.

Manx: *Laagh Lheeah*

Common Scoter
Melanitta nigra

Regular winter visitor, recently occurring during the summer and on autumn passage.

Ralfe's assertion that the Common Scoter was probably 'of sparing but regular occurrence' has remained valid throughout this century. Scoters are certainly under-recorded because of the difficulty of identifying the small parties of dark duck which are quite often seen well off the west coast during the winter.

The pattern of occurrences has changed during the last 45 years. Until 1938 records had been strictly confined to the period December to February. Drakes were seen in Peel Bay in April and on 12th May 1938 after which late January to March became the most favoured period, in fact the occurrence of 10 off the Jurby coast on 22nd November 1953 was at that time the earliest Manx record. A Common Scoter was found dead at Smeale on 25th June 1957, and since then records for the main island for the period June to September have exceeded those for the winter months – records between March and May are decidedly rare. Peel has always been the best place for Common Scoters both as winter visitors and during autumn movement. Autumn movement from mid August to the end of October is a regular feature of Calf

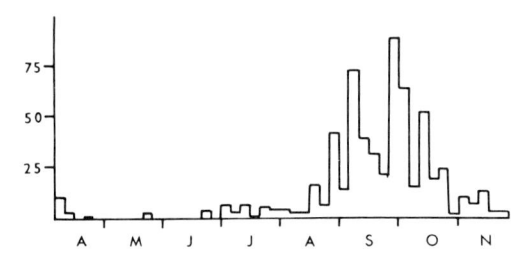

Common Scoter. Total bird days per 5 day period. (Calf).

sea-watching as can be seen on the histogram. When Scoters do come into the bays they are usually seen singly or in pairs, while records of birds in transit are typically of small parties of up to 14. There have been just three inland records of single birds – at the Bishop's Dub on 1st January 1975 and at Kionslieu on 24th August 1981 and 8th October 1983.

Velvet Scoter

Melanitta fusca

Infrequent winter visitor.

The Velvet Scoter was not recorded until 1932 since when there have been 20 records involving 29 birds. With the exception of 2 at Langness on 1st September 1963 all these records have occurred between 26th October and 2nd March. Derbyhaven and Carrick Bay have been particularly favoured and there are 3 records for Peel and 2 for Douglas. Individuals have lingered for several weeks viz., in Douglas Bay from 16th November to 4th December 1962 and at Derbyhaven from 2nd to 22nd January 1972 and from 1st December 1974 to 7th February 1975. From the Calf 1–2 southbound birds have been seen on 4 occasions between 26th October and 15th November.

Goldeneye
Bucephala clangula

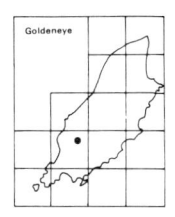

Common winter visitor.

Although he had little to write about the Goldeneye, Ralfe nevertheless regarded it as the commonest of the diving ducks.

As with a number of other ducks there was an apparent increase in abundance in the late 1920s, indeed the period 1929–36 was noted for some substantial gatherings which were not to be approached for a further 40 years. At that time Derbyhaven was the most favoured area and the bay held over 20 on 19th January 1936. Between 1938 and 1953 many records of 1–5 birds (and on one occasion 8) came from Peel and the west coast between Niarbyl and Gob y Deigan; while during the same period and continuing to the late 50s the Foxdale dams were regularly visited. Nineteen-fifty-five to nineteen-sixty-one was a period in which Port St Mary and Carrick Bay were visited by up to 8 Goldeneye in the winter. They were clearly becoming commoner in the middle sixties and this increase in abundance continues to this day.

The most important sites are just to the west of Castletown, where there is a January peak of up to 18 and Douglas Bay where 9 were recorded in 1984 and 13 in 1985. Kionslieu is still regularly visited, particularly in late autumn with counts of 12 on 15th November 1977 and 26th October 1980. Kerrowdhoo, the Mooragh Lake and in particular the trout farm at St John's John's have 6–9 birds in the early winter most years, while on the coast similar numbers are again regular at Strandhall; and Niarbyl had a peak of 12 on 23rd January 1982. During the winter Goldeneye occur irregularly

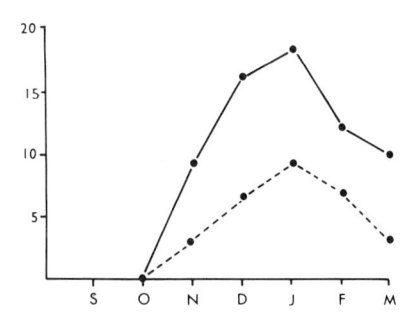

Goldeneye: West of Castletown 1974–83. Upper line = monthly maxima – all counts. Lower line = average mid month counts.

and in small numbers all round the coast and at any of some 20 inland waters ranging from farm ponds to reservoirs. On the Calf millpond a bird present on 17th and 18th October 1968 fed on eels.

Inland waters are visited principally between October and January with a very obvious peak in November, while on salt water, although records do occur occasionally in the autumn the majority occur between November and March with a striking January peak.

First Goldeneye are usually seen in mid October, although there have been at least 6 September records in the last decade, including 15 flying through the Calf Sound on 15th September 1982. There are two August records – 5 off the Point of Ayre on 5th (1951) and 1 at Derbyhaven on 26th (1973). Last birds are seen between mid March and mid April, extreme dates being at Baldwin Reservoir on 27th April 1975, on 8th May 1934 and a drake at Kionslieu on 20th June 1978.

Manx: *Laaghag Hooillagh*

Smew

Mergus albellus

Scarce winter visitor.

Ralfe was only aware of 2 Manx records, but between 1927 and 1934 the Smew was a regular visitor at Derbyhaven with as many as 10–12 on 3rd January 1928. There were also records for Peel and Perwick during this period. No Smew were seen for the next 10 years and the period 1945–78 saw just 11 records. In the winter of 1981–2 1 was seen on the Mooragh lake from 20th December to 6th January, with 2 on 30th January. Most records have occurred between 25th November and 16th March and particularly from December to February. More than any other duck its visits coincide with very cold weather. Almost half of the records have been in Derbyhaven Bay. Of the remainder, half have been on salt water and half on fresh. A drake flew through the Sound on 30th September 1978 while late records were of one at Peel on 30th April 1931 and a pair which arrived at the Clypse Reservoir in late April 1945 – the duck eventually being shot on 5th May.

Red-breasted Merganser

Mergus serrator

Regular winter visitor. Has bred once.

In the late 19th century the Red-breasted Merganser was a scarce winter visitor which had been recorded on both salt and fresh water, but by the late 1920s its visits, particularly to Derbyhaven and Carrick Bay, had become regular. The 1930s were notable for the biggest gatherings in Carrick Bay and neighbouring Chapel Bay (Port St Mary), where there were 11 in December 1934 and 12 between 6th and 10th of the following April. In the early part of 1936 there were up to 12 at Poyllvaaish and Madoc had a record 14 some years earlier. On 19th November 1938 there were 4 on the Clypse Reservoir, which, with the exception of one or two occurrences on the Mooragh Lake, is the only fresh water record this century.

Between 1940 and 1960 mergansers continued to frequent the same coastal locations and occasionally turned up at Ramsey and Peel – but numbers never exceeded 6, 2–3 birds together being typical. Up to 1960 they were rarely seen before the last week in October – the earliest date being 6th October – or after the last week in April – 15th May being the latest.

Increasingly since 1960 Red-breasted Mergansers have been seen in July and to a lesser extent in June, August and September. Many such records have been of birds flying past (especially from the Calf), but birds have also settled for short periods during the summer in Derbyhaven and Peel Bays. Summer records usually involve single birds – very occasionally 2 or 3, while in winter, although seen around the coast at many sites in addition to the traditional ones, 4 birds is a rather rare maximum.

The relatively recent occurrence of summer records has coincided with the colonisation of the Lake District and Anglesey as breeding areas during the 1950s and breeding on the Isle of Man was finally proved when a duck was flushed from 5 eggs in a burrow of marram grass bordering the southern Point of Ayre gravel pit on 15th June 1985 (Cullen 1985).

Manx: *Thunnag Cleeau Yiarg*

Goosander

Mergus merganser

Rare winter visitor.

Ralfe considered the Goosander as being of very casual occurrence – 2 had been shot in Peel Bay in November 1881 and ducks were also shot at Santon and St John's in January 1894. Between 1926 and 1934 this otherwise rare duck was recorded on about 18 occasions, mostly at Derbyhaven but also in Douglas Bay, off the Ballaugh coast and inland at Kionslieu, Tromode and on the Silverburn. In contrast none were seen between 1935 and 1946 since which there have been just 8 records, usually of single birds but on one occasion 2 drakes and a duck at Langness on the late date of 11th May. Of these 8 records, there was one other for Langness/Derbyhaven, one each for the Cluggid, Clypse Reservoir and Baldwin Reservoir and 3 for the Calf. Goosanders are usually seen between November and March although south-bound individuals have been seen from the Calf on 28th September and 17th October.

Manx: *Laagh 'Eeacklagh*

Honey Buzzard
Pernis apivorus

Rare passage migrant.

There are 6 Manx records. One was shot in Glen Auldyn in June 1907, the remainder were all seen on the Calf. On 16th July 1974 1 flew along the east coast of the Calf and disappeared to the south-east. Six weeks later, on 27th August, another flew over the highest point and away in a south-westerly direction. Individuals were seen on 10th and 11th July 1979 and rather a late immature bird flew up and down the Glen on 5th October 1982.

Black Kite
Milvus migrans

Rare passage migrant.

Recorded twice on the Calf. On 3rd June 1976 1 flew across the islet leaving in a north-westerly direction and on the same date in 1982 another was seen over the cliffs of the east coast.

Red Kite
Milvus milvus

Vagrant.

Following an attempt to introduce game birds to the Isle of Man in the late 17th century payments were made for killing various vermin. Included in this category were Kites, and the Castle Rushen papers reveal that birds were killed in all parishes except Andreas, Ballaugh, Michael and Onchan in 1689. The Kite was thus a plentiful species at that time and according to Fisher (1966) nested in the Isle of Man (but never in Ireland) until the 19th century. It receives no mention by Ralfe however and the only record for this century is of one present near Ballaugh from late December 1958 to early February 1959 (Crellin 1960).

White-tailed Eagle
Haliaeetus albicilla

Probable former breeding bird.

On the west coast is a near vertical north-facing precipice, surmounted by a grassy ledge and jutting out from the brows which fall very steeply for almost 300 m from the summit of Lhiattee ny Beinnee. The precipice, which is about 60 m high, is known as Ernery (sometimes spelt Eairnyerey) and was the nesting place of the White-tailed Eagle. The name is Norse and must have been acquired prior to the extinction of the Norse language in the 14th century.

Bishop Wilson (1722) provided the first, and indeed the only, historical reference when he wrote that the Island had 'one airy of eagles'. As Ernery is arguably the most remote place on the Isle of Man, the lack of documentation is understandable.

Ralfe quoted information from 3 different sources who had first or second hand details of eagles nesting on sea cliffs, specifically identified as Ernery in one instance and more vaguely as 'at the south end of the Isle of Man' in another. The eagles were eventually destroyed in a snow storm in about 1815, two sources relating how they were found under snow in a farmyard. The third informant, who lived at Lingague, a farm on the eastern slopes of Lhiattee ny Beinnee, told Ralfe that his father recalled the eagles perching on an outlying mass of rock near the foot of Ernery which was known as Eagle Rock.

During the last 170 years the only definite record of the White-tailed Eagle was one obtained at Greeba on 12th December 1907 and this may well have been an escape. It had been in the area for 2 or 3 weeks and had already been pursued and wounded. It was an immature bird whose tail feathers were said to have been considerably abraded as if it had been kept in captivity.

Manx: *Urley Erne*

Marsh Harrier

Circus aeruginosus

Rare passage migrant only recorded in spring.

The first Manx record concerned a female which was seen on the Calf on several occasions between 9th and 29th May 1967. A Marsh Harrier seen at Fleshwick a few days later on 5th June was almost certainly the same bird.

Another bird, considered to be an immature male, hunted over the Glen and the Heath for an hour on 19th May 1974. On 27th and 29th May 1976 a female was seen near the Braaid and it seems very likely that it was the same bird which hunted over the Langness salt marsh one day in early June. A female was seen over the Calf on 14th May 1982 and the 5th Manx record was of another female or immature bird on 30th May 1985.

One to two Marsh Harriers are usually seen each year in south-west Scotland almost entirely in the period mid May to early June.

Hen Harrier
Circus cyaneus

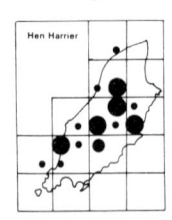

Resident and common winter visitor.

Although Kermode listed 2 Hen Harriers seen at Maughold in December 1900, the first unequivocal record was of an adult male, which was shot in the gareys of Ballagarraghyn in the early spring of 1906. Two further records followed in 1921 and the next 40 years produced some 18 records between late August and early May and mostly from the northern plain. Between 1963 and 1971 Hen Harriers appeared almost annually in spring and autumn on the Calf and from 1972 occurred with increasing frequency on the main Island in areas of moorland, and to a much lesser extent curragh.

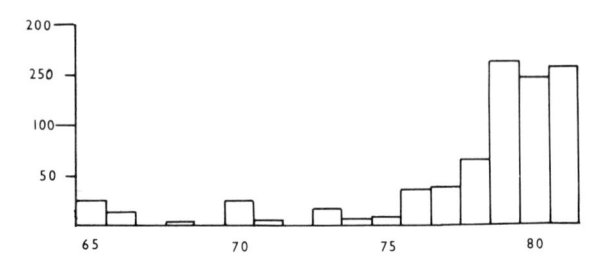

Hen Harrier: Annual bird days 1965–81. (Calf).

The very large majority of these records came from the southern hills and it was here, in Glen Rushen Plantation that the first breeding in the Isle of Man took place in 1977 (McIntyre et al. 1978). Until 1977 there had been no records between 20th May and 27th August.

It is possible that nesting also took place in the Cringle area in 1977 and Hen Harriers were seen in the Blaber River area during that summer and probably nested there the following year. Nineteen-seventy-nine saw a remarkable extension of the summer range – nesting probably took place at Conrhenny and additional pairs were noted in summer at Archallagan and Druidale. In the Sulby Glen area young were reared at Killabregga and a pair may have nested on the opposite side of the glen at Ballakerka plantation. Breeding was proved at Glen Crammag in 1980 and there were several summer reports from Slieau Whallian. Two pairs bred in Druidale in 1981 and 5–6 pairs now breed on the Island each year. Hen Harriers are now a very typical feature of the Calf and breeding there is anticipated with some confidence but so far records between the end of May and beginning of August are very rare. Manx nests are usually in long heather either in open moorland, or, as at Glen Rushen in failed conifer plantation irregularly scattered with trees up to 2 m in height. Most nest sites have been between 200 and 270 m above sea level but in 1985 a pair bred close to sea level in the Ballaugh Curraghs. Four is the most usual clutch size and 3 young have flown from the majority of nests observed. Young are usually able to fly during the first half of July.

Throughout the winter Hen Harriers may be seen over a variety of habitats. In the north they favour all varieties of low-lying farmland as well as the Curraghs of Ballaugh and, particularly, the Blue Point brooghs. They are seen less frequently over the southern lowlands and along the central valley. Moorland remains a popular habitat, especially the lower slopes of the southern hills and recently the Calf. No communal winter roosts are yet known.

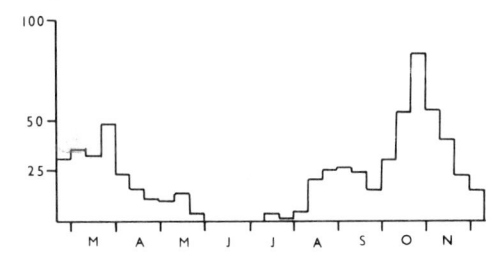

Hen Harrier: Total bird days per ten day period (Calf).

The pattern of Hen Harrier passage through the Calf is well illustrated on the histogram. The greater number of bird days in autumn is attributed to some extent to the dispersal of young birds reared on the Isle of Man.

There are two ringing recoveries – one ringed as a pullus in Wigtownshire in early August was found dead at the Lhen 5 months later, while another nestling ringed at Slieau Moar in early July was controlled on the Calf 12 weeks later.

Goshawk

Accipiter gentilis

Vagrant.

An adult female was seen over Sartfell on 23rd April 1975 and a juvenile female flew north over Langness on 27th August 1980.

Sparrowhawk
Accipiter nisus

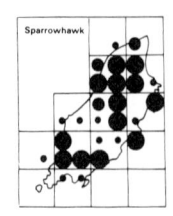

Well represented resident.

Ralfe described the Sparrowhawk as being fairly abundant, many plantations all over the Island having pairs regularly nesting in the same neighbourhood. It is likely that the species enjoyed the same sort of prosperity throughout the first half of this century, but as in Britain as a whole, so in the Isle of Man, a catastrophic decline took place in the late 1950s. This was due to the use of organochlorine insecticides in agriculture. In 1959 the scarcity of Sparrowhawks had been noted, especially in the north of the Island and it was during the same year that the Bird Observatory opened on the Calf of Man. In Britain Sparrowhawks are remarkably sedentary and ringing data suggest that Manx birds are no exception, thus birds occurring on the Calf originate from the main island and the number of bird days recorded at the Observatory is an accurate gauge of the prosperity of the Manx breeding population. It can be seen that in the 11 years 1959 to 1969 there was an average of only 4 bird days per annum. Nineteen-seventy provided the first hint of recovery with 11 bird days, revival was in full swing by 1972 when there were 60 and between 1973 and 1981 the yearly average has been 87. Since 1972 breeding records on the Isle of Man have been plentiful and the Sparrowhawk is now probably as abundant as at any time this century.

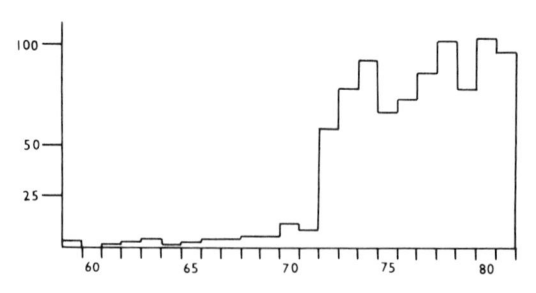

Sparrowhawk: Annual bird days 1959–81 (Calf).

Sparrowhawks probably breed in all the island's mature conifer plantations as well as in a number of glens and in scattered clumps of woodland in the vicinity of farmland. They are perhaps commonest in the wooded hillsides overlooking the northern plain. A number of sites such as Gob y volley, Skyhill, Ballachurry, Lambhill and Port Soderick Glen have a long tradition of Sparrowhawk nesting stretching back many decades. A realistic estimate of the present breeding population would be between 20 and 30 pairs. As in Ralfe's time most eggs are laid in mid May – the earliest laying date is 30th April (St Judes 1957) and it is very unusual to find young still in the nest after mid July. Four to five is the usual clutch size although there are 1 or 2 records of 6 eggs.

While Sparrowhawks are often seen in highspeed flight low over a roadside sod hedge they also frequently hunt the bushes scattered over the coastal brooghs. Nearly all prey items are birds but there is a record of a cock bird taking a bat at Ballachurry (Andreas) in August 1946 (Crellin and Crellin 1947).

On the Calf Sparrowhawks are often seen in spring, but occur much more frequently in autumn from mid August to mid November. Records during June and July are almost unknown.

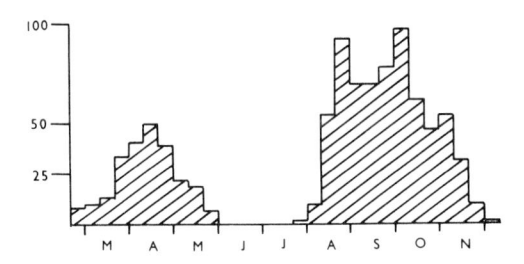

Sparrowhawk. Total bird days per ten day period (Calf).

Of 57 birds ringed on the Calf there have been 5 recoveries and there have been a further 6 recoveries of birds ringed on the main island. There have been no recoveries of Manx-ringed Sparrowhawks away from the Isle of Man and while 4 birds showed movement of 30–39 km, 6 were recovered 5 or less km from where they were ringed. A bird ringed as a nestling at Langholm (Dumfriesshire) was found dead at Jurby 5 months later. The longest time between ringing and recovery is 6 years.

Manx: *Shawk, Shirragh* = Hawk, *Shirragh ny Giark* = Hen Searcher.

Buzzard

Buteo buteo

Irregular and transient autumn visitor.

The ulna of a Buzzard was among bones found at the Perwick Cave midden deposit dated at approximately AD 90 (Garrad 1972).

Ralfe's only record was of an adult, killed at Earystane, Arbory in October 1902.

Buzzard records in each month.

	J	F	M	A	M	J	J	A	S	O	N	D	Total
Up to 1959			3				1			3	2	3	12
1960–1982	2		1	4	3	2	1	8	4	3	1		29
Total	2		4	4	3	3	1	8	4	6	3	3	41

The table illustrates the increased frequency of records and the recent predominance of August records. Nineteen-seventy-six was a notable year with a single bird in April and late August, followed by 1 in the north and 4 over Ballasalla on 18th September and a further individual 1 week later. In 1977 it is likely that a pair summered on the Island – two were seen in display flight over the northern plain on 17th April and at Round Table on 2nd May when aggressive display between one of the Buzzards and a male Hen Harrier was seen. One week later an individual was seen over Glen Helen and between 22nd and 26th June one (and on 1 occasion 2) was often seen at Gob y Volley.

The first Calf record was of 1 taken alive on the rocks at Amulty in June 1907 and there have been 7 records (included in the table) since the opening of the Observatory. Two were seen on 6th April 1961, otherwise Calf records have been of single birds in January, May, June, August (twice) and early September.

Rough-legged Buzzard

Buteo lagopus

Vagrant.

The four Manx records are all from the Calf.

In 1963 1 was seen on 15th and 16th March and from 25th April to 4th May. On 25th September the same year 1 was seen high overhead flying west and the fourth bird was present on the Calf from 7th to 15th October 1982.

Golden Eagle

Aquila chrysaetos

Vagrant.

Occasional historical references do not of course distinguish between this species and *H. albicilla*, but there is reasonable evidence that in the 17th century the Golden Eagle was an occasional visitor and rather less convincing evidence that a pair bred on the Isle of Man in the early part of the 19th century. In 1676, in a letter to the Marquis of Ormonde (guardian of William,

Earl of Derby and Lord of Mann), Henry Nowell wrote 'And I cannot also omit but give your Grace an account that there is of late an eagle coming into this Isle, which is a fowl that very seldom and scarce in age cometh here, it being a place where never any such birds useth to breed, and that there is all possible care taken for to preserve her here, it being observed to be very lucky when any such is seen in the island.' (Wood 1917).

Ralfe (1924) mentions two people who had told him that their parents knew of eagles nesting on Greeba. About 1817–19 an attempt was made to take an eaglet from the nest, but it retreated into a crevice and the old birds made repeated attacks on the intruders. The other witness, who regularly visited a farm below Greeba, knew of eagles nesting there until probably as late as 1835. The unwooded crag on the southside of Greeba, overlooking the central valley, was certainly the most suitable site for a Golden Eagle's eyrie and it is improbable that eagles were confused with any other raptor. The repeated attacks of the adults seems to detract from the authenticity of the earlier record and it is certainly strange that the nesting of such a conspicuous bird should not have received a mention from contemporary writers. Train (1845) referred to eagles nesting on Snaefell in Bishop Wilson's time (early 18th century) – surely he would have mentioned the Greeba nest had it existed.

In the winter of 1881–2 one or two eagles were seen on several occasions in the north of the Island between November and February by apparently reliable observers, and over the last 100 years there have been occasional unconfirmed reports. However the only generally accepted record is of an immature bird seen at very close quarters on 9th October 1949 (Rogers and Cowin 1952).

Manx: *Urley*

Osprey

Pandion haliaetus

Scarce passage migrant.

Although the Manx Museum possesses an adult male shot in a tree at Ballamenagh, Lonan on 26th March 1924, the fairly regular occurrence of Ospreys is a recent development. One was seen over the Calf on 30th August 1961 and in 1965 one stayed there from 6th September to at least 14th October, when the Observatory closed. Since 1973 when there were 3 Calf records, an Osprey has been seen there or on the main island each year except 1978 and 1979 until 1982 when there were two records. There is a total of 14 Manx records (9 being from the Calf) with a monthly distribution of March 1, April 2, May 2, June 1, July 1, August 2, September 4, October 1 (excludes the 1975 bird). The latest record was of a first year bird seen over Tholt y Will on 22nd October 1976 and found dead there 2 days later. Clearly the relative frequency during the last decade can be linked with the increasing breeding success of the Osprey in Scotland.

Kestrel
Falco tinnunculus

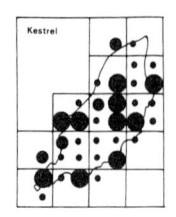

Well represented resident and passage migrant.

Ralfe wrote of the Kestrel – 'This is one of our characteristic birds, the Manx coast abounding in localities which suit it. At short intervals along our rock-bound shores a pair of these beautiful Hawks may be met with, and soon attract notice by their graceful motions and keen cries. The Kestrel loves a rock half covered by ivy and with grassy ledges, where in some earthy hollow sheltered by the herbage the richly coloured eggs are laid usually early in May.' Eighty years later, these evocative remarks are still true as indeed is the Kestrel's liking for slate quarries, although other inland nest sites are probably commoner than in Ralfe's time. While Ralfe knew of no tree nesting, this has occurred from time to time since first reported at Ballachurry (Andreas) in 1944, but is still uncommon. Buildings are used sometimes – favoured sites being pigeon holes in barns, ventilation holes in St Michael's Chapel on Fort Island and (with repeated success) in the belfry of Malew Church. There are instances of Kestrels laying in old Ravens' nests on the coast at Onchan Head and in quarries at Folieu, near Ramsey and Stoney Mountain. The tree nest at Ballachurry was in the old nest of a Hooded Crow, while at the Guilcagh an old Magpie's nest has been used. Perhaps the most typical nesting site is the river gorge, where eggs may be laid on a narrow ledge partly covered by soil and usually overhung by a bank above. Nesting has been described within 5 metres of a Barn Owl's nest, and Ravens, Choughs and Kestrels all nested in the little Vaaish Quarry one year. Four or five eggs are usually laid, although there are records of complete clutches of 3 and 6 eggs. Laying takes place in the first half of May and the earliest date of which young have been found is 29th May. Four young were still in a nest at Niarbyl on the late date of 30th July. On the Calf Kestrels breed occasionally with, in 1964, as many as 3 pairs. There is no evidence that the Manx Kestrel population was significantly affected by organochlorine residues in the 1960's. It is likely that 25–40 pairs breed in the Isle of Man.

Kestrels are present on the main Island and on the Calf throughout the year – Calf numbers are significantly higher from August to October when 5–10 in a day are often seen with some visible passage to the south and west. During August and September good numbers are often seen hovering at intervals along the mountain road between Onchan and Ramsey – the best counts were 27 on 16th September 1972 and 30 on 19th September 1985.

The Kestrel has been seen following the plough with gulls in February and Madoc has described a Kestrel feeding on a dead bird with two Hooded Crows on Langness.

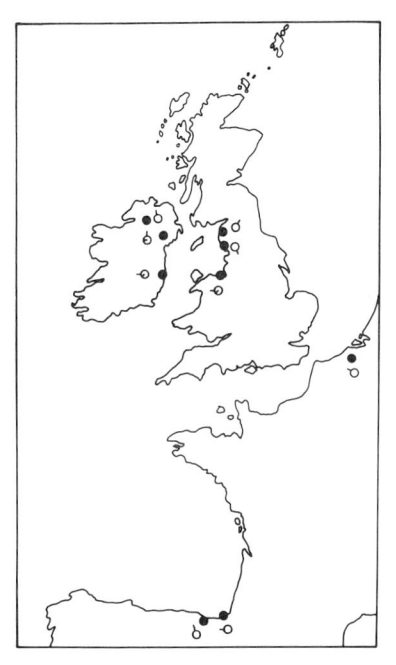

Kestrel. Recoveries of birds ringed on the Isle of Man. All were ringed as pulli except the three where the month of ringing is indicated.

It is well recognised that young Kestrels tend to disperse in a mainly southerly or south easterly direction in autumn (Snow 1968). Five Manx fledglings have been recovered during their first winter – one was in Belgium, one was at the extreme south of the French Biscay coast and another was just over the border in Spain. Two days after the Spanish recovery another young Kestrel from the same Onchan Head brood was recovered in Co. Tyrone, Northern Ireland illustrating most impressively how nests-mates may migrate in totally different directions. In contrast the 5th bird was shot on the Island in mid January just 10 km south of its fledging place. South-easterly dispersal was also illustrated by a 1st winter bird ringed on the Calf in mid August and recovered on the Wirral 17 days later, but a Cumbrian fledging was found dead on the Island the following March. Of Kestrels recovered after their first winter 2 were recovered in Cumbria, 2 in Ireland (September and December) and 4 were on the Isle of Man together with a further 3 Calf retraps. The longest gap between ringing and recovery is $6\frac{1}{2}$ years.
Manx: *Stannair Ruy*

Red-footed Falcon

Falco vespertinus

The only Manx record is of a male seen on the Calf over Gibbdale on 4th June 1978. (Jennings 1981).

Merlin

Falco columbarius

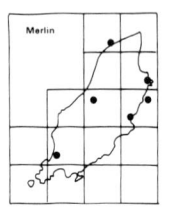

A regular passage migrant and winter visitor, which may occasionally have bred.

In the Isle of Man the status of the Merlin as a breeding bird is shrouded in more mystery than any other species, except possibly the Twite. As long ago as 1656 Chaloner wrote 'In the summer time there arrive here out of Ireland and the west parts of Scotland, many of those small Hawks called Merlyns.' Did Merlins breed quite widely in the 17th century or do these remarks simply refer to autumn migration? It seems very likely that about 1860 Merlins did nest on the southern slopes of Peel Hill – 'a small blue hawk, no bigger than a Wood Thrush' nesting in ling could hardly have been any other bird. There is similar information from two other sources. A hawk's nest was found in heather in 1893 between Honey hill and Glen Roy and in 1899 two young were caught in heather on Slieau Ruy above Agneash. No observations were made about the parent birds, but J. J. Gill, a careful and accurate observer, did report a nest in heather in the northern hills about that time – it contained 4 eggs.

The Manx Museum has a clutch of 5 eggs taken from a nest in Druidale in 1909 and Ralfe's supplement reports that young were taken from a nest on the Carnanes (Rushen) 'years ago' without supporting evidence.

In the period 1929–36 both Madoc and Rogers were confident that Merlins bred both on the main Island and on the Calf. Pairs were seen in June at several places, but the evidence is only presumptive, more especially on the Calf where summer records were of individuals only. A pair was often seen at Glen Helen in early June 1947 and the last 10 years have seen a notable increase in summer records. Although most of these are isolated records a pair was seen high on the west side of Colden in late June 1973 and a Merlin was present for much of the summer at Barony (Maughold) in 1975 and at Ballamodha (Malew) in 1979.

Calf records show the Merlin to be a regular spring and autumn migrant. Spring passage is seen mainly from mid March to the end of April and heavier autumn passage is from late August to the latter half of November with a definite October peak. As the Observatory is not manned through the mid-winter period the histogram will not reveal wintering birds. On the main Island Merlins are certainly commonest in autumn, but this abundance extends through December.

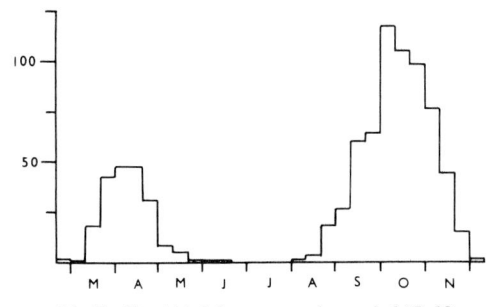

Merlin. Total bird days per ten day period (Calf).

Main island Merlin records in each month 1972–82

	Jan	Feb	Mar	Apr	May	Jun	Jly	Aug	Sep	Oct	Nov	Dec
High moorland	1	0	1	2	6	4	2	2	4	1	1	1
Inland lowland	2	6	6	3	0	2	2	3	2	5	2	5
Coast	3	2	2	3	1	0	2	5	8	5	9	8
Total	6	8	9	8	7	6	6	10	16	11	12	14

High moorland records are unusual during the winter when Merlins are most commonly seen on the coast – Langness is a particularly favoured area in autumn.

Thirteen birds were ringed on the Calf in the period 1959–82 – one was recovered, dead at Jurby Head in late June 21 months after ringing.

Two of the five specimens in the Manx Museum are of the Icelandic race *F.c. subaesalon*. Both had been shot on 21st April – the other three are of the European race *F.c. aesalon* (Williamson 1960). Birds showing characteristics of the Icelandic race have recently been seen on the Calf in both spring and autumn.

Hobby

Falco subbuteo

Uncommon passage migrant.

The first Manx record was of an immature male at Santon Gorge on 10th September 1972. Since then individuals have been seen on 6 other occasions between 17th May and 1st October – 5 of these were on the Calf, the other was at Poyllvaaish. June has 2 records, the other months in this period one each.

Gyrfalcon

Falco rusticolus

Vagrant.

The only occurrence in the Isle of Man was in 1884. It was eventually shot by a gamekeeper on Douglas Head on 8th April, but had previously been seen at Ballaglass (Maughold) and at Bradda Head. It hawked Rooks on Douglas Head and Kermode related how, a day or two before being shot, it struck one which fell close to a man who picked it up, whereupon the falcon swooped and struck the Rook out of his hand.

During the winter of 1883–4 at least 8 Gyrfalcons were obtained in Ireland. (Ussher and Warren 1900).

Peregrine

Falco peregrinus

Resident and partial migrant.

Joalf's huge cross slab, which is preserved at Kirk Michael and dates from the late 10th or early 11th century depicts a number of hunting subjects. On one face, above the head of the cross, are two birds which Williamson and others considered to represent a Peregrine stooping on a smaller bird. This is thus one of the earlier records of falconry in the British Isles (Williamson 1944).

In 1405 King Henry IV gave the Isle of Man with all its rights to Sir John Stanley on condition that he paid homage and gave two falcons to him and to every future King of England on his coronation day. Sir John's descendants ruled as Kings or Lords of Mann for 360 years until George III assumed the Lordship, while the presentation of two falcons continued up to the coronation of George IV in 1821. In 1422 the fine for taking a hawk was £3 and in 1577 the same sum was payable for each adult, young bird or egg taken. During the 17th century the first wardening took place with the employment of a falconer who carefully watched the Peregrines' eyries. In 1656 Chaloner referred to 'some Ayries of mettled Falcons that breed in the Rocks', half a century later Bishop Wilson wrote of at least two such eyries, while Train (1845) specifically mentions Maughold Head and the Calf. Coronation falcons are known to have been taken from both these sites and indeed it was Maughold that provided the birds for George IV.

During the 1880s Manx Peregrines were ruthlessly persecuted by collectors: an adult was shot at each of two sites leading to abandonment for several years, while one site was robbed of either young or eggs on five occasions during the decade. Ralfe knew of 10 or 11 coastal sites but none inland and suspected that most had existed since time immemorial. During the present century eleven basic coastal sites were used in most years up to the mid 1950s and all have been reoccupied at some time since the recovery began in 1973. Inland, 2 quarry sites were regularly used before the slump, two others occasionally and 2 or 3 natural sites equally infrequently.

Organochlorines affected Peregrines more than any other raptor in the Isle of Man. Three pairs nested in 1962 (two successfully), but in the years 1963–72 no Manx Peregrines bred. During 1972 they had become notably more conspicuous and in 1973 2 pairs bred successfully, the beginning of a pleasing renaissance.

Ralfe considered 4 to be the usual clutch size, eggs being laid at the end of March or beginning of April. Of a number of nests studied by Cowin between 1938 and 1958 nearly all had clutches of 3. During the last 45 years laying has usually started between 14th and 25th April – the earliest first egg dates have been 23rd March 1960 and 30th March 1952 and occasionally laying has been delayed until the first week of May. At inland quarry sites there has been a notable tendency to use old nests of Ravens, a habit Ralfe had also noted at coastal sites.

Although Peregrines usually nest close to seabird colonies, Ralfe and his contemporaries considered that gulls and auks were rarely if ever preyed upon. A recent study on the Calf however has shown that 15 out of 94 kills were auks, which seemed to be the favourite prey of the female. In contrast the male selected doves and to a much lesser degree Starlings, Blackbirds and Skylarks (Jennings 1983). Neither rabbits nor Choughs appeared in this study, but elsewhere on the Island rabbits are very commonly taken and there are several records of Choughs being killed. The same study included only 2 Jackdaws, generally regarded as the most common Manx Peregrine

Peregrine prey recorded on the Isle of Man

Rabbit	Redshank	Rock Pipit
Leach's Petrel	Turnstone	Wren
Wigeon	Black-headed Gull	Blackbird
Teal	Herring Gull	Fieldfare
Mallard	Kittiwake	Redwing
Red Grouse	Guillemot	Mistle Thrush
Grey Partridge	Razorbill	Magpie
Moorhen	Puffin	Chough
Oystercatcher	Domestic/Feral/Rock Dove	Jackdaw
Golden Plover	Woodpigeon	Rook
Lapwing	Collared Dove	Hooded Crow
Dunlin	Turtle Dove	Raven
Whimbrel	Cuckoo	Chaffinch
Curlew	Skylark	Goldfinch

kill, but it should be remembered that although large numbers of Jackdaws are seen on the Calf in the autumn, they do not breed there.

An interesting incident was witnessed on the coast north of Derbyhaven when a pair of Peregrines selected a Greenshank from the assortment of birds which rose in panic at their approach. The Greenshank responded by climbing higher and higher into the sky and remaining above the falcons, which after a token chase gave up and half heartedly buzzed a small pack of Wigeon which were resting on the sea. Peregrines have taken newly fledged Ravens, but although often seen in apparent aerial combat with adult Ravens this seems to represent mutual antipathy rather than prey seeking. In the Manx Museum is the skin of a Kestrel which died after being struck by a Peregrine. There are records of a Peregrine being killed attacking a Heron, leading ultimately to the transfixing of the falcon by the Heron's bill, and of a Peregrine being killed by a Raven as the two birds were fighting over a dead rabbit (Williamson 1944).

In Ralfe's view Peregrines were rarely seen away from their breeding haunts and did not occur in winter. Nowadays Peregrines are seen in the Isle of Man throughout the year and over all habitats, including towns. In Britain young Peregrines disperse for distances up to about 300 km, but although 5 nestlings were ringed in the period 1949–52, none were recovered and there is no evidence regarding movement of Manx bred birds. One Peregrine has been recovered on the Island – ringed as a nestling in Cumberland, it was found at St John's nearly six years later, while another bird from the same brood was recovered in Ayrshire.

It might be expected that such a celebrated member of the Manx avifauna would be represented in local place names. In fact the only place which probably has such a derivation is Wallberry, which is thought to be derived from the old Norse Vala-berg = Falcon Cliff. Marstrander knew of seven examples of this common name in Norway (Kneen 1925, Marstrander 1932). Wallberry, south of Douglas is known to have been the site of an eyrie in the 19th century.

Manx: *Shirragh y Ree*

Red Grouse

Lagopus lagopus

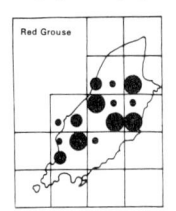

Well distributed resident.

Denton wrote in 1681 'They have store of moor-game both gor and gray' and during the second half of the 18th century Manx literature contains frequent references to grouse, but although formerly abundant they were extinct by 1835. In 1880 they were reintroduced in Druidale and were well distributed through the northern and southern hills by 1903, although in that year Manx birds only constituted $2\frac{1}{2}$% of the total registered under the Game Act.

Red Grouse can now be found on virtually all heather-covered moorland above 200 m. In the southern hills they are found from the Sloc and Slieau Eairystane north over Cronk ny iree laa, South Barrule and Dalby Mountain to Slieau Whallian. North of the central valley they occur from Dowse over Beary Mountain, Greeba, Colden, Carraghan to Creg ny baa and Conrhenny. They are also found on Sartfell, Slieau Dhoo and Slieau Curn, all over the Sulby watershed and east to Clagh Ouyr and North Barrule. There are no recent reports from the hills between the Laxey and Corrany valleys. Grouse have also been seen outside these areas, notably in 1973 when there were records from Peel Hill and Barony. Two were flushed from heather near the Point of Ayre on 23rd March 1951 and Madoc had a record from Clay Head. In the late 18th century John Quayle had attempted to introduce Grouse (and deer) to the Calf but failed totally. There are however 2 recent Calf records of single birds on 25th October 1971 and 2nd March 1976.

Grouse are regularly released in the Manx hills and are subject to rough shooting, but it seems that the quite widely varying population from year to year is more related to weather and heather burning. Eggs are usually laid in late April or early May but a Glen Roy nest held 3 eggs on 23rd March 1952.

Manx: *Kellagh Ruy* = Red Cock. *Kiark Freoaie* = Heath Hen

Black Grouse
Tetrao tetrix

Former resident, now extinct.

The Denton manuscript (1681) implies that grouse 'both gor and gray' existed on the Isle of Man. Ralfe had doubts about the authenticity of this statement but was certain that Black Grouse were introduced when the Scottish Dukes of Atholl were Lords of Mann (1736 onward). He only had details from the hills between the valleys of the Cornaa and Laxey rivers from which the Black Grouse probably became extinct about 1842. Prior to this date up to 20 black cock might be seen together. In 1880 Kermode listed it as 'recently introduced and not yet become extinct' but the Black Grouse does not appear in his 1901 list. Further introductions were made in the north, but although 4 Manx birds appeared in the 1921 Game list by 1924 Ralfe considered the species once more extinct.

Red-legged Partridge
Alectorix rufa

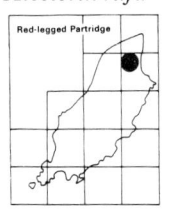

Recent introductions produced occasional sightings in the Poyllvaaish area in 1973–4 and near Aust, north of Ramsey where young were reared in 1980 and 1981. One seen at Park Llewellyn (Maughold) in March 1981 may have come from Aust.

Grey Partridge
Perdix perdix

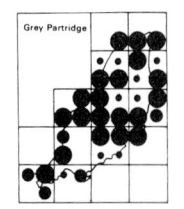

Fairly common resident.

Attempts to introduce the Partridge to the Isle of Man in the early part of the 17th century were unsuccessful but by 1693 Sacheverell was able to write that birds sent over by the Earl of Derby were thriving well. In 1687 a law had been published at Tynwald stating 'That whosoever shall be found to destroy, annoy, or kill any of the Partridges either young or old that are set forth in or about Ballakillingan, in Kirk Christ Lezayre, or in any other place where they do frequent, such person or persons are to be fined in £3 to the use of the Rt. Honble. Lord of this Isle, and to endure a monthe's imprisonment by way of corporal punishment besides.' Although the Game Act of 1835 suggested that Partridges were very scarce, Forbes (1839) found them 'not uncommon' and Ralfe considered that they had maintained this status to the beginning of the present century.

The Grey Partridge is still, as described by Ralfe, '– very fairly distributed, though perhaps hardly to be called abundant. A favourite refuge, as expressed by the Manx name *Kiark-rhennee*, is the bracken on the lower hillsides and the selvages of rough land along the coast.' A typical bird of farmland and its uncultivated fringes it occurs up to about 180 m above sea level.

Pairing starts in mid January although sizeable coveys may be seen into the second half of February. Eggs are rarely laid before the last week of April, the majority of clutches being started in May. At Ballachurry (Andreas) young hatched on the very late date of 25th August 1973. A typical clutch is of 16–22 eggs, the largest number of eggs – 27 in a nest at Jurby in June 1941 – were probably laid by 2 birds. The population is very much dependent on the climate and cold, wet weather in June and July consistently leads to poor numbers in autumn. In contrast the fine summers of 1975 and 1976 produced large winter coveys with 30–40 birds together on several occasions. Casual recording in the spring of 1976 revealed over 40 pairs. The largest gathering recorded on the Isle of Man was 54 birds flushed from a field at Bride on 23rd September 1953.

On the Calf Partridges were plentiful at the end of the eighteenth century (Robertson 1794) and may have existed 100 years later although the only evidence was some feathers found in 1901. Partridges were also noted by Calf visitors in 1936 and 1939 and have been recorded there every year since 1960. In 1961 the first breeding took place on the Calf and a peak of 11 pairs was reached in 1965. From 1966 to 1969 there were 3–5 pairs, in 1970 and 1971 8 pairs and a record 16 pairs in 1972 and 1973. Nine to ten pairs continued to nest up to 1977, there were 6 in 1978 but no breeding records since.

There is an almost complete albino example in the Manx Museum.

Manx: *Kiark Rennee* = Fern Hen

Quail
Corturnix coturnix

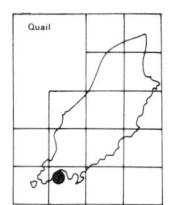

Very scarce and irregular summer visitor.

The Quail was included in the Manx Game Act of 1835 and around the same time it was described by Forbes as not uncommon. The next 40 years saw a notable decline probably culminating in its temporary extinction so that it did not deserve a mention in the Game Act of 1882. This closely resembles the situation in Ireland where Quails enjoyed increasing abundance leading to peak numbers between 1845 and 50, followed by a decline starting about 1865, leading to almost total disappearance by the 1880s (Ussher and Warren 1900). The number of Quail visiting Britain is notoriously variable from year to year, but from time to time, perhaps related to warm dry spring weather in southern Europe, there are considerable invasions. 1870 was a 'Quail year' which made no apparent impact on the Isle of Man, but in 1893 the invasion was seen throughout the British Isles and Quail were widely heard in the Isle of Man. Occasional records followed during the next 10 years and in 1902 six Manx Quail were registered under the Game Act. Since then Quail have been recorded in 27 of the 81 years. Notable Quail years in Britain were 1947, 1953, 1964 and 1970, but in the Isle of Man the best of these years, 1953, was probably inferior to 1952 when 4 separate calling males were noted. The large majority of calling males have been heard in the three most northerly parishes and certain small areas have been favoured particularly. Birds were heard all summer at Andreas in 1931 and 1937 and a nest was found at Ballavarry just south of the village in 1940. Ballavarry had Quails in the summers of 1950, 1952 and 1953 as did nearby Ballaghaue in the latter two years. Quail were heard at Ballamoar (Jurby) throughout the summer of 1947 and 1950, while in Bride they were heard at 2 sites in 1953, bred in 1964 and were heard in June 1967. More recently one was heard at the Dog Mills on 2nd August 1979. There have been sporadic records from other parts of the Island during the last 20 years, notably at St Marks in 1967, Ballamodha in 1975 and Ballafesson in 1977. These were all records of males calling in June.

From the relatively small sample of Manx records it can be seen that Quails are heard mainly in June and to a lesser degree in July. There is one record of calling from mid May and several for the first few days of August up to 11th. It is difficult to know how often Quails have nested on the Island because prolonged calling may simply mean that a male has failed to find a mate, while it is known that successful nesting can take place without any calling (Moreau 1951). The only nest to be found this century contained 8 eggs on 31st July 1940, while 3 birds at Ballaskilley, Bride on 20th September 1964 might have been a family bevy.

The Quail has been recorded 4 times on the Calf – on 22nd September 1944, 10th May and 3rd June 1970 and 21st May 1981. Quails habitually wintered in Ireland during the last century and while the Isle of Man has no records for December or January a male was seen in the Bride hills as recently as 27th March 1983. There are just 3 late autumn records – the latest being 14th November.

Manx: *Eean Feie*.

Pheasant

Phasianus colchicus

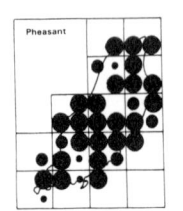

Well represented resident.

It is most unlikely that attempts were not made to introduce Pheasants in the 17th and 18th centuries, but they were not included in the 1835 Game Act. By 1880 however Kermode was able to write 'Introduced at different times, for the amusement of poachers. I am told that there is still *one*, which may be seen occasionally.' Attempts at introduction at the Nunnery, Bishopscourt, Orrisdale, Ballakillingan and Ballagawne (Rushen) in the late 19th century all failed. Later, considerable numbers were released at Ballamoar (Jurby), but although more than 20 Manx birds appeared in the Game Lists of 1921 and 1922 numbers gradually dwindled so that by 1934 Madoc was confident that there were no Pheasants on the Island.

Because of its dubious credentials as a wild bird the Pheasant was rarely mentioned in the annual bird reports but by 1956 the species was becoming established through the importing of eggs. Even 16 years ago Pheasant were described as few, but increasing. Since 1971 they have been well distributed through the Island and locally very common. They are particularly conspicuous in Stanton parish, the Baldwin valleys and the curraghs of Greeba and Ballaugh. There is now a well established wild population which is regularly fortified by introductions. They occur in farmland and particularly favour the bracken covered fringes of the coastal brooghs and the foothills up to about 260 m above sea level.

Three males have been recorded on the Calf from 8th April to 25th June 1976, from 14th May to 1st June 1977 and on 13th October 1977.

Water Rail

Rallus aquaticus

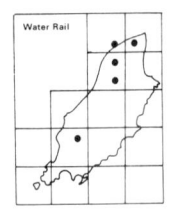

Regular passage migrant and winter visitor – breeds in small numbers.

'The retiring nature of the bird and the haunts it inhabits makes it very difficult to judge of its distribution and abundance...' – Ralfe's observation 80 years ago is no less applicable today and there is nothing to suggest that the elusive Water Rail is any more or less common than it was then. At the end of the 19th century it was recognised as a game bird and Ralfe used to see specimens for sale in poulterers' shops from time to time. He quoted breeding records from Congary near Peel and the Ballaugh Curraghs where 3 nests were found in 1903.

As a breeding bird the Water Rail has a very local distribution. Over the last 40 years nesting has only been confirmed at Ballaugh Curraghs, the Dog Mills and Congary. To these sites one might add with reasonable confidence the marsh land between Eairy and Kionslieu, several pieces of marshland in the northern plain and Lough Cranstal.

During winter Water Rails occur in a great variety of habitats throughout the Island – extreme examples are one found in *S.S. Tyrconnell* in Ramsey Harbour in 13th March 1927 and another on Ramsey Quay in November of the same year. In recent years the Water Rail has been a regular visitor to a Port Erin garden during the winter months, while at the other extreme one was shot in a marshy part of the hills 400 m above sea level in March.

A review of records for the main island this century shows that there is a sudden influx in October and records continue through the winter with much the same frequency, although January is the poorest month possibly indicating cold weather dispersal further south. Good March numbers, comparable to those in October, reflect migration. On the Calf, when the picture is not distorted by wintering birds, there is a very small passage of spring birds, but an impressive October peak.

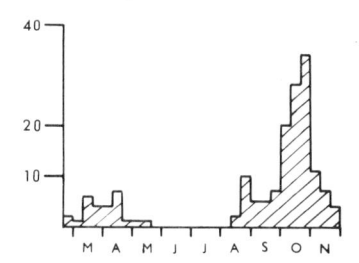

Water Rail. Total bird days per ten day period (Calf).

Twenty-four Water Rails were ringed on the Calf between 1959 and 1982 – there have been no recoveries, but 3 birds have been retrapped one or two years after ringing. There is one recovery of a Manx ringed bird – this was an adult caught at Ballachurry (Andreas) on 28th December 1950 and recovered at Alkamar (Holland) on 8th November 1952.

Manx: *Drean Ushtey* = Water Wren

Spotted Crake
Porzana porzana

Formerly a very rare passage migrant.

There were three late 19th century records, but none since.

In the 1870s one was shot in the autumn near Castletown, another was shot at Greeba in February 1885 and the third was killed, probably against telephone wires, in Onchan village in September 1892. This species declined markedly in Britain during the 19th century, but bred in Dumfriesshire at the time of these records – and indeed did so in the period 1968–72 (Sharrock 1976).

Baillon's Crake
Porzana pusilla

Very rare vagrant.

The only record is of one shot at the Dog Mills in 1847. The only two Irish records were in 1845 and 1858.

Corncrake
Crex crex

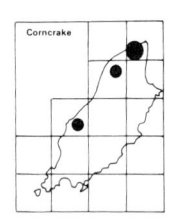

Scarce and irregular passage migrant which breeds occasionally.

Feltham (1798) had commented on the abundance of the Corncrake but although still a common and regular summer visitor, both Kermode and Ralfe suspected that it was decreasing by the turn of the century. This suggests that a diminution in numbers preceded the decline in the eastern counties of Ireland which began in the early 1900s. Nevertheless for the next 30 years the Corncrake remained a very common bird until numbers began to fall away quite markedly in the mid 1930s. It seems that a period of relative stability followed with many sites occupied year after year until about 1956 when a further decline became apparent. This continued through the 1960s to 1976 when it is reasonably certain that for the first time no Corncrakes bred on the Island. Since then regular crekking has only been heard at two sites – at Kerrowgarrow in the central valley in 1979 and 1983 and at the Guilcagh in 1980.

Until the mid 1950s the Corncrake was well distributed throughout the lowlands, though always commoner in the north where the Ballaugh Curraghs and Sulby meadows were traditionally well populated. Elsewhere Pulrose and Ronaldsway airfield were 2 sites which were deserted in the mid fifties. Over the last 25 years during which the Corncrake has become increasingly rare 1967 and 1973 stand out as good years for the species. In the latter year they were heard regularly at Croit e Caley (Colby), Ballakilmartin (Onchan), Cooilroi (Lonan), Ballacorteen, Thalloo queen and Rhenab (all in Maughold), the Garey ford (Lezayre) and at Barregarrow (Michael), where 3 individuals were heard on 13th July; there were thus reports of 11 birds and others must have gone unrecorded. Barregarrow and Cooilroi were both occupied for many years prior to their desertion in 1976. In the period 1968 to 1972 breeding was confirmed in 10 of the Island's 14 10 km squares and probably took place in two others (Sharrock 1976) but this gives a false impression of abundance.

The Corncrake's decline in Britain is usually attributed to the use of mechanical hay cutters and to the earlier cutting of grass for silage. Both factors are applicable in the Isle of Man where grass is cut from about 28th May onward. Nevertheless the Corncrake deserted one of its most favoured haunts, the marshy curraghs of Ballaugh, where more modern grass management does not apply, in the early 1960s.

Corncrakes were usually first heard between 22nd April and 4th May, the earliest dates being 16th April 1888 and 17th April 1951. Crekking continued for varying periods through May, June and to a lesser degree July, the latest date being 3rd August 1933. The earliest date on which young have been seen was 5th June 1945 at Ballachurry (Andreas) while a very late nest at Corvalley (Marown) held 13 warm eggs on 10th August 1913. At this nest the bird remained sitting although the hay had been cut, dried and cleared. The nest was covered with cut hay through which a tunnel passed.

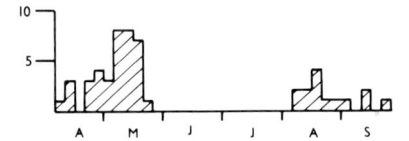

Corncrake. Total bird days per five day period (Calf).

On the Calf the Corncrake is infrequently seen on passage – more often in spring than autumn. Six have been ringed. The distribution of records since the Observatory opened in 1959 provides further evidence of the decline of this species – in the period 1959–70 there were 43 records but between 1971 and 1982 there were only 9. On passage Corncrakes have been found in a variety of unusual situations such as the Quays at Ramsey and Castletown, on moorland at up to 400 m and, on the Calf, down a rabbit hole and hiding among tins in the Lighthouse paint store. There have been several winter records – in the 1920s one was shot on the Rheast at the head of Sulby Glen on 9th November, another was seen at Harcroft near Douglas on 23rd November 1893, while on 15th December 1934 one was shot at Onchan. At the end of January 1915 one was caught alive at Shenvalla, near Peel (the same record was given as the end of February in Ralfe's supplement) and around the same period in early February one was arrested by a police constable in Castle Street, Douglas.

Manx: *Eean Raip* = the bird (which cries) 'raip'

Moorhen
Gallinula chloropus

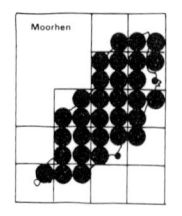

Common resident

Ralfe wrote of this species 'Though common in suitable localities, the Water-hen is in Man by no means the familiar object of rural life that it is in many parts of Britain.' Nevertheless it was clearly very plentiful along the Dhoo valley, the lower reaches of the Sulby and the small ponds of the north, although relatively scarce in Ballaugh Curraghs. Madoc felt that the Moorhen was becoming commoner and it is now resident on all the smaller pieces of still water throughout the Island. Such sites vary enormously from tiny farm dubs with little shelter, where the nest may be built on a half submerged bicycle frame, to shallow pools covered with bogbean and surrounded by willows as at the Dollagh. Seasonally variable waters in marshland such as the Ballaugh Curraghs and Lough Cranstal have a good population, while near the coast the Ayres back slacks, the Calf millpond and the Langness saltmarsh are all traditional sites. The Eairy dam with its rich vegetation is about the largest piece of water with resident moorhens and they are rarely seen on the reservoirs. They are common along many of the streams notably the Dhoo throughout its length, both in the Greeba curraghs, in the farmland of its lower reaches and at Kirby. They are plentiful on the Lhen and Killane Rivers and along the lower parts of the Sulby, Glass, Neb, Santon, Silverburn and Colby Rivers. In 1975 4.5 km of the Glass, upstreams from Quarterbridge held 7 territories. This was a stretch flowing mostly through farmland and contrasted with only 2 territories on 4.2 km of the Glenmaye River and only 1 on 5.6 km of the Laxey River. Both these latter waters are fast flowing rocky moorland streams with scarcely any aquatic vegetation and a history of mining.

First clutches are usually laid during April, but with a notoriously high failure rate up to 3 repeats may be made extending the breeding season to early August. The earliest egg date is 11th March (St John's 1928) and clutches later in March are not rare. Six is the commonest clutch size followed equally by 5 and 4 eggs. There are a few records of clutches of 7 and 8 – a nest in the north containing 8 eggs on 13th August, an unusually large clutch for so late in the season. Ten eggs in a Ballaugh Curragh nest had been laid by two hens. While many nests are on or just above the water, nests have been found in trees up to 5 metres above the ground and Moorhens have used the old nest of a Magpie.

Good numbers congregate in autumn and winter. Up to 20 are regularly seen at Kirby and Tromode Dam, with 31 at the latter site on 5th March 1974, but the biggest count was at Ballasteen near Andreas with 52 on 25th July 1975. Although notably sensitive to hard winters, the mild Manx climate seems to have little impact on the Moorhen. Nevertheless a number were found dead in the great frost of 1895 when the Sulby River froze. On the Calf, where 1–2 bred annually up to 1979, spring and autumn migrants are occasionally seen. Thirty-three Moorhens were ringed on the Calf in the period 1959–82. Several have been retrapped, in fact less than 50% of those ringed were on passage. The only ringing recovery was one ringed as an adult at Ballachurry (Andreas) and found dead at Jurby East, 3½ km away, 6 years and 7 months later.

Manx: *Kiark Ushtey* = Water Hen

Coot
Fulica atra

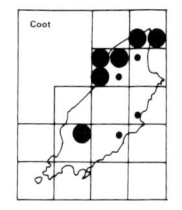

Fairly common resident.

Although the Coot had probably been resident in the Ballaugh Curraghs since at least the mid 19th century and was also presumed to breed on the Onchan pond, Ralfe did not consider it common. He suspected that it might have been overlooked as a breeding bird at several northern sites and by 1890 it was certainly nesting at Lough Cranstal. During the late 1920s it became much more common and colonised the Eairy Dam and the Bishop's Dub. It was found nesting at the Lagagh in 1935 and Ballacain in 1939.

The Onchan pond was drained long ago and the Ballaugh Curraghs were probably deserted early this century, but the Coot continues to breed at the other 5 sites and has further extended its range recently with nests at the Dollagh, Lough Dhoo, Bishopscourt Glen, several of the small northern dubs and Kerrowdhoo. At the Standing Stone pool just west of Ballaugh a pair of Coots have built a massive nest 1 m high. With 2–4 pairs at the Eairy, 2 at the Bishop's Dub, 3–4 at the Lagagh and at least 1 pair at 5–6 other sites a breeding population of about 15 pairs seems likely. Most clutches are started during the last 10 days of April, the earliest egg date being 7th April. Although Madoc described tiny young as late as 15th August there are no other records of nests in June or July – this may be an artificial impression due to summer growth of vegetation (such as Water horsetails at the Eairy Dam) concealing the sitting bird.

Outside the breeding season Coots gather particularly at the Eairy Dam, where a peak count of 31 was made in October 1938. At least 20 wintered there in 1972 but the last 10 years have seen a definite decline with annual peaks varying between 7 and 15 birds. This decline has been balanced by increasing numbers at Kerrowdhoo, where there were up to 16 during the 1981–2 winter and utilisation of fresh sites for wintering such as the Billown Quarries, Crogga and Kirby. During very cold weather 1 or 2 Coot are occasionally seen on the sea. There is no evidence that the Isle of Man receives winter visitors from elsewhere and the only two Calf records are of single birds on 7th May 1963 and 27th June 1973.

Crane

Grus grus

Vagrant.

One was seen at Scarlett on 22nd October 1978 and had probably been in that area during the preceding week (Marshall 1979). Earlier there was an unconfirmed but seemingly authentic record of one in Santon parish on 4th May 1978.

Locally the Grey Heron is often called the Crane and was referred to as such by Townley in 1791.

Oystercatcher

Haematopus ostralegus

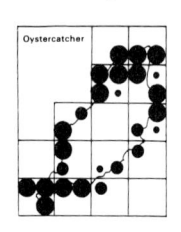

Common breeding bird, passage migrant and winter visitor.

Ralfe described the Oystercatcher as a familiar and dominant species occurring in comparable numbers in both summer and winter. He described nesting along the beaches from Orrisdale north round to Ramsey and on the Ayres heath. Breeding also took place at Dalby, White Strand, Maughold, the Kitterland and the Calf, but although plentiful along the coast from Santon to Perwick it did not nest between those points.

By 1923 Langness and Poyllvaaish had been colonised as breeding areas and Oystercatchers now nest in modest numbers around the rocky coast wherever there are platforms of upturned jagged slate. Many pairs nest in land adjacent to the shore, most typically on the Ayres where nests are attractively sited on scrapes in the sand in the carpet of burnet rose. On the sandy warren forming the northern part of Orrisdale Head and adjacent fields of pasture and stubble they breed freely and each of the Ayres gravel pits has a few pairs. Between Derbyhaven and Santon there are nests on the waste ground at the top of the precipitous walls of a slate quarry and they nest all over the Calf in the old pastures. With the virtual saturation of coastal breeding sites small numbers now breed well inland. One of the first such instances was on Dalby mountain where a pair nested in the late 1950s in rough moorland pasture 2 km inland. This was followed by nesting in a field north of Eary Cushlin, and in 1972 four eggs were laid in very rough pasture on the south-west slopes of Slieau Whallian more than 3 km inland (L.S. Garrad *pers.com.*). These sites were between 150 and 250 m above sea level and do not appear to have been occupied during the last decade. In 1974 two eggs were laid in a ploughed field at Barregarrow and since 1979 there has been nesting at a number of sites on the northern plain, including 3 pairs in adjacent fields or rough pasture near Lough Dhoo and a pair at Ballachurry Fort $4\frac{1}{2}$ km inland. There have as yet been no breeding records from the lower parts of the Sulby River.

On the Calf breeding numbers have increased from 10 pairs in 1959 to about 25 pairs since 1979. The Langness breeding population is about 20 pairs, that of the Ayres heath at least 30 pairs with perhaps another 10 pairs in the adjacent gravel pits. Twenty pairs nested along a 3 km stretch of the Ballaugh shore in 1978 and it is likely that the total number breeding along the shore from Orrisdale to Ramsey is in the region of 200 pairs. A fair estimate of the Manx breeding population would be 350–400 pairs. Three eggs are usually laid, although complete clutches of 2 and 4 eggs are not uncommon. The only clutch of 5 eggs was unquestionably laid by 2 hens. Most eggs are laid during May, occasionally laying starts as early as 20th April, replacement clutches are laid in early June and eggs have been seen as late as 15th August.

Along the northern shores the breeding population disperses during August, and winter parties are mostly of about 30 birds although there were 200 on the Lhen Ayres in early December 1975. There is a regular winter flock of up to 100 at Ramsey and 40 at Port Grenaugh while parties of about 30 are commonly seen on coastal fields north of Peel and Ramsey and in Santon Parish. In the south east a flock of 100 assembles on the Airfield in early July. Numbers here and on the adjacent shores of Derbyhaven and Langness may reach 250 by late August and almost 400 during September. Many of these are thought to move southward as numbers usually decline in October and November before peaks in excess of 400 are seen in late December and early January. Thereafter numbers in February, March and April are in the region of 100 and there is a regular flock of 60 non-breeders at Langness during May.

There have been 14 recoveries of Manx ringed Oystercatchers, 9 being during the first 9 months after ringing as pulli. Of these nine, two were recovered within 1 month of ringing close to the ringing place, the other 7 were recovered well to the south with 2 in Caernarvon, 1 in Carmarthen, 1 in Wexford, 1 in Cornwall and 2 in France. One was recovered in its 3rd February in Cornwall, another in its 2nd February in Co. Cork, while

Oystercatcher. Recoveries of birds ringed as pulli and first autumn.

1 ringed as a pullus on the Calf in June 1953 was recovered at Morbihan, north-west France in late August 1963. One was recovered where it had been ringed at Rue Point $6\frac{3}{4}$ years later and the only recovery of a bird ringed as a juvenile (Calf, late September) came from Jedburgh in the Scottish borders $2\frac{1}{2}$ years later – probably its natal area.

Manx: *Garee breck* = Pied creature (north). *Bridgeen* (south)

Little Ringed Plover
Charadrins dubius

There are two Manx records of this species which since 1938 has been extending its breeding range in Britain in a north-westerly direction. One was seen on Langness on 5th and 6th May 1969 and another flew up the Glen on the Calf, settling briefly on a field near the Observatory on 5th May 1974. The actively worked gravelpits of the Ayres must be a potential breeding site for the species.

Ringed Plover
Charadrius hiaticula

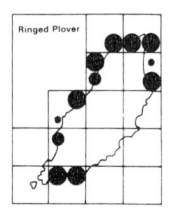

Common resident and passage migrant.

From Ralfe's remarks about this species it would seem that it has shown a small increase, certainly as a breeding bird, during the last 80 years. In 1904 it was a common breeder along the coast from Michael to Ramsey, including the sandy warren of the Ayres. Ralfe could only credit it with 'probable breeding' in Castletown Bay, but 4 pairs bred at Poyllvaaish and he also cited recent breeding records from the coast north of Derbyhaven, from Traie Vane south of Dalby and from Scarlett.

The majority of the Manx breeding population is still to be found along the northern shores. No attempt at an accurate census has been made, but the 6 pairs along 3 km of the Ballaugh shore in 1978 is typical for most of this shore line. Nests are much more frequent between Rue Point and the Point of Ayre – in places as often as one every 15 metres and there is a record of 2 birds sitting 115 cm apart. A few pairs nest in the sandy Ayres heath and the gravel pits, where a nest on the raised edge of a track was 'rumbled' by the wheels of heavy lorries passing only 50 cm away every few minutes without any parental concern. South of Ramsey Ringed Plover nest at Port Lewaigue while north of Peel there is the odd pair at Will's Strand and White Strand. In the south east they ignore the beaches, 6–8 pairs nesting at both Poyllvaaish and the Pool/Saltmarsh area of Langness on short maritime turf and on patches of gravel which appear in this terrain. Nesting has also occurred at the edge of a runway on Ronaldsway Airfield.

Eggs are laid throughout May and June. April nests are quite common, the earliest being 8th April (Ayres 1933), while the latest hatching date recorded was 31st July. Although 2–4 eggs are usual there is one record of a clutch of 5.

Outside the breeding season Ringed Plover can always be seen in the large bays of the south and east coast. At Langness/Derbyhaven 50–80 birds are usual from August to October, swelled at times by passage birds to 130 in August. Numbers rarely exceed 30 between November and March, 100 on 12th December 1976 being exceptional. Spring passage produces fair numbers in late April and May, the best count being 200 on 24th April 1981. Wintering numbers at Strandhall are comparable while in Douglas Bay 30–40 birds (with a like number of Dunlin) are present from November to early February, resorting to roost at high water on the rocks south of Onchan Harbour. Up to 40 Ringed Plover winter in Ramsey Bay, but the exposed beaches

123

of the north west coast are usually deserted from late September to early April. On the Calf it occurs as a passage migrant in spring and to a much greater extent in autumn, when the bulk of birds pass through during August.

There have been two recoveries of Manx-ringed Ringed Plovers – a first winter bird ringed on Langness on 20th August was recovered 14 days later in Manche, north west France and a Rue Point pullus was controlled in Co. Down 7½ weeks later. One bird ringed on Sylt, off the north German coast, in late May was recovered at Douglas in October of the following year.

Manx: *Feddag Ainnit*

Kentish Plover
Charadrius alexandrinus

Vagrant.

The only Manx record is of one on the Sandwick shore, Langness on 15th April 1966.

Dotterel
Charadrius morinellus

Rare passage migrant.

In the autumn of 1896 a female was shot in cultivated upland near Ballacutchal (Santon) and another autumn bird was seen at Jurby on 16th October 1935. More recently there have been 3 spring records – 6 were seen in the hills 3 km north of Laxey on 21st May 1974, a very windblown bird was watched for sometime in a field above the Chasms on 3rd May 1981 and one flew low over the Observatory on the Calf on 29th April 1983.

Golden Plover
Pluvialis apricaria

Common winter visitor.

Although Feltham (1798) particularly commented on its abundance, from Ralfe's description it seems likely that the Golden Plover, although a well-known winter visitor, did not occur regularly in such large numbers as it does now. He implied that great numbers only appeared during very cold weather, visiting lowland pastures and, exceptionally, the coast. Although there was never any hint of breeding in the late 19th century the aged J. C. Crellin had heard of nests and young being found in the northern hills. It seems likely that the Golden Plover formerly nested in the Isle of Man as three localities have the name Cronk Fedjag or Cronk ny Fedjag (= Hill of the Plover). (Kneen 1925). Cronk Fedjag in Arbory is a heather covered plateau 340 m above sea level, while Cronk ny Fedjag in German is a hill of rough, hummocky grass rising to 250 m north west of Little London, listed in the Diocesan Register of 1742. The third locality is an area of extensive heather near Spanish Head. Wintering Golden Plover are virtually unknown in the Manx hills so that the development of the name Fedjag almost certainly arose from birds frequenting these sites in the breeding season. There have been two recent records of Golden Plover in high moorland. In late July 1973 a bird behaved in a way that suggested there might be young nearby at the top of Colden and on 30th August 1981 a party of 11 was seen on the moors west of Slieau Ruy.

The Golden Plover is now known as an abundant winter visitor to the coast and neighbouring lowlands, numbers being fairly evenly divided between the south east and the northern plain. In the south east they feed on the weed covered rocks of Langness and Derbyhaven Point at low tide, moving to the fields adjacent to the Haunted House and to Ronaldsway Airfield to roost. Sometimes there are considerable numbers in the fields near Scarlett. In the north a considerably larger area is occupied. The most favoured stretch of shore is in the vicinity of Sartfield, although there are often good numbers at the Lhen and along the Ayres coast. Ramsey Bay also has a regular flock. Inland the fields between the Dollagh and Ballaugh Cronk and the grassy expanses of Jurby airfield are probably the roosting areas for the Sartfield birds while the rest of the population is often found in fields adjacent to the Ayres and to the north and west of Glascoe.

At Langness and Derbyhaven very small numbers first appear during July – the earliest date is 5th July 1981 and between 1972 and 1982 the mean arrival date was 12th July. Numbers increase during August but rarely exceed 100 before September when maxima of 300–800 are usual. Peak winter numbers are seen mostly in early January followed by a slow decline although flocks of up to 600 continue to the second week of April and as many as 250 have been seen at the end of that month. The latest record for Langness is a party of 10 on 9th May 1977 although in the north there were 5 at Jurby and 20 at Rue Point on 31 May 1981 and 2 on the Ayres heath at Ballaghennie on 18th June 1985.

An attempted count of the Manx population on 9th January 1977 yielded 1,700 on Ronaldsway Airfield, 350 on Langness, 1,200 on Jurby Airfield and 300 near Ballaugh old church giving a total of 3,550. During the last decade there have been two other counts of single flocks in excess of 1000 in the south east during November and several in the north, notably over 2000 at the Dollagh on 13th November 1973, 1,100 at Ballaugh Cronk on 1st December 1977, up to 1,300 in the Crawyn/Jurby Airfield area in early

January 1978, with over 2,000 on the Sartfield shore 2 weeks later. There were also 2 separate flocks of 1000 in fields west of Glascoe on 6th January 1980.

On the Calf a few birds are seen in spring and fair numbers in autumn, especially between late August and early October. There were 150 on the Calf heath on 17th August 1974. Both *P.a. apricaria* and *P.a. altifrons* have been identified.

Manx: *Ushag Reeast* = Bird of the Waste. *Fedjag Reeast* = Whistler of the Waste

Grey Plover
Pluvialis squatarola

Regular passage and winter visitor in small numbers.

There does not seem to have been any significant change in the status of the Grey Plover during the last 100 years. Up to 4 birds can nearly always be found during the winter months at Langness or Derbyhaven – the Sandwick shore and adjacent weed covered rocks, the sandy eastern part of Derbyhaven Bay and the rocks below the Golf Links Hotel being the best places. Less frequently they visit the coast from Poyllvaaish round to Port St Mary and the Ayres shore, although at the latter site they occur mainly on autumn passage, particularly during October. To the rest of the coast the Grey Plover is only a very casual and transient visitor.

At Langness single birds have been seen on 26th June 1931, 10th July 1981 and 31st July 1948. There have been a few August records but in most years they are not seen before mid September. Although the second half of September is the main passage period on the Calf of Man, October is easily the best month on the north and south east coasts of the main island. Always present in December and January they then occur less frequently as the year advances, April records being on a par with those for August. There have been three May records, the latest being one at Langness on 19th May 1942. Spring passage is barely recognisable. Parties of 5–10, although rare, have been seen in all months from September to April, there were 17 at Poyllvaaish on 23rd February 1985, 15 at Port St Mary Point on 2nd February 1956 and 20 at Rue Point on 27th December 1982.

Lapwing
Vanellus vanellus

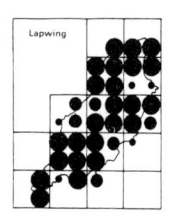

Common migrant breeder and winter visitor showing notable cold weather movement.

Ralfe described the frequent but erratic visits of large numbers of Lapwing to the Isle of Man during winter, but considered the species much less common than on the mainland. Although breeding in most of the Island's parishes, only a few pairs would be found in each locality. He considered the typical nesting habitat as the rough and damp wastes in the lower parts of the hills as well as the Ballaugh Curraghs and the Ayres. In 1901 the highest concentration of breeding birds was probably on the Calf.

By the late 1930s much the greater part of the breeding population was confined to the northern alluvial plain, being divided between the Ayres and the Curraghs of Ballaugh (Williamson 1948). Langness had also been colonised, but Lapwings were only known to breed at 3 localities in the hills – in stony hill pasture near the Braaid Circle at around 150 m and in wet rush-grown garey near Creg ny baa and at Park ny Eairkan, probably a site of some antiquity as the name is derived from the gaelic name for Lapwing *Eairkan*.

As in other parts of northern Britain the Lapwing is now a more abundant breeding bird than previously. Numbers on the Ayrelands and in Ballaugh Curraghs have probably changed little but the wet rush-grown fields of which the northern plain has no shortage have been widely colonised. Some 20 pairs nest in the vicinity of Ballacain Dubs and there are others to the west and east of Jurby, at the Guilcagh and neighbouring Kerrowmoar and around Lough Cranstal. Ten or more pairs nest on Langness, while on the Calf numbers fluctuate with peaks of 8–10 pairs in 1938–9 and 1969–74. There has been notable expansion in the lower parts of the hills, notably in Rushen and Arbory where the population is in the region of 50 pairs. In the northern hills there are 3–4 pairs at Eary ny suie (175 m) Druidale (275 m) and above Agneash (200 m) and rather more at Ballacarooin, west of Creg ny baa (265 m). An interesting development is the recent colonisation of the Point of Ayre gravel pits where 6 pairs bred in 1980.

The habitat preference of breeding Manx Lapwings was considered by Williamson (1948). On the Ayres they shunned the hummock-heath subject to severe rabbit attack, but favoured the grass-heath clearings where a poor turf had developed. They also nested freely in the once-cultivated fields on and near the inner edge of the heath. Here, and in the Curraghs (and also in the hills) the partly rush-grown field is the characteristic habitat, but ploughed land and the margins of dubs are quite often used, while good pasture is shunned. Williamson noted that on the Ayres margins late breeders moved into territories vacated by birds which had already brought off their broods. At Langness he thought that birds nested on the saltmarsh following loss of earlier nests on ploughed fields when harrowing took place. Nowadays the Langness saltmarsh is used from an early stage in the season as are the grasssy hummocks which fringe Poyll Breinn.

Although eggs have been found as early as 23rd March very few clutches are started before the second week in April. Laying after the end of May is unknown on the Isle of Man.

Flocks gather in the north and south east after the breeding season and as many as 200 have been seen at the Point of Ayre by 7th July. From September onwards flocks of up to 70 are quite widespread and in particularly favoured localities such as the fields to the north of Ballaugh village, Jurby airfield, farmland around Glascoe, the margins of the Ayres and the south east of the Island flocks of up to 500 are not unusual and 1000 or more have been noted in each month between September and February. The greatest numbers are seen during very cold weather when the Isle of Man is usually notably warmer than Scotland and England. Under such circumstances visible westward passage towards Ireland is sometimes seen and may exceptionally involve as many as 5,000. The most notable influx was seen in late January 1933 when thousands arrived in the Peel area and there were hundreds of birds in every coastal field between Glenmaye and Dalby – the following day a further 2,000 were seen moving west over Onchan Head, Lapwings were also plentiful in the south of the Island, yet a few days later the invasion was over.

There have been just three recoveries of birds ringed as pulli on the Isle of Man – all came from Ireland one was recovered in Co. Limerick during its first winter, another came from Limerick in its second winter and the third was recovered also in its second winter in Co. Down.

An albino was seen at Kirkmichael in 1947.

Manx: *Earkan*

Knot

Calidris canutus

Regular passage visitor occurring less frequently in winter.

Almost unknown to Ralfe in 1905, he recognised the Knot as an irregular autumn visitor by 1923. Since 1960 it has occurred with much greater frequency.

Although there is a questionable record of 'about 20' at Ramsey on 26th June 1962, one was present on Langness on 13th July 1985 and 25 flew south past the Calf on 17th July 1964, the first individuals are usually seen during the last 10 days of July. August and September, and to a lesser extent October, are the main passage months and small parties of up to 6, occasionally as many as 24, are present most days. Nearly every year a few Knot will be seen during the period November to February, but occurrences between March and May are rather infrequent. Derbyhaven and the Sandwick shore are the most frequented sites, while Knot are seen occasionally on the Ayres shore mainly on passage, in fact there are only 2 records for the north coast between 7th November and 12th March. There are a few records from Ramsey and Carrick Bay and 12 from the Calf between 17th July and 30th October. There is one inland record of a bird in a ploughed field near the dub at Ballamona Moar on 6th January 1985.

Sanderling
Calidris alba

Regular passage migrant in moderate numbers and scarce winter visitor.

Although in 1905 Ralfe knew of only two records, by 1923 he was able to describe the Sanderling as being of regular though sparing occurrence both on the northern and southern coasts associating with Dunlins and Ringed Plovers in spring and autumn. Until 1945 most reports were of parties of up to 5 birds, with on one occasion 11 together. Since then flocks have frequently exceeded 20 and during the last decade flocks of 30-60 have been seen most autumns in the north.

On passage Sanderlings occur almost exclusively along the sandy shore from the Lhen to Ballaghennie in the north and at Sandwick in the south east. At both sites autumn passage is much heavier and more prolonged, the northern beaches having much the larger flocks. Although they have been seen as early as 10th July, they are not common until the last week of July, during which period the heaviest passage occurs – the largest flock reported consisting of 81 birds on 27th July 1980. Passage continues to about 22nd September with occasional flocks of 30-40 birds, after which a few stragglers may be seen to mid November. At Langness passage over the same period is much lighter, parties of less than 10 being usual and flocks of 22 on 26th July 1980 and 24 on 21st August 1977 being exceptional.

In contrast Sanderlings seem to visit Sandwick in rather larger numbers than the Ayres coast in spring. At Sandwick the main passage period is from 30th April to 18th May, parties of up to 20 birds are usual and there were 30 on 11th May 1979. In the north spring visitors are later, occurring mainly between 10th and 23rd May and no recent flocks have exceeded 20. At both sites modest flocks are seen up to the second week of June. Sanderlings are occasionally seen in the Strandhall area on passage and there is one Calf record of a single bird on 5th August 1972.

As a winter visitor the Sanderling is decidedly scarce occurring, mostly singly, at Sandwick, Derbyhaven, Port St Mary and Douglas. There are three records of small parties during the winter in the south east – 12 on 23rd February 1947 and 8 on 7th March 1933 and 20th March 1942.

Although overland migration has not been seen on the Island there is an interesting record of 9 Sanderlings found dead below wires at the Bungalow on 30th May 1919.

Little Stint

Calidris minuta

Regular on autumn passage in very small numbers.

Until 1928 there had only been 3 records, but since then it has been seen almost every year during the autumn. The Little Stint is almost exclusively a visitor to the Langness pool and Sandwick shore – in the period 1928–58 there were a few records from the north coast but there have been only 2 singles there since. It has also been seen twice at Strandhall and twice on the Calf. At Langness passage is seen mainly between 16th August and 16th September, with a small cluster of records for the last week of September. The earliest autumn date is 27th July 1945, when 4 were seen at Rue Point and there are a few records for October up to 12th (1978). On autumn passage 1–3 birds are usual, the biggest party being 9 together at Sandwick on 29th September 1973.

At other times the Little Stint is rare – there have been three November records up to 18th, 1 at Langness on 14th February 1979, two April records on 15th and 24th and a record of 2 on the Ayres on 18th May 1929.

Temminck's Stint

Calidris temminckii

Four were seen in the Langness pool on 13th and 14th July 1976 (Cullen 1977) and another was present there from 28th August to 3rd September 1985. Madoc's record of one from 2nd to 9th September lacks any detail which might make the record acceptable.

Curlew Sandpiper

Calidris ferruginea

Irregular visitor of autumn passage.

Ralfe knew of only two definite records of the Curlew Sandpiper but it has been recorded in most of the last 60 years. There does however seem to have been a change in the pattern of records since about 1936. Until then, although principally an autumn visitor there had been about 6 records for the period 27th April to 31st May at a time when there had never been a spring record for Ireland (Witherby et al. 1940). These, and the majority of autumn records for the early 1930s came from the Ayres where there were large numbers, especially in September, in 1929 and 1934. On one occasion in September 1934 Madoc saw over 50 feeding on a bank.

Since 1936 there has only been one record for the Ayres and Curlew Sandpipers have not been seen in spring anywhere since 1966. One to three birds are now seen irregularly from late August to early October, the only flocks having been 15 at Langness on 15th September 1960 and 26 at Derbyhaven on 29th September 1963. They are rarely seen other than on the Sandwick shore or in Derbyhaven Bay although there have been a few records for Carrick Bay and between 1958 and 1967 it occurred annually at Port St Mary Point. There have been four mid November records, the latest being 2 at Derbyhaven on 22nd November 1930. In spring the earliest record was 1 at Port St Mary Point on 21st March 1966 and during the 1960s there were also 3 other spring records between 14th April and 1st May. The earliest autumn date is 24th July 1934.

On the Calf the Curlew Sandpiper has occurred singly from 14th to 16th April 1966, on 8th August 1969 and on 11th September 1978.

Purple Sandpiper
Calidris maritima

Fairly common passage migrant and winter visitor.

Ralfe knew of a number of sites frequented by Purple Sandpipers, although nowhere were they abundant. In the early 1890s a flock frequented a particular reef in Douglas Bay during the winter, tide permitting; up to 15 birds were seen in 1893 while in February 1905 he saw a party of 6 at Scarlett. Other localities included Port Lewaigue, Port St Mary and, in the spring, Langness and Spanish Head.

It is difficult to know whether this inconspicuous bird has become more common or whether it was overlooked previously. By the winter of 1922-3 a party of 6 was present on the rocks behind Peel Castle and this site, together with the rocks at the northern end of Douglas Bay and Port St Mary Point have remained the most favoured localities for Purple Sandpipers. More recently the Calf has proved to be an important site and Niarbyl also has a small wintering population as well as larger numbers on passage. Single birds and sometimes very small parties also turn up occasionally on passage at a number of other places around the coast.

Peel Castle rocks

During the last decade the first birds of the autumn have been seen regularly during the first three weeks of July – the earliest date was 1st July 1975, and numbers during this month are very small, 9 on 16th July 1973 being very unusual. Similar small numbers continue through August, but the average maximum in September is 10, with 19 the best count. Numbers increase through October and more especially in November, when there is an average maximum of 18 and a peak count of 35 in 1981. Here December is the best month with recent maxima of 40 in 1981 and a record 52 on 4th December 1982. January numbers are comparable to November and there is a further small decline in February and March. With presumed departure of most of the winter visitors during March. April numbers are low, sometimes up to 20 may be seen later in the month or in early May. Purple Sandpipers have not been seen at Peel after 13th May. A. S. Moore has an unusual record of 5 birds leaving the wave swept rocks and probing the turf behind Peel Castle and finding food during a very stormy day in mid January.

Niarbyl

Although little watched, Niarbyl has a small wintering population of perhaps 4–6 birds – a maximum of 17 being seen on 6th February 1973. It is also visited on autumn passage in August and early September, the best count being 23 on 8th September 1980.

Calf of Man

The earliest autumn date is 12th July, but first arrivals are more usually seen in August. Numbers are usually less than at Peel although there were counts of 48 on 20th September 1981 and at Cow Harbour during a south-westerly gale on 15th November 1978, indeed November is usually a good month on the Calf with many counts of 20 birds. As the Observatory is not manned during December and January the wintering population is not known, but there were 20 on 10th December 1980, up to 16 during February 1979 and 33 on 6th March 1979. As at Peel April is a month of few Purple Sandpipers and the latest date is also 13th May. As long ago as 1912 Purple Sandpipers were regularly visiting the Chicken Rock at low tide from August to December and records in November and January 1933 led Williamson (1940) to conclude that the Rock was visited by birds wintering on the Calf. Nowadays parties of up to 20 are still sometimes seen flying to or from the Chicken Rock in calm weather at low tide.

Port St Mary

There is one record for 9th July, otherwise Port St Mary has a varying winter flock of 10–20 birds which traditionally occupy Kallow Point although up to 24 birds have recently been seen in winter at Gansey on the north side of the bay. Counts of 20 in late April up to 6th May suggest a fair presence on spring passage. Port St Mary has the latest Manx spring record – 19th May 1957.

Douglas

At the northern end of Douglas Bay Purple Sandpipers are seen mainly from November to March, frequenting the rocks at Derby Castle and around Onchan Head from Port Jack to Onchan Harbour. At Onchan Head they share the high tide roost with Dunlin and Ringed Plover. Ten to twenty birds are usual, but on 5th December 1929 during a south-westerly storm Madoc found over 50 lined up on the ledges below the sea wall of the Loch Promenade. As many as 20 have also been seen below Douglas Head at the south end of the bay. Douglas seems to be little used on passage.

At migration time Purple Sandpipers are sometimes seen away from the wave-splashed margins of the rocky coast and on the Ayres shore it is probably regular in small numbers in April and May and August and September. The best flock was 8 on 11th May 1944 and the latest a single bird on 10th November 1980.

Dunlin
Calidris alpina

Common passage migrant and winter visitor.

In the absence of numerical data it is difficult to compare the abundance of the Dunlin 80 years ago with the situation today, although in the mixed winter flocks Ralfe found that Ringed Plover outnumbered Dunlin, a situation which no longer obtains. The best flocks were, as now, seen on spring and autumn passage.

The Dunlin has never been proved to breed on the Isle of Man, although it has been suspected on a number of occasions. Early in May 1931 J. J. Gill found a pair by the Ballure Reservoir – the only Manx record of this species in a moorland habitat. On 28th June 1942 a bird performed a broken wing act on the Langness saltmarsh and during the summer of 1947 breeding was suspected by P. R. Foulkes Roberts on the Ayres and two young birds were captured alive on 27th July. Dunlin records are very rare between 5th June and 5th July but there have been two recent records from the Ayres shore during this period – 3 were seen at the Rue Point Lagoon on 24th and 25th June 1979 and there was a flock of 19 on 17th June 1981.

Although a few birds may be seen earlier in the month first flocks on autumn passage are usually seen about 20th–25th July. Good numbers are then seen until the end of September. At Langness parties of about 100 are common throughout August and there have been notable peaks of over 200 on 13th August 1973 and over 500 on 21st September 1966. On the Ayres shore flocks of 10–40 are usual, the best count being a late flock of 120 on 7th November 1982. The winter period October to March is characterised by regular flocks of 20–60 at Langness/Derbyhaven and Douglas and Ramsey Bays. Nevertheless in some years they may be almost absent for several weeks while in others flocks of up to 200 may appear briefly in the south east in mid winter. On the north coast Dunlin are very scarce between December and March, yet 300 were seen at the Lhen on 18th February 1977. Everywhere they are notably scarce for most of April but spring flocks are sometimes seen at the end of that month continuing to the end of May. Again Langness numbers of 150–300 birds greatly exceed those along the Ayres shore.

On Langness Dunlin are seen not only on sand and fine shingle, but also on the mud of Poyll Breinn, the intertidal rocks and reefs, the saltmarsh and occasionally on neighbouring Ronaldsway Airfield. At Douglas the

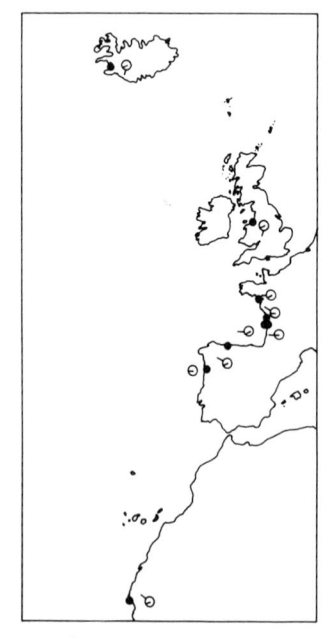

Dunlin ringing recoveries.

wintering flock feeds at the north end of the bay flying to roost with Ringed Plover and Purple Sandpipers on the rocks just south of Onchan Harbour. At Ramsey the sands of the bay are deserted for the Mooragh Lake when it is drained early in the year. Other localities visited by small parties are the damp surrounds of the Glascoe Dub, Strandhall and occasionally Peel and Niarbyl. On the Calf the Dunlin is a regular spring and autumn migrant in small numbers, the maximum day count being 27.

G. D. Craine has ringed Dunlin on autumn migration at Langness and Derbyhaven and had 9 recoveries. Six of these (5 ringed during their first year) were recovered in their first autumn – 4 on the Biscay coast of France 5, 10, 16 and 27 days later, 1 on the north coast of Spain 43 days later and 1 at Port Etienne, Mauritania (4,000 km to the south) after 47 days. Of the remainder 1 survived 5 years before its recovery in Portugal, 1 was controlled at Hoylake almost 6 years after ringing and the other was controlled in Iceland 3 years 11 months later.

Manx: *Breck ny Traie*

Buff-breasted Sandpiper
Tryngites subruficollis

Vagrant.

One was watched for over 4 hours on the Calf during the afternoon of 17th September 1973. It was resting and feeding on short heather near one of the highest points on the islet and was quite tame, allowing observation down to 13 metres. During September 1973 there were about 20 records in Britain of this North American wader which breeds between latitudes 69°N and 74°N and migrates to South America. (Wright 1975)

Ruff
Philomachus pugnax

Regular on autumn passage in small numbers.

Recorded first in 1929 and twice in 1938, the Ruff has occurred annually on autumn passage since 1960. Although the earliest autumn bird was seen on Langness on 10th July 1981 and there have been two other records for late July, Ruff are most often seen between about 6th August and the end of September. There have been a few October records up to 24th. The majority of records are of 1–2 birds, indeed this has been exclusively so in July and August, but parties of 3–9 have occurred on several occasions during the second half of September and in 1967 up to 7 were quite often seen at Langness during October. On spring passage the Ruff is a rare visitor, there having been just 4 records of single birds between 26th March and 9th April. There have also been 3 winter records – 1 was seen on Ramsey North shore on 28th December 1982, K. Williamson found a party of 6–7 on a reef near

Derby Castle (Douglas Bay) on 9th January 1938 and there were two at Rue Point on 30th January 1966.

In the early 1960s Ruffs were seen regularly at Port St Mary Point, apparently lingering for up to 12 days. More recently there have been several records from Strandhall and Poyllvaaish, but the Langness area is easily the best place for this species. Here they frequent the Pool, the scattered collections of brackish water, the Sandwick shore and occasionally Derbyhaven Bay and flood water on Ronaldsway Airfield. The same, or perhaps different birds are sometimes seen for several weeks, e.g. in 1973 when 1 or 2 were often seen from 24th July until 26th September. There have also been 6 autumn records for the Ayres, including 6 on 19th September 1980 and 4 ruffs and 5 reeves on 13th September 1981. The Calf has just 2 spring records and 1 in September – all single birds.

Jack Snipe

Lymnocryptes minimus

Regular passage migrant and rather scarce winter visitor.

Although difficult to assess, there is nothing to suggest that Ralfe's view that the Jack Snipe was far from rare is not still applicable. This species is often overlooked and probably more familiar to the sportsman than the ornithologist. The most useful information comes from the Calf where it occurs regularly on passage. Autumn birds predominate with 42 bird days in the period 1959–81 – the earliest date is 5th September and the latest 16th November with an obvious peak around mid October. During the same period there have been 17 bird days in spring between 5th February and 25th April. The Jack Snipe is usually seen singly, often in the company of *G. gallinago* with which it shares the same habitat. The most notable gathering was of about 20 birds which were flushed from the Lagagh on 24th April 1938. There has been no more than a handful of records for December and January.

Snipe

Gallinago gallinago

Common passage migrant and winter visitor. Rather local breeding bird.

Ralfe described the Snipe as 'A fairly plentiful game-bird in Man, and at times is found in considerable abundance about the many little wild damp tracks interspersed over the country. ... The spring flight passes through the island in March or the beginning of April, and the autumn migrants are numerous in October and November.' He considered that Snipe bred 'very sparingly in Man, as in the Ballaugh Curraghs, in the 'moaneys' in the upper part of Lonan, and the marsh land at Greeba.' The game returns of 1902 and 1903 listed 252 and 207 Manx birds.

There is some evidence that both before and since Ralfe's time snipe have been rather more abundant in the Island. On 14th January 1841 for example 15 were shot on the Calf (Williamson 1940) while in two seasons in the late 1840s 'an old hand at snipe shooting' killed 800 in marshes neighbouring the Point of Ayre (Hadfield 1856). By 1923 Ralfe was able to add the moors about Foxdale, the neighbourhood of the Lhen Trench and the bogs above Glen Auldyn as breeding sites and the winter flocks now seen at Langness and the Eairy Dam seem much larger than any occurring at the beginning of this century.

Although a drumming Snipe is one of the commoner Manx sounds it was only noted in fourteen 5 km squares in the period 1977–81. Nesting is probably fairly widespread in the numerous marshy areas of the northern plain and to Ralfe's breeding areas one can add the Sulby watershed above Tholt y Will and the Cregneish area. In 1980 a pair attempted to breed near the millpond on the Calf. Although noted for the length of its breeding season, Manx nests with eggs, though admittedly rather few, have only been found between 16th April and 5th June.

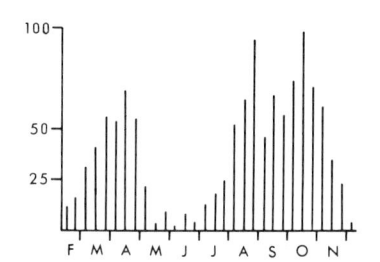

Snipe. Total bird days per ten day period (Calf).

The passage periods, rather more extensive in both spring and autumn than suggested by Ralfe, are well illustrated on the histogram for the Calf. On the main island readily visible flocks are noted from October to February at Langness/Derbyhaven, the Eairy Dam and near Jurby Church. On the Langness saltmarsh and at Derbyhaven Point 30–80 birds are not unusual, while peaks of 60 have been seen at the Eairy and 50 on the margins of flood water below Jurby Church. Such numbers are no doubt typical of other areas where the birds are less conspicuous. Much of the Island's moorland is quite boggy during the winter and individuals are repeatedly flushed when one walks in the hills.

The ring, placed on an adult snipe on the Calf in July 1960 was found in an old Peregrine's eyrie at Jokkmokk in northern Sweden 19 years later, one of the most northerly recoveries of a British-ringed Snipe. One ringed as a chick in Iceland was shot at the Calf Sound during its first winter; although the race breeding in Iceland is *Gallinago g. faeroeensis*, this bird was attributed by R. Wagstaffe to the nominate race *Gallinago g. gallinago* (Williamson 1960).

Manx = *Coayr Heddagh* = Spear-face

Great Snipe
Gallinago media

Very rare autumn visitor.

Madoc wrote of the first Manx record – 'I approach this record with some diffidence ... (but) in the belief that, without personal examination, the birds which have been seen by me could be nothing else'. On 30th November 1930 he and a companion put up a heavy looking snipe from high dry ground on the centre of Langness. After a short straight flight, when some white about the tail was noted, it dropped and was then flushed again. He recorded another bird with the same characteristics in the same location on 15th January 1933. On 12th November 1934 Madoc watched one on a rock on Langness before it flew away and the breast markings and white tail feathers were very noticeable.

Long-billed Dowitcher
Limnodromus scolopaceus

Vagrant.

One landed briefly in front of a hide by the mill-pond on the Calf at 0900 on 28th September 1980. By good fortune the hide was occupied by the assistant warden (Jennings 1981). At 1630 the same day, what must surely have been the same bird was seen on the Langness pool by a number of observers, remaining until at least 7th October (Cullen 1981). Was it a coincidence that one arrived at Tacumshin, Co. Wexford on 8th October, staying there until 26th October?

By the end of 1980 this Alaskan and north east Siberian breeding species had been specifically identified in the British Isles about 70 times. Ralfe placed in square brackets a specimen of the 'grey long beak' shot in a marsh near the Point of Ayre in 1847 (Hadfield 1856).

Woodcock
Scolopax rusticola

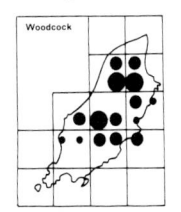

Well distributed breeding resident. Regular passage migrant and winter visitor.

Two late 18th century references imply that the Woodcock occurred on the Island as a passage migrant and by 1888 Kermode was able to write that it had occasionally been known to breed, although this statement did not appear in his list of 1901. Ralfe knew of no breeding records but around the turn of the century there were records for August and September, well before the period of autumn passage.

Throughout Britain the Woodcock was originally known exclusively as a winter resident and although breeding became established in many parts of England during the 17th and 18th centuries it was not until the end of the 19th century that virtually all counties in the British Isles had breeding populations. (Alexander 1945-7). In the Isle of Man breeding was not finally confirmed until nests were found in Greeba Plantation in 1906.

The wooded parts of Glen Roy and the Ballaugh Curraghs were the next areas to be colonised and a steady but definite increase in the breeding population is still continuing. Woodcock now breed in all the mature conifer plantations and in the wooded parts of the Curraghs of Ballaugh and Greeba and the gareys at Ballacreetch (Onchan) and Ballacoine (Michael). There is insufficient data to give any estimate of the total Manx breeding population, although a guide to numbers in some areas is provided by the number of birds seen roding. Thus in 1972 5 roding birds were seen in Glen Auldyn and in 1975 9 were seen from the old railway track over 1 km of Greeba Curragh.

The Woodcock has a long breeding season and in the Isle of Man calculated first egg dates range from 9th March (Narradale 1959) to at least 2nd July (Eary Beg Plantation 1973).

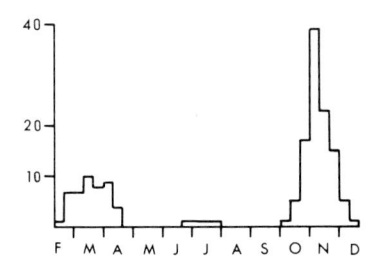

Woodcock. Total bird days per ten day period (Calf).

The pattern of passage is well illustrated by the histogram of Calf records — modest numbers in spring from mid February to mid-April and greater numbers in autumn from October to early December with a notable early November peak.

During winter Woodcock numbers vary greatly so that on a traditional Boxing Day shoot in the centre of the Island an average of 20 birds is usually seen, but in 1983 the same terrain produced 60–70 birds. Many wooded areas are frequented by Woodcock both during the breeding season and in winter, but during cold weather they occur in a rich variety of situations such as gardens, the uncultivated fringes of farmland, in damp moorland and in the sand dunes of the north coast. Unusually 9 were seen in Langness Pool on 6th August 1936.

From ringing recoveries of Woodcock bred in northern England, Scotland and Ireland it might be supposed that over 70% of Manx bred birds would be resident (Kalchreuter 1982). Perversely the only recovery of a Manx ringed pullus was in Wigtownshire during its first January. The recovery in December of a bird ringed as a pullus in Co. Durham suggests that some birds from northern England winter on the Island, while a mature bird ringed on the Calf in late June (and so probably a Manx breeder) was killed in Co. Fermanagh six months later. Ireland is the great receptacle of wintering Woodcock taking many birds from Norway and Western Sweden and it seems likely that a good proportion of birds visiting the Isle of Man in autumn and winter are of Scandinavian origin.

Manx: *Ushag Rennee* = Fern Bird

Black-tailed Godwit

Limosa limosa

Passage migrant occurring regularly in small numbers in autumn and infrequently in spring.

First recorded in mid November 1931 and again in the autumn of 1932, 20 years elapsed before the Black-tailed Godwit was once more seen on the Isle of Man. In the period 1952–56 all records were, in view of the bird's present status, unusual. Single birds were seen in the south east on 10th and 11th December 1952 and between 28th January and 1st February 1954. An individual on Langness on 25th May 1954 remains the latest spring record for the Island, while the two seen in Castletown Bay on 1st March 1956 constitute the only record for that month.

Since 1957 Black-tailed Godwits have occurred with increasing frequency in the autumn and occasionally in spring. The earliest autumn date was 5th July 1969 and records continue up to the end of September, with 7 in July and September and 14 in August. In 1979 there were additional records for 4th November and 2nd January. There have been separate records for 6th and 7th April and six others between 18th April and 3rd May. Rarely has the Black-tailed Godwit been seen other than in the Langness/Derbyhaven area, the Sandwick shore and the saltmarsh being particularly favoured. Elsewhere, the Sound has 1 record, Strandhall/Poyllvaaish two, the Ballalough meadows near Castletown one, Ronaldsway Airfield one, Ramsey two and the Glascoe and Ballakinnag Dubs one each. Single birds are usual but up to 4 have been seen together in August. Black-tailed Godwits had only been recorded on the Calf singly on 3 occasions until 1983 when 3 fed in the lower glen fields on 8th and 9th July, to be followed by 2 more on 17th September and single birds on 23rd and 26th September.

The only bird to be examined in the hand had been shot near Castletown on 28th October 1957 and was found to belong to the nominate race *Limosa l. limosa*, yet it is the Icelandic race *Limosa l. islandica* which has wintered in increasingly large numbers in Ireland and southern England since the 1940s. (Williamson 1960).

Bar-tailed Godwit

Limosa lapponica

Regular on autumn passage and as a winter visitor in small numbers. Irregular on spring passage.

Ralfe knew of the Bar-tailed Godwit as a regular visitor to the coast between Derbyhaven and Poyllvaaish in autumn and early winter. He never saw more than five together and could only produce two records for mid winter and one for early April. During the early part of the present century a regular wintering habit in the same area became established, but it is really only during the last decade that Bar-tailed Godwits have started to appear rather erratically in spring.

Individuals are seen most years during the second half of July, the earliest date being 12th July, but it is not until late August that they occur in any number. Notable records during this period were 24 on the Calf on 16th August 1974, 44 flying over the islet on 23rd August 1974, 18 flying south past Contrary Head on 30th August 1975 and 14 on the Ayres on 31st August 1981. September is the principal month for passage, movement continuing into October although the picture is complicated by the presence some years of birds in late September which are destined to remain through the winter. During September parties of up to 6 birds are present most days on the Sandwick shore – 1979 was exceptional with 29 on 9th, 31 on 20th and still 25 on 30th September. There were also 17 there on 7th October 1982 and 23 on 22nd September 1985.

Wintering birds are largely confined to Langness and Derbyhaven where 2–5 birds are present from October to March, occasionally lingering until early April. The best winter count was 16 on 11th February 1934 although the following description by Madoc deserves special mention – 'Once, on 18th January (1933) . . . quite a thousand, or more, of these birds flew close along the shore at the Point of Ayre in great packs and hordes and in complete silence; travelling from east to west presumably making for Ireland. The last letter I had from the late T. A. Coward referred to the sudden cold snap in England and the absence of bar-tails; and this was no doubt part of their movement to warmer climes.' April records are becoming more common and recently birds have been seen in May up to 25th. The only June record is of one which flew past the Calf on 13th (1982).

Away from Langness and Derbyhaven, Bar-tailed Godwits occur with reasonable regularity on the shores of Carrick Bay and the Ayres during autumn and occasionally at other times. They have occasionally been seen at Ramsey and Douglas and about a dozen times on the Calf between 15th July and 17th September.

Whimbrel

Numenius phaeopus

Fairly common passage migrant and very rare winter visitor.

Ralfe regarded the Whimbrel as a regular visitor on passage to the coast around Castletown and to the northern shores of the Island, being more plentiful in spring than autumn. Small parties frequented the salt pools of Langness and 20 on Fort Island was exceptional. As a passage migrant the present status of the Whimbrel is unchanged although there have been 3–4 records for each of the months November to March since 1929.

Although there are a few records for early April the main spring passage period is from about 27th April to 19th May. Parties of 5–10 are usual with occasionally as many as 20. On 7th May 1980 an exceptional flock of 70 was seen on the sands below Hango Hill, with 30 still there 3 days later. Whimbrel are occasionally seen in June on the Calf and the main island and in one or two instances have probably summered. Autumn passage is seen mainly from about 18th July to the end of August with frequent records continuing until the first few days of October. Although the period of autumn movement is much longer, numbers actually settling on the main island are small, a party of 6 being quite unusual. Larger numbers are seen and heard flying over the island both around the coast and inland and considerable night passage is quite often heard during spring and autumn. Whimbrels were heard over Douglas at night on the unusually late date of 11th November in 1972.

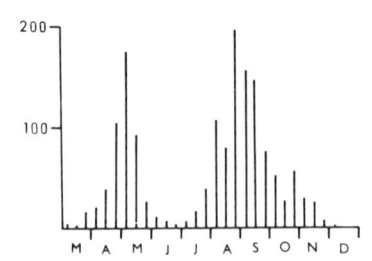

Whimbrel. Total bird days per ten day period (Calf).

In contrast to the pattern on the main island, the histogram clearly shows that on the Calf larger numbers are seen in autumn than spring – here the maximum spring count was 14 on 8th May 1962 while in autumn there were 20 on 23rd August 1964.

In 1983 a single Whimbrel was seen on the Calf up to 11th November and then again when the Observatory opened on 21st February, raising the possibility of over-wintering.

The few other winter records are of 1–3 birds making brief appearances at Langness, Derbyhaven and Poyllvaaish. There are also single records from the north west coast for late February and early March.

Curlew
Numenius arquata

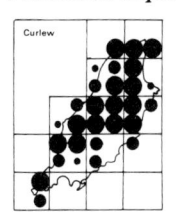

Common resident. Abundant on autumn passage and as a winter visitor.

By tradition the Curlew was the first bird heard by St Patrick when he landed on the Island in the early 5th century, but despite this and other legends, evidence that the saint actually visited the Island is lacking. Apocryphal as this story may be the song of the Curlew in spring is *the* most characteristic sound of the Manx hills.

According to Ralfe Curlews were common along the shores of the north and south coasts, a few even being seen there during the breeding season. They occurred in great numbers on migration and night movement was often heard; in contrast very few nested on the Island, indeed in 1862 it was not regarded as a breeding bird. By 1903 however Ralfe was able to describe a few pairs breeding on the swampy moorlands in which the branches of the Sulby rise, the head of Glen Rushen and in the Ballaugh Curraghs. Twenty years later considerable numbers nested in the Curraghs and hilly wastes of Ballaugh and Lezayre. As in other parts of Britain there has been a marked increase in the breeding population during this century with spread over damp grass and heather moorland throughout the northern and southern hills. Greeba Curraghs have been colonised and from the initial settlement in the Curraghs of Ballaugh and Sulby there has been a spread into most of the rushy pastures of the northern plain. The overgrown fields bordering the Ayres heath were colonised in the 1930s and nesting now takes place in the marram-covered dunes around Rue Point. Although breeding has yet to be confirmed Curlews are regularly seen displaying over the gareys of Malew and Santon and on the Calf a pair has attempted to breed each year since 1963, with 3 pairs in 1964. Eggs have been found as early as 14th April and as late as 24th June.

Numbers occurring on passage and during the winter probably increased in the early part of this century, but although quantitative comparisons are very difficult the period 1930–1980 has seen no obvious change. Madoc wrote that autumn numbers were vast and, according to Coward, far greater than in Cheshire. Flocks of 2–3,000 in the Dee and Mersey estuaries in the early 1930s (Bell 1962) may provide a pointer to Manx numbers at that time. The considerable passage of Curlew from late June to early October is well illustrated by the Calf histogram.

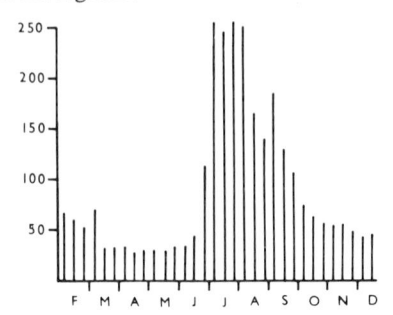

Curlew. Average bird days per ten day period (Calf).

A widely distributed bird both on passage and in winter – the following are the most important sites:

Ronaldsway Airfield, Langness and Derbyhaven: Flocks of 100 may form as early as the last week in June and during July 200 are regular with a peak count of 600 on Langness on 14th July 1983. From August to October flocks of 3–600 are usual and there have been counts in excess of 1,000 in each month. Numbers in November and March are generally less, 500 being exceptional, but by far the greatest numbers are seen from December to February. At high tide the Curlew form large flocks together with Golden Plover and Lapwing on the airfield, moving to the rocks of Derbyhaven and Langness as the tide recedes. Peak counts for the area were 2,235 on 25th December 1983, 1,180 on 22nd January 1978 and 2,300 on 24th February 1978.

Douglas Bay: 130–200 birds are regularly seen from November to early March, frequenting the rocks to the north of Onchan Harbour and the Conister.

Glascoe area: During the period of autumn passage flocks of 80–200 are usual and from late October to late January the fields between the Dog Mills and the Bride hills usually hold flocks of 3–400 with an early January peak of 1500 in 1980.

North coast: The coast from Orrisdale Head to the Point of Ayre attracts considerable flocks on autumn passage. Madoc found thousands on the sands below the Ayres as early as 19th July and on 31st July 1975 there were 1,500 at Orrisdale Head and a further 2,000 below Knock e Dooney. There are records of 1,500 at Blue Point in August and September, but this area is little used later in the year, a flock of 1,000 at Rue Point in December 1982 being exceptional. On the other hand flocks of 1–300 are plentiful in fields all over the northern plain during winter.

Will's Strand to Glen Wyllin: Flocks of up to 400 are regularly seen on the coastal fields from mid July to late February.

Because of its easily recognisable call the Curlew is particularly conspicuous during night passage, heard most often during March but also in February, April and October.

Two ringing recoveries suggest that Curlew bred on the Island are sedentary – both were ringed as pulli and recovered in the same area, in January eight years later and in May at the age of 13. Birds ringed as pulli in Sweden and Finland have been recovered on the Island in January, while another young bird ringed in Kirkcudbrightshire was recovered 3 months later, in late August in Michael.

Manx: *Crottag* i.e., *Cruittagh* = Humped

Spotted Redshank
Tringa erythropus

Uncommon passage migrant.

First identified in 1934, there have been 23 Manx records of the Spotted Redshank – 13 on Langness, 2 at the Jurby Dub, 6 on the Calf and one at Aldrick and Kentraugh. One, and occasionally two, birds have occurred principally on autumn passage between 8th July and 21st September with late individuals on 2nd and 20th November. The three spring records have been on 27th March, 26th April and 9th May.

Redshank
Tringa totanus

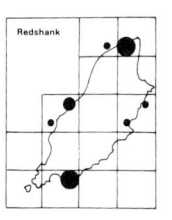

Scarce but regular breeding bird. Common passage migrant and winter visitor.

During the latter part of the 19th century the Redshank could only be regarded as common in the south east of the Island between Cas ny Hawin and Kentraugh, being absent only at the height of summer. Although once common at Ramsey, there, and along the north and west coasts it was only occasionally seen.

In May 1915 'a pair was certainly breeding (though the nest was not found) at the Lagagh Moar' and by 1923 it was a much more common bird, small parties being regularly seen at Ramsey, Douglas and the Dalby coast, with considerably increased numbers in the south (Ralfe 1923). Madoc was able to describe it as 'very common round the coast of the Island throughout the non-breeding months.'

Breeding was eventually confirmed in 1928 when a nest was found in wetlands near the Ayres coast. During the next decade, up to 4 pairs nested in this area in a variety of habitats 250–400 m apart, and 1–2 pairs have nested there annually since. In 1932 three young, just able to fly and accompanied by their parents, were found at Pooyl Dhooie, about 2 km upstream from the mouth of the Sulby River and in 1935 young were hatched from a nest at the Lagagh. During 1934 and 1935 Redshanks summered at Kionslieu, young hatched there in 1936 and nesting probably took place in 1937 too. Since 1942 1–3 pairs have nested regularly on Langness and in 1975, after summering birds had been seen during each of the four previous years, a pair brought off 3 young at Harstal, south of Dalby. Thus over the last 55 years the total breeding population has been remarkably stable at 4–5 pairs, yet even this small population has shown a notable diversity in its choice of habitat. On the Ayres nests have been found in rush grown fields, around the slacks and on the heath itself, while on Langness they have nested among rushes in wet ground at the edge of the saltmarsh, in the dry hummocks around the Pool and on the top field – a dry well-grazed area. Williamson (1938) has described how one year he was reasonably certain that a single male mated with 3 females, each of which reared young. During a fairly short breeding season the earliest and latest calculated dates for first eggs have been 17th April and 25th May.

From mid July parties begin to gather in the south east but rarely exceed 50 until early October. From October to December 50–100 birds are usual and peaks of 200 have occurred in each month. Numbers are only marginally less in January and February but rapidly dwindle in March. Douglas Bay and Onchan Harbour have fair numbers from August to March with 20–30 in autumn and up to 80 during the winter. Ramsey has a variable winter population with peaks of 80 birds frequenting the drained Mooragh Lake in February. 20–40 are seen on the Ayres shore in the autumn and at Peel, Port Grenaugh and Strandhall in winter. The Redshank seems equally at home on shores of both sand and shingle. Like the Turnstone it feeds busily among the masses of seaweed stacked along the highwater mark, while the intertidal mud of Derbyhaven Bay is one of its favourite resorts as are the weed covered rocks of Castletown Bay and Derby Castle. Inland they are sometimes seen in parties of up to 25 on school playing fields in Douglas and in small numbers on flood water at Kirby. The most favoured inland resort in winter is the Glascoe Dub, where as many as 60 may be seen in January. The pattern of occurrences on the Calf is illustrated on the histogram. Numbers there have decreased considerably since about 1970.

One bird ringed as a chick in Cumberland was killed by a Sparrowhawk on Langness the following April.

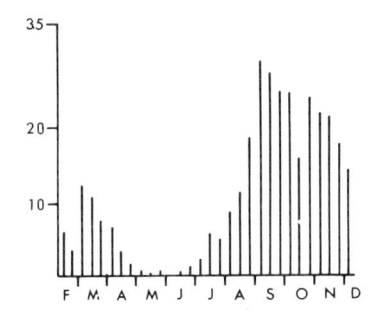

Redshank. Average bird days per ten day period (Calf).

Examples of the Icelandic race *T.t. robusta* and the *britannica* form of *T.t. totanus* have been identified in the hand.
Manx: *Goblan Marrey* = Beaked bird of the sea

Greenshank

Tringa nebularia

Regular passage migrant and rather scarce winter visitor.

Ralfe believed that the Greenshank was a regular visitor in very small numbers, and it seems that during the last 50–60 years it has occurred with much greater frequency, although nearly always singly.

On migration the Greenshank occurs almost exclusively in the autumn. It has twice been seen as early as 24th June, but the first bird is more usually seen during the second half of July. The great majority of Greenshank records occur in August and to a notably lesser extent in September. October numbers are comparable to those in July, while the aggregate of monthly records from November to March is remarkably constant. On any day during the winter period it is now usually possible to find a Greenshank. Spring passage is barely recognisable, the Greenshank is scarcer in April than in any winter month and there have only been 4 May records up to 24th. Records of 2 and 3 birds together are unusual – greater numbers exceptional. There were 7 in the south east in late 1934, 5 at Derbyhaven in February 1936, 15 at Ramsey on 13th April 1962 and 6 at Langness on 7th August 1984. The best day total for the Calf was 6+ on 7th August 1980.

On autumn passage the Greenshank occurs most frequently at Langness/Derbyhaven and on the Calf (up to 23rd September). It is also a fairly frequent visitor to the north coast and Ramsey Bay and has been seen once at Tromode, Glascoe Dub, Lough Cranstal and Ballamona Moar. During the winter it is rarely seen away from Langness/Derbyhaven, although the drained Mooragh Lake proves attractive in late January and early February and there have been a few records from Port St Mary Point, Carrick Bay and Cas ny Hawin. Inland, there is a solitary record for Kirby in early January 1945.

Lesser Yellowlegs
Tringa flavipes

Vagrant.

Madoc's record of one on 27th October 1935 on Langness was accepted by Witherby. H. M. Rogers reported another on Langness on 2nd May 1936 and a third bird was seen by Madoc, also on Langness from 19th to 25th July the same year.

Green Sandpiper
Tringa ochropus

Irregular passage migrant.

The visits of the Green Sandpiper are very largely confined to the period 3rd July to 28th September with late birds on 23rd October and from 7th to 14th November when in 1982 one was regularly seen on the saltmarsh at Langness. In spring it is rare with just 4 records between 10th April and 11th May. The only true winter occurrence was at Ballacross Dub (German) on 18th January 1922.

Unlike most sandpipers this species is very rarely seen on the Manx coast. On the Calf, which accounts for 70% of all records and some 34 bird days in autumn between 1959 and 1981, it has nearly always been seen by the millpond, usually singly but on 3 occasions 3 together. On the main island Green Sandpipers have turned up at a variety of dubs, drains and ditches – the Dollagh Dub with two records being a very typical site. On Langness, where it has occurred 3 times, it favours the saltmarsh.

Wood Sandpiper
Tringa glareola

Rare passage migrant.

First reported from the Calf in 1966, there has been a total of 7 records for the islet involving 10 birds. The one spring record was on 29th May 1977, the remainder have been on 5th August, 8th August (2), 13th August (3), 22nd August, 7th September and 2nd October. In addition two were seen at Poyllvaaish on 12th August 1980.

Common Sandpiper
Actitis hypoleucos

Common passage migrant. Has bred.

The status of the Common Sandpiper in the Isle of Man has not altered during the last hundred years. It is one of the anomalies of Manx Ornithology, puzzling Ralfe no less than present day students, that it is not a regular breeding bird. Cumbria, which has many geographical similarities to the Island has a good breeding population as does south west Scotland, yet in Co. Down the Manx situation seems to prevail.

The brief breeding story is as follows. On 5th June 1910 a nest with 4 eggs was found on a fern clad bank close to the Baldwin Reservoir. The eggs were accidentally broken the following day but on 23rd June a replacement clutch of 4 eggs was found near the first site. In the late 1920s a nest with eggs was found by a fisherman beside the River Glass close to Tromode Dam and on 17th July 1932 three downy young were found at the Clypse Reservoir. On 23rd June 1948 a bird disturbed at Pooyl Dhooie near the tidal limit of the Sulby River appeared very distressed but no sign of nest or young was found.

It is a common passage migrant, numbers in autumn greatly exceeding those seen in spring. Spring passage is seen mainly from mid April to mid May with occasional stragglers to the end of that month. Exceptionally early birds were seen on 4th and 5th April 1967. In a number of years recently there have been two distinct periods of spring migration separated by 10–14 days. In 1905 Ralfe wrote 'On passage the Sandpiper is found along the lower and wider portions of our principal streams, as the Silverburn, the Glass, whose shingly and gorse-bordered margins above Douglas are an unfailing resort, and the Sulby, where Mr Kermode says the ford near the head of the tide (Pooyl Dhooie) west of Ramsey is a favourite haunt. But the species is also extremely characteristic of a 'burn-foot' where there is a gravelly beach, as at Glenmay Strand, Cas ny Hawin in Santon, and Groudle. I have seen it on similar ground on the shore at Grainsh, near Ramsey (where there is no stream); but it is also found on the zone between high and low water mark at the base of our steepest sea-promontories like Bradda, Contrary Head, and Stroin Vuigh, where it creeps over the sloping weedy surface like a Purple Sandpiper, and I have observed it on the rocks of Peel Castle Island, and of the Calf.' On spring passage Common Sandpipers occur much more frequently inland than they do in autumn, yet they are still twice as common on the coast. The Neb, Glass and Silverburn together with Ballamoar Reservoir and the Eairy Dam are all regularly visited in spring, while Fleshwick and the Ayres shore are very easily the best coastal sites. At this time they are usually seen singly although there are a few records of 5–6 together and recently parties of 10 and 11 have been noted at Fleshwick.

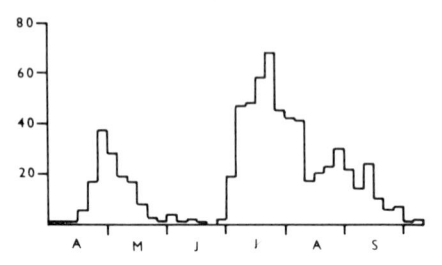

Common Sandpiper. Total bird days per five day period (Calf).

June records are uncommon and while first returning birds are sometimes seen during the first week of July, their arrival may be delayed by up to 3 weeks. Nevertheless in most years the peak of autumn movement occurs in late July, with passage continuing to mid-September. As in spring a gap of 2 to 4 weeks may occur during August and early September before a second smaller movement of birds. Common Sandpipers are rarely seen in the second half of September and there have been four or five October records up to 9th. Coastal records predominate very strongly in autumn although the favoured localities are quite different to those used in spring. Cas ny Hawin is *the* site, yet it does not feature at all in spring, and they are common all along the coast as far as Black Head. They are also regular at Peel and along the adjacent coast to the north, but quite uncommon on the Ayres shore. Small parties of 5–10 are commonplace in autumn and occur particularly in late July – the biggest gatherings were 14 at the Clypse Reservoir on 12th July 1976, 17 on the rocks at Spaldrick on 17th July 1956 and 19 at Strandhall on 13th July 1985. On the Calf the best day totals are of 5–10 birds.

Percentage of Common Sandpipers reported from inland and coastal sites on the main island in spring and autumn

	Spring	Autumn	Combined
Inland	15	7	22
Coast	29	49	78
Total	44	56	100

There have been just 4 winter records of individuals by a pond at the Nunnery on 12th December 1946, at Cas ny Hawin on 28th February 1925, at Port Moar (Maughold) on 18th March 1945 and at Fleshwick on 18th March 1978.

Manx: *Looyran*

Turnstone
Arenaria interpres

Common passage migrant and winter visitor. A very few probably summer annually.

Ralfe regarded the Turnstone as a regular, though not abundant, visitor to many parts of the coast between 20th August and 16th May. He considered the Conister rock and the rocky shores on either side of Castletown Harbour as the most favoured localities and parties were usually of 6–20 birds. Thirty years later Madoc's description suggests no change in the Turnstone's status although by now June records were occurring occasionally and parties of up to 30 could be found on the Ayres shore at any season. There is no doubt that in the early 1960s there was a notable increase in numbers visiting the island. A flock of 2–300 was seen at Sandwick on 19th December 1963 and since then counts of 150–200 birds have been made at Langness/Derbyhaven in all months between October and May.

Apart from Langness, where it is very difficult to distinguish between passage birds and winter visitors, Onchan Harbour is a favourite locality with 50–100 birds present from September to April. 20–70 Turnstones can usually be found along the Ayres shore, between Castletown and Scarlett and in Carrick Bay. Port Grenaugh regularly has a small party during the winter and parties of up to 30 are sometimes seen north of Peel, though at Peel itself they are rather scarce.

June records are always of interest and recently it has usually been possible to find between 2 and 6 birds at Langness and on the Ayres shore.

On the Calf spring and autumn migration is quite obvious although numbers are not great with the highest day count only 50. 20–30 birds have recently wintered on the Calf. In 1940 Williamson could only cite one Calf record although small parties were regular at the Chicken Rock during migration time. Nowadays up to 10 can regularly be found on the rock in quiet conditions at low tide.

Although much of their feeding is done on the weed covered rocks at low tide, they can also be found on shingle and to a lesser extent sandy beaches, especially when storms have stacked masses of seaweed along the tide line. At high tide they retire to rocks at such places as Fort Island, Derbyhaven Point and Derby Castle.

Turnstones have never been seen inland on the Isle of Man although one was found dead in Slieau Whallian plantation on 28th November 1929.

Manx: *Goblaghan*

Red-necked Phalarope
Phalaropus lobatus

Very rare autumn passage migrant.

The first known occurrence was on 23rd September 1926, when one was killed against the Point of Ayre Lighthouse. One was present in the Outer Harbour at Port St Mary from 16th to 18th September 1956 and it was perhaps the same bird which was present for two weeks in Castletown Harbour during the same month. On 14th and 15th October 1967 one was seen in Chapel Bay, Port St Mary and on 25th October 1980 one was seen swimming on the sea at Will's Strand.

Grey Phalarope
Phalaropus fulicarius

Rare autumn passage migrant.

Since 1860 there have been 18 Manx records of the Grey Phalarope between 11th August (1979) and 12th December (1860). The monthly distribution of these records is August – 2, September – 4, October – 4, November – 5 and December – 3. Four examples were obtained between 1891 and 1898, there were single records in 1929, 1942 and 1967 and a further 10 since 1972. At Langness, where it has been recorded 8 times, it has been seen on the Sandwick shore and on the Pool and was on one occasion a Lighthouse casualty. Five Calf records involving 8 individuals, have been of birds flying past in a southerly direction. A north-westerly gale on 20th October 1984 brought four individuals. The only inland record was of one found dead below wires on the railway line at Union Mills.

(Phalaropes not specifically identified, have been seen flying past the Calf on 3 occasions in September and once in mid November during the last decade and there have been single records from the main island in October and November).

Pomarine Skua
Stercorarius pomarinus

Uncommon passage migrant.

First recorded in October 1890 and not again until 1963, there have been 37 records involving 55 birds between 1972 and 1985. All records have been between 23rd July and 16th November – the majority occurring between 13th August and 11th October. The Pomarine Skua is most often seen from the Calf, with 3 birds being seen on 3 occasions and 5 on 16th October 1983. Elsewhere there have been records from near the Chasms, Peel Castle and several from the Ayres coast, where 4 were seen together on 29th August 1972. In 1985 alone there were at least 10 records – 5 involving 7 birds from the north west coast between 31st July and 1st September and a further 5 from the Calf (8 birds) between 5th September and 5th November.

Arctic Skua
Stercorarius parasiticus

Regular passage migrant.

Although only rarely seen from the Manx coast Ralfe believed that the Arctic Skua was probably much more common a little out to sea being a familiar bird to the Manx fishermen who called it the Shirragh Varrey (Sea Hawk).

During the first half of this century there was no more than a handful of records and Williamson (1940) did not list it among the Calf birds. Since 1947 however, the Arctic Skua has been seen with increasing frequency, mostly along the west coast from the Point of Ayre to the Calf during the autumn months.

From about the second week in July until the end of August 1–2 birds can often be seen close to the Ayres shore harrying terns, the most being 11 on 7th August 1984. These birds do not seem to be passing through – they are transient visitors. There have been a few June records for this part of the coast – the earliest being 12th June 1947 and, in comparison with Peel and the Calf, September records are rare. In contrast Arctic Skuas are unknown off the Calf in July, are rather uncommon there in August and reach their greatest numbers in September, passage slowly falling off through October. A similar pattern is also seen at Peel. The best day totals for the Calf were 15 on 12th September 1980 and a remarkable 45+ on 16th October 1983. The latest autumn records were of one on 23rd October 1977 and 2 on 11th November 1972. East coast records are quite rare.

Arctic Skuas are rare in spring, but between 1972 and 1984, there were 6 Calf records between 17th April and 12th June and one from the Groudle coast.

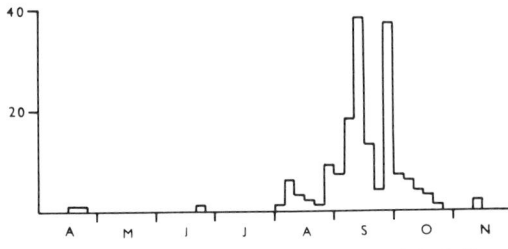

Arctic Skua. Total bird days per five day period (Calf).

Two were shot at Douglas on 26th April 1880 and there have been just two other early records for May.

The majority of birds seen from the Isle of Man are dark-plumaged.

Manx: *Shirragh Varrey*

Long-tailed Skua

Stercorarius longicaudus

Rare autumn passage migrant.

The first record was of a juvenile found dying in a Douglas school playing field on 5th October 1960 (Williamson 1962). There have been five subsequent records from the Calf. On 3rd October 1975 another immature bird was seen from Cow Harbour flying south behind a flock of Kittiwakes (Haycock 1978). On a day of quite exceptional sea passage which brought 800 Fulmars, one Sooty and 650 Manx Shearwaters, 2,000 Gannets, 2 Pomarine, 15 Arctic and 23 Great Skuas, 2 Black Terns and a Little Gull an adult was seen flying south on 12th September 1980. On 21st September 1982 a juvenile flew westward close to Cow Harbour, a day of good auk passage on which the three other skua species were seen. In 1984 a sub-adult bird flew through the Sound on 30th September and an immature flew south off Culbery on 14th October.

Great Skua

Stercorarius skua

Regular passage migrant.

Mentioning just one bird, caught on a hook in Douglas Bay in November 1903, Ralfe wrote that 'this apparently disappearing species is a rare bird around the Irish sea.'

Around the Calf of Man the Great Skua occurs with a frequency comparable to that of *S. parasiticus* and the histograms for the two species are remarkably similar. Elsewhere it has been only irregularly seen during the last 60 years with a hint of greater frequency in the last decade.

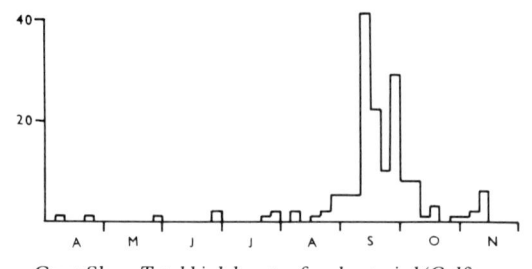

Great Skua. Total bird days per five day period (Calf).

Great Skuas are occasionally seen off the Ayres in late July and are commonest off Peel in September. The latest of several November records on the Calf was 12th (1977), but elsewhere there have been single records for December, January, February and March.

As with *S. parasiticus*, spring records are rare with 4 in April, 3 in May and 3 in June.

On the Calf of Man the highest day counts were on 12th September 1980 when 23 flew south and that great day of skua passage, 16th October 1983 when at least 48 birds were seen in association with large Kittiwake flocks.

Manx: *Maarliagh Marrey*

Mediterranean Gull

Larus melanocephalus

Vagrant.

The two Manx records occurred in 1981 with one between Peel and White Strand on 30th July and another, a first winter bird, flying south and close to Cow Harbour on the Calf on 28th September (Jennings 1982). This species has occurred in north west Europe with much greater frequency during the last 30 years.

Little Gull

Larus minutus

Regular autumn passage migrant and winter visitor in very small numbers.

First identified near Derbyhaven on 25th October 1934, there were no further reports until 1971. In this and the next two years there were single records and varying numbers have been reported annually since 1976. All records have occurred between 4th August (Calf 1977) and 12th April (Peel 1985). On the Calf the Little Gull has been seen 12 times – the records being equally divided between August, September and October, the latest being one flying south east through the Sound on 20th October 1982. There have been two other August records, both from the south – 6 were moving south about 2.5 km off Castletown Bay on 23rd August 1978 and an adult was seen at Port St Mary on 22nd August 1982. Although recorded on several occasions off the Ayres each year since 1976 it is very likely that single birds have wintered off this coast with frequent reports from mid September through to mid February. In addition there have been reports of individuals at Douglas in December, and Scarlett and Peel in January. Also at Peel were two on 13th and 14th February 1985, one from 8th to 29th March 1982, one on 11th April 1985 and two flying south the following day.

Sabine's Gull
Larus sabini

Rare passage migrant.

First identified in 1950 when an immature bird was seen from a boat 1.5 km west of Peel on 24th September. This followed 2 days of westerly gales in the Irish sea (Moss 1953). There have been four other records – an adult flew south with Kittiwakes close to the Calf during a westerly gale on 1st October 1977, a juvenile lingered for 30 minutes off the Calf on 26th September 1978, an adult was seen from the Calf on 9th May 1983 and another adult was watched for 20 minutes working the sea off Peel Castle on 25th August 1985.

Black-headed Gull
Larus ridibundus

Common summer visitor and abundant passage migrant and winter visitor.

Ralfe thought it likely that when the Island's marshes were more extensive the Black-headed Gull probably nested, although there was no record of it ever having done so. He described it as 'very abundant upon our coast during the greater part of the year, though almost wholly absent during the nesting season.' Commonest in the larger bays it also occurred inland 'sometimes in big flocks, and mingling with Rooks and Lapwings, as as much of its food is doubtless derived from the fields as from the shores. During the winter months a flooded meadow is a favourite haunt, and the species appears in flocks or small parties on such meagre sheets of water as our island affords.' Except for a few stragglers Black-headed Gulls were absent from the end of March to mid June, but in late June he did note agitated behaviour, as if at the nesting grounds at both the Jurby coast and the Lhen.

In the early 1930s Madoc wrote 'Sooner or later they will breed here, I am sure. I have found them on sheltered ground in the central Ayre, in pairs very late in April.' Yet it was not until 1947 that a nest with 3 eggs was found on the Ayres back slacks (Ladds 1948). Since then Black-headed Gulls have probably bred annually, although up to 1963 this was limited to about 3 pairs at various points along the inland margin of the Ayres. 1964 saw a notable extension – 60 birds were present at the Lagagh in early May, and although breeding does not appear to have taken place there, at least 10 pairs nested at Ballawhane/Gat y Whing 1 km to the west. In 1965 there were 3 separate small colonies with 10 nests at Gat y Whing, 5 at the Lagagh and a further 10 below Knock y Dooney. Gat y Whing had a peak of 25 nests in 1966 and during the next few years colonies of about 10 pairs appeared briefly at dubs near Smeale and Ballagarrett. In 1973 there were 18 nests in a flooded field south of Glascoe and the following year 30–40 nests on shallow slacks to the south east of Ballamoar; but the greatest expansion occurred in 1975 when 140 pairs bred in the gravel pits to the south west of the Point of Ayre. The 1976 colony was comparable, yet 3 years later this site had been deserted. Meanwhile the Lagagh colony had grown with 26 nests in 1976 and around 50 nests in each year since. The odd pair still nests by the Ayres back slacks and there have also been recent nests in the Ballaugh Curraghs and at a small dub north of Andreas. 1980 saw the colonisation of another gravel pit to the south of the Point of Ayre with a present population of some 60 pairs. The last 35 years have thus seen the establishment of the Black-headed Gull as a Manx breeding species with a total population possibly approaching 50 pairs by the late 1960s, reaching a peak of about 170 pairs in 1976 and probably varying between 60 and 90 pairs since.

Breeding success has usually been poor. At sites such as the Ayres the nesting area has sometimes dried off completely by early June and in some instances the nests have been trampled by cattle. The Lagagh has been consistently unsuccessful, perhaps due to egg-collecting, on the other hand the Point of Ayre gravel pits have usually produced a fair number of flying young. Typically nests are made on hummocky islands in shallow water, although in the gravel pits groups of nests are scattered over mounds of gravel, some of which are surrounded by water while others are in dry terrain. There is no obvious explanation for the inconsistency in gravel pit nesting. The chosen pits have been worked each year, but there has been no obvious change in the extent of human disturbance. Arctic Terns have always nested in the pits occupied by the gulls and have continued to do so in the years following desertion by the gulls. There is no record of eggs being laid before 8th May.

Away from the northern plain one or two individuals may be seen here and there from late March to early July, the arrival of a flock of 100 at Derbyhaven on 27th June 1974 being quite exceptional. More usually in the south east there is a gradual increase in numbers during July with as many as 300 present on Ronaldsway Airfield or in Derbyhaven Bay by mid August. Such numbers remain typical through the autumn and a flock in excess of 1,000 at Derbyhaven on 30th September 1977 was remarkable. Through December and January four figure counts are commonplace with a record 1950 on 1st January 1983, but numbers dwindle during February although a 1,000 strong flock has been seen as late as 24th of that month. The largest gatherings often follow a south westerly gale when large numbers may be seen fluttering over the Sandwick shallows dropping repeatedly to pick up flotsam. During March it is very unusual to see more than 30 anywhere.

While the south-east of the Island attracts the greatest numbers, in winter flocks of 1–300 are common in many places – notably Scarlett and Strandhall, Port Grenaugh, Douglas Bay (up to 1,000 in January), Garwick and Ramsey as well as Kerrowdhoo Reservoir, school playing fields and the type of inland site described by Ralfe. The extreme scarcity of Black-headed Gulls anywhere in early spring suggests that the breeding population consists of summer visitors rather than residents.

Very few Manx young have been ringed and surprisingly there have only been 4 recoveries of pulli ringed elsewhere. One ringed in Co Antrim was found dead in late September 6 years later and another from central Sweden was recovered during its fourth October. Two Norwegian birds recovered in late May and early June three and one year after ringing. An adult breeding at one of the Point of Ayre gravel pits had been colour-ringed at Ravenglass.

Manx: *Pirragh*

Common Gull

Larus canus

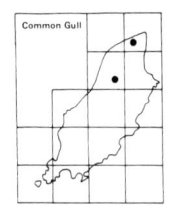

Common on autumn passage and as a winter visitor. Has bred once.

Ralfe described small numbers appearing on the coast in autumn, winter and spring and in 1923 implied that it now occurred more regularly especially on the sandy northern shore. Madoc's earliest date was 15th July after which Common Gulls would be seen in increasing numbers. Hundreds might be seen at Derbyhaven after storms, but numbers clearly varied markedly. He regarded it as rare after the beginning of March.

Around the coast there has been no obvious change. The Common Gull shares with the Black-headed Gull a liking for the Island's sandy beaches and from late July to early March a few may be picked out at Sandwick and Derbyhaven – rarely are there as many as 10, and 20 on 16th February 1975 was exceptional. Further north, at Douglas, much bigger flocks are seen from time to time notably 300 on 12th February 1966 and 230 on 16th November 1967. The sands of Ramsey Bay have held fair numbers in the past but there are no recent details. Along the north coast from the Lhen to the Point of Ayre there have been sporadic records of individuals during May and June during the last 50 years. Hopes that a pair might be breeding in the Point of Ayre gravel pit in 1975 and 1976 were not realised, but on 12th June 1983 a nest with 3 eggs was found in the Rue Point gravel pit – two young being subsequently reared (Cullen 1984). Small flocks of up to 20 birds are sometimes seen on the Ayres shore in August and 60 there on 7th January 1984 was the largest coastal flock for many years.

The regular occurrence of winter flocks of Common Gulls at inland sites appears to be a recent development, there being no such published records prior to 1972. Such flocks are usually of 30–60 birds and the principal sites are the Douglas High School playing fields, the fields around Cronk ny Mona (Onchan) and farmland of the northern plain. Similar numbers also occur on certain inland waters with maxima of 150 on Baldwin Reservoir in January 1979, 76 at Kerrowdhoo Reservoir in January 1973 and 60 at Kionslieu Dam

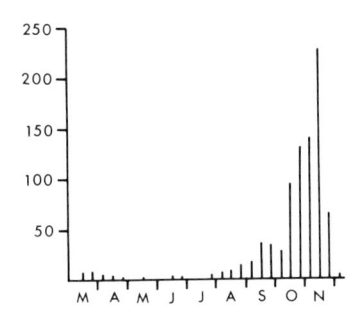

Common Gull. Total bird days per ten day period (Calf).

in February 1973. Late autumn movement past the Calf is well illustrated in the histogram which excludes an exceptional count of 500 flying south during the huge gull movement of 13th November 1972. In general it can be said that the Common Gull is absent from the first week in April until early July.

Manx: *Foillan Vane*

Lesser Black-backed Gull
Larus fuscus

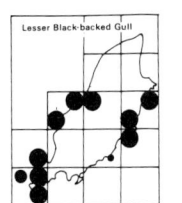

Rather scarce summer visitor.

In the late 19th century Lesser Black-backed Gulls nested in considerable numbers on the Calf with colonies at the south end of the islet and on the isolated rocks of the Burroo and the Stack. Ralfe noted that, although nesting in close proximity to Herring Gulls, the Lesser Black-backs tended to form groups of their own. On the main Island a few nests occurred in some of the big colonies of *L. argentatus* and he specifically mentioned 1 pair at Pistol Castle, 1-2 pairs at Knocksharry and a few pairs at Stroin Vuigh. (Ralfe actually described the last site as Tring Vuigh, but according to Kneen Tring and Stroin are the same word!). By the early 1920s comparatively few bred on the Calf, but a pair had been found nesting at the Ladder below Peel Hill. In 1930 F. Wilkinson found no fewer than 20 pairs nesting on the Lonan coast, presumably in the Bulgham/Dhoon area. Visiting the Calf in 1936 H. M. Rogers only found 3 nesting pairs, but the situation had probably improved by 1938 when Williamson described colonies at Caigher Point and between Kione ny Halbey and South Harbour with odd pairs only between these two sites. He thought that even where their numbers were densest Lesser Black-backs were outnumbered by Herring Gulls by twenty or thirty to one.

There is no evidence of any significant change in the Calf population up to the early years of the Observatory when there were about 8 pairs near South Harbour, but in 1963, 1964 and 1965 the population virtually doubled each year and an ultimate peak of 100 pairs was reached in 1967 only to halve inexplicably the following year. Since then the breeding population has fluctuated between 30 and 50 pairs, mostly in the South Harbour colony.

On the main Island 1 pair started nesting on the Marine Drive in 1938, and there was still a small colony at the Dhoon in 1941. Counts in 1956 and 1957 suggested an east coast population of 25 pairs made up of 3 on the Santon coast, 2 on the Marine Drive, 3 between Clay Head and Groudle, 8 at Bulgham, 7 to the north and south of Port Cornaa and 2 at Maughold. By 1959 east coast numbers were down to 10–11 and 10 years later only 5 and a solitary nest in the inland gull colony on Slieau Freoghane. Recently the main island population has increased again to at least 40 pairs in 1985. Along the east coast from Port Moar to Port Grenaugh (35 km) there were 25 pairs, but the best concentration was along 2 km of the west coast between Gob ny Creggan Glassey and Gob y Deigan with 11 pairs and the population was completed with a few isolated pairs from Peel south to the Chasms.

On the Calf birds begin to arrive in late February, building up to the full breeding population by early April. Departure often starts in early July, continuing through August. One or two may be seen there up to mid November. Elsewhere scarcely a year goes by without an individual being seen in December or January, but Lesser Black-backs are very scarce before mid March. In 1978 a non-breeding group of at least 6 was present at Kionslieu from 25th April to 1st July and although large numbers are not often seen on passage 100–180 were recorded on the Calf between 13th and 23rd March 1982 and over 150 were seen there on 24th August 1978.

There have been 5 recoveries of birds ringed as pulli on the Calf. These have come from the extreme south west of Spain in August, Portugal in July (when 7 years old) and January, Co Wexford in September and Greater London in August (19 years after ringing).

The Manx breeding population belongs, as do all British breeding birds, to the race *L.f. graellsii*, but some birds passing through between September and November, and at least one in March were of the jet-black backed race *L.f. fuscus* which breeds in northern Scandinavia and around the Baltic.

Manx: *Foillan Saggyrt* = Priest Gull

Herring Gull
Larus argentatus

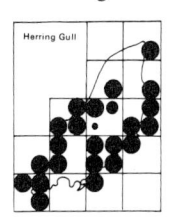

Abundant resident.

Ralfe's description of the Herring Gull as 'perhaps the dominant bird of Man' is no less applicable today, indeed although there are no numerical data with which to compare the census of 1969 (Slinn 1970) there seems little doubt that the population increased during the first half of this century. Earlier Ralfe had attributed the increase during the late 19th century to the Seagull Preservation Act of 1867, but there is nothing to suggest that the legalisation of taking gulls' eggs in 1917 had the reverse effect.

Although the 1969 census yielded 10,000 breeding pairs Slinn considered the figures for the main island to be an absolute minimum and thought the total Manx population was nearer 12,000. On the Calf Ralfe described 'immense numbers' and Williamson (1940) regarded the coastline, with the exception of a small area to the east of the Sound landing places, as practically a continuous gullery. When the Observatory opened in 1959 the Calf population was estimated at 1,500 pairs, but it was not until 1968 that a careful count was made revealing 1,900 pairs – a figure which was matched the following year, when there were an additional 148 pairs on the Kitterland. There was little detectable change during the next few years but by 1975 the population had reached 2,100 and this level has been sustained most years since although there have been inexplicable drops in 1978 and 1982 to only 1,200 pairs. Ralfe commented that very few nested between the Sound and Port Erin, but there were 278 pairs in the 1969 survey and 428 around Bradda, a well tenanted area 80 years ago. Fair numbers continue to breed between Fleshwick and Dalby and the colony described by Ralfe as 'great' between Glenmaye and Peel Hill had a breeding density even heavier than the Calf. Ralfe considered that the small numbers on the German coast were increasing in 1903 and Slinn found 600 pairs along this 5 km stretch of coast. Neither Ralfe nor Slinn described breeding north of Kirkmichael and Ramsey but in 1979 eight pairs had young at Cranstal and in 1985 a nest with eggs was found in a gravel pit near the Point of Ayre. Maughold remains an important site, but although there has probably been some expansion between Port Moar and Laxey 550 nests over 8.5 km represents the lowest density on the Manx coast. Clay Head was first colonised in 1895 and Onchan Head rather later, while Ralfe mentioned only a few nests along the Marine Drive – these sections now hold the densest populations on the east coast. Between

Port Soderick and Port Grenaugh a colony was centred on Pistol in 1903, had extended round Santon Head by 1923 and held 612 nests in 1969. From about 1910 there were a few nests on Langness, but this must have been a very brief colonisation. The abundance of nests described by Ralfe between Perwick and the Sound is perhaps the only section of coast showing a decline this century with a very modest average of only 82 nests per km in 1969. In 1969 60 pairs nested in the quarry behind South Quay, Douglas, a colony which had altered little by 1978 when 70 sites were occupied.

Inland nesting, having been previously rumoured, was eventually confirmed in 1923 when 2 nests were found on the slopes of a valley at about 250 m above sea level and some 6 km inland. The same year two more nests were found at an even higher level in the same area. Another nest was found at Lhergyrhenny in 1943 and the first colony of any substance was discovered on the northern slopes of Slieau Dhoo at over 300 m in 1951. This colony contained about 25 nests and a second colony was found on Slieau Freoghane (Moss 1952).

The Slieau Dhoo colony was of a similar size in 1966 but by 1969 had grown to 100 nests, with a further 130 on Slieau Freoghane. Nesting in this range of hills has continued with reports also coming from Sartfell to the south (200 nests in 1984) and Slieau Curn to the north.

Census of breeding Herring Gulls 1969 – after Slinn.

Location	Coastline length	Total sites 1969	Ave. prs/km
Calf of Man	6.5 km	1900	292
Sound – Port Erin	3 km	278	93
Bradda	3 km	428	143
Fleshwick-Niarbyl	7 km	552	79
North of Niarbyl	—	39	—
Glenmaye-Peel	5 km	1604	321
White Strand-Glen Moar	5 km	600	120
Maughold	5 km	775	155
Port Moar-Port Cornaa	3.5 km	209	60
Port-Cornaa-Laxey	5 km	340	68
Clay Head-Howstrake	4.5 km	878	195
Douglas Head Quarry	—	60	—
Marine Drive	4.5 km	920	204
Port Soderick-Port Grenaugh	4.5 km	612	136
SW of Port Grenaugh	—	39	—
Perwick-Sound	5 km	411	82
Slieau Dhoo	—	100	—
Slieau Freoghane	—	130	—

In 1924 an unsuccessful attempt was made at nesting on the chimney of a house in Laxey and more recently roof top nesting has been noted at Douglas, Port Erin and Port St Mary.

Eggs are normally laid in early May, eggs in late April are not uncommon and the earliest date recorded was on 14th April 1932 at Peel.

Examination of pellets on the Calf has shown that breeding Herring Gulls there are largely dependant on offal, undersized fish and Norway Lobsters (King Prawns) scavenged from trawlers. The sea to the west of the Isle of Man is an important fishing ground for the Norway Lobster and the close-meshed nets used by the Northern Irish trawlers up to 1979 retained huge numbers of small fish which were then discarded. It was estimated that 34 million Whiting were rejected by these vessels in 1973 (Watson 1981) – a staggering source of food for Manx Herring Gulls, which can often be seen in their hundreds streaming out past the Stack in the direction of Ireland.

Considerable numbers gather around the coast outside the breeding season, Peel Hill with its abundance of fish offal being a particularly favoured area. Of inland waters Kerrowdhoo Reservoir and Kionslieu Dam have flocks of up to 300 during the winter, they visit refuse tips in huge numbers and 6,000 gathered in a field near Braddan Church on 26th August 1973.

Southward movement is sometimes seen from the Calf in autumn e.g., 2,500 flew south in 8 hours on 11th November 1972.

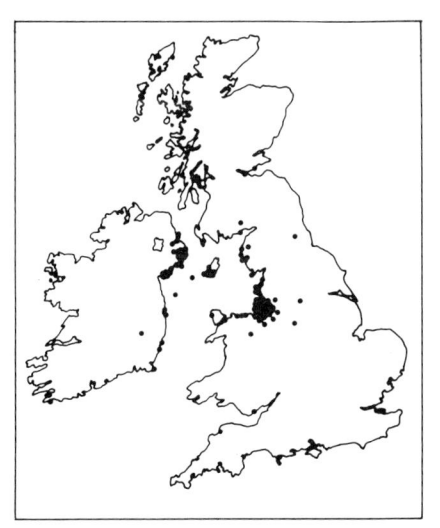

Herring Gulls ringed as pulli and recovered when immature, excluding birds from Morbihan (NW France) and Jylland (Denmark).

Herring Gulls ringed as pulli and recovered when adult. (Total for Isle of Man = 53.)

There have been nearly 200 ringing recoveries, 95% coming from north-west England and the Irish Sea coasts. Two birds, both ringed as pulli, have been found in Denmark and one has been recovered in north west France. A bird found dying near Manchester in 1980 had been ringed as a chick in 1959.

Manx: *Foillan*

Iceland Gull

Larus glaucoides

Rare winter visitor.

The first Manx record was in 1931 when a bird spent its second winter in the Ramsey area, being seen frequently from 5th October to 15th March. A first winter bird was found dead at Jurby Head on 24th February 1935, another bird in its first winter flew south past the Calf on 11th November 1972 and a second year bird was seen from the Calf on 30th August 1974.

A minimum of 9 individuals have been recorded since 1982. A second year bird was reported from the Calf on 3rd April 1982 and one was present at Peel from 29th January to 13th March 1983. An adult flew south past Peel on 16th October 1983 and between 20th January and 14th April 1984 at least three birds were seen periodically at Douglas. In 1985 individuals were seen at Peel on 11th April and near Glen Moar on 9th and 19th June.

In spite of its name the Iceland Gull breeds no nearer than Greenland, small numbers straying as far south as the British Isles every year.

Man: *Foillan Loughlinagh*

Glaucous Gull

Larus hyperboreus

Rare winter visitor.

Ralfe collected records of 4 examples of the Glaucous Gull between 1880 and 1903. During the last 60 years there have been 29 documented occurrences, 10 of these being from the Calf during the period 1969–82. The earliest autumn record was on 1st October 1934 and the last in spring 10th May 1983.

Numbers of Glaucous Gull occurrences in each month in the Isle of Man 1880–1985

Oct.	Nov.	Dec.	Jan.	Feb.	Mar.	Apr.	May
6	2	1	3	4	5	9	3

On a number of occasions birds have been present for a few days and sometimes several weeks. Certain of these records may have involved the same individual in different years – at Ramsey for example one was present from 25th February to 3rd March 1935 and 21st to 23rd February 1937, and also from 2nd to 20th April 1945 and from 23rd February to the end of March 1946. Similarly a first winter bird was seen often in the Sound from 18th October to 2nd November 1975 and the following year a 2nd winter bird visited the Kitterland on 18th November. The ages recorded for 10 of the Calf birds were as follows 3 first year, 5 second year and 2 adult.

The Glaucous Gull has a circumpolar breeding range, the nearest breeding grounds being in Iceland and the east coast of Greenland.

Great Black-backed Gull
Larus marinus

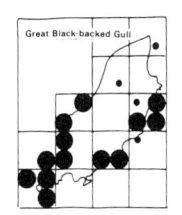

Common resident with most of population showing some dispersal. Fairly common winter visitor.

Ralfe regarded the Great Black-backed Gull as not uncommon in winter when most birds were seen singly particularly in the bays of Douglas, Peel and Ramsey. It was only occasionally seen in summer and he had no convincing evidence of breeding, although according to Williamson (1940) fishermen from the south of the Island maintained that the big 'Parson Gull' had nested on the Calf Stack since the end of the 19th century.

In 1911 a pair was found nesting at the Sloc and continued to do so annually until 1920 when there were 2 pairs and another nest was found on a stack off Bradda in 1922. Ralfe was satisfied that breeding occurred on the Calf from (at the latest) 1914. By 1923 there were 6 pairs nesting in the south-west and a further pair on the north east coast. Subsequently the first nest in the Peel area was found in 1924 and there were nests at Spanish Head in 1930 and the Marine Drive in 1931. The Calf was now the principal breeding site with 19 pairs in 1935. In 1938 there were 4–5 pairs on the Marine Drive, 6 pairs between The Chasms and Spanish Head and probably 10 pairs on the Calf. This same year saw the first reference to the Kitterland with 2 breeding pairs but in 1939 this rock had, according to Williamson, 'quite a colony' and the Calf population had probably trebled.

A census of breeding Great Black-backed Gulls was carried out in 1956 and 1957 (Slinn 1957 and 1959) and in 1969 (Slinn 1971). These studies showed a steady increase in the main Island population as can be seen in the following tables. On the Calf however peaks of about 200 pairs were reached in 1963 and 1965, the 1969 count coming during a decline which was to continue until 1974.

Only on the Calf and Kitterland have regular breeding surveys been carried out since 1969. On the Calf numbers have fluctuated between 170 and barely 100 – sinking to just 70 pairs in 1982. In contrast the Kitterland population has been stable between 50 and 60 pairs, but must now be at its accommodation limit with 70 pairs in 1982. Thirteen pairs on the coast north of Peel in 1976 and 15 pairs at Maughold in 1980 are evidence of continued expansion in these areas, while in 1984 breeding was proved on the sand cliffs north of Shellag.

Between Peel and Contrary Head there have been counts of between 66 and 106 individuals during June in recent years. Inland two pairs were found in the Slieau Freoghane Herring Gull colony in 1969 and there were at least 3 pairs there in 1981.

Slinn found that 3 was the most usual clutch size and out of 359 eggs examined in 1956 four were of the pale blue almost unmarked variety. Such eggs were found singly among clutches of normally marked eggs. The first date on which young have been found was 27th May.

In view of the well known predatory nature of the Great Black-back it

Pairs of breeding Great Black-backed Gulls–1956, 1957 and 1969 (after Slinn).

	1956	1957	1969
Sound to Port Erin	5	10	6
Bradda	12	*	30
Fleshwick to Niarbyl	3	10	18
Glenmaye to Peel	11	*	21‡
Peel Headland to Ladyport	*	4†	9
Maughold	8	*	7
Port Moar to Laxey	*	11	14
Clay Head to Onchan Head	*	4	5
Douglas Head to Port Soderick	7	*	7
Port Soderick to Port Grenaugh	8	*	5
Perwick to Sound	1	1	8
Main Island Total	55		130
Kitterland	23	25	56
Calf of Man	113	86	100
ISLE OF MAN TOTAL	191		286

* *no count*   † *1958 count*   ‡ *includes 1 nest between Niarbyl and Glenmaye.*

is interesting to note that it's prosperity on Peel Hill has failed to halt the definite increase in breeding auks in this area. They also approach carrion with a gluttonous voracity and a pair has been seen to take precedence over 4 Ravens at a sheep's carcase.

After the breeding season adult Great Black-backed Gulls appear in increased numbers both in breeding areas and at other points on the coast in August and September. The best count for Peel Hill was 267 on 11th September 1976 and counts in excess of 150 are usual there. Almost 100 have been found between Peel and Gob y Deigan and 74 on the Ayres coast in late August, while in the south there have been 120 between Strandhall and Port St Mary and nearly 50 at Derbyhaven in September. Stormy weather can bring up to 800 on to the Calf to roost.

Numbers during winter are less – up to 150 have been seen on Peel Hill in December but 30–70 birds are more usual, while elsewhere a few may be found among Herring Gulls both on the coast and inland.

There have been some 60 ringing recoveries, nearly all coming from Irish sea coasts as well as two from south west Ireland and two from the Bristol Channel. About 15 birds ringed on the Island as pulli have been recovered on the Isle of Man, but nearly all have been in spring or summer with just one in early February and another in early March the exceptions. This suggests a high degree of winter dispersal of the Manx population. One bird ringed as a nestling at Tranøy, Northern Norway, was recovered on the Isle of Man in its first December.

Manx: *Juan Mooar* = Big John

Kittiwake
Rissa tridactyla

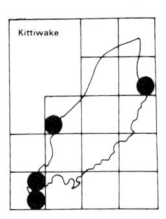

Common breeding bird and abundant passage migrant.

Ralfe described the only colony existing in the late 19th century with some of his most evocative prose. 'On the Calf of Man, a little east of the Stack, a recess in the high sheer cliffs ends in a cave, and around the entrance to this the nests are placed on the usual little shelves, the lowest being some twenty feet above high water. The deep green sea washes up to the precipices and covers the floor of the cavern, over the gloom of which the beautiful dove-like birds flit like spirits of whiteness. A little further to the east is another group of nests, but the whole form practically one settlement.' This colony, which was known to exist in the early 1860s, contained about 30–40 nests and by 1903 was thought to be declining. Ralfe later described this site as directly under the lighthouses and Williamson (1940) was told of an inlet on this part of the coast known locally as Giau Pirragh, where the Kittiwake colony used to be.

This colony was finally abandoned sometime between 1911 and 1921 and during the present century colonies have been established at Spanish Head and Black Head, Maughold, Peel Hill and at new locations on the Calf and in the Sugar Loaf area.

Spanish Head and Black Head

Coinciding with the decline of the old Calf colony a new colony was established over the mouth of the cave next to Slea ny bery (also called Slegaby) below Black Head. Although in 1907 and 1909 this was only small, by 1923 it contained hundreds of pairs and had a few years earlier overflowed to Spanish Head where a settlement appeared below the old slate quarry. Of these colonies Madoc wrote '...the numbers which collect at Black Head – part and parcel of Spanish Head – are enormous and appear to get larger every year. They nest all up the precipitous sides and on ledges within the caves which run in here; and, standing up on the cliffs of Spanish Head, one is nearly deafened.... by an ever-increasing volume of sound.' Yet counts of only 70 nests at Black Head and about 20 at Spanish Head in both 1933 and 1934 are evidence of a decline here. Varying numbers continued to occupy Spanish Head through the 1940s, but by 1947 Black Head had been deserted (Moss

1949). Nevertheless Black Head did hold 12 nests in 1952 and was occupied by between 5 and 15 pairs during the next 5 years (Slinn 1960), being finally abandoned in 1959. In 1955 Spanish Head held 78 nests, but here too numbers declined with only 43 in 1956, 32 in 1957, 36 in 1958, 30 in 1959 and only 8–10 in 1960. By 1964 the Spanish Head colony had also been abandoned.

Maughold

Kittiwakes were first noted at Maughold during the breeding season in 1945 and may have nested in 1946 (Crellin 1948). In 1948 nests were seen on the north face of Gob ny Strona and by 1951 this colony held about 50 pairs, with a further 20 pairs on a stack below the lighthouse, and there were 3 small colonies in the St Maughold's Well area (Crellin 1952). In 1953 the three areas contained 67, 22 and 22 nests, in 1955 an aggregate of 126 nests and in 1959 23, 2–3 and 40 nests. By now St Maughold's Well was becoming the principal settlement and this site accounted for most of the 160 nests counted in 1969 (Slinn 1971). Although there were only 33 pairs at Gob ny Strona and 20 pairs at the Well in 1973 it appears that the Maughold colony has increased considerably during the last decade. There were 70 nests at the Well in 1978, a total of 430 pairs in the whole area in late July 1979 and 689 birds in mid May 1980, while in 1982 there were 79 nests below the Lighthouse (the more populous Well colony not being counted).

Peel Hill

A small colony was discovered between Thistle Head and Cashtal Moar in 1947 and the following year 11 nests were counted from the sea (Moss 1949). Although perhaps overlooked, there were no further records until 1959 when 3 nests were seen. In both 1960 and 1964 there were very few nests but by 1969 there were 3 small but separate colonies. The old one persisted but there was a new settlement at Cashtal Moar – the two colonies totalling 14 nests, while 2 more nests were found on the south side of Contrary Head (Slinn 1971). In 1973 there were at least 51 occupied sites on Peel Hill, increasing to 70 in 1974 and over 100 at the colony between Thistle Head and Cashtal Moar in 1975 and 1976, when there were 11 more nests on the south side of Contrary Head. By 1980 there had been further increases with 103 nests at Cashtal Moar, 24 on south Contrary Head and a few more at Thistle Head, while the figures for these areas in 1982 were 107–111, 18 and 12–15.

The Calf

It will be recalled that the Calf was deserted as a breeding location during the second decade of the present century. However fishermen had been aware of autumn gatherings at Caigher Point and in 1955 Kittiwakes were present during the breeding season, with some 13 nests being found the following year, 20 in 1957 and 136 in 1959. The 1960's saw a remarkable increase in the Calf breeding population – by 1962 the Caigher colony had reached a peak of 162 nests and fresh colonies had appeared at Ghaw Lang and Kione Roauyr adding a further 23 nests to the total. Breeding success was abysmal, yet in 1963 the new colonies were responsible for the addition of 77 nests and in 1965 211 out of a total population of 374 pairs were at Ghaw Lang. Breeding numbers continued to increase until a peak of over 700 nests in 1969 and 1970 – by now Ghaw Lang had 445 nests and two colonies at Caigher Point held 148 and 103 nests – there were also small numbers at Culbery, Clet Elby and Kione Roauyr. Even more striking than the increases of the 1960s were the losses of the early 70s. Most marked in 1971 and 1972, there has been a slow recovery since the token presence of 1978. Ghaw Lang was deserted by 1975 and although it held a few nests in 1976 and 1977 has not been occupied since. The Caigher colonies have continued to be regularly tenanted as has Kione Roauyr but there has been no recent occupation of either Culbery or Clet Elby.

Sugar Loaf and Anvil

In 1969 2 nests were seen at the Anvil, also known as the Pulpit, and about the same time a colony was established on the cliffs opposite the Sugar Loaf rock. In 1972 and 1973 some 80 pairs were nesting at the second site, including a few nests on the rock itself. In 1975 there were 165 nests at the Anvil and 200 in the Sugar Loaf area, with about 650 young fledging from the two colonies. Numbers were appreciably less during the next few years, in 1979 there were 80 and 98 nests respectively, but in 1982 there were 227 nests in the Sugar Loaf area alone.

In summary it seems likely that the old Calf colony was gradually replaced by the Black Head/Spanish Head colony over a period of several years, starting in 1907. The latter colony probably enjoyed its greatest prosperity in the 1920s, declining gradually during the next 3 decades. Almost simultaneously during the late 1940s colonies were established well away from the south west at Maughold and Peel, with rapid increases at Maughold although the Peel settlement developed in a very hesitant fashion until the 1970s. Meanwhile the recolonisation of the Calf began in 1956 and with this development Spanish Head was soon deserted. The Calf colony increased enormously in the late 1960s only to decline just as dramatically in the early 1970s when it seemed likely that the Kittiwakes moved across to the Sugar Loaf area. At the same time the colony on Peel Hill expanded appreciably. It is tempting to suppose that Maughold and Peel were colonised from St Bees Head and southern Scotland respectively and the recovery of a Maughold ringed pullus breeding on the Calf six years later in 1959 shows that the Maughold colony contributed, at least in part to the recolonisation of the Calf.

In 1959 Slinn assessed the Manx population at 230 pairs and this figure had increased to 900 by 1969, the main island population having doubled while that on the Calf had increased almost six-fold. There seems little doubt that there was a substantial overall decline in the early 1970s but by 1975 the population was in the region of 750 pairs and had increased to 1,272 by 1985 (A. S. Moore *pers. comm.*).

Regular observations by A. S. Moore on Peel Hill have shown that Kittiwakes usually reoccupy the nesting cliffs between 17th and 23rd February. Eggs are laid from the second week in May until mid June and first young will be fledged by mid July. The last young usually get away between 6th and 16th August, but many adults linger on through August, finally leaving the cliffs during the first 2 weeks of September. In years when there is complete breeding failure at a colony the cliffs may be deserted as early as the middle of July. Breeding success on the Calf has been well documented since 1959 and it is interesting to note that during the great expansion of the Calf colonies in the 1960s there were several abysmal years in which very few young were reared. In 1968 and 1969 the number of young fledged was about half the total number of breeding pairs. Heralding the slump in years to come the majority of some 700 nests were never properly built up in 1970, less than 100 eggs were laid and only 3 young flew. In 1971 111 young fledged from 450 nests, but during the next 8 years breeding effort was very half-hearted with just a few young in 1973, 1975 and 1976. In the other years few or no eggs were laid, yet 5 km away the Sugar Loaf/Anvil colonies were enjoying tremendous success. 1980–82 has seen a revival of the Calf colonies with breeding success similar to that of the late 1960s.

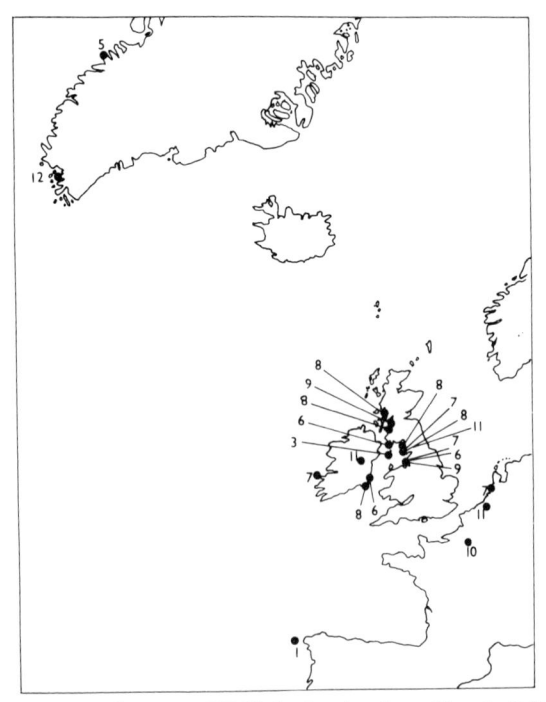

Location and month of recovery of 22 Kittiwakes ringed as pulli on the Calf of Man.

During June a flock can usually be found resting on the Ayres shore – on 19th June 1983 150 were counted at Blue Point. During August and September a large flock is present in the Caigher Point area (Calf) – 1–2,000 have been usual in recent years but formerly up to 4,000 were regular and 12,000 were seen on 2nd October 1966 although even this figure was exceeded by the 13,000+ of 16th October 1983. All age groups are present with adults usually predominating. Large movements occur in autumn, most birds flying south along the Island's west coast and past the Calf. This is seen particularly in September, but also through October to mid November, with rates sometimes exceeding 500 birds per hour and over 5,000 on the late date of 11th November 1972.

In the period 1959–82 912 Kittiwakes were ringed on the Calf producing 22 recoveries. Five of these were recovered within 4 months of ringing as pulli and had moved up to 175 km. Another bird was found off north west Spain during its first January and another on the Dutch coast in its first May. Five more recovered at ages 12–14 months were found on the coasts of Cumbria, Lancashire, Wicklow, Wexford and Kerry. The 3 Kittiwakes recovered during their third year came from Greenland and France. The remainder aged betwen 4 and 16 years came, with one exception, from the Irish sea coasts, Ayrshire and Argyllshire. The remaining bird was recovered during its 8th winter in Belgium.

Manx: *Perragh*

Sandwich Tern
Sterna sandvicensis

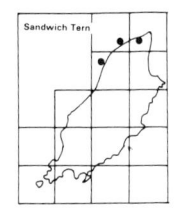

Common passage migrant.

A Sandwich Tern shot at Ramsey on 23rd August 1892 was the first Manx record, but this species receives no mention in Ralfe's supplement of 1923 so that if there were any further occurrences up to that time they must have been very rare. During the period 1925–37 1–3 birds were seen from time to time each year on spring and autumn passage and it was even claimed that a nest was found on the Ayres in 1931 and 1932. Larger parties were seen in the autumn of 1938 and then on 3rd August 1940 there were over 200 on the shore at Rue Point, the flock including many young birds. H. M. Rogers described how adults were 'feeding youngsters unable to fly' but at a later date he clearly had doubts about the veracity of this statement and in his list of 1956 wrote 'No record of breeding.' From 1940 onward Sandwich Terns did occur more frequently on passage and a few birds may have summered, but flocks of 50 at Spaldrick in late April 1947 and 110 at Langness in September 1960 were exceptional. Increasing numbers were seen during the 1960s and since 1972 it has been very easily the commonest tern occurring on passage.

Sandwich Terns have been recorded 4 times in March, the earliest being

2 over Derbyhaven Bay on 12th March 1925. This was for 33 years the earliest ever record for the British Isles. (Hudson 1973).

Parties of 30 are common from mid April onwards, the best count being 102 at Rue Point on 29th May 1980, while in 1981 there were 219 birds along the coast from Ballaugh Cronk to Ramsey, including 120 off the Ayres, on 17th June. It is not known if these birds summered on the Island or had deserted some nearby colony as a result of disturbance. The same could be said of a party of 40 on the Rue Point shore on 25th June 1979. A few birds can usually be found in early July but it is not until the last week of the month that flocks of between 150 and 200 birds arrive off the Ayres shore. These flocks, which are of adult and immature birds, may be present for several weeks, resting on the beaches in the Rue Point neighbourhood. The adults fish the shallow waters, returning frequently with sand eels to feed the young birds on shore. The earliest date for such a mixed flock was 19th July 1976 and the latest 1st September 1979. The highest count was 300 on 16th August 1984. Although the vast majority are found off the Ayres, good numbers also occur from Ballaugh round to Ramsey and parties of up to 20 frequent Langness during the autumn. During September Sandwich Terns are seen in good numbers moving south west off the Ayres coast e.g., 220 flew south west in 15 minutes on 6th September 1980. October records are not uncommon, the latest being 10 on 19th October 1976.

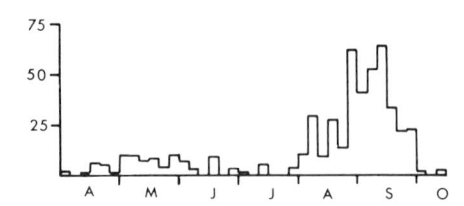

Sandwich Tern. Total bird days per five day period (Calf).

Williamson (1940) did not include the Sandwich Tern in his Ornithology of the Calf of Man and even now numbers seen from the islet are not great. Spring passage is very light, autumn (mostly early September) much heavier, but the highest day count is only 11.

A solitary ringed bird has been recovered on the Isle of Man: one ringed as a nestling on the Farne Islands in late June was found at Blue Point 10 weeks later. Most of the young birds viewed through a telescope one day in July 1979 had been ringed and dazzling or clap-netting on the Ayres could be very interesting.

Roseate Tern
Sterna dougallii

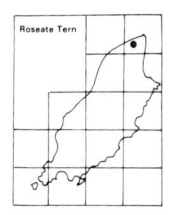

Rare passage migrant.

The first Manx records were in 1955 when on 28th July two were seen at Rue Point and three days later near the Point of Ayre (Cowin 1956). Two years later Cowin described in his diary (unpublished) how he and a companion were almost certain that a nest with one egg at Smeale Ayres on 21st July was that of a Roseate Tern. In 1975 three independant observers suspected that a pair was present at Rue Point in late May and early June – courtship feeding was observed and a nest was alleged to have been found. Most of the small breeding population of Britain and Ireland is to be found around the Irish sea in colonies in Co Wexford, Northern Ireland and Anglesey.

There have been 7 other records of 1 or 2 birds – 3 being from Langness, 3 from the Calf and one from the Ayres. The earliest date was 15th April 1960 and the latest 29th September 1978. There has been one other April record, 1 in mid June (Ayres 1979) and 2 in late August.

One bird, ringed as a nestling in Wexford Harbour, was recovered when 6 years old on the Ayres.

Common Tern
Sterna hirundo

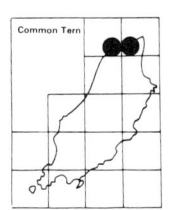

Regular passage migrant and scarce breeding species.

Only very occasionally was the Common Tern identified during the 19th century and it was not until 1911 that a small colony was found breeding close to a larger collection of Arctic Terns. A few years later small numbers were widely scattered over a considerable area of the Ayres. During the early 1930s both Common and Arctic Terns had a number of successful breeding seasons, although the former remained in the minority continuing to nest in small scattered colonies. By 1938 Common Terns had become the more abundant with over 50 pairs at Rue Point and more at Ballaghennie (Williamson 1939) and Glasman (1944) provided the first accurate figures for this species when he found 24 pairs nesting on the Smeale Ayres and another 12 pairs at Ballaghennie compared with 13 pairs of Arctic Terns at the Point of Ayre and a small colony some miles down the coast. Comparable numbers nested in several years up to 1948, but numbers then declined and it seems that no more than 7 pairs have nested in any of the last 30 years. The majority of breeding records come from the beach between Rue Point and Ballaghennie although Common Terns did breed in some numbers at the Point of Ayre during the thirties and early forties and there have also been recent nests between Rue Point and Blue Point. At least one pair nested in the gravel pit south west of the Point of Ayre in 1976 and 4 nests were located in the southern pit in 1985. In an average year eggs are laid during the first two weeks of June, the earliest recorded date being two clutches of 3 at Rue Point on 29th May 1938. When nests have failed repeat clutches may be laid in July and eggs of this species have been found up to 25th July (1941).

On passage medium sized terns are seen mainly along the south coast between Port St Mary and Derbyhaven and on the northern coasts from Peel round to Ramsey. Rarely are they specifically identified. In some years 'Commic' terns first appear during the second half of April, while in others they may not be seen until well into May. There is an exceptional record of 2 over Peel Bay on 11th February 1926, otherwise the earliest record is of one, also at Peel, on 11th April 1972. In the autumn there have been a few records during the last week of October 4 (identified as *S. hirundo*) were at Peel on 11th November 1940 and one was seen off the Lhen shore on 31st December 1972. Small parties of 2–6 birds are usual on passage, so that 50 at Poyllvaaish on 29th April 1947 and 17 at Derbyhaven on 12th

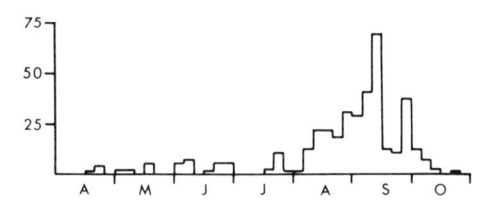

Common/Arctic Tern. Total bird days per five day period (Calf).

September 1965 were quite noteworthy. On the Calf 'Commic' terns are occasionally seen in spring, but occur principally in September flying south through the Sound.

Manx: *Gibbyn Gant* = Gannet of the Sand-eels. *Spyrryd. Spithag*

Arctic Tern
Sterna paradisaea

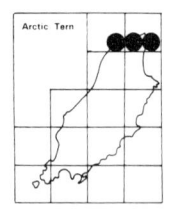

Regular passage migrant and not uncommon breeding species.

During the second half of the 19th century the Arctic Tern suffered a marked decline in abundance as a Manx breeding bird. In 1862 J. C. Crellin wrote 'There are generally hundreds of birds of this kind come to breed, but this year the people in the neighbourhood said that there were very few. Indeed though I was in the midst of them and their breeding ground for several hours, I think that I never saw more than eight at a time. Of course there were a great many more than that number, but there used to be dozens of them in sight at once.' Between 1896 and 1905 the breeding population was steady at about 30 pairs, the majority being in one colony with a few nests some distance away. The inference from Ralfe's supplement is that the terns enjoyed only mixed success over the next 2 decades, but with a succession of good breeding seasons between 1929 and 1935 numbers increased considerably, although the only published numerical data was a reference to over 40 pairs at a new nesting site in 1935. There were many nests at the Point of Ayre in 1939, but this site (at that time the principal one) held only a dozen pairs during the early forties, a period during which the Common Tern was the more abundant species. Typical of the fluctuating breeding numbers were two colonies of 25 pairs at the Point of Ayre and Ballaghennie in 1945, but numbers seem to have been low throughout the early fifties. During the last 25 years between 25 and 50 pairs have bred along the shore in a rather scattered fashion from Blue Point to the Point of Ayre, with a further more compact colony (first mentioned in 1955) on the east coast $1\frac{1}{2}$ km from the Point of Ayre. During the period 1939–65 the main colony seems to have been at the Point of Ayre, but recently the beach there has been untenanted although there have been colonies at two gravel pits south west and south of the Point. The pit to the south west had 25–30 pairs in 1975 and 1976, when there was also a substantial Black-headed Gull colony, but only 8 in 1979 by which time the gullery had disappeared. In 1982 and 1983 the pit to the south of the Point has held up to 25 pairs together with a rather larger colony of Black-headed Gulls. At Rue Point another gravel pit has been occupied by up to 7 pairs since at least 1979 (Cullen 1980). A few pairs nested inland at Ballakesh Ayre in the early 1970s.

As with the other terns breeding success has varied considerably due sometimes to freak tides or inclement weather and sometimes to excessive human disturbance or wholesale egg collection. Eggs are usually laid during the first fortnight in June, the earliest date being a clutch of 2 on 26th May 1908. Repeat clutches may be laid well into July and a bird has been seen sitting as late as 2nd August (1967).

The remarks relating to extreme dates under Common Tern apply to birds not specifically identified as *S. hirundo* or *S. paradisaea* – the earliest definite Arctic Terns were several at the Lhen on 16th April 1944 and the latest were one over the Calf on 27th October 1981 and 3 over Derbyhaven Bay on 4th November 1948. Three birds ringed as pulli on the Ayres have been recovered. All were found dead in the same area 10, 10 and 16 years later.

Bridled Tern

Sterna anaethetus

Very rare vagrant.

An adult Bridled Tern flew through the Sound on 5th September 1980. This was the 7th British record and only the second Bridled Tern to be identified in vivo. (Jennings 1981).

Little Tern
Sterna albifrons

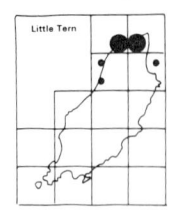

Not uncommon summer visitor.

The Little Tern was first identified on the Isle of Man in 1898 when Ralfe found a colony of about 20 nests, almost certainly at Rue Point. During the next 25 years several sites along the Ayres shore were used and numbers were sometimes 'very considerable'. As with the larger terns the thirties were years of increasing prosperity and it is only very recently that anything approaching the figures for 1938, when there were 50 pairs at Rue Point and another colony at Ballaghennie, has been achieved since. It is likely that the annual number of breeding Little Terns was between 10 and 25 pairs during the 40 years up to 1979 when a complete census in late June yielded 43 pairs (Cullen 1980). In 1985 there were 57–60 breeding pairs. Rue Point has been the most consistently tenanted site, but Little Terns have bred at least once to the west of the Lhen (5 nests in 1951) and as far east as the Point of Ayre. In the summer of 1979 there were two isolated nests and 7 groups of between 2 and 10 nests between the Lhen and a point half way between Ballaghennie and the Point of Ayre, with the greatest concentration between Blue Point and Rue Point. Here there were 10 nests over a 50 m stretch of beach with 7 of these in a 15 m stretch. South west of the Lhen the coast has received little study and it is possible that nesting has taken place unnoticed. Thirteen birds were seen over the Sartfield shore on 1st June 1975 and 2 pairs were present between Glen Wyllin and Orrisdale during the 4 weeks up to 14th June 1977.

May is often well advanced before the first Little Terns are seen, there have been occasional records during the last 3 days of April and the earliest date was 23rd April 1944. In some years they are not seen after mid August and September records are very rare – the latest being 19th September 1935. Unlike the larger terns, Little Terns are scarcely seen away from the breeding area, in fact Ramsey Bay is the only locality where they occur regularly. There is just one record for the Calf – 4 birds on 29th August 1963.

It thus seems that birds breeding elsewhere do not pass through the Island. Just 2 pulli ringed on the Ayres have been recovered. One was found dead at Douglas 26 days later, suggesting that southward passage may take place down the Island's east coast, while the remains of the other were found in a nearby Kestrel's nest on the day of ringing.

Manx: *Gant Beg*

Black Tern
Chlidonias niger

Uncommon passage migrant.

Ralfe described an immature bird shot on Langness on 15th October 1903. An adult was seen at Port St Mary in May 1913 (the only spring record), but 54 years were to elapse before the Black Tern was again seen on the Isle of Man. Between 1967 and 1984 9 years produced records of this species, the earliest was on 31st July 1975 and most have been seen between 3rd September and 16th October. Although sometimes seen singly, small parties are perhaps more typical. In 1969 6 or 7 were seen at Langness on 22nd and 27th September and in 1977 there were 3 at Port St Mary on 3rd September, 5 off the Ayres on 25th September, 3 at Derbyhaven on 29th September and 2 at Langness on 1st October. There have been no inland reports and the 17 records have come from the north coast (4), Peel (2), the Calf (2), Port St Mary (3) and Langness/Derbyhaven (6).

Guillemot
Uria aalge

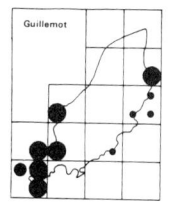

Common summer visitor and abundant passage migrant.

Remains were identified in the Perwick midden deposit of approximately AD 90.

The breeding of the Guillemot in the Isle of Man was mentioned by Willughby, who described the method by which the eggs, young and adult birds were harvested in the 17th century (Ray 1678), but it was the writers at the end of the next century who described the quite incredible numbers which bred on the Calf. Townley (1791) wrote vividly of his visit to the Calf 'We then went down to the boat and rowed round the greatest part of the Island, which presented us with some of the most striking, romantic scenes I ever had met with; and with so great and such a mixed multitude of birds, as no one spot in the universe can (I believe) exhibit, for their numbers were so astonishingly great indeed, that I do not know how to liken them, but by Scriptural comparison, as the stars of the firmament, or the sands upon the sea shore, which are beyond the art of numeration.'

Likewise Feltham (1798) wrote 'In the west side of the Calf the rocks are stupendous, and the quantity of birds called muirs etc., incredible; whether sitting on the rocks with their young, floating on the surface of the sea, or filling the intermediate air they give vivacity to the scene; and their shrill voices "which carol aloud and in chorus join," arrest attention and please one from its novelty.'

Ralfe described the Guillemot as nesting almost exclusively on the high cliffs of the south west part of the Island. On the Calf they were particularly plentiful on the Stack and the precipices under the lighthouse, and also nested on the east coast of the islet. There was a colony to the west of Spanish Head and they were numerous on the Sugar Loaf and adjacent cliffs. Some 150 birds nested in a picturesque cavernous situation on Bradda (identifiable as Amulty) with a few more a little to the west. A few birds nesting with Razorbills at Stroin Vuigh in 1894 were no longer present in 1899, and he thought that a few bred on Peel Hill, a site which had 2 dozen pairs by 1923. By 1934 Madoc was able to describe considerable numbers breeding at Maughold Head and in 1953 they were thought to be nesting on the Marine Drive.

Bourne (1956 and 1957) counted the *Alcidae* in the south west of the Island in 1955 and 1956 and Slinn (1971) conducted complete censuses in 1967, 1969 and 1970. Since 1974 H. S. Collister has carried out a number of counts in the Sugar Loaf area and A. S. Moore has made repeated counts of sea birds on Peel Hill throughout several seasons. These have been published in the appropriate Manx Bird Reports, while on the Calf successive Wardens have furnished figures since 1959. A selection of these results are tabulated opposite illustrating the Guillemot's varying prosperity at different colonies. The historic settlement around Spanish Head (and at Black Head) was the Island's largest in 1956 but was virtually extinct in 1967 and is not known to have been occupied since 1970. The Sugar Loaf area, which includes the Rock itself and the adjacent coast from the Chasms to Kione ny Ghoggan, has, allowing for yearly fluctuations, remained fairly stable.

Numbers on Peel Hill were at their lowest in 1970 and have increased steadily since, more especially since 1979. On the Calf a peak of 250 pairs was reached in 1964 but there were little more than 100 pairs from 1970 to 1977, since which there have been steady increases to 250 pairs in 1982 and 350 by 1985. Counts at the smaller mainland colonies have been less frequent, but at Maughold 445 birds in 1985 represented a dramatic increase on the 80 birds of 1982 and the 16–25 noted in 1967–70. Bourne and Slinn found 32–54 birds at Amulty, where there were 40 in early June 1984, while south of Contrary Head, where there were 10 birds in 1967 and 16 in 1970, there were 64 in early July 1982. Slinn's counts included 8 at Aldrick, up to 23 near Bay Fine and 14–15 at Stroin Vuigh, but there are no recent details. Overall the Guillemot population of the Isle of Man declined markedly between 1956 and 1970 but has recovered and is now greater than at any time during the last 30 years – this is due in part to increases on the Calf, but mainly to the considerable expansion on Peel Hill.

Guillemots, like Razorbills, start to reoccupy the cliffs of Peel Hill, some-

Guillemot: Counts of birds at the principal Manx colonies during the breeding season. Figures for the Calf other than 1955–6 refer to breeding pairs

	'55 '56	'67 '69 '70	'74 '75 '76	'79 '80 '81 '82	'85
Peel Hill	NC NC	273 197 105	137 180 229*	312*490 542 645	698
Spanish Head	380 493	5 5 2	0 0 0	0 0 0 0	3
Sugar Loaf area	530 421	443 369 284	438*510*467*	NC NC NC 423	677*
Calf of Man	235 214	148 125 100	100 100 100	180 170 215 250	350

* *Late June or early July counts, perhaps inflated by non-breeding birds. NC = No count.*

times in late January but more often during February, and after a peak in late June or early July they have all gone by the beginning of August.

Autumn movements are not separable from those of the Razorbill. Rarely are Guillemots seen on land in early winter, but there were 10 on the cliffs south of the Ladder on Peel Hill on 15th December 1974.

Guillemots no doubt featured in the great sea bird wreck following the gales in January 1839 and Kermode mentions 700 being found dead on Douglas shore for no obvious reason around 1869. During the present century there have been a number of oiling incidents, but in autumn of 1969 there was an immense disaster in the Irish sea for which no cause was found. Over 15,000 seabirds were found on the beaches of both sides of the Irish Sea and the total kill may have been in excess of 50,000 (Cramp et al. 1974). On the south and west coasts of the Isle of Man almost 400 seabird corpses were found between 29th September and 30th November, over 370 being Guillemots. Slinn (1971) estimated that the true death toll was 600–700 birds. Some were oiled but the majority were completely free or only had traces of oil in their plumage. A sample of 52 Guillemots were weighed, all were under weight, the majority being between 550 and 700 Gm (the usual range being 800–1150 Gm).

The Manx breeding population belongs to the southern race *U.a. albionis*, but the northern race *U.a. aalge* occurs frequently in winter and has been seen offshore in summer. The racial characteristics were examined in 98 birds from the autumn wreck of 1969 and the results are tabulated below.

Race	Adult	Immature	Juvenile	Total
Southern	36	24	8	68
Intermediate	4	13	2	19
Northern	5	5	1	11
Total	45	42	11	98

Occasional examples of the 'bridled' form are identified at Manx colonies. According to Southern (1939) they constitute 0.5% of the Manx population and this form becomes increasingly common further north and to some extent west e.g., Islay 8.0%, St Kilda 16.5% and Shetland around 25%.

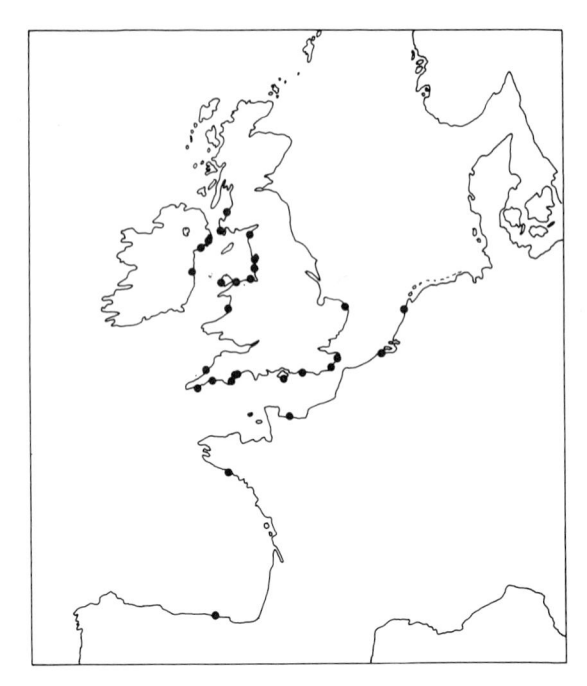

Guillemot ringing recoveries.

The ringing of 504 Guillemots on the Calf between 1959 and 1982 produced 31 recoveries from many parts of the coast south and west of a line from the Kintyre peninsula to Norfolk (including 3 on the Isle of Man) and abroad from northern Spain to Holland. Eight of the 31 were recovered 8 or more years after ringing, the Manx longevity record being held by a bird ringed as a pullus in July 1967, which was found dead in County Dublin 11 years 10 months later.

Manx: *Stronnag. Chennell*

Razorbill

Alca torda

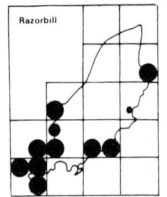

Common summer visitor and abundant passage migrant.

The Razorbill, present in the Perwick midden deposit dated AD90, has been recognised as a plentiful breeding species since Willughby's visit to the Isle of Man in 1660. Ray (1678) gives a rather quaint account of the Manx auk colonies under the heading of Razorbill although the description applies principally to the Guillemot. 'It lays, sits, and breeds up its Young on the ledges of the craggy Cliffs and steep Rocks by the Sea-shores, that are broken and divided into many as it were stairs or shelves, together with the *Coulternebs* and *Guillemots*. The *Manks* men are wont to compare these Rocks, with the Birds sitting on them in breeding time to an Apothecaries shop, the ledges of the Rocks resembing the shelves, and the Birds the pots. About the Isle of *Man* are very high Cliffs, broken in this manner into many ledges one above another from top to bottom. They are wont to let down men by ropes from the tops of the Cliffs to take away the Eggs and young ones. They take also the birds themselves when they are sitting upon their Eggs, with snares fastened to the tops of long poles, and so put about their necks.'

Feltham (1798) specifically mentioned Razorbills and Puffins among the plentiful rock birds of the Calf and 100 years later Ralfe was able to describe the Razorbill as more widely distributed, if not more abundant than the Guillemot. The main breeding colonies were at Spanish Head and on the Calf, where they were plentiful on the western cliffs and the Stack and at Kione Roauyr. They also nested at Amulty (Bradda), in small numbers between Fleshwick and Stroin Vuigh and between Glenmaye and Peel Hill. Kermode knew of one or two nesting around Laxey and Maughold but by 1903 Ralfe believed that they no longer did so.

During the present century the breeding population on Peel Hill increased from about 12 pairs in 1921 to 84 pairs in 1969 with little recent change. The 1969 survey yielded colonies of 26 at Traie Lagagh, 11 at Stroin Vuigh, 6 at the Sloc, 23 at Amulty, 7 at Bradda Head, 17 near Bay Fine and 11 at Aldrick (Slinn 1971). Although Ralfe gave no figures it seems likely that the colonies at Traie Lagagh and between Port Erin and the Sound have increased, the others altering little. Bourne (1956) carried out a survey of the south west and the Calf in 1955 and found 185–205 birds in the Spanish Head/Black Head area, almost 300 in the Chasms/Sugar Loaf area and 221 at more than a dozen small settlements on the Calf. He considered that these figures represented a severe reduction in the population and Slinn's figures for 1969 confirmed this trend with totals of 46, 121 and 150 apparently occupied sites for these three areas. Since then Calf numbers have been relatively stable but there have been further reductions in the other two areas. In contrast the east coast has seen definite expansion. By 1931 Maughold had been re-colonised and had 53 pairs in 1969. A colony was established at Wallberry on the Marine Drive about 1965 and had 12 pairs in 1969, while between Gob Lhiack and Pistol Castle there were 5–7 pairs in the period 1967–70 and probably more than 20 by 1981. 1969 remains the only year in which there was a complete census and Slinn put the total Manx population at 576 pairs.

At Peel the first Razorbills arrive in early February. Peak counts in excess of 300 birds are usually achieved in late March or early April and there is a further mid-summer peak before numbers decline quite quickly during July, and August records are rare.

Autumn passage of Razorbills and Guillemots off the Calf from late September to the end of November is often heavy with 1–2,000 birds per hour flying south, usually soon after dawn. Day counts of over 6,000 occurred on 8th and 9th October 1980. During the winter months Razorbills are

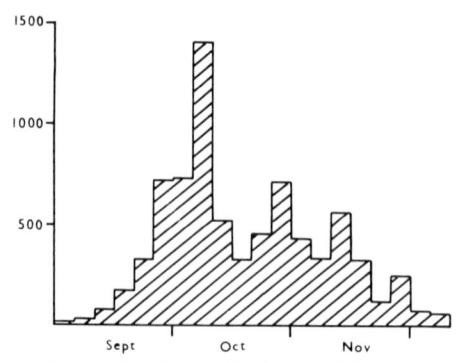

Razorbill/Guillemot. Average bird days per five day period during autumn passage (Calf).

plentiful further out to sea and large numbers of auks have been seen over the Wart Bank in mid January.

Wrecks of auks occur from time to time, the first such event being recorded by Train in 1845. He relates how thousands of sea-birds were found dead on the beach, mainly around Spanish Head after the great tempest of 6th and 7th January 1839 and that among them Razorbills were very numerous.

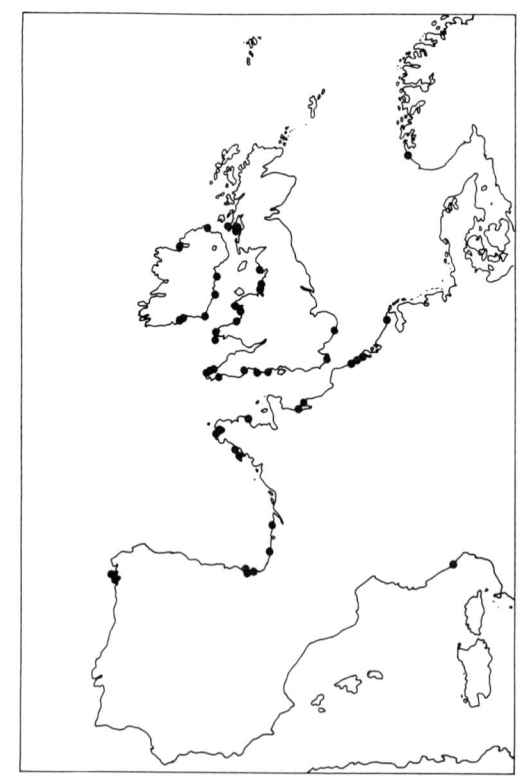

Razorbill ringing recoveries.

In the period 1959 to 1982, 834 Razorbills were ringed on the Calf yielding 47 recoveries ranging from Donegal to south west Norway, the low countries, Italy and north west Spain. One bird ringed as a nestling on the Calf was found breeding at Skokholm 5 years later and again the following summer. The retrapping of more than 40 Calf-ringed birds has produced two notable longevity records – one ringed as a pullus in 1960 bred close to its natal site until at least 1980, while another first ringed in 1959 was retrapped in 1984.

Manx: *Coltrag*

Great Auk

Pinguinus impennis

Extinct. Probable former summer visitor.

Among the remains of many birds and animals found in a midden deposit in a cave at Perwick Bay by F. J. Radcliffe in 1969 were 2 bones of a Great Auk. One was a furcula or wish-bone (formed by the fusion of right and left clavicle) identified by D. Bramwell by comparison with an almost identical specimen in the Zoological department of the Manchester Museum. The other – a femur, 72.4 mm long, was recognised on the basis of its auk features and great size. The date yielded by C14 radiography was approximately AD90. (Garrad 1972).

Some thirty years before this find Williamson (1939) had identified a sepia-drawing in the British Museum as the earliest illustration of the Great Auk made in the British Isles. It was one of a number of drawings made by Daniel King in 1652 for his *Vale-Royall of England, or, The County Palatine of Chester Illustrated* to decorate the 34 page appendix by James Chaloner *A Short Treatise of the Isle of Man*. Unlike King's other engravings of Manx scenery the Great Auk (and another picture of Gannets) did not eventually appear in the book. The drawing shows an easily recognisable adult Great Auk in breeding plumage on a flat seaside rock and bears the caption 'Theis Kind of birds are aboute the Isle of Man.' Earlier students, including Ralfe, had assumed it to be a misshapen Puffin *Fratercula arctica*. Manx historical literature contains no reference to the species.

Prompted by Williamson's paper John Gawne (1944) wrote 'This must be the bird Bill Corlett, a Port St Mary fisherman, told me about in the summer of 1895. It was a flightless bird which used to come at a certain time to the Flat Rocks south of the Point, and Bill Corlett pronounced the name as 'Big Uig.' He had been told about it when a boy (perhaps about 1840–50) by old men, the same as he told me when I was 13 years and he 65. He was a very intelligent old man and died, aged 90 years, in 1920. I think the time of year those old fishermen would be likely to see the birds would be between April and the end of July, as that was the time they would be passing the Flat Rocks on their way to the fishing-grounds. From August to the end of September they went to fish off Douglas in the opposite direction.'

This suggests that the Great Auk could have been a summer visitor to the Isle of Man up to about 1790. One was caught at Waterford in 1834, the last British Great Auk was captured on Stac an Armin, St Kilda in 1840 and done to death as a witch, and ultimate extinction was achieved on Eldey, Iceland, when a male and female and their egg were destroyed in June 1844.

Black Guillemot

Cepphus grylle

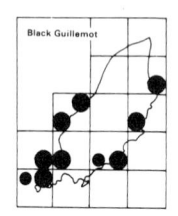

Not uncommon resident.

Jardine's assumption that the Black Guillemot bred in the Isle of Man (1838–43) was confirmed by Crellin some 20 years later, although numbers were only small. Kermode (1901) listed the Sea Pigeon as breeding in small numbers at Maughold, Clay Head, Peel and the south of the Island and in 1905 Ralfe knew of four or five nesting localities, some very close together, on the west coast and at least 2 on the east side of the Island. Ralfe's largest colony held about 20 pairs and was probably one of several between Raclay and Eairnyerey below Lhiatte ny Beinnee. Here they nested in holes under the top of a 60 ft cliff and at another site among fallen boulders just a few yards above high tide. He thought that Black Guillemots had probably increased during the previous 20 years. One of the east coast sites must have been Maughold, where Bell obtained eggs in 1905 and 1908, but clearly fear of egg collectors was responsible for Ralfe's unwillingness to reveal precisely the nesting sites of this singularly attractive seabird. Whether at this time Peel Hill was a breeding station is not clear, but from 1921 to at least 1934 numbers increased steadily in this area. Counts of 20 birds in March and April were typical and in 1932 58 were counted along the Patrick coast on 6th May and 35 on the sea opposite the Peel nesting site on 2nd July. 40–50 were present off Peel Hill during the summer of 1934 but the paucity of subsequent records suggests a considerable slump. During the same period there are records of up to 8 birds at Maughold and in 1932 a new colony was discovered on the east coast, probably at Clay Head, where 4 years later 50 were seen on the sea in early April. Published breeding records for Clay Head continued until 1939 and 3 were seen near Port Soderick in May 1940, but from that date until 1952 breeding records of just a few pairs came exclusively from Peel and Maughold.

During the last thirty years breeding has been reported from about ten locations.

Bradda

Slinn (1964) listed 2 pairs at Amulty in each year from 1953 to 1956 and 8 birds were seen in 1954 and 1955 (Bourne 1955 and 1956). In 1969 there was only one apparently occupied site, but there was one count of 12 birds the following year (Slinn 1971). There were counts of 30 birds in mid April 1975 and early August 1979 and regular study throughout the breeding seasons of 1981 and 1982 by H. S. Collister produced 15 and 11 pairs respectively. Although most of these were around Amulty there were also at least 3 pairs between the Carn and Bradda Mines (west coast) in 1981.

Fleshwick to Eairnyerey

Between 1952 and 1958 2–4 pairs were found north of Fleshwick by Slinn and in 1969 he again thought 2 sites were occupied, although in the following year his best count was 13. August counts of 14 in 1977 and 45–50 in 1978 give little indication of breeding numbers, but Collister found 13 breeding pairs in 1981 and 16 pairs in 1982. He had a peak count of 60 birds on 19th July 1981.

Glenmaye to Contrary Head

Slinn found 2 pairs at Traie Lagagh in 1969 since which peak counts during the breeding season have steadily increased so that 36 birds were counted along this stretch of coast on 21st June 1981.

Peel Hill

Only 1–2 pairs nested on Peel Hill during the 1950s but a flock of 17 was seen in early May 1964 and by 1969 there were 7 occupied sites. A. S. Moore has done repeated counts along this coast most years since 1973 and numbers have steadily increased with peaks of 30–40 birds during June from 1976 to 1981, 54 in late May 1982 and 78 on 8th May 1985. He assessed the breeding population between Peel and Glenmaye during the 5 km square Atlas Survey at 28 pairs. The colony to the north of Thistle Head is now the most important Manx breeding site.

Maughold Head

Slinn found 5 pairs in 1953, but only 3 in 1955 and 2 in 1961 and 1969. Five to six birds were occasionally seen during the breeding season and there were 13 on the sea in mid June 1978. Since then up to 16 have been seen in July perhaps reflecting a slight increase in breeding numbers.

Clay Head

One to two pairs were present in 1959, 1961 and 1970. Few recent figures are available but 40 were seen on 19th April 1976 and there have been counts of up to 20 birds in early July 1981 and mid April 1982. During the 1977–81 Atlas survey the population was estimated at 10 pairs.

Gob Lhiack

Two pairs were present in 1961 and 3–4 pairs in 1974. Counts of 14 in early May 1977, 16 in late June 1981, and midsummer counts of 21 in 1983 and 1984 suggest that breeding numbers are also increasing here.

Perwick Bay

Five to six birds have been seen during the breeding season since 1979 with a peak count of 12 on 20th June 1982.

Bay Fine

Up to 5 birds are usually seen from boats going from Port Erin to the Calf during May and June probably indicating a breeding population of 2–3 pairs.

During the breeding season there have been occasional records from *Stroin Vuigh*, *Laxey Head*, the *Marine Drive* (where one pair at least has bred recently), *Santon Head*, the *Chasms* and *Spanish Head*. One to two pairs have bred south of *Ballanayre Strand* since 1980. On the *Calf* Black Guillemots have been prospecting potential breeding sites for many years on the northwest coast and in 1978 an attempt at breeding may have taken place near Culbery, where a bird on the sea and another somewhere in a deep fissure ashore were heard calling to each other. Sightings from the Calf were rare before 1969 – further evidence of increases on the Isle of Man since then.

In summary the Manx population suffered a marked decline in the early 1940s, which continued for about 30 years, but from an admittedly underestimated 17 pairs in 1969 there have been steady increases and 80–85 pairs now probably nest on the Isle of Man.

Nest sites are usually hidden in holes and behind boulders and access from the land is often tricky so that relatively few nests have been inspected. Eggs have been found as early as 21st May (Peel 1932) and as late as 31st July, when two eggs hatched at Maughold Head in 1947 (Crellin 1948).

Black Guillemots start to move away from Peel Hill in late July and rarely are more than one or two birds seen there from about 10th August until mid October. Some are then present through the winter months, increasing during February and March and reaching a peak at the end of that month or in early April. Numbers in early spring have increased during the last decade with counts of 61 in both 1979 and 1981 and a record 114 on 31st March 1982. Parties are seen off the precipitous west coast during winter and are regular in Derbyhaven and to a lesser extent Douglas Bay from October to February. At Derbyhaven 2–6 birds are usual and there have been peak counts of 15 on 28th November 1976 and 12 on 13th January 1974.

A few Black Guillemots have been ringed at Peel and Maughold, but there have been no recoveries.
Manx: *Caillagh Ghoo*

Little Auk
Alle alle

Rare winter visitor.

Ralfe described the Little Auk as a rare straggler which was the victim of winter storms, and by 1923 had only collected 5 records involving 6 storm-driven birds, 3 of which were found at inland locations. The last 60 years have produced a further 61 records involving 94 individuals.

Birds are most often seen close to land following gales and a number have been washed ashore dead or dying. The majority of records are however of healthy birds such as those often seen in Peel Bay by Clementson (1946) – 'it is an enjoyable sight to watch this small sea-bird complacently "ducking" up and down as it rides the rough waves, now and then diving into the midst of an oncoming breaker, and always appearing to be "calm, cool and collected," whatever the weather conditions may be.' It was sufficiently familiar at Peel to have earned the name *Yeean Saggayrt Beg* or Little Parson Bird. Inland records have been surprisingly scarce – one was found dead below wires at Sulby in December 1938 and another was found in a Port Erin street in January 1975, but the most notable record was of a party of at least 11 birds flying over the northern slopes of Cronk Fedjag (Patrick) on 26th January 1944, one being struck down by a Kestrel (and now preserved in the Manx Museum).

A few periods have produced more records than usual, most notably the autumn of 1927 when 4 were seen off Fort Island on 28th October, with 2 more on 6th November, 2 at Onchan on 10th November and 1 off Fort Island on 26th December. Four corpses were found at Derbyhaven on 4th January 1930 with 4 more on Douglas shore in February 1935, while in 1955 individuals were seen at Port Erin on 4 dates between 8th January and 7th March. Most records have occurred in December and January and extreme dates were 1 off Caigher Point on the Calf on 9th September 1965 and one off Maughold Head on 30th May 1946. They are most commonly seen at Peel and Derbyhaven with most of the remaining records coming from the intervening west and south coasts.
Manx: *Coltrag Veg*

Puffin

Fratercula arctica

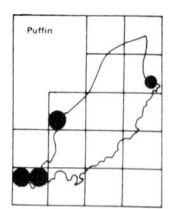

Not uncommon summer visitor.

The earliest evidence of the Puffin's presence on the Isle of Man comes from the midden deposit in the Perwick Bay cave dated at AD90 (Garrad 1972). Willughby, distinguishing this species from the Manx Shearwater (for long known locally as the Puffin), described it as breeding yearly in great numbers on the Isle of Man (Ray 1678). Recalling his visit to the Calf on 11th July, Townley (1791) wrote 'We got a second refreshment from our stores, to which was added, by the very civil old lady, a dish of cold parrots, with an assurance from her that they were excellent food, and that they afforded a broth, or soup, that was uncommonly good and nourishing. I tasted one of the birds and found it savoury, not ungrateful to the palate, and was therefore induced to purchase the new-taken ones, in order to try their excellency in the article of broth, or soup, which was so highly commended by the old lady.' Later he wrote 'We had our parrot soup for dinner, and better was never tasted, turtle soup excepted.' In 1903 Ralfe wrote that they were still very common on the Calf, especially around Kione Roauyr – 'in the season the agitated tideways of the Sound are dotted with their swarming multitudes.' They also nested in smaller numbers at Spanish Head and in 1896 a large colony had been noted among the fallen stones at the bottom of the cliff at the Chasms. Puffins had also been seen during the breeding season at Bradda, Peel Hill and Maughold. By 1923 the breeding grounds in the south west had extended and numbers increased, while at Maughold there was a growing colony with about 30 pairs in 1922 and 60 pairs the following year. This was probably the peak of the Puffin's expansion on the Calf and in the south west because by the 1933 it was no more than 'quite common' on the islet and in 1939 there were very few, Kione Roauyr and Culbery being virtually deserted, while there are no published records for the adjacent mainland until 1940. At Maughold the decline was later with good numbers in the early 1930s and an estimated 60 breeding pairs in 1941; the subsequent fortunes of the several Manx colonies are as follows:

Calf

No details are available for the forties and early fifties but counts of 12 and 16 birds in 1955 and 1956 (Bourne 1956 and 1957) are evidence of the very tenuous hold of the Puffin on the islet. When the Observatory was established in 1959 there were at least 8 breeding pairs and numbers steadily increased to 24 pairs in 1965, 30 pairs in the early seventies and about 65 pairs in 1979. Since then about 40 pairs have bred annually. The best count was 153 birds on 5th July 1976.

Spanish Head

There were a few birds in the early forties and a small but thinning colony in 1947. Although about 10 birds were present in 1950 and 1955, there were none in 1956. Puffins were present in 1966 and 1967 and Slinn found 9 occupied sites in 1969 and 14 in 1970. Counts of 24 birds in 1976 and 1982 suggest that numbers have at least been maintained.

Chasms and Anvil

Occasional counts between 1941 and 1952 never exceeded 16 birds and although 28 Puffins were seen off the Anvil in late July 1955, subsequent counts have been of 10–20 birds, mostly in the Anvil area with an estimated 8 occupied sites in 1970.

Maughold Head

This colony declined sharply from 60 pairs in 1941 to a very few in 1944. Small numbers continued to breed with a minimum of 5 pairs in 1956 and 16 occupied sites in 1969. Numbers have since declined with a probable population of just 3 pairs during the Atlas survey of 1977–81.

Peel Hill

Up to 6 were seen at Contrary Head in 1933, but counts in 1934, 1942, 1955 and 1956 did not exceed this figure. There may have been a slight increase since – 12 birds were seen in 1959 and Slinn credited Peel Hill with 9 occupied sites in 1969 and 1970. A count of 39 birds was made in 1975 and, numbers having approached this figure in several years since, a peak of 53 was achieved on 21st July 1983. During the Atlas survey of 1977–81 it was thought that up to 14 pairs bred.

The decline of the Puffin between 1925 and 1940 was much greater than that of the larger auks. In 1959 there were probably less than 20 breeding pairs on the Isle of Man, but a modest recovery has taken place with a probably under-estimated 59 pairs in 1969 (Slinn 1972) and perhaps 100 pairs in 1979.

Birds first appear on the sea close to their breeding stations during the last 2 weeks of March, coming ashore in early April. Their disappearance in late summer is synchronous with that of the other auks and Puffins are rarely seen after mid August. During autumn and winter records are rare – occasional Calf records have occurred up to 9th November (1976). Winter records are almost unknown, although one was seen at Port Erin on 14th February 1956 and another from a boat in the same area on 28th February 1978.

As Puffins nest in burrows there is very little information regarding laying and hatching. Very few have been ringed and there have been no recoveries. There is little evidence of passage past the Isle of Man, but over 100 were seen flying south past the Calf on 5th October 1982.

Manx: *Pibbin. Poltrag*

Pallas's Sandgrouse

Syrrhaptes paradoxus

Very rare vagrant.

Pallas's Sandgrouse breeds on the steppes of central Asia whence it erupted westward as far as the British Isles in a number of years between 1859 and 1909. During the great invasions of 1863 and 1888 birds reached the Isle of Man. In 1863 they reached the Wirral in May and Dublin in June, but the only Manx record was of 4 shot from a flock of 16 at the Point of Ayre on 22nd September, although Ralfe mentions that others were sold by a Ramsey butcher. The greatest irruption occurred in 1888 with birds arriving on the east coast of England in early May and reaching Lancashire and Cumberland by 20th. Two were shot from a party of 8 at the Lhen on 26th and another was killed from a flock of 15 in a turnip field at Maughold on 28th, the day on which one was shot in Co. Down. There were no records through that summer but 1 was shot from a flock of 11 at the Lhen on 21st October and Ireland received a further wave of immigrants in November. One was shot at Ramsey in January 1889 and others were seen in June and July. Meanwhile a large colony was present on the Wirral in 1888 and 1889. British records for 1890 were confined to the eastern counties from Suffolk to Yorkshire except for the Isle of Man where 7–11 were present in the Lhen district during November and December, the last record being of one shot at Maughold in January 1891. No birds reached the Island from the last major invasion of 1908.

Rock Dove and Feral Pigeon

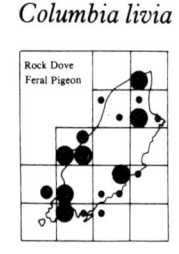

Columbia livia

Formerly an abundant resident, the Rock Dove is probably now extinct. The Feral Pigeon remains a common resident.

Rock Dove bones have been identified from a midden deposit in a cave at Perwick Bay dated at AD 90. Rather surprisingly 17th century writers make no mention of the Rock Dove but its almost unbelievable abundance between Port Erin and the Calf at the end of the 18th century is well described by Townley (1791). 'After we had doubled the first point in the main island, we saw great numbers of wild Pigeons, that lodge and breed in the holes of the tremendous rocks which surround and guard that westerly peninsula of Mona; but they were so very wild as not to allow us to come within gun-shot of them. They appeared entirely to resemble the blue dove-coat Pigeon, but smaller.' While visiting Peel he was given wild Pigeons to eat. He continued '... they were darker than the dove-coat Pigeon, legs and feet red, beaks yellow and were good eating. Vast quantities breed in the high rocky cliffs all the way from Peel Island to the Calf. They are a very shy bird, not easily approached by a gunner, but boys scramble up the rocks and take the young ones out of the breeding holes.' About the same time Robertson (1794) classed wild Pigeons with Gulls and Puffins as the most numerous birds on the Calf. Ralfe learned from several sources that up to the 1860s they remained numerous on the west coast between Fleshwick and Dalby and in the east between Port Moar and Dhoon and on the Santon coast. But they were energetically pursued as a source of food both by shooters and by parties in boats who netted the breeding caves so that by 1905 it was Ralfe's belief that pure-bred Rock Doves no longer existed on the Isle of Man.

During the last eighty years a few individuals, having all the characteristics of pure Rock Doves, have been seen quite often around the coast, but equally wild and unapproachable are other individuals which are clearly derived from Feral Pigeons.

There is very little historical information about the Feral Pigeon in the Isle of Man. The so-called Pigeon Tower at Rushen Abbey was built in the 12th century alongside the infirmary, but according to Butler (1978) it was probably only converted for use as a dovecote after the dissolution of 1539. At Ballachurry (Rushen) there is a fine pigeon house of unknown antiquity and the same farm has 150 pigeon holes of brick construction set into the slate walls of one of the farm buildings. Such pigeon holes are common in farms throughout the Island and were probably built about 1830–40. At Ballacoar (Lonan) there are no less than 177 holes while at East Lhergydhoo (German) there are 60–70 holes in a single line below the eaves of one wing of a building. Fifteen to forty holes are probably typical, but as few farms are without them it is clear that the dovecote pigeon population was at one time very considerable. Pigeons were kept principally as a source of food, but they proved to be a mixed blessing as they could in no time clear the farmyard of food put out for poultry. Nowadays flocks of up to 20 pigeons are resident in a number of farms although they tend to nest in the rafters of dutch barns – only at Ballachurry do they exist in their former numbers. There they continue to nest in the pigeon holes and in spite of the culling of 200 birds the previous winter there were considerably more than 200 around the farm in the summer of 1984. These farm birds, like those that occur in considerable numbers in Douglas and less plentifully in the other towns, are very tame.

The Isle of Man therefore possesses two populations of *C. livia* – a small number of very wild birds nesting in caves on the coast and a much greater number of farm and town nesting birds. Both populations contain birds with all the features of pure Rock Doves but their relative proportion is decidedly greater in the wild population.

C. livia is very easily the most commonly taken prey of the Peregrine.

A little to the south of Douglas Head a small stream passes under the Marine Drive entering the sea through a steep sided gully. This is Strooan Calmane, the Pigeon Stream, and surely derives its name from the Rock Dove.

Manx: *Calmane ny Creggey*

Stock Dove
Columba oenas

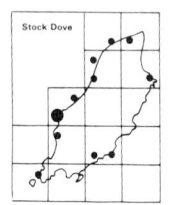

Rather local, but not uncommon resident.

There are conflicting views as to whether the Stock Dove was resident in Cumberland prior to 1870, but by 1875 it had expanded its breeding quarters there in a most remarkable degree (Macpherson and Duckworth 1886). It was first recorded in Ireland in 1875 and first bred in Kirkcudbrightshire in 1876. In the Isle of Man it was unknown until 1885 when 'Rock Doves' breeding on Greeba were tentatively attributed to this species, similarly grey pigeons on the south Lonan and Santon coasts in 1895 were not satisfactorily identified, but the following year breeding was confirmed when 2 young were taken from a cliff top hole south of Port Grenaugh. As in other areas the colonisation of the Isle of Man in the next few years was comprehensive and rapid so that by 1902 they were plentiful along the coast from Peel to Fleshwick and at several places between Maughold and Dhoon. Around this time Stock Doves gathered in good numbers in the south west during winter, 4 being shot in October 1899, 3 out of a flock of 60 in November 1900 and others were shot from considerable flocks in December 1904 and January 1905. Stock Doves nested at Glen Auldyn in 1907, Clay Head in 1911 and had colonised the rocky parts of Sulby Glen by 1923.

The occupation of nest sites in trees from 1930 provided evidence of further expansion, in 1938 they were present on the Marine Drive and in South Barrule quarry and appeared in the extreme south west in the early 1940s. Williamson (1940) did not list the Stock Dove among the Calf's birds and it was not recorded there until 1960 with a pair breeding in 1973 and 1974. During the last 10 years they have been often reported from Ballaugh Curraghs and have remained faithful to Sulby Glen and the old east coast sites. In the west they are regularly seen along a 3 km broad coastal belt from Gob yn Ushtey to the Point of Ayre and in Patrick parish, but everywhere numbers are small.

In spite of the definite colonisation of an increasing number of areas it seems that there has been an overall decline in numbers if winter flocks can be regarded as a guide. Madoc wrote of flocks of up to 50 in the Baldwin valley, yet since 1935 nearly all reports have been of parties of up to 6 birds with the exception of flocks of over 20 on the Ayres in June 1965 and February

1966, 14 near the Arrasy plantation in January 1983 and 18 at Dollagh Moar in February 1985.

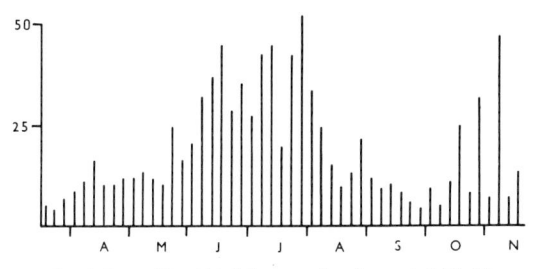

Stock Dove. Total bird days per five day period (Calf).

The Stock Dove is regarded as a sedentary species and the pattern of Calf records supports this view although there is a suggestion of autumn passage with Woodpigeons, the best day count being 19 on 10th November 1976.

Manx: *Calmane Gorrym*

Woodpigeon
Columba palumbus

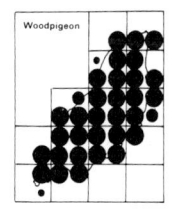

Abundant resident and passage migrant.

Amongst several superbly depicted creatures on Sandulf's 10th century cross slab at Kirk Andreas is an unmistakable dove whose neck ring clearly identifies it as *C. palumbus*.

Ralfe considered the Woodpigeon to be comparatively less abundant than in England and when he visited the Island in early November 1928 A. W. Boyd commented on its relative scarcity. Constantly failing to merit inclusion in the annual Manx Ornithological Notes assessment of any change in status is difficult. Nevertheless consistent increases were noted in the years up to 1940 and it does seem that this has continued with increasing afforestation and despite a 35% reduction in cereal production and a 65% reduction in root crops in the period 1945–81.

Although renowned for its long breeding season the extreme dates on which two eggs have been found are 9th April (Kirby 1974) and 22nd September (Malew 1968). In treeless areas a number of interesting nesting sites have been found – on the Ayres one nest was in a bush only 15 cm from the ground, while another was on the ground beneath gorse. On the Calf, where 1 or 2 pairs bred annually from 1969 to 1975, Woodpigeons nested successfully on a rocky ledge near the Observatory and on the ground under thick bracken near the Mill Giau, but deserted a nest built in the Heligoland trap.

In the autumn considerable numbers gather in areas of deciduous woodland and in conifer plantations and westward passage is regularly seen from the Calf, mostly during the last week of October and the first two weeks of November. Maxima in excess of 400 are not uncommon and 1840 flew west on 9th November 1977. Flocks of Woodpigeons remain plentiful on the main Island throughout the winter.

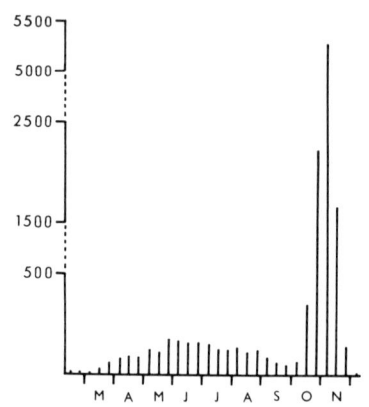

Woodpigeon. Total bird days per ten day period (Calf).

Six Woodpigeons ringed as nestlings on the Isle of Man have been recovered during their first January: one was on the Isle of Man, the others came from Hereford, Shropshire, Chesire, Anglesey and Co. Antrim. A second winter bird was shot in Co. Down and two others in their third winter were recovered on the Isle of Man. Three birds have been recovered during the summer within 1–3 years of ringing, all were on the Isle of Man and one was within 300 m of its natal site.

Manx: *Calmane keylley*

Collared Dove

Streptopelia decaocto

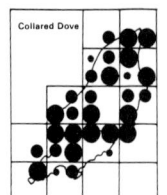

Common resident and spring passage migrant.

Until 1930 the Collared Dove bred no nearer than Belgrade in Yugoslavia, but there followed a remarkable north westerly expansion reaching Holland in 1947, Norfolk in 1955 and three Irish sea counties – Cumberland, Down and Dublin in 1959 (Hudson 1965).

The first Manx record was on 31st May 1962, when one was seen on the Calf and in 1963 the Calf produced 3 more spring records, while one was found shot at Castletown on 29th April. Breeding first took place north of Ramsey in 1964 and for 3 years resident birds were confined to this area with 2 pairs nesting in the same garden in 1965 and a flock of 48 there in February 1966. Meanwhile the Collared Dove was occurring in increasing numbers on spring passage on the Calf and 9 migrants were seen at Fleshwick on 11th April 1967. By the autumn of 1968 birds had settled at Ballasalla and were seen in Castletown during the following summer. Two were seen in Laxey in March 1970 and a flock of 16 was present at Baldrine that autumn. Douglas was probably colonised about the same time and in the autumn of 1972 there were flocks of 110 at the foot of Richmond Hill, and regular parties of up to 30 birds in gardens in Onchan, Douglas and Union Mills. By now there were a few at Port Erin, the Eairy and Kirkmichael and the populations in Ramsey, Laxey and Castletown were substantial. 1973–5 saw a general spread into small villages and farms and the long-delayed colonisation of Peel.

Since 1975 the Collared Dove has been generally distributed in the Isle of Man with an apparently stable population. It is a typical bird of the gardens and streets of residential areas as well as villages and farms where grain is available. In the hills they are sometimes seen over moorland and plantation and have been recorded up to 400 m above sea level. A flock of 60 or more can always be found at the Laxey flour mills.

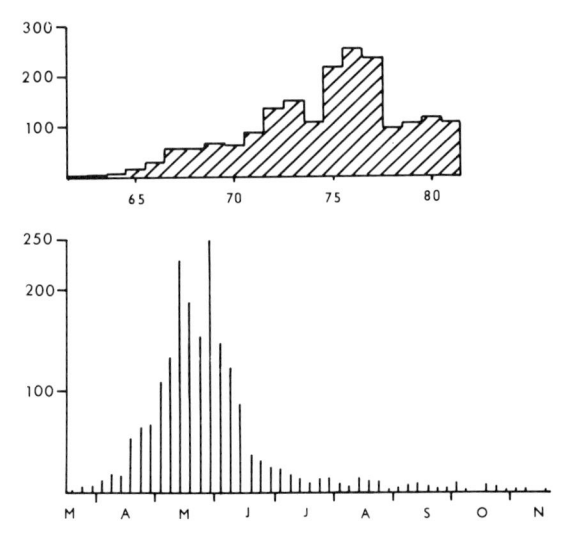

Collared Dove. Total bird days per year 1962–81 (Calf) – upper figure.
Total bird days per five day period 1962–81 (Calf) – lower figure.

On the Calf the Collared Dove occurs commonly on spring passage but since 1980 numbers have been notably lower than in the expansionist years from the late sixties to late seventies.

Turtle Dove

Streptopelia turtur

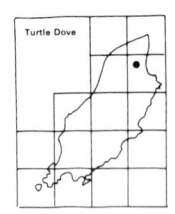

Uncommon passage migrant.

To Ralfe, who could only find four Manx records, the Turtle Dove was no more than a rare straggler and during the last 60 years there have been about 40 records for the main island. The earliest was one on the Marine Drive on 17th April 1934 and this remains the only April record. There have been 4 May records, 18 evenly spread through June, 9 in July, 4 in August, 3 in September and the latest was one shot from a flock of Woodpigeons at Knockrushen (Castletown) on about 20th November 1918. Turtle Doves are seen much more commonly on the Calf, the majority of records occurring between 10th May and 20th June, appreciably earlier than on the main island. On the Calf 1979 was an exceptional year with 47 bird days compared with a previous best of only 19 – it also produced the best day count with at least 7 on 13th May. In contrast there were no Calf records in 1982 and only 2 in 1983. The Calf peak in early June is even later than on Skokholm and Bardsey, where passage is greatest in late May. These Irish sea observatories are beyond the normal breeding range and late birds are thought to be inexperienced first-summer birds overshooting their English and Welsh breeding areas (Riddiford and Findley 1981).

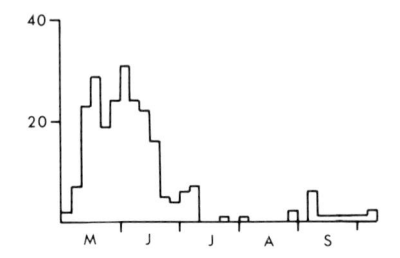

Turtle Dove. Total bird days per five day period (Calf).

Turtle Doves breed in Lancashire and rather unevenly along the north Welsh seaboard. There have also been breeding records in counties Down and Dublin. On the Isle of Man records have been concentrated on the Colby area in the south and in the northern parishes of Bride, Andreas and Jurby and although breeding has never been proved it always remains a possibility. In 1931 one or two were present in the south west throughout June and July with 3 birds at the end of August. Two immature birds with 2 adults at Bride on 5th August 1963 might have been Manx bred. More recently one lingered at Colby from 27th June to 3rd July 1979.

An adult Turtle Dove ringed on the Calf in late May was shot in northern Spain in mid September the following year.

Manx: *Calmane Coe*

Rose-ringed Parakeet
Psittacula krameri

One was seen briefly outside the Calf Observatory on 29th July 1975.

Great Spotted Cuckoo
Clamator glandarius

Accidental.

A freshly dead female was found at Ballajora, Maughold on 12th March 1963, having overshot its Iberian breeding area. At the time it was the 11th record for the British Isles (Foulkes Roberts and Williamson 1963) although by 1982 the total had increased to 26.

Cuckoo
Cuculus canorus

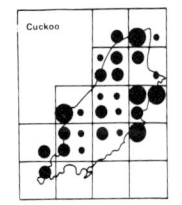

Fairly common passage migrant but rather scarce summer visitor.

Described by Ralfe in 1903 as common and well distributed, the Cuckoo has become much scarcer as a breeding bird over the last 80 years. Between 1927 and 1938 there were a number of years in which Cuckoos were relatively scarce, the first indications of a trend which gathered momentum in the middle 1950s and echoed that seen in Ireland (Ruttledge 1966).

As breeding numbers have declined so the Cuckoo has withdrawn from such habitats as suburban gardens and well cultivated farmland and is now largely a bird of curragh, lowland heath and moorland. Thus Cuckoos are still found in Ballaugh Curraghs, the central valley, the inland margins of the Ayres and in the hills and probably bred on the Calf in 1965, 1971 and 1973. As in Ireland Meadow Pipits are the commonest hosts, but others recorded in the Isle of Man are Dunnock, Sedge Warbler, Yellowhammer, Robin and Skylark. Song, usually the first sign of the Cuckoo's arrival, is heard throughout the day and there have been several records between midnight and 3 a.m.; it has not been heard after 30th June.

Between 1928 and 1982 the mean date of first arrival was 21st April, while on the Calf between 1962 and 1983 it was 25th/26th April. The earliest record was of one at Langness Lighthouse on 28th March 1887, one was calling at Crogga on 31st March 1934 and Cuckoos have been seen on several occasions between 7th and 11th April. On the Calf passage reaches a peak around 20th May, although the best day count was 7 on 29th April 1966. Return passage is seen from mid July with a peak of juveniles in early August. September records are scarce, but there have been a few records between

5th and 13th October and one very late bird at Peel on 12th November 1921.

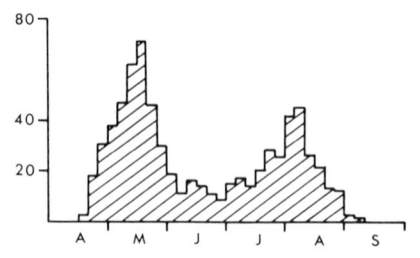

Cuckoo. Total bird days per five day period (Calf).

Seventy-seven Cuckoos have been ringed on the Calf with just one recovery. Ringed as an adult in early May it was found dead near Düsseldorf, West Germany on 26th August 2 years later.

Manx: *Cooag*

Barn Owl
Tyto alba

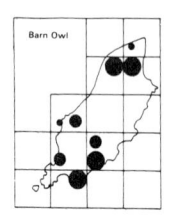

Scarce resident.

The Barn Owl was not listed by Kermode, but during the final two decades of the 19th century it does appear to have been a very scarce resident. The first record was of one found dead on the shore at Castletown about 1880 and further corpses came from the Nunnery and the Garth (Marown). About 1895 a pair nested in the ruins of Eyreton Castle (Marown) and Ralfe mentioned a nest from one other locality. By 1930 there had been just four more published records – two from Malew and one each from Maughold and Ballaugh, but the early thirities were to see a quite dramatic increase with no less than 6 nests being recorded in 1933 alone. This period of prosperity lasted for about 20 years with a breeding population of perhaps 20 pairs (Garrad in Bunn et al. 1982). The main areas where nesting has been well documented were in the southern part of Andreas parish and in the Crosby/Braaid/Douglas area, but breeding was quite widespread with records from Onchan, Bride, Jurby, Kirkmichael, the St. John's/Patrick area and Malew, where there were 2–3 pairs within a 1 km radius of St Lupus' Church. From the early 1950s the species has been in retreat and published records have contained a disturbingly high proportion of corpses since 1964. Between 1973 and 1976 the yearly total of records was between 16 and 19 with between 3 and 5 corpses, while from 1977–82 the annual score was only between 7 and 10. The low point was perhaps reached in 1980 when there were 5 corpses in a total of 10 records. Early in 1983 the membership of the Royal Manx Agricultural Society, representing a significant cross section of the farming community, was circularised with a request for information about the species. This revealed evidence of continued regular nesting at 5 widely separated locations and surprisingly little evidence of desertion of farms previously tenanted. There were also 5 instances of regular occupation of a building by a single unmated owl.

There does not seem to be a single explanation for the Barn Owl's decline. The most tempting is of course the use of toxic pesticides. The notable reduction in numbers during the sixties coincided with declines in the population of Sparrowhawk and Peregrine and owls dying at Dreemskerry (Maughold) and Ballachurry (Andreas) in 1973 and 1974 contained lethal amounts of Dieldrin. On the other hand, the Ballachurry bird, along with another found in the same barn a little later, was emaciated and apparently suffering from starvation and there was a drastic shortage of rodents in the 1973/74 winter. Indeed successful poisoning of rodents with Warfarin may have contributed to the Barn Owl's decline both through food shortage and perhaps the effects of Warfarin on the owls. An owl found dead at St John's in March 1977 contained very low residues and was thought to have died of starvation and two more from Regaby (Andreas) and Ballanard (Onchan) in January 1980 also contained very low chlorinated hydro-carbon residues. Other causes of death having no bearing on long-term trends are traffic, entanglement in netting and drowning in a water butt – a notoriously frequent cause among Barn Owls. One first year bird was rescued from a bucket of treacle!

The Barn Owl has a remarkably long breeding season – eggs have been found as early as 15th March in 1933 while in 1948, 3 young flew from a Bride nest at the end of November (Foulkes-Roberts 1949). First clutches are usually laid during the first half of May and the earliest date on which young have been seen was 31st May (1936). Four to six eggs are usual and there is one record of a clutch of 7, but fledging success is poor, 2 being the commonest number to leave the nest.

In the Isle of Man farm buildings and hollow trees are used almost equally as nest sites. Barns as such are not very often used, but various forms of housing for pigeons have consistently found favour with nests in pigeon holes (commonly), a pigeon loft, a dovecote and the Pigeon Tower at Rushen Abbey. Other man made sites have included disused farm chimneys, a hen house, the old cock-pit at Ballamoar and St Barnabas's Church, Douglas. In 1936 Barn Owls nested in one fork of a hollow tree and Jackdaws in another fork of the same tree, both birds successfully rearing their young.

Although hunting mainly over farmland and in woods, Barn Owls are sometimes seen on the coast and have been found roosting in a rocky alcove on Peel Hill and in a hole in the Shellag sand cliffs. It is an occasional visitor to the Calf and may possibly have bred. On 17th June 1943 three birds were present in one of the old lighthouses and another was found dead in the barn by the farmhouse. Between 1959 and 1972 there were five further records for the islet in May, June and September, but there have been none since.

There have been eight recoveries of Manx-ringed Barn Owls, the greatest movement, 18 km being shared by three birds.

Manx: *Screeaghag oie* = Night-screecher.

Scops Owl

Otus scops

Vagrant.

On a day which brought such other continental European species as Hoopoe and Wryneck to the Calf, a Scops Owl was found sitting in the catching box of the Heligoland trap at the head of the Mill Giau on 29th April 1968 (Wright 1973). It was also seen twice in flight the following day. (Another probable Scops Owl landed in the rigging of a fishing boat about 14 km south of Port Erin in late April 1983. After resting for about ¾ hour it flew off towards the Island. This record was not accepted by the Rarities Committee).

Snowy Owl

Nyctea scandiaca

Vagrant.

A Snowy Owl, formerly preserved at Orrisdale, was shot on the rabbit warren nearby in about 1844. Another bird was shot about 1855.

Little Owl

Athene noctua

Very rare visitor.

The first definite record was of one seen on the Calf on 25th March 1960 and there have been two records for the main Island since. (Ralfe had rejected a record of one shot near Creggans, Malew in 1883). Introduced to Britain in the late 19th century, the Little Owl is resident along the coasts of Cumbria, Lancashire and north Wales but has only occurred as a rare vagrant in Ireland.

Tawny Owl

Strix aluco

Vagrant.

Unknown in Ireland, there has been only one definite record of the Tawny

Owl on the Isle of Man, a bird being present around the Leodan on the Calf from 2nd to 9th September 1961 (Craine 1962).

(During the last decade hooting has been heard on several occasions in residential areas of Douglas but there have been no sight records.)

Long-eared Owl
Asio otus

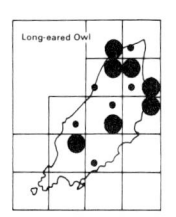

Well distributed resident.

The Long-eared owl has long been regarded as the typical owl of Ireland and the Isle of Man. Considering the meagre amount of Manx woodland 80 years ago Ralfe regarded it as well distributed, being found all over the Island wherever there were plantations, nesting sometimes in very small patches of timber. Madoc was particularly familiar with the Long-eared Owl describing it as 'almost common' and the species undoubtedly increased during the first 30 years of this century with the population being maintained during the next 30 years. During the 1960s only one nest was reported and, while a nocturnal inhabitant of woodland is clearly liable to be overlooked, such a poor return must have reflected a significant decline. During the years 1964–71 only one Long-eared Owl was recorded on the Calf – further evidence of low numbers on the main island. The last decade has seen a notable recovery and they now nest in a number of the Island's plantations and small stands of conifers. As recently as 1981 two occupied nests at the Guilcagh (Andreas) were only 250 m apart.

Although primarily a bird of coniferous woods Manx birds also nest in damp lightly wooded Curragh, especially at Ballaugh but also in other smaller tracts of marshy ground, and large gardens, notably at Ballagawne (Rushen) and Lambhill (Bride) where in 1946 two occupied nests were only 80 m apart. The large majority of nests are in the old nests of Magpies, but in Ballaugh Curraghs Madoc found that nests of Sparrowhawk and Hooded Crow were usually used. In 1944 and 1945 Long-eared Owls nested in the rookery at Ballachurry (Andreas) and in the first year a nest contained 2 Rook's eggs and 3 owl's eggs. Most eggs are laid during March and April – the earliest, a clutch of 6 on 5th March, was probably started on or before 23rd February. There are two other recorded instances of laying in late February, while 2 young in a nest at Knocksharry (German) on 30th June indicate a last egg being laid no earlier than 10th May. Nests with only one egg have been found on 19th and 21st May but it is not known if they were incomplete clutches. Four is the most usual clutch size on the Isle of Man, but several nests with 5 and 6 eggs have been found and 7 eggs have been recorded once. The most common brood size is 2–3, 4 young are unusual, but there is one record of 6 young in a nest.

The Wood Mouse is easily the most commonly taken prey. Other species which have been identified in pellets include the House Mouse, the Brown Rat and the Short-tailed Vole.

The vole was found in a pellet from a Glen Auldyn roost (Nuttall 1981) and is of interest because voles are not known to occur on the Isle of Man (see also under Short-eared Owl). Small bird and beetle remains have also been found in pellets.

Outside the breeding season Long-eared Owls occur in a wider range of habitats such as coastal brooghs, harbours and town parks – indeed Madoc found a pair in the Villa Marina gardens (Douglas) in late March, a date not incompatible with breeding. In winter parties roost together, the largest being a gathering of 11 at a Santon site in November. On the Calf they are seen most years and have been found roosting by the Observatory (3 together on 7th November 1975) and the Withy. One ringed there on 26th May was retrapped 7 weeks later and another ringed in mid June was recovered at Colby in July two years later.

Manx: *Hullad. Kione chayt* = Cat's Head.

Short-eared Owl
Asio flammeus

Uncommon summer and winter visitor and regular passage migrant.

During the latter half of the 19th century the Short-eared Owl was a regular autumn and winter visitor. In 1892 when the vole plague brought considerable numbers to south-west Scotland a Douglas taxidermist had 4 birds at one time during January. Ralfe had one summer record and knew of owls' nests being found on the ground near Injebreck, twice in the young plantation on South Barrule and at Greeba although they may well have been attributable to *A. otus*. By 1908 further nests had been found at Archallagan, Greeba and Ballaugh Curraghs and eventually in 1921 the shooting of both parents in the Curraghs left no doubt that a nest with 2 eggs was of this species.

Short-eared Owls were occasionally seen in the summer up to 1930 but during the next 16 years they were not seen between early April and late August, most records occurring in February and to a lesser extent November. During the mid 1940s they started to occur with increasing frequency in April and May and eventually a pair nested on the Calf in 1959. In 15 of the 21 years up to 1980 1–3 pairs nested on the Calf, in 1962 and 1964 a pair nested on the Ayres and in 1971 a nest was found in the Ballaugh Curraghs. Probable breeding pairs were found on Stoney Mountain in 1972 and near the Sloc in 1975. Single birds had been seen between Round Table and Eary Cushlin during several summers from 1964 onward and breeding has probably taken place annually since 1977 with nests found in 1980 and 1982. Pairs summered at Conrhenny plantation each year from 1976 to 1979 and during the last 10 years breeding at several localities in the central hills may well have occurred. The last 25 years have thus seen the establishment of the Short-eared Owl as a regular Manx breeding species.

Haycock (1974) analysed the Short-eared Owl's prey from pellets collected at nest sites on the Calf.

Prey species identified from 243 pellets collected at nest sites of Short-eared Owl on the Calf of Man in 1973 and 1974 (after Haycock)

Species	Total no. individuals	% of Total	Conversion factor	Total prey units	% of Total prey weight
Pygmy Shrew	184	54.3	0.20	36.80	5.80
Natterer's Bat	1	0.3	0.25	0.25	0.04
Rabbit	17	5.0	10.00	170.00	27.10
Short-tailed Vole	1	0.3	1.00	1.00	0.16
Wood Mouse	9	2.7	1.00	9.00	1.40
Brown Rat	71	20.9	5.00	355.00	56.50
Bird spp.	56	16.5	1.00	56.00	9.00

Although the Pygmy Shrew was easily the most commonly taken prey, the Brown Rat was nutritionally the most important. The rabbits were all young animals and birds included Wren, Blackbird, Wheatear, Dunnock, Meadow Pipit and Linnet. In addition the remains of at least 20 beetles were found in the pellets. The Short-tailed Vole, supposedly absent from the Isle of Man, joins those found in owl pellets at Crogga and Glen Auldyn to provide an intriguing riddle for students of Manx natural history.

Interesting examples of opportunistic feeding by this species have been observed at lighthouses. In August 1938, on a night of thick fog and heavy small bird passage a Short-eared Owl perched at the top of the flagpole at the Chicken Rock, returning repeatedly to kill and swallow migrants at the lantern (Williamson 1940). Nowadays thrushes are often hunted around the Calf light, one or two owls being present regularly through the autumn, especially on foggy and drizzly nights.

Outside the breeding season Short-eared Owls are seen in all months, but are commonest from August to November. They occur mostly around the coast and in the Curraghs of Ballaugh and Greeba. Since 1958 one or two have occurred annually on Langness in early autumn, the earliest arrival date being 17th July. Fleshwick and the Ayres are also visited in autumn. From December to February Short-eared Owls are now rather scarce but in early April they start to occupy potential breeding areas in the hills. Although usually seen singly, winter parties of 4–6 are sometimes seen and there are two records of 10 together – over a turnip field at Ballatrollag (Malew) in November 1907 and over the heath on the Calf on 22nd October 1978.

Fifty-seven Short-eared Owls were ringed on the Calf between 1959 and

1983. One of the first brood of 1959 was recovered at Fleshwick during the same August, while another ringed as a nestling was recovered off the north Irish coast in August of the same year.

Nightjar

Caprimulgus europaeus

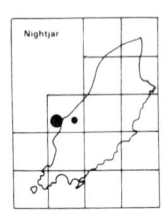

Rare summer visitor.

In the late 19th century the Nightjar was a regular summer visitor in small numbers. A nest was found at Gob y volley in 1895 and it probably bred on the bracken covered hillsides of Ravensdale and Greeba and on the Ayres. It seems that Nightjars passed through the Island in some numbers during September.

During the present century the Nightjar bred regularly at two or three sites until about 1940, continuing for a further decade at Peel Hill. Since 1950 it has been an infrequent summer visitor.

On the Ayres the first nest was found in 1908 and breeding probably continued without interruption until 1941. Nests were found on bare stony ground (Madoc 1934), on the open heath and in the bracken covered fringes (Williamson 1938). On the southern slopes of Greeba nests were found in 1904 and 1905 and there were further records in the early 1930s. In spite of the maturing of the plantation there remain clearings and bracken covered slopes suited to the Nightjar and birds were repeatedly seen by forestry workers during the summer of 1973. During the period 1919–26 they probably bred on the Lezayre hillsides overlooking the northern plain and in Laxey Glen and Glen Roy there was a regular summer presence from 1923 until 1932 when breeding was confirmed. On Peel Hill Nightjars are likely to have bred annually from 1931 until 1949 and as recently as 1980 one was found dead in Peel Harbour on 5th August. Indeed all but one of the handful of records since 1974 are from the Peel area with birds present near St Johns in June and late August 1974 and song records during May from Glen Maye in 1980 and neighbouring Raby Beg the following year. In the plantations above Foxdale Nightjars had been reported in 1920 and 1935 and were heard nightly during the summers of 1962 and 1963. Isolated song records which have come from Congary Curragh (June 1938), Baldwin (May 1938), the Calf (late May 1943) and Ballachristory (Jurby) and Bride in late May 1955 probably point to irregular and scattered breeding. Manx Nightjar habitats have altered little in the last 100 years and indeed the clearing of timber from parts of the older plantations has created additional suitable sites. The decline is similar to that seen in Scotland, north west England and North Wales which started about 1930.

Nightjars have only very rarely been seen on passage in the last 50 years – one was seen at Ballabrooie (Patrick) on 22nd April 1968, another was seen resting on the lantern grating of the Chicken Rock Lighthouse on 28th May 1955 and 1 was flushed at Barony (Maughold) on 18th September 1947.

There have been no records for the Calf of Man since the Observatory opened in 1959.

Manx: *Ushag ny Hoie*

Swift
Apus apus

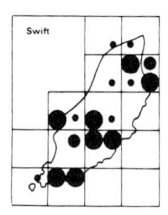

Common summer visitor and passage migrant.

Swifts were described by Townley (1791) as occurring at Douglas Head and Onchan, but Ralfe regarded the species as rather scarce. In Douglas they nested in three churches and at Peel in the walls of the Castle and possibly (according to F. S. Graves) in the cliffs at Contrary Head. Castletown, deserted as a breeding station by 1903, was reoccupied in 1918, while at Ramsey nesting was first noted in 1915. In 1931 Swifts were found nesting at Union Mills and Madoc implies that they also did so in fair numbers around Ballamona Hospital at the Strang. In the late 1920s and early 1930s numbers increased in the Douglas area and, judging from the size of flocks now seen in June, numbers may well have increased further during the last decade.

Douglas continues to accommodate the major bulk of the Manx population, but there are one or two long-established sites at Port St Mary and Swifts continue to breed in Castletown, Peel, Ramsey and at the two Strang hospitals. At Douglas and Ramsey most nests are under the high roofs of Victorian boarding houses, but at Castletown they have nested in the curtain wall and high under the arch of the Keep at Castle Rushen.

In the Douglas area parties of Swifts congregate particularly over Port e Chee meadow and its recently created lake and over Tromode Dam, but during the breeding season substantial flocks may appear anywhere and there are recent records of up to 200 in late June over Castletown. They are often seen in fair numbers in aerial gymnastics over hilltops, the most notable gatherings being 200 over Slieau Ruy in late June 1975 and over 100 over Beinn y Phott in early July 1976.

Between 1928 and 1982 the average date for first arrival was 3rd May with the earliest being 8 at Kirby on 18th April 1948 and 1 over the Calf on 24th April 1978. Usually main arrivals are not seen until well into the second week of May and in some years Swifts are scarce or absent until

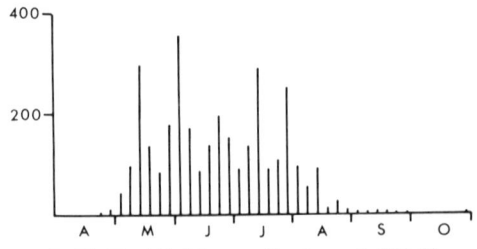

Swift. Total bird days per five day period (Calf).

the last week of that month – on the Calf the best day count was 500 on 3rd June 1962. A few Swifts have been ringed from the Manx Museum nests in Douglas – one ringed as an adult was retrapped exactly a year later, while another was found dead under wires in Somerset in mid May. In the towns numbers start to diminish in mid July and Swifts are very scarce during the second half of August. A few stragglers are often seen in September and there have been occasional October records, the latest being two at Douglas on 30th October 1960.

Manx: *Gollan ny Greg*

Alpine Swift

Apus melba

Rare passage migrant.

Recorded at Port St Mary in late May 1931 and again on 17th May 1933, there were two at Niarbyl on 18th May 1934. There were then no further reports until 1978 when at Maughold Head one was seen on 9th June and two on 11th June (Cullen 1979). There have since been two records from the Calf – 1 flew south over the Stack on 10th July 1979 and another was seen over the Burroo on 13th June 1982; one seen the previous day at Ballamodha was probably the same bird.

Kingfisher

Alcedo atthis

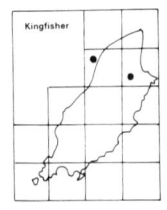

Infrequent visitor.

In the early part of the 19th century Forbes described the Kingfisher as 'not scarce if sought for', a description which Ralfe still considered to be appropriate in 1903. Although Kermode wrote that it was resident in small numbers throughout the island he could produce no evidence of breeding and Ralfe commented that definite records of specimens 'obtained' belonged almost entirely to the winter months.

Unknown to these writers a nest with eggs was found by the Sulby River west of Ramsey about 1893 and in 1920 an adult bird was seen in the same locality with 2 young birds. The streams in the Douglas neighbourhood were much frequented in the late 19th century and a nest with 3 eggs was found in a hole in the bank of one such stream by H. M. Rogers during the second decade of the present century.

It is hard to escape the conclusion that there was a very small breeding population during the 1930s. There were unconfirmed reports from the Neb at Glenfaba during several summers and Kingfishers were alleged to have nested regularly near Sir George's Bridge on the Glass. In the north a pair was seen at Glen Auldyn in late August 1932 and there were several reports from Ramsey in 1934, including a story of breeding under the boathouse on the Mooragh Lake. Since 1940 summer records have been very rare – one was present at the Nunnery during 1944, a pair was seen on the Killane Trench in late June 1951, two were seen at Sulby Bridge in mid July 1976 and 1 was seen on the Neb on two dates in mid July 1978. Two birds probably summered on the Sulby in the Garey/Ballakillingan area in 1984, but it seems very unlikely that Kingfishers have bred on the Isle of Man during the last 40 years. The lower stretches of the Island's four principal rivers are not unsuitable, but these waters are well fished and the regular presence of Kingfishers during the trout season could hardly pass unnoticed.

From August through to February Kingfishers are recorded annually on the lower stretches of the rivers, in harbours and on the rocky coast. The Nunnery, the millstream above Tromode laundry, the Mooragh Lake and the harbours of Ramsey, Douglas and Peel are particularly favoured winter resorts. Kingfishers have been recorded twice on the rocky shores of the Calf on 12th September 1961 and 24th August 1970 and one was seen twice at Langness Pool in October 1976.

Although considered to be a sedentary species there is quite marked autumn dispersal of British Kingfishers, and according to Morgan and Glue (1977) almost 10% of ringing recoveries showed movements of 50–99 km and one bird was recovered 555 km from its ringing site. There is thus every reason to suppose that Manx autumn and winter records relate to visitors from the adjacent larger islands.

Manx: *Ushag Awiney* = River Bird

Roller

Coracias garrulus

Vagrant.

One was shot in Marown parish about 5th August 1834, a good description appearing in Mona's Herald (Stevenson 1941) and on about 20th June 1984 one was found drowned in a farm trough between Port St Mary and Port Erin.

Hoopoe

Upupa epops

Fairly regular passage migrant in very small numbers.

The first documented record of the Hoopoe was in 1835 when one was shot on Langness. The frequency of records of such a conspicuous bird is unlikely to be influenced by the diligence of observers and as the histogram shows there has been a notable increase in records over the last 20 years.

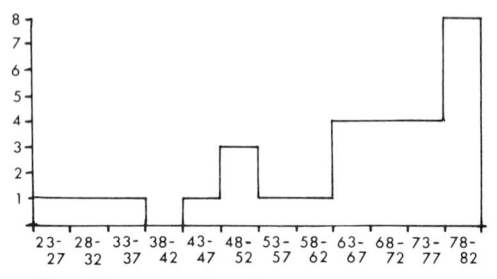

Manx Hoopoe records per five year period 1923–82.

To the Isle of Man the Hoopoe is principally a bird of spring passage. Although there are two March records – 1 was seen in a Castletown garden on 24th March 1973 and another lingered at Ballagawne (Rushen) from 25th March to 8th April 1950 – the majority have been seen between 12th April and 23rd May (about 16 records). There have been three June records and one each for July and August. During October 1965 one was present for several weeks at Braddan and the latest record was of one above Port Moar (Maughold) on 2nd November 1967. On the Calf there have been just five records between 12th April and 25th June and one on 9th October.

Wryneck

Jynx torquilla

Irregular autumn passage migrant which has occasionally been seen in spring.

Until 1963 the only record had been of one killed at Abbeylands in 1896, but it has occurred on the Calf in twelve of the last 22 years with some 34 records in all. Autumn records have been spread evenly from 21st August (1977) to 10th October (1983). On 18th September 1969 there were at least 4 individuals on the Calf and on two other days in early September two have been seen on the same day. Although most Calf visits are brief, one bird ringed on 28th August 1963 was retrapped on 10th and 13th September and one ringed on 8th September 1970 was retrapped 10 days later. Several other birds have lingered for up to 4 days.

Spring records are rare – one was present from 9th to 15th April 1969 and other individuals were recorded on 29th April 1968, 18th May 1974 and 24th June 1977.

There have been three records for the main Island – a road casualty on Langness on 25th August 1973 and individuals at Port Erin on 28th and 29th August 1985 and on Peel Hill on 2nd September 1985. Seventy-one birds recorded in Ireland up to 1981 showed a seasonal bias similar to that seen on the Calf with just 9 spring records (Preston 1982).

Green Woodpecker
Picus viridis

Rare autumn visitor.

The Green Woodpecker was first recorded in 1952 when early on an autumn morning one clung to the wall of the Chicken Rock Lighthouse for about 2 hours. In 1958 one was heard at Orry's Mount in mid October and again at Ballachurry (Andreas) on 14th November.

One was seen near Monk's Bridge, Ballasalla on 13th August 1960, another at Ballachurry on 22nd September 1972 and at neighbouring Close Lake the next day and the most recent was one at Port e Vullen on 24th August 1977. These records have occurred since the colonisation of west Cumbria in the late 1940's which was followed by an extension into Dumfries and Galloway in the 1950s.

Manx: *Snoggeyder Glass*

Great Spotted Woodpecker
Dendrocopos major

Irregular winter visitor.

Ralfe knew of only three records of the Great Spotted Woodpecker, the earliest being one shot at Orrisdale in September 1849, the other 2 being killed at Ballakillingan and the Nunnery during the winter. The first half of this century saw only 5 further records, but they have occurred in 14 of the last 32 years. During three winters several birds were present in different parts of the Island following irruptions of northern European birds. In the autumn of 1962 vast numbers of woodpeckers moved from north-east Europe westward through Scandinavia reaching the observatories in the north and east of the British Isles in September and, more notably, in October. In the Isle of Man one was seen at Lezayre on 9th September and two were present at Ballavale (Santon) throughout October. During December one was again seen at Lezayre but individuals also appeared at Laxey, the Patrick area and Douglas. The Laxey bird was often seen up to 9th March, when there were two together, in the west there were sightings from St Johns to Glenmaye, involving one or two birds up to 8th February and in Douglas, where there were certainly two birds, records continuing up to 11th April (Bracegirdle 1963). The last bird was seen at King William's College on 25th April. In

1968 there was an almost identical movement through Scandinavia with arrivals in eastern Britain between 7th and 15th September, individuals reaching the Calf on 17th and 22nd. During the winter birds were present at the Raggatt (Patrick) and at Sulby, and one remained on the Calf from 26th April to 9th May. During the winter of 1972–3 at least 4 birds were present. More than one was seen in south east Andreas on 2nd October, to be followed by records from Ballamodha on 14th, Kirkmichael on 19th and 20th (two birds) and Andreas village on 26th. During November and December individuals were seen at Santon and Greeba. One was present at Ellanbane (Lezayre) in early January and came regularly to a bird table at Ballakillingan through February and March to 9th April when there were two, the last sighting being at Sulby on 20th April. At Ballamoar (Patrick) one was seen regularly through January and February and there was a very late record from the Raggatt on 23rd May. Again there were two in the Douglas area from early February to the end of March. In each year 1979–82 a bird has been recorded, sometimes for several days, at Ballachurry (Andreas): it is conceivable that this is a resident bird but sightings from May to October have been lacking. In the Isle of Man Great Spotted Woodpeckers have consistently favoured a small number of localities namely the Raggatt, Ballavale, the Nunnery and Glencrutchery (Douglas), Ballakillingan and Ballachurry.

A bird shot at the Nunnery in February 1899 was an example of the northern race *D.m.major* and it is likely that most, if not all, of the other Manx records relate to this race.

Manx: *Snoggeyder*

Woodlark

Lullula arborea

Very rare passage migrant.

Ralfe rejected a record of a Woodlark on the lantern of Langness lighthouse on 21st October 1886 and Madoc's description of a tired storm-driven bird, seen at close range on Clay Head on 26th October 1930 is not very convincing although accepted by Witherby. A wing was found at Cranstal on 24th September 1978 and in 1981 there were two records from the Calf – one flew north singing on 16th April and one flew west with Skylarks on 16th November.

Skylark
Alauda arvensis

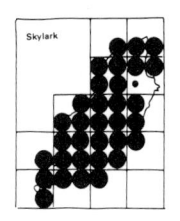

Common summer and winter visitor and abundant passage migrant.

There is no evidence of any change in the status of the Skylark during the last 100 years. It breeds plentifully on the sandy wastes of the Ayres, where 84 territories were located in an area of 565 hectares in the Common Bird Census of 1965 (Wallace 1965), on the wide expanses of grassland of the airfields and golf courses and on pastures from sea level up to 425 m. Since the opening of the Observatory in 1959 between 2 and 15 pairs have nested on the Calf with a stable population of 9–10 pairs since 1977. Nests with eggs (usually 3–4) are found throughout May and June, extreme dates being clutches of 3 on the Ayres on 28th April 1946 and at Peel on 22nd July 1931.

It is thought that the breeding population leaves the Island in the autumn and that wintering birds are of northern European origin, although there are no ringing data to confirm this. Autumn movement is seen from late September and it is very heavy throughout October with dwindling numbers through to the end of November. Day counts of 500 are not uncommon on the Calf and there have been a few records in excess of 1,000, the most being 1,500 flying south west over a 3 hour period on 28th September 1965. Flocks of wintering birds are often 50 strong and can reach 200. Light spring movement is seen during February and March when lighthouse casualties used to occur at the Chicken Rock and at the Point of Ayre, where 23 were killed on 20th February 1890. Even earlier movement has been noted and Ralfe mentions Skylarks being killed at the Bahama light vessel (12 km east of Ramsey) on 5th and 10th January 1887.

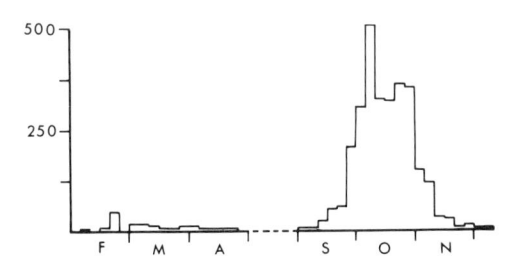

Skylark. Average numbers on passage per five day period (Calf).

Betweeen 1959 and 1983 47 Skylarks were ringed on the Calf, but there have been no recoveries.

Manx: *Ushag Tappagh, Ushag y Tappee, Ushag Happagh* = Crested Bird. *Ushag Cabbagh* = Stammering Bird

Shore Lark
Eremophila alpestris

Very rare passage migrant and winter visitor.

The first record of the Shore Lark was on 16th January 1942 when two were seen on the Ayres shore (E. F. Ladds. *pers. comm.*). This same shore produced two more on 5th November 1961 and further records in the spring of 1973 with three on 20th April and two on 6th May. On the Calf one was seen at the Burroo on 15th October 1976.

Sand Martin
Riparia riparia

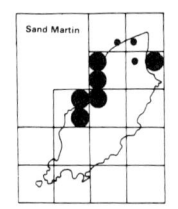

Common summer visitor and passage migrant.

The Sand Martin has only nested in fairly modest numbers during the last 100 years, the larger part of the population using natural sites on the coast, the remainder breeding inland at sites which in recent times have been exclusively man-made. Ralfe described the sand cliffs from Orrsdale to Jurby Head and those of Bride as being used abundantly, while at Douglas Head they nested until about 1885 in the earthy top of the large quarry behind the Battery Pier. Inland they were found in a sandbank at the present site of Hutchinson Square in Douglas, at Ballacreetch (Onchan) and at Ballafletcher (Braddan). At Mount Gawne (Rushen) nesting attempts failed through removal of material and the Ballaharra sandpit in German had been deserted by 1905, although by 1928 it had been recolonised and remains to this day the most important inland site with some 40 nests in 1983. Other sandpits in the Peel area have been used from time to time, notably Ballacross in 1938, Poortown in 1955 and Lhergydhoo (very small) since at least 1981. Bride Sandpit was occupied in 1946 and 1951 and Braddan (perhaps the same as Ballafletcher) in 1943 and 1949. At Peel power station the colony was deserted in 1975. Coastal cliffs still account for the bulk of the breeding population with greatest numbers to the north and south of the Dog Mills in Bride parish. On the north west coast colonies continue to appear at various places between Jurby and Orrisdale although as Madoc said they do get spoiled by erosion of the sand cliffs. At Kirkmichael there have been colonies, not always occupied, for at least 60 years at Ballyra and Glen Mooar. Further south Sand Martins have nested recently at Ballaquine and Lynague.

There are only a few published counts from nesting colonies, but clearly 40 nests is about the maximum achieved at individual settlements in the Isle of Man. Typical of the difficulties in assessing the true population at a colony is the situation at Lhergydhoo where there is little doubt that only 2 or 3 of some 20 burrows are occupied in any one year. Britain saw a marked reduction in the breeding population between 1968 and 1969, perhaps due to drought in the Sahel zone of West Africa, but although 1969 was a poor year in the Isle of Man the really bad years were 1973 and more especially 1974. Since 1976 it seems that numbers have recovered, 1979 saw the heaviest ever passage in May and breeding numbers in the early 1980s have been reassuringly good.

Both on the coast and inland nest sites are very similar being close to the top of a vertical sandy face whether it is a true sand cliff as on the northern coasts, an inland sandpit or a shallow sandy zone on top of a rocky cliff or quarry.

Betweeen 1928 and 1982 the mean first arrival date was 2nd–3rd April and while Sand Martins were seen in March in 24 of the last 55 years there were March records in 9 of the last 12 years suggesting a tendency to earlier northward movement. Early dates have been 8th March 1977, 10th March 1948, 11th March 1978 and 18th March 1961. Often these early birds pass through 2–3 weeks before any others and main movement usually starts in the second or third week of April continuing to mid May. The best day count on the Calf was 400 on 25th April 1975. Much lighter autumn passage (best day count on the Calf 40 on 8th September 1965) is seen from mid July to mid September, late dates being 16th October 1960 and 29th October 1978.

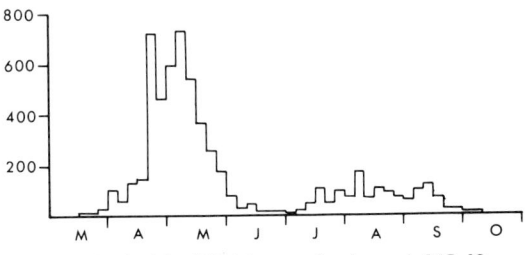

Sand Martin. Total bird days per five day period (Calf).

Forty-seven birds have been ringed on the Calf with no recoveries.
Manx: *Gollan Geinnee*

Swallow

Hirundo rustica

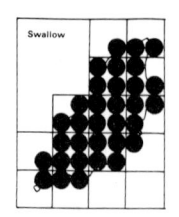

Common summer visitor and passage migrant.

The Swallow was one of the 'seven sleepers' *Ny shiaght cadlagyn* of Manx folk-lore, supposedly hibernating in winter. The other sleepers were *Foillycan* (the Butterfly), *Shellan* (the Bee), *Jialg lheer* (the Lizard), *Craitnag* (the Bat), *Cooag* (the Cuckoo) and *Clogh ny cleigh* (the Wheatear) (Kermode 1885). Ralfe quotes another source which substitutes for Butterfly, Bee and Lizard: *Hullad* (the Owl), *Eean raip* (the Corncrake) and *Coar heddagh* (the Snipe).

Ralfe believed that the Swallow was distinctly scarce as compared with its abundance on the mainland, but in the absence of any Manx census data it is difficult to say whether this is still the case. It is certainly a well distributed breeding bird, whose numbers are greatly augmented during spring and autumn passage. From time to time during the last 60 years there have been periods when Swallows have been absent from farms where they traditionally nest – this was so in 1930–32 and very notably in 1973–77. A good recovery was seen in 1978 and they probably regained their former breeding strength in 1980.

Although now nesting exclusively in buildings, cave nesting formerly occurred with a record from the Santon coast in 1886 and from Langness in 1946. The Langness nest was partly supported by a small ledge 10 m inside the cave (Crellin and Crellin 1947). Most nests are found in farm buildings which are still in use, but deserted farmsteads and shelters in wild moorland localities are quite widely used. On the Calf one or two pairs regularly nest in the outbuildings of the Observatory, another pair can often be found at Jane's House, there have been occasional nests in both the old lighthouses and they have nested once at the old smithy. Two pairs nested on the islet in 1939 and since the Observatory opened in 1959 1–4 pairs have bred with 5 pairs in 1969. Nest sites in more urban localities include public lavatories, sports pavilions, boathouses, bus shelters and railway buildings. In rural areas there are probably very few farms occupied or deserted which do not receive a breeding pair in summer. In the Isle of Man they have nested in a shelter on Snaefell at an altitude of 380 m. At Fleshwick Swallows built a nest in a bowl lying on a shelf in an outhouse and at Bride on the outside of the big church bell (Creer 1952). On the Calf a cock Wren built his nest over a freshly constructed Swallows' nest during one morning forcing the Swallows to rebuild in another building where they successfully reared a brood. Laying usually starts in mid May and a proportion of birds will start second clutches in early July. Third clutches are not uncommon and in 1944 three such clutches were found at northern localities – two had been started in late August, but in the third nest the first egg was not laid until 4th September (Glasman 1945). Four to five eggs are usual and there is at least one record of a Manx clutch of 7.

During the period 1928–82 the mean first arrival date was 7th April. March records are rare and have only been noted in 8 of the 55 years under review – the earliest being 15th March 1931, 19th March 1929 and 24th March

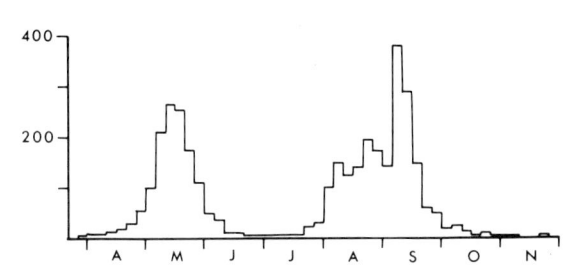

Swallow. Average bird days (passage only) per five day period (Calf).

1982. The peak of spring passage is from about 5th to 25th May with a maximum day count on the Calf of 600 on 9th May 1975. Southward movement is mostly during August and September (2,500 passed the Calf during 11th September 1966) with small numbers in October and in most years in November. A flock of over 100 migrants over Castletown on 4th November 1937 was quite exceptional as no other party during that month has exceeded 15. The mean date for the last Manx Swallow during the period 1928–82 was 7th/8th November and the latest records were 11th December 1980 and 2nd December 1959. Kermode gives two interesting winter records – a certain John Quayle told him that after a snowstorm (no date) he found about 20 huddled together inside the window of an old house, he released some which flew about in an aimless and sluggish fashion: in 1899 'one or two were seen about Douglas in January and February'. At Castletown Mill Swallows roost in a reed bed which in late August 1976 contained 500–1,000 birds.

In the period 1959–83 1,583 Swallows were ringed on the Calf and the total Manx aggregate is well over 3,000 yielding 52 recoveries. Of these 16 were recovered in the Isle of Man during the same year, 20 in the Isle of Man during a subsequent year and 16 were recovered elsewhere. A nestling ringed at Philip the Ploughman's cottage, Ballaugh, was recovered in late June the following year breeding near Trondheim, Norway. Two juveniles ringed on the Calf within two days of each other in late August were controlled at Dawley, Salop on successive days one month later. Twenty swallows have been retrapped at their place of ringing in a subsequent year, the most notable being one ringed on the Calf as a juvenile in late July 1966, which was retrapped on both spring and autumn passage in 1968. One bird ringed elsewhere as a juvenile was controlled on the Isle of Man 4 years 8 months later.

Manx: *Gollan geayee* = Fork of the Wind

House Martin
Delichon urbica

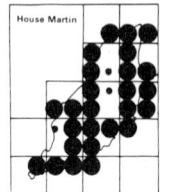

Common passage migrant and summer visitor.

The present century has seen the House Martin's status change from that of a scarce visitor, nesting with almost equal frequency on cliffs and buildings, to that of a very plentiful breeder on man-made structures with a very small number continuing to nest on coastal cliffs.

The first man-made site known to Ralfe was the Central Hotel at St Johns where House Martins nested in 1884 and three years later they started to nest at several localities in Douglas, where the Loch Promenade was later to become an important site. Buildings around Castletown Post Office were colonised in 1916 and later Castle Rushen itself, and for a while there was a small colony on the Golf Links Hotel beside Fort Island. Even as late as 1934 breeding numbers, according to Madoc, were not great and cliff nesters still constituted a significant proportion, but during the thirties the population began to expand appreciably with colonies appearing at a number of farms, especially in the north. Notable among these was Staward (Sulby) which supported a colony of up to 30 pairs from 1930 to at least 1952. At Ellerslie (Marown) there were 20 nests around the great concrete silo in 1945 and at Druidale Farm (Michael), 210 m above sea level, there were 25 nests in 1960. The largest recorded farm colony was at Billown, where in 1963 there were 47 nests. During the last 20 years it seems that House Martins have been lured away from farms by the building of new housing estates where pebble-dashed walls seem irresistable. The birds are quick to appreciate a new estate and a colony can become established before the houses are complete. Such colonies are present on estates throughout the Island. Few older buildings now seem to be used, the most notable being the white washed Jurby Church where there were 14 nests in 1984 and 1985.

Eighty to ninety years ago coastal colonies existed at Contrary Head (20 nests), Pistol Castle, Port Soderick, Skinscoe (20 nests) and Maughold Head. Another colony just north of Port Soderick had been deserted. The colony at Contrary Head was still in existence in 1932, while those at Port Soderick and Maughold survive to this day and for the last 15 years at least there has been another east coast colony at Port Soldrick. For a period during the late 1930s they may have nested over coastal caves in Rushen parish and there are probably other colonies, so far overlooked, such as the 3 nests west of Port Grenaugh in 1969. Cliff nests are often situated above the entrance to a cave – at Port Soderick they are on the cliff face well above the cave, while at Port Soldrick they are just under the arch of the cave as were the nests in the old Skinscoe colony. According to Ralfe nests at Contrary Head and Maughold (also over the entrance of a cave) were at a great height, but at Port Soderick they are at very modest elevations of between 7 and 15 m and those at Port Soldrick are not much higher. The nests are usually built beneath a protruding piece of slate which forms a sort of porch. The three known surviving colonies are small – Maughold had 12–15 nests in 1973, Port Soderick 8 in 1984 and Port Soldrick 6 in 1982. There is one record of nesting in a stone quarry on Douglas Head, where there was a large colony in 1950 – it has not been recorded since and was certainly not present in 1984.

Between 1928 and 1982 the mean first arrival date was 13th April and early dates have been 16th March 1977, 17th March 1964 and 23rd March 1974. Calf passage is at its height from mid May to the first few days of

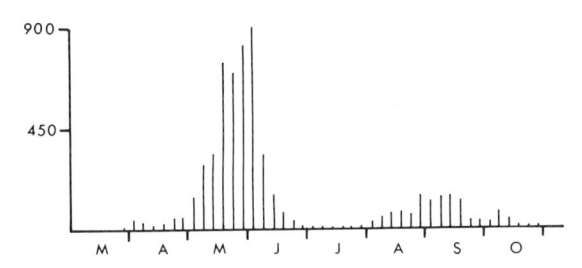

House Martin. Total bird days per five day period (Calf).

June, with a best day total of 200 on 20th May 1979, and autumn movement, mostly in August and September is much lighter (maximum 100 on 5th September 1973). The mean latest date is 18th/19th October and stragglers have been seen on 18th November 1967, 28th November 1897 and 3rd December 1940 (3 at Peel).

The ringing of 51 House Martins on the Calf has only produced one recovery – in Port Erin 34 days later. Ringing on the main island has produced just 12 retraps, one being caught at Port Erin in three successive summers.

Manx: *Gollan Thie*

Richard's Pipit

Anthus novaeseelandiae

Vagrant.

The only record of this large pipit which breeds on the steppes of central Asia and across Siberia was one seen on the heath close to the track down to Cow Harbour on the Calf on 1st October 1972 (Wright 1973).

Tawny Pipit

Anthus campestris

Vagrant.

A Tawny Pipit was seen near the Calf of Man Observatory on 6th October 1971 (Wright 1973) and two other individuals occurred on the islet in 1985 on 23rd September and 7th October.

Tree Pipit

Anthus trivialis

Fairly common passage migrant which has bred.

Unknown to Ralfe a Tree Pipit's nest with one egg was found at Thornhill near Ramsey in about 1890. In June 1911 one was seen and heard for several days at Injebreck and breeding was strongly suspected, but it was not until about 1928 that Madoc established that the Tree Pipit occurred regularly in small numbers on spring and autumn passage. At coastal locations such as Langness and Clay Head a few birds could be found among large flocks of Meadow Pipits up to mid October. More recently observations on the Calf have revealed that there is a token presence in spring and much heavier movement in autumn.

In 1958 a bird held territory on the eastern slopes of Slieau Whallian and from 1959 until the early 1970's up to three pairs bred regularly in this area. They usually arrived during the last week of April, a number of nests were found and the earliest date for young was 16th May. In 1963 a pair was seen at Cronk y Voddy in May and mid June and in 1966 breeding was reported from Little London.

On the Calf passage of small numbers is seen from mid April (earliest 6th April 1980) to the beginning of June and much heavier autumn passage in late August and stragglers continue into October, the latest being on 9th October 1976. The best day count in Spring was 15 on 15th May 1979 while in autumn over 100 were seen on 4th September 1979 and 40 or more have been seen on several other occasions. In 1932 Madoc described passage as continuing into November but his exceptionally late record for 27th November seems as improbable as the two allegedly seen at Slieau Whallian

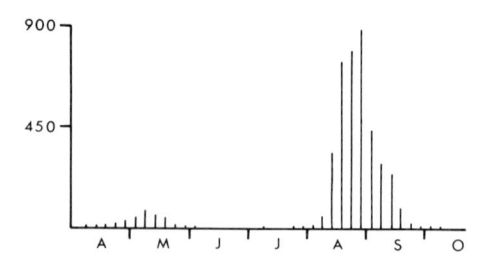

Tree Pipit. Total bird days per five day period (Calf).

on 7th March 1964 (Hudson's extreme dates for the British Isles are 12th March and 18th November.)

Between 1959 and 1983 358 Tree Pipits were ringed on the Calf yielding one recovery, a bird ringed on 19th August 1970 and found dead ten weeks later at Nouakchott, Mauritania is the only British ringed Tree Pipit to be recovered south of the Sahara.

Meadow Pipit
Anthus pratensis

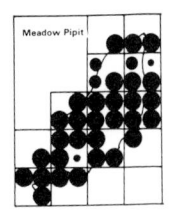

Common summer visitor, passage migrant and winter visitor.

'This is one of the very common and familiar birds of the island, abundant on every bit of grassy waste and in summer at least extending up to or nearly to its very highest ground; on the mountain land it is often the only species met with over miles of country. On the selvages of the coast its domain overlaps that of the Rock Pipit.' This description by Ralfe is equally applicable today.

The peak of immigration is seen at the beginning of April and by the middle of that month many clutches are complete – some broods are still in the nest at the end of July. In the early days of the Calf Observatory some 25 pairs were thought to breed, but since 1971 80–100 pairs have nested annually. While it is likely that the earlier figures were underestimates, there has been a real increase probably due to the cessation of farming and a gradual increase in rankness of vegetation, especially heather, in which the majority nests. In 1965 41 territories were found on the Ayres between Blue Point and the Point of Ayre (Wallace 1972).

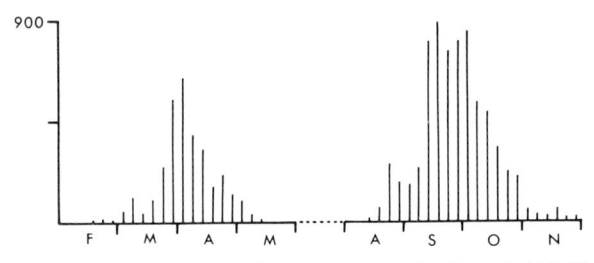

Meadow Pipit. Average numbers on passage per five day period (Calf).

Southward movement starts in late August and is at its maximum from mid September to early October. On the Calf the greatest day count was 5,000 on 19th September 1966. On the main island there is a definite tendency for southbound flocks to follow the hill tops and connecting ridges. The winter population is relatively small and is concentrated mainly in the vicinity of the coast. It is at this time that they are found on the lawns of Douglas Promenade and individuals are often found in the quieter residential streets. Spring passage is much lighter than autumn with a maximum day count on the Calf of 750 on 31st March 1979.

From 6,555 Meadow Pipits ringed on the Calf there have been 29 recoveries. Only 4 of these were on the British Isles and mid winter returns have come from north-west France to Southern Spain and Portugal, with the majority from the latter area. Several birds have been retrapped locally on the Calf when six years old.

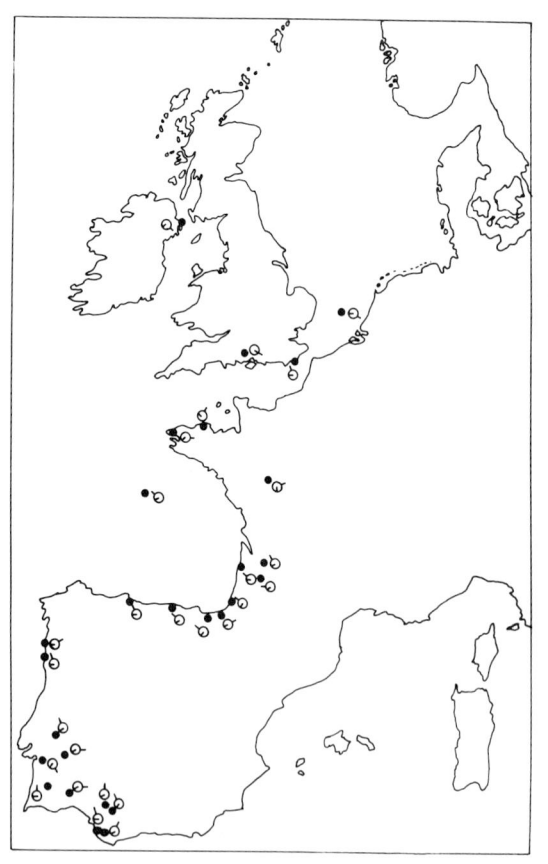

Meadow Pipit ringing recoveries.

As well as the nominate *A.p. pratensis*, the larger, brighter plumaged race *A.p. theresae* is of regular occurrence, especially in autumn, usually in the

company of White Wagtails *Motacilla alba alba*, of presumed Icelandic origin.
Manx: *Tweet* or *Cheet. Ushag y Veet*

Rock Pipit
Anthus spinoletta

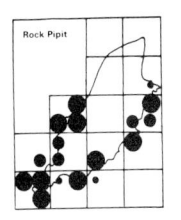

Common resident which also occurs as a passage migrant.

'In its peculiar locality the Rock Pipit is just as common as the last named. All along the rocky coast, high or low, it is abundant, among the little crags and sea-pink swards of Scarlett, on the tide-rocks at the foot of the great cliffs of Bradda and Spanish Head, and far amid the gloom of cavernous recesses, as the Ooig Mooar and the "Hall", near the Chasms, where it flits high over the deep green water that fills the cave. It flies and runs about the piers and sea-walls of Douglas, and seeks its food among the pools and little weedy reefs below them, in company with Ringed Plovers and Purple Sandpipers, a very tame and familiar but little-noticed bird.' Again the passage of time has in no way invalidated Ralfe's evocative words.

As a breeding bird it occurs with few interruptions from Glen Mooar south and round to Maughold. On the Calf there has for many years been a breeding population of 45–50 pairs and Langness is another stronghold. The nest is usually within a few metres of the sea, typically in a rocky defect well protected by vegetation, but on the Calf a few birds nest a little inland in stone walls and heather and a nest has been found on Langness 200 metres from the coast in gorse. Although nests have been found on the extreme dates of 4th April (Langness 1974), and 28th August (below Cronk ny iree laa 1902), early clutches are sometimes completed by mid April with second attempts during June and early July.

Some migrants probably pass through the Calf regularly and night migration of parties of 10–15 birds has been observed in March and September at the Chicken Rock Lighthouse.

From September to February Rock Pipits are more gregarious, loose flocks feeding along high water mark in the sandy bays and favouring particularly the pebbly coves of Port Grenaugh and Onchan Harbour where winter parties of up to 30 are regular. On the west coast Niarbyl is particularly favoured with a winter flock of up to 60 birds.

Ninety-four Rock Pipits have been ringed on the Calf, but none have been recovered. A bird of the nominate race *A.s. spinoletta*, the Water Pipit, was found feeding among Meadow Pipits in the Calf Lighthouse fields on 8th April 1977 (Haycock 1978) and on 19th February 1981 during a period of easterly winds a flock of about 15 Rock Pipits was found feeding in the Glen, this was an unusual site for Calf residents and all those examined showed the characteristics of the Fenno-Scandian race *A.s. littoralis*.
Manx: *Fushag Varrey*

Yellow Wagtail
Motacilla flava

Regular passage migrant in small numbers.

The first published record of the Yellow Wagtail was not until 1900 when there was a report from Maughold Head on the remarkable date of 8th December (Hudson 1973). At the time it was the latest ever record for the British Isles. Yellow Wagtails were seen in the autumn on a number of occasions during the next 20 years and it was even claimed that a pair bred at Maughold, one of several highly suspect records almost certainly referring to *M. cinerea*. Others probably in this category were 3 at Gansey on 23rd January 1931, although the observer stressed the correctness of his identification, a pair collecting food among the rocks at low tide at Traie Vane on 27th June 1934 and one at the Dhoon Quarry on 5th February 1942.

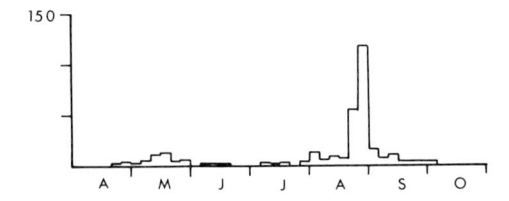

Yellow Wagtail. Total bird days per five day period (Calf).

Since about 1925 Yellow Wagtails have passed through the Island regularly in spring, and, in greater numbers, autumn. On the Calf, where the earliest date was 23rd April 1978, most spring birds are seen during May – the maximum day count of 3 being recorded on many occasions. The earliest unequivocal Manx record was one of 4 amongst grazing cattle on 16th March 1934 and other early birds were 2 on 31st March 1936, 1 at Onchan on 12th April the same year and 2 at Langness on 15th April 1966. Yellow Wagtails are occasionally seen in June and July but the main autumn movement is in late August. This coincides with the beginning of the main period of migration of *M. alba*, whose much larger gatherings often contain the odd representative of *M. flava*. Records after mid-September are not common and the latest Calf record was on 4th October 1981. (One or two records for the main island up to 10th October are questionable.) The highest day count on the Calf was 42 on 27th August 1966.

The vast majority of those birds sub-specifically identified have been of the race *M.f. flavissima*. A male Blue-headed Wagtail *M.f. flava* was present on the Calf on 15th May 1979 and the Grey-headed race *M.f. thunbergi* has been seen on the following occasions: single males on Langness on 5th August 1969 and on the Calf on 16th June 1972 and from 16th to 18th May 1974. Two birds were also seen on the Calf between 23rd and 28th August 1978.

Grey Wagtail
Motacilla cinerea

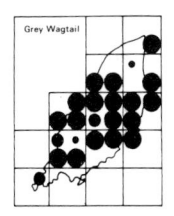

Fairly common breeding bird, occurring also as a passage migrant and winter visitor.

Ralfe implied that the Grey Wagtail was a rather scarce breeding bird because although he knew of several instances of nesting he had himself never seen one between April and late August. In his 1923 supplement he acknowledged that he had previously overstated its scarcity, but even then it was clearly very much less common than it is today. The rocky streams of the Isle of Man are ideally suited to this delightfully elegant wagtail and there are few if any which do not support at least one breeding pair. The only serious attempt at assessing the population was during the summer of 1975 when accurate surveys revealed 7 pairs on the Laxey River from Snaefell mines to the sea (5 km) and 5 pairs on the Glass between the Baldwin confluence and Quarterbridge (4.6 km), while on the Neb there were 3 pairs between the head of Glen Helen and Tynwald Mills (2.5 km) and 5 pairs from the Foxdale River junction to the sea (4.6 km). Twenty breeding pairs in 16.7 km is equivalent to 120 pairs in 100 km. Comparable figures in 1974 for other parts of Britain were Midlands and East Anglia 31, Northern England 37, Southern England 49, Northern Ireland 91 and North Wales 114. (Sharrock 1976)

Although the majority of nests are built very close to running water, at Middle Farm, Braddan a pair bred successfully in an open fronted farm building 320 m from the nearest stream and nests up to 40 m from water have been found at Garwick, Foxdale and Ballasalla. In many places adjacent to mills, weirs and bridges, the river bank is supported by a wall and this is arguably the prime nesting site. Because of this some sites have been used annually for many decades: Ballaugh Bridge has been regularly occupied for 80 years, Tromode falls for at least 45 years and the Foxdale railway bridge for at least 25 years.

Young have been found as early as 27th April, giving a first egg date on or before 11th April, but laying usually starts during the last week of April. Occasionally treble brooded, young have been found in the nest up to 21st July.

On migration Grey Wagtails pass through the Calf in fair numbers mainly during September. During the autumn there are day counts of 30 or more most years, the best being 58 on 13th September 1980. The latest Calf bird was on 17th November 1980. Thirteen were seen together at Glenfaba Weir on the River Neb on 24th September 1985.

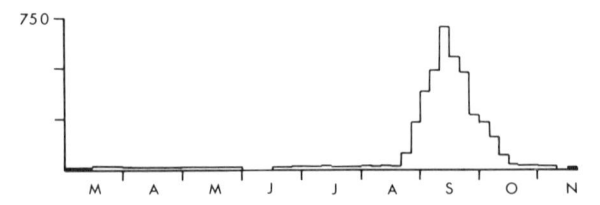

Grey Wagtail. Total bird days per five day period (Calf).

During winter they are much scarcer along the streams, but occur at certain points on the coast, in particular Port Grenaugh, Onchan Harbour and Niarbyl, and are often seen in the towns both in the gardens of residential areas and the streets of the more urban parts. Winter observations are nearly always of just one or two birds, but K. Williamson recorded an exceptional flock of about 40 feeding on the shore at Port Soderick on 2nd January 1938.

Three Grey Wagtails ringed in May in Scotland have been recovered on the Isle of Man during the same year – two of these were controlled on autumn passage, the third was found dead in mid December. There have been no recoveries from 64 birds ringed on the Calf.

Manx: *Ushag Ghlass*

Pied Wagtail

Motacilla alba

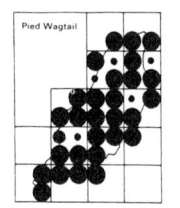

The Pied Wagtail *M.a. yarrellii* is a common breeding bird and passage migrant.

The White Wagtail *M.a. alba* is a common passage migrant.

In 1903 Ralfe knew the Pied Wagtail as a common resident, which was nevertheless much commoner as a migrant, but probably due to difficulties in separating the subspecies was only able to cite three records of the White Wagtail – all from the seashore during spring. Yet in 1923 he was able to say of *M.a.alba* that it appeared regularly at Castletown in considerable numbers on spring migration and yet more numerously on the autumn migration, a situation which obtains to this day.

The Pied Wagtail is very widely distributed as a breeding bird. Five is the most common clutch size although 6 eggs are not uncommon and smaller clutches are produced especially later in the season. On the Calf the first egg in a nest near the Observatory was laid on the very early date of 18th April 1981, but few eggs are laid before the second week in May. Most young are away before the end of July although a Strandhall nest still held young on 15th August 1946. On the Calf it has been a sporadic breeder, the first record being of a successful nest in a wall near the farmhouse in

1956. In 1976 two broods were reared in the out-buildings of a derelict lighthouse and between 1980 and 1983 two to four pairs nested regularly favouring particularly the upper lighthouse and the Observatory, but also Cow Harbour, South Harbour and Culbery.

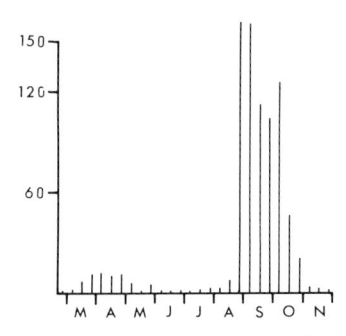

Pied Wagtail. Average passage numbers per ten day period (Calf).

M. alba is a common passage migrant, although autumn birds far outnumber those seen in spring. On the Calf Pied Wagtails have been recorded between 28th February and 30th November, the best day counts being 21 in spring and 100 in autumn. White Wagtails have not been seen before 6th April nor after 10th October – the best spring day count was only 10, but 300 have been seen in autumn. On the main island Derbyhaven Bay, the Sandwick shore and Fleshwick are particularly favoured. Spring peaks are usually of about 25 birds, although there were 50 at Sandwick on 30th April 1979. During the last few days of August a scatter of 30–100 birds at these southern bays is a regular feature. They hurry over the sands over weed-covered rocks, along the shingle beaches and onto the adjacent golf course. Elsewhere the muddy floors of the harbours of Peel, Castletown and Ramsey are also attractive to these energetic little birds.

In winter Pied Wagtails are plentiful in the towns, feeding fearlessly in busy streets on the quieter avenues of the residential areas and in particular on the sea side promenades. In spring they become more widely distributed and Kermode described how farmers used to await their appearance before beginning to plough. In 1901 he wrote 'Only a few years ago a farmer in Andreas started out to plough and put back again because the Wagtail had not come.' Its eager accompaniment of the ploughman remains one of the most attractive sights of the Manx spring. A number of roosts have been located from time to time, the best known being one in an ash tree by the Court House in Ramsey. This was occupied definitely from 1912 to at least 1947, birds being present from early September to the end of October and sometimes on to the beginning of December with peak counts of about 300. In the early 1930s there was an autumn roost in Castletown Square and in 1948 a roost of several hundred birds in trees bordering Noble's Park along the Glencrutchery Road in Douglas. In the mid 1950s Pied Wagtails roosted throughout the winter on the Mooragh Island at Ramsey and recently over 70 were found roosting in the Cringle Quarry (an unusually wild location 300 m above sea level) on 7th October 1978 and another roost has been found at Onchan Stadium. A small spring roost was also found at King William's College – 20–30 birds collecting in mid March in 1945 and 1951. There is just one record of Pied Wagtails roosting communally in summer – 28 occupying an old mineshaft near Foxdale on 28th June 1932.

Although 289 White/Pied Wagtails have been ringed on the Calf and many pulli of *M.a. yarrellii* have been ringed on the main island there have been no recoveries.

Manx: *Ushag Vreck* = Pied Bird. *Ushag voltee* = Weather Bird

Waxwing
Bombycilla garrulus

Irregular winter visitor in very small numbers.

To the British Isles the Waxwing is an irregular winter visitor which in some years occurs in considerable numbers when a poor crop of rowan berries coincides with high breeding success in its north-east European nesting grounds. During the last century there were notable invasions in 5 winters, and in the last, that of 1892–3 there were records of 4 birds reaching the Isle of Man. Eastern Britain had always received much greater numbers and there had only been 2 previous records for the Isle of Man. Although good numbers reached Ireland during the major influx of 1903–4, none were seen in the Isle of Man in that winter or that of the 1913–14 invasion. At Ramsey one had been taken in 1906–7 and several were seen in December 1921 when the British Isles witnessed another invasion. The irruption of 1932–3 reached Ireland and produced one record of 2 birds at Kirkmichael during November and since then all the major British invasions have penetrated to the Isle of Man. Thus in 1937 early March produced several records of 4–6 birds in the Laxey area, 2 more at Cornaa and others at Ramsey, while an invasion extending to west Scotland coincided with 2 birds spending November 1941 at Laxey. At the time the irruption of 1946–7 was the greatest in Irish history and was heralded on the Isle of Man by a single bird at Sulby on 19th November. There was a scatter of single birds in the Ramsey area from early January and a flock of 9 gathered by 19th February. That winter also brought records from Maughold, Kirkmichael and St John's, but with the onset of the thaw they all disappeared (Cowin 1948). In March and April 1952 single birds were reported in the Douglas area and when Ireland next enjoyed a substantial influx in the winter of 1957–8 there was another good showing on the Isle of Man with 3–4 at Bride, 2 at Lewaigue and 6 at Ramsey all on 19th November, to be followed by single birds at St John's in mid December and at Douglas at the end of March. In Ireland Waxwings were reported annually from 1955 and this was nearly true on the Isle of Man where there were some 7 records during 1959, 1 in 1962, 6 in 1963 (which included the only Calf record) and 1 in 1964.

The unprecedented invasion of western Europe in 1965–6 was remarkable for its magnitude and its earliness (Cornwallis and Townsend 1968). First was a party of 13 in Morvern (Argyll) from 22nd September, but the next record came surprisingly from the Isle of Man, a single bird feeding on *Cotoneaster* berries at the Beary (German) on 8th October. A further week was to elapse before numbers began to increase considerably in Scotland and arrivals took place along the east coast of England. Towards the end of October a flock of 200 appeared at Derry, Northern Ireland, there were good numbers along the coast of Lancashire, Cheshire and North Wales and a number of flocks were seen on the Isle of Man, all these birds having probably moved on from Scotland. The Manx invasion probably began between Michael and Peel to be followed by fresh arrivals in the Bride area. They became widely distributed mostly in parties of 5–7 birds but there were several reports of 20–30. There were good numbers up to mid November, but it seems that by early December the Waxwings had moved on to Ireland where peak numbers were seen in late November and in December. Last records of the invasion were in Douglas where there were birds on 21st and 27th April. In 1966, 1967, 1968, 1973, 1974, 1975 and 1977 1–3 records of single birds or pairs have occurred mostly in November and December, although one was present for a few days in early January and another stayed for 10 weeks from 20th January.

With the exception of the great invasion of late 1965 the Waxwing has been a rare visitor and it is interesting that Ballakermeen School in Douglas was visited in February 1952, November 1968, December 1974 and during early 1977 with a further record from very nearby in late December 1973/early January 1974.

Dipper

Cinclus cinclus

Former resident breeding bird, now a rare visitor.

Towards the end of the 19th century the Dipper was a resident of the Laxey and Cornaa valleys. It had been seen on the headwaters of the main Laxey River near Snaefell Mines and on its minute tributary the Glen Foss stream which joins it near Laggan Agneash. Further downstream the main river is joined by the Agneash stream, which provided water for the Laxey Wheel, and there seems little doubt that Dippers bred below the Wheel and also in Glen Drink near Agneash itself, a nest being found there in 1897. During the same period nests were found on several occasions, usually under bridges, on the Cornaa River. Unaccountably there have been no records of Dippers in either valley during the last 80 years.

Cadman (1898), having fished the Sulby, Neb and Glass Rivers virtually from their sources and with great regularity since 1859 stated 'There are not any Water Ouzels in Man' and this must have been an accurate observation for these rivers. In 1901 however a Dipper was seen on the Rhenass branch of the Neb and nests were later found in several years up to 1907. In 1912 an unfinished nest was found in the Cluggid Gorge, a branch of Sulby Glen and the following year Dippers nested under the bridge at the entrance to East Baldwin. In 1934 Madoc was able to write that he had found nests at Tromode and at West Baldwin village, but there have been no breeding records since.

During the period 1937–48 Dippers were recorded most years including pairs at an undisclosed site in May 1937, on the Silverburn at Ballasalla in April 1939 and at Druidale (Upper Sulby) in May 1940. This period also produced spring records for the Middle River and the Dhoo at Kirby.

Dippers have been recorded less than ten times during the last 35 years in March, April, May, August, September and November, a remarkably barren era for a bird which is such a characteristic resident of streams similar to those of Man on the adjacent islands.

Careful examination of six specimens from the Isle of Man has shown that both the British race *C.c. gularis* and the Irish form *C.c. hibernicus* have occurred. British birds came from Tromode in November 1880, from the Sulby, from an un-named location in the summer of 1928 and from a fourth undisclosed site, while examples from Castletown (November 1915) and the headwaters of the Sulby (November 1923) resembled the Irish race.

Manx: *Lhondhoo ny Hawin* = Blackbird of the Stream

Wren

Troglodytes troglodytes

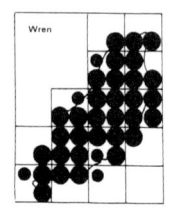

Very common resident.

Ralfe described the Wren as being common and well distributed, without being really numerous – 80 years later it is unquestionably very common and as Ralfe so aptly wrote 'it is at home among the heather and brambles overhanging the course of the mountain stream through the rocky ravine, amidst the boulders and bracken of the rough hillside, and in the rock fissures of the wild coast, as well as in the neglected garden hedge with its mossy hawthorn stumps, or the farm-steading, where in winter it finds its food. A steep, shaded, and overhung bank is perhaps its favourite home.' Although sensitive to hard winters it has been noted on the Calf to suffer much less than the Stonechat.

Eggs are laid mostly from early April through to late May, but fresh eggs have been found in August. An exceptionally early nest was found near Ormly Hall, Ramsey on 12th January 1908: it contained 2 eggs considered to be 6–8 days incubated (Bell 1908). The commonest site for a nest is either behind the roots of a stream-side tree, undermined by spates, or against the vertical surface of the table of earth and roots of a fallen tree. More unusual situations have been in a jug on a hook in an outhouse and in the sleeve of a jacket hanging in a shed. Sayle (1980) described how a Wren visited a Blue Tit's nest during the summer and was later seen feeding a juvenile Blue Tit away from the nest.

A Common Bird Census in Cooıl Dharry in 1975, 1976 and 1977 revealed 21 territories in an area of 14 hectares (Cain 1978). This is no doubt typical of other wooded glens such as Port Soderick, Silverdale, Glenmaye and Groudle. Along a 4 km stretch of the River Glass from the Baldwin Junction to Quarterbridge, a mixture of wood and farmland, 22 territories were located in 1975, while on the Calf (246 hectares) there was an apparent increase from 8 territories in 1959 to at least 73 in 1974. Since then the Calf breeding population has been between 45 and 75 pairs with a notable slump to 25 pairs in 1979 followed by a swift recovery.

Although the Manx population is regarded as resident there is definite movement in spring and autumn although there is no evidence as to whether this involves only Manx birds or those from further afield. Birds have been seen at the Chicken Rock in October and the Calf witnesses regular influxes in March and April and in September and October. In the period 1959–83 2,125 birds were ringed on the Calf, yet only one was recovered – at Port Erin. During an 11 year sample period over 8% of birds were retrapped on the Calf one or more years after ringing.

Wrens retrapped after year of ringing on the Calf of Man 1969–79

Years after ringing	1	2	3	4	Total retrapped	Total ringed
Number retrapped	59	25	12	4	100	1198
% of total ringed	4.93	2.09	1.00	0.33	8.35	100

Wrens ringed in Laxey and Castletown in autumn were recovered nearby during the same winter.

One of the best known seasonal Manx customs is 'Hunt the Wren' celebrated on 26th December. It is not peculiar to the Isle of Man as it used to be practised in Ireland and has been described in a different form in England and France. William Harrison (1869) wrote 'This custom is still kept up on St Stephen's Day, chiefly by boys, who at early dawn sally out armed with long sticks, beating the bushes until they find one of these birds, when they commence the chase with great shoutings, following it from bush to bush, and when killed it is suspended in a garland of ribbons, flowers and evergreens. The procession then commences, carrying that "King of Birds", as the Druids called it, from house to house, soliciting contributions, and giving a feather for luck. These are considered an effectual preservative from shipwreck, and some fishermen will not venture out to sea without having first provided themselves with a few of these feathers to ensure their safe return. The "dreain" or Wren's feathers are considered an effectual preservative against witchcraft. It was formerly the custom in the evening to inter the naked body with great solemnity in a secluded corner of the churchyard, and conclude the evening with wrestling and all manner of sports.' According to Townley (1789) if the Wren could be caught before sunrise good herring fishing during the next season was assured. Although the habit of killing a Wren had probably died out by 1900 Ralfe knew of many parties scattered

around the Island in 1904, and the custom can still be witnessed, notably in Peel, to this day. Its origin remains a mystery.
Manx: *Drean*

Dunnock
Prunella modularis

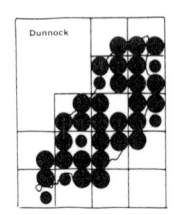

Common resident which also occurs as a passage migrant.

Kermode believed that the Hedge Sparrow became less plentiful towards the end of the 19th century but there is no evidence of any significant change since then. It is widely distributed as a breeding bird in gardens and hedgerows, in the more open wooded glens and all around the coast especially where there is a rich straggling growth of brambles. In the Isle of Man it is found up to about 230 m above sea level in such localities as South Barrule plantation and the open woodland below Kate's Cottage. In 1965 a Common Bird Census of the Ayres, where the heavily overgrown margins between heath and pasture form such an excellent habitat, yielded 6 territories and in 1975–7 2 territories were found in Cooil Dharry. During the 1960s the Calf population varied between 6 and 16 pairs and reached a peak of 33 pairs in 1972. From then until 1981 when there were 20 pairs breeding numbers varied between 15 and 27 but following the severe winter of 1981–2 there was a dramatic crash to only 8 pairs. Kermode had seen eggs on the early date of 20th March, but most are laid during April and May and young may still be in the nest up to the end of July.

Minor passage is sometimes seen on the Calf in spring and most autumns during September and October – there was a flock of 24 at Jane's House on 3rd September 1961 and 30 in the Glen on 1st October 1978 – the best day count. Day arrivals of 15–20 new birds occur on a few days each autumn.

Dunnocks seem scarcer during winter, not perhaps on the coast but certainly inland, so some of our breeding birds may migrate although ringing recoveries give little support to this. Between 1959 and 1983 1,190 were ringed on the Calf with just 6 recoveries – 4 in the Port Erin/Port St Mary area, 1 at Foxdale and 1 at Walney, Lancs.

Of birds ringed on the main island five have been recovered – all within 5 km of their ringing site. During a sample 9 year period almost 18% of Dunnocks ringed on the Calf were retrapped during a subsequent year.

Dunnocks retrapped after year of ringing on the Calf of Man 1969–77

Years after ringing	1	2	3	4	5	6	Total retrapped	Total ringed
Number retrapped	48	21	9	4	6	2	90	501
% of total ringed	9.58	4.19	1.80	0.80	1.20	0.40	17.97	100

Manx: *Drean mollagh* = Rough Wren. *Bogh Keeir* = Grey Poor One

Robin
Erithacus rubecula

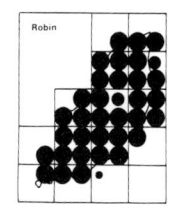

Common resident, passage migrant and winter visitor.

There is no evidence of any change in the Robin's status during the present century. It is a common inhabitant of all varieties of woodland, of hedgerows and bramble covered walls and of rural and suburban gardens. Cooil Dharry, a typical wooded glen of 14 hectares, held 20 territories during the summers of 1975–7, while a 4 km stretch of the River Glass from the Baldwin junction to Quarterbridge held 15 summer territories in 1975. On the Calf, where breeding was first proved in 1967, 4–6 breeding pairs were usual up to 1977 since which they have failed to nest in two years with only 2–3 pairs in the other years.

One of the more appealing features of this favourite among song birds is its often highly original choice of nest site. In 1932 the Vicar of Castletown discovered a nest with five eggs on books laid flat on the top shelf of a bookcase in his study and in 1974 a pair nested in a gap between tins of paint in a busy Onchan warehouse. A nest with two eggs was found in Glen Auldyn in 1932 on the very early date of 2nd March, but first eggs are usually laid towards the end of the first week of April. The latest date for young in the nest is 23rd June. Five is the commonest clutch size, closely followed by 4, 6 eggs are rather unusual and 7 exceptional.

On the Calf spring passage is from March to mid-May with 50 recorded on two dates in early April. Autumn movement is seen from late July to mid-November with a peak in mid-September. The maximum day count was 140 on 13th September 1976.

Smith (1973, 1975, 1976) made a study of autumn territories on the Calf. He surveyed the whole island and found 31, 43 and 58 territories in successive years. He admitted that his technique improved each year and did not feel that these figures represented an increasing population. He was confident in the accuracy of his last figure (autumn 1975). Seven territories were located around the Observatory where tree and shrub cover is richest. There was a good population through the Glen and a number of others were found along the boundaries of the old field systems, where brambles grow against dry stone walls. About $\frac{1}{4}$ of the territories were coastal. Smith's analysis of the ringing and recapture logs showed that the autumn population was made up of resident adults and of migrants, some of which would move on while others would winter on the Calf.

Between 1959 and 1983 3,123 Robins were ringed on the Calf and many others have been ringed on the main island. The very few recoveries of birds ringed as pulli suggest that they are resident. Many birds passing through the Calf are destined for Ireland and others have been recovered during the winter in other parts of the Isle of Man. Breeding season returns from the Isle of Man have come mostly from Scotland. An example of the continental race *E.r. rubecula* was ringed on Fair Isle on 27th September and controlled on the Calf 20 days later. This race is recognised as a scarce Calf migrant in April/May and October/November. The only continental recovery was of an immature bird ringed on the Calf in late August and found in Utrecht (Holland) 4 months later.

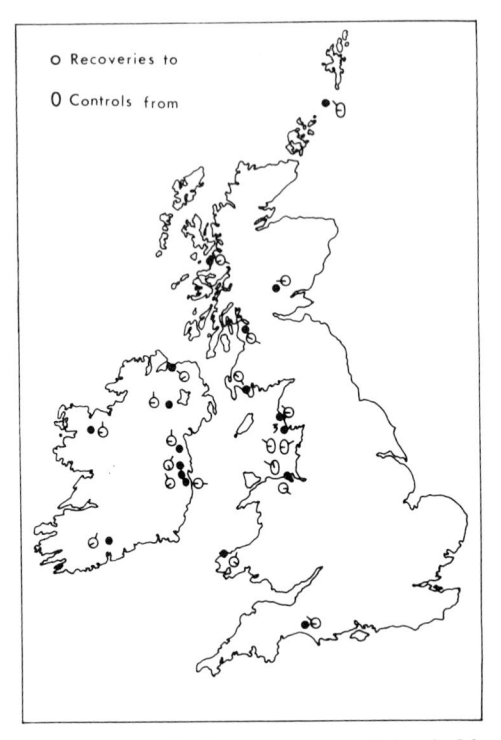

Recovery sites and origins of Robins ringed or controlled on the Isle of Man.

Manx: *Cleean jiarg* = Redbreast. *Spittag*

Nightingale

Luscinia megarhynchos

Uncommon passage migrant.

The first Manx record was of one trapped on the Calf on 15th May 1966 (Bennett 1968). Individuals have since been recorded on the Calf on 3rd, 5th (two on the same day), 16th, 17th and 30th May and on 20th and 27th June. The only autumn record was of an unidentified Nightingale seen on 27th September 1976 which was either this species or a Thrush Nightingale *L. luscinia*.

Bluethroat

Luscinia svecica

Rare passage migrant.

The first Manx record was of an immature female trapped near the Calf of Man Observatory on 14th November 1975 (Haycock 1978). There has since been one other autumn record from the Calf (an immature or female) on 9th October 1983 and four in spring between 12th and 19th May. In 1977 an immature male was seen in the Glen on 17th and 18th and in 1981 there was a female by the millpond on 12th, an adult male at Cow Harbour the following day and a second year male in the Glen 6 days later. Bluethroats occurred in exceptional numbers in north and east Scotland in mid May 1981, but surprisingly there were no records for the western side of Scotland or Ireland at that time.

All three males seen on the Calf were attributable to the red-spotted race *L.s. svecica*.

White-throated Robin

Irania gutturalis

Vagrant.

The only record for the British Isles is of a male seen near the Observatory on the Calf of Man on 22nd June 1983. The White-throated Robin breeds in Asia Minor, Iran and Afghanistan, wintering in Arabia and north-east Africa (del-Nevo 1983). At the time of going to press this record was still under consideration by the British Ornithologists' Union.

Black Redstart

Phoenicurus ochruros

Regular passage migrant in small numbers, individuals wintering in some years.

First recorded on the Isle of Man in February 1848, the next 50 years produced only one definite record – two birds frequenting the shipyard at Ramsey in late January 1895. During the following three decades there was just a handful of winter records, but since 1927 one or two birds have been recorded almost annually on the main island. With one notable exception its appearances on the Calf were similar up to 1973, but since then it has become decidedly more plentiful on both spring and autumn passage.

Although occasionally noted from as early as 1st October, most autumn records fall within the period 15th October to 30th November and four autumn invasions deserve special mention. In 1939 a small party was present near Langness Lighthouse on 12th November and was followed by an astonishing movement on the Calf during the last week of that month. Some 250 Black

Redstarts appeared suddenly about 24th November, coming in on a north-westerly wind and remaining in similar numbers until 28th, when they decreased, vanishing altogether before the end of the month. Scores of birds were seen along the Glen and the wall running from Gibbdale almost to South Harbour (Williamson 1940 and 1947). Strangely no such invasion was witnessed in any other part of Britain at this time. Between 26th and 28th October 1975 there was a much smaller influx on the Calf with a peak of 18 birds on the latter date – to the south west at Hook Head (County Wexford) there had been 9 birds on 24th October and 75 on 26th, but the only records for the main island were 3 on the Chasms beach on 3rd November. 1977 saw a fair passage through the Calf between 15th and 27th October (maximum 9 on 21st October). Slightly later, between 17th and 20th October there were a few in the Castletown area and there followed frequent records of 1–2 birds from many parts of the Island up to 26th November. Again this movement occurred a few days earlier in south east Ireland, Great Saltee witnessing movement from 14th to 21st October with a peak on 18th. The largest invasion of recent years was in 1982 starting with an influx of 27 birds on the Calf on 30th October and 35 the following day – 7–18 were then seen daily through November. On the main island 1–2 were present at Scarlett, Derbyhaven, Onchan Head and Peel during the last days of October and at Port St Mary 1–3 were present from 2nd to 13th November with 5 on 3rd. One to two Black Redstarts were reported quite widely up to 14th November. In Ireland the invasion was seen at two localities in Co. Cork on 30th October and there were over 40 at Hook Head on 30th and 31st while on Bardsey rather smaller numbers peaked between 29th and 31st. This pattern of autumn records shows that Black Redstarts reach the most southerly parts of the Isle of Man from the south and south west, consistently moving in the opposite direction to that in which most other passerine migrants are travelling. There also appears to be a closer link with records from Ireland than those from West Wales and small numbers at Hilbre and other Cheshire localities can in no way be related to Manx occurrences. It is also noticeable how very few Black Redstarts have been reported in southern Scotland in the wake of Manx invasions.

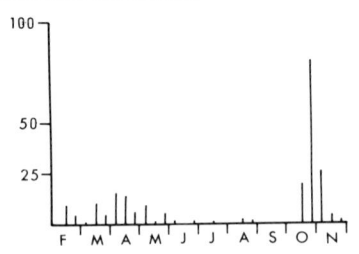

Black Redstart. Total bird days per ten day period (Calf).

Late autumn migrants will often linger for a few days or even 2–3 weeks at the same location and there are a few instances of Black Redstarts remaining from December to mid February and on two occasions until mid March.

Port St Mary has consistently attracted wintering birds, notably in 1937/8 when up to 7 were present, with 1 in 1939/40, 1974/5, 1978/9 and 1981/2.

In spring birds have been seen on the Calf from as early as 11th February, but small numbers (highest day count only 4) are seen mainly from mid March to early May. Spring records for the main island are decidedly few and the rare occurrences between the end of May and the beginning of October are as follows: 1 on the Calf on 27th and 28th June 1972, 1 on the Marine Drive on 4th July 1974, 1 on the Calf on 13th July 1981, another frequenting the garden of the Calf Lighthouse from 19th July to 27th August 1982, 1 at Knockaloe Beg on 30th July 1968 and 2 on the Calf between 17th and 23rd August 1975.

On passage Black Redstarts are found on rocky shores and beaches, sometimes in quarries, and in towns where gardens, allotments, shipyards, timber yards and fairgrounds have all been visited. Particularly favoured localities have been Port St Mary, the Chasms, Langness, the Marine Drive, Onchan Head and Peel Castle rocks.

Redstart
Phoenicurus phoenicurus

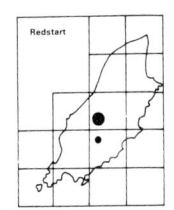

Regular passage migrant which has bred.

In 1905 Ralfe wrote of a few occurrences of the Redstart in spring and autumn, but it is clear that it was an uncommon bird which had so far eluded him. By 1923 he was able to upgrade its status to that of a regular passage migrant and so it has remained. Although the establishment of the Calf Observatory has produced a huge increase in the number of records (an average of 34 Redstarts are ringed there annually), the number of records for the main island has altered very little. The Calf appears to be very much at the western limit of Redstart migrations as it is clearly a much rarer bird on passage in Ireland. Strangely the numbers ringed on Bardsey (whose annual ringing effort is very similar to that of the Calf) are only just over 40% of the total of Calf-ringed Redstarts.

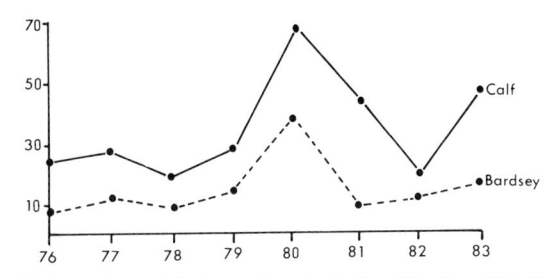

Redstart. Annual ringing totals on the Calf and Bardsey 1976–83.

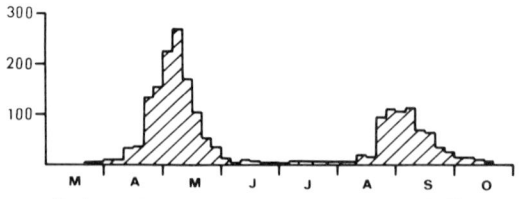

Redstart. Total bird days per five day period (Calf).

Rather commoner on spring than autumn passage, the earliest date is of three near St John's on 19th March 1961 and 1 on the Calf on 24th March the same year. The main spring movement is seen from mid April with a peak in early May. Thirty on 26th April 1966 and 7th May 1967 were the highest day counts on the Calf, where there have also been occasional records during June and July. Autumn passage is from late August to the end of September with a few birds occurring in October in most years. The latest Calf record was on 17th October 1977, but on the main island there is an exceptional record of a male at Surby on 7th November 1980. Although on the main island records from close to the coast predominate it is clear that Redstarts on passage pass through the centre of the island halting here and there. Typically they are found along the hedgerows of farmland and curragh and on the edges of plantations.

Between 1968 and 1971 at least one pair bred annually in the hills of the Sulby watershed, nesting in the stone walls near the Druidale ford and a few km north at Killabregga. In Ireland the Redstart is a very scarce breeding bird, but the period 1968–72 saw more breeding records than in any comparable period this century (Sharrock 1976) – since then up to four pairs have continued to breed in Co. Wicklow.

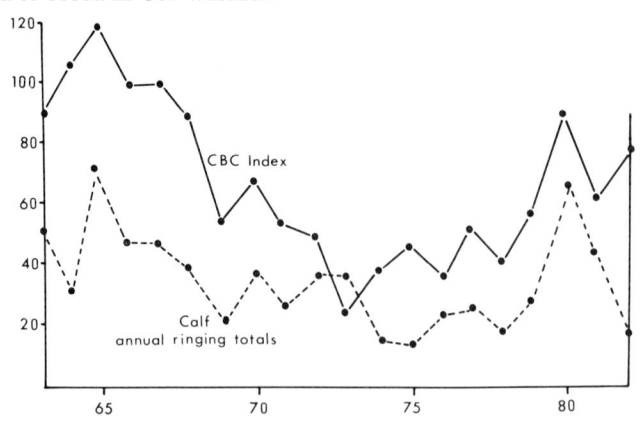

Redstart. Annual ringing totals (Calf) and national CBC indices, 1963–82.

In the period 1959–83 846 Redstarts were ringed on the Calf with 6 recoveries coming from Algeria, Morocco, Portugal, Spain, Lundy and Northern Ireland. In addition birds ringed on the Isle of May, Northumberland (a pullus) and Beachy Head (Sussex) were controlled on the Calf.

Whinchat
Saxicola rubetra

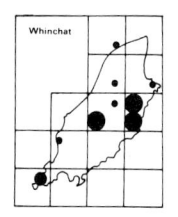

Scarce summer visitor and regular passage migrant.

First identified by Ralfe in Laxey village in late April 1897, the Whinchat was recorded with increasing frequency during the next 25 years so that he could describe it as a regular migrant in his supplement. There is nothing to suggest that it is any more or less common on passage now than it was 60 years ago. Whinchats have bred very spasmodically since 1909 and regularly and in increasing numbers at one locality over the last 10 years.

James Bell's collection contains a clutch of 4 eggs taken from a nest at the Point of Ayre on 27th May 1909 and attributed to this species, but the Winchat's Manx breeding history really started in 1926 when Madoc found two pairs in the Laxey valley in June, one of which was feeding young. Around the same time he located two singing males in late June in the Corrany valley. In 1932 and again in 1936 young were seen being fed near Cregneish, while in the north a pair was present at Knock e dooney throughout the summer although breeding was never proved. On the Calf Whinchats have bred at least twice, a pair being seen with young on 12th June 1943 and a brood of 4 near the nest on 26th June 1957. On 8th June 1952 a female was seen visiting a nest beneath heather at Kionslieu which was found to contain 5 newly hatched young and 1 egg. In 1964 a pair was seen at Injebreck on 28th June and in 1976 one young bird fledged from a nest on Peel Hill on 28th July – two years later Whinchats bred at Conrhenny Plantation and very probably in Sulby Glen and above Greeba Bridge. In 1985 a nest on the lower slopes of Slieau Meayll held 5 young on 14th May.

While most of these have been casual instances of breeding, the Laxey valley now has a history of regular breeding for 10 years and quite possibly for considerably longer. Nesting there in 1926 has already been mentioned and in 1965 a pair was seen with 2 juveniles on 8th August. Since 1975 Whinchats have nested in the vicinity of Laggan Agneash – early reports probably referred to a single pair, but in 1980 three pairs were thought to have produced young and in 1984 a pair had 2 fledged young on 30th June and at least four other pairs were holding territory over a distance of 1 km. Here the northern side of the valley is clothed in dense bracken interrupted here and there by bushes and outcrops of rock about 200 m above sea level.

The main period of spring passage is during the first two weeks of May with fair numbers continuing to the end of that month. The earliest record

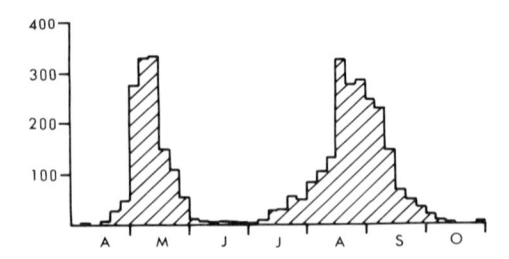

Whinchat. Total bird days per five day period (Calf).

was of a female at Cregneish on 3rd April 1960 and there have been a further 5 records before 12th April. The highest spring day count for the Calf was 50 on 12th May 1965, while on the main island 13 on the Andreas Ayres on 14th May 1943 and at least 15 on Langness on 4th May 1985 were exceptional. Returning birds are seen increasingly from early July but the peak is between mid-August and mid-September, with occasional October records most years. In both 1975 and 1976 late birds were seen on the Calf on 28th October, but on the main island there was one at Kentraugh on 5th November 1967 and another at King William's College on 20th November 1966. The highest autumn day count on the Calf was 40 on 19th August 1966.

On passage Whinchats are seen mostly at coastal sites but occasionally in the hills. Although a more familiar bird than the Redstart on the main island, only 503 were ringed on the Calf between 1959 and 1983 with recoveries from Algeria, Spain and France. One bird ringed on 24th August was retrapped on 6th September the following year.

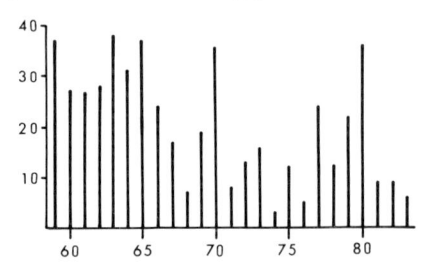

Whinchat. Annual ringing totals 1959–83 (Calf).

Stonechat
Saxicola torquata

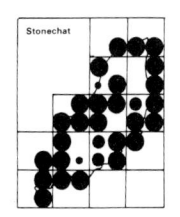

Common resident, summer visitor and passage migrant,

The delightfully uninhibited, not to say flamboyant Stonechat is a Manx speciality. As Ralfe wrote 'the isle abounds in the kind of ground suited to it – the untilled borders of the coast, the bushy strips along the course of the streams, the patches of "garey", rough and often somewhat wet land overgrown with gorse, the lines of huge and furze-beset hedging; and the mild climate of our winter is attractive to the somewhat tender nature of the Stonechat.'

While the present century has seen a considerable reduction in Stonechat numbers in mainland Britain due largely to habitat destruction (Magee 1965) this does not appear to have happened on the Isle of Man. Unfortunately no numerical data prior to 1937 are available. Ralfe described it as very common and Madoc wrote of 'big numbers in the Island, in some places it swarms.' The Stonechat is notoriously sensitive to sustained cold weather so that the population is subject to marked fluctuations but in the long term there seems to have been no significant change. This is well illustrated by breeding numbers on the Calf over the last 25 years. On Peel Hill there were 8 pairs in the summer of 1937, but recently there have been as many as 18 territories there in 1976 but only six in 1981. Similarly there were 4–6 pairs along the Marine Drive in the early 1940s while recent counts have varied from 2–7 pairs. The national census of 1961 revealed 35 pairs on the Isle of Man of which at least 14 were on the Calf which had a fairly good year. There seems little doubt that this was a very considerable under-statement of the true Manx population which in an average year is probably between 100 and 150 pairs.

Severe winters have from time to time almost wiped out the Manx population. Particularly lethal were the winters of 1894–5, 1916–17 and 1962–63, after which full recovery on the Calf took a decade. On the main island there is a sparse but quite widely distributed inland breeding population when overall numbers are high as in 1977, when there were 20 or more pairs, but two bad winters resulted in a total absence from inland sites in 1979 and 1980.

On the Calf the breeding population is known to be partly resident, full numbers not being present until mid-April, and this is probably true on the main island too. The Stonechat has a long breeding season and is usually triple-brooded. Early eggs are laid during the last few days of March and while most breeding activity is over by the end of July there is a record of a Poortown nest containing four eggs on 2nd September 1928. Five is the most usual clutch size, but 4 or 6 eggs are not uncommon and there is one record of a nest with 7 eggs at Andreas in June 1938. Polygyny is well known in the Stonechat and has been noted on the Calf. During periods when Stonechats are found inland certain localities remain tenanted in both the breeding season and in winter at altitudes up to 300 m. Sometimes the traditional gorse bushes of rough country are forsaken in favour of man made lookout posts such as television aerials or the rigging of a ship in harbour and in winter they readily resort to the stacks of dry seaweed along the high water mark.

On passage Stonechats move through the Calf between March and May and in greater numbers from July to November. One thousand three hundred and ninety birds were ringed on the Calf in the period 1959–83 and 8 have been recovered. Most of the birds ringed are locally bred and juveniles. Juveniles ringed in June were recovered at Port Erin the same November and at Peel the following September, while another juvenile (probably Manx-bred) was recovered in southern Portugal 6 months later. A juvenile ringed in late August was found dead at Port Erin 3 months later and the other 4 recoveries were of birds ringed during their first September, their natal area being unknown. One was recovered at Jurby 12 months later, another was found in Cheshire 14 months later while the other two were recovered in Spain and France the same winter. It is interesting to note that although a fair proportion of our Stonechats appear to winter in southern Europe ringing totals on the Calf relate remarkably closely to breeding numbers and in particular mirror the slumps related to unusually cold British winters.

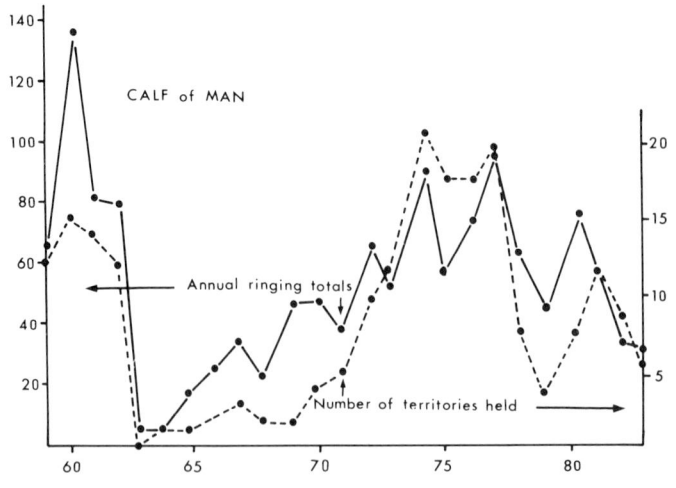

Stonechat. Annual ringing totals and territories held 1959–83 (Calf).

Manx: *Boid y chonnee* = Point of the gorse. *Kione dhoo y eeigyn* = Black head of the stacks

Wheatear
Oenanthe oenanthe

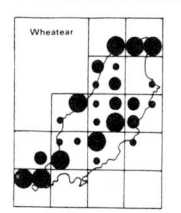

Rather scarce, but regular summer visitor and common passage migrant.

Although common on passage, the number of Wheatears which remain to breed varies quite markedly. In general Ralfe's statement that comparatively few do breed is applicable today, but Madoc, writing of the 20s and early 30s, believed that 'quite a considerable number stayed to nest.' More recent observations have shown that localities tenanted by several pairs one year, may be deserted the next – the Calf, where 0–8 pairs have nested during the last 25 years, provides a good example.

Wheatears nest in cavities under slabs of stone, in recesses in stone walls and in rabbit holes. The Isle of Man is rich in rocky moorland and whether coastal or inland this is the chosen habitat of the majority of our breeding

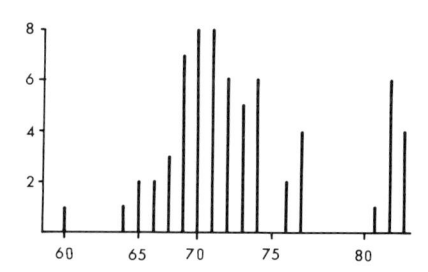

Wheatear. Breeding pairs on Calf 1959–83 (excl. 1966 – no data).

birds. Apart from the Calf the coast of Rushen, especially Bradda Hill, is a favourite area. They have also bred from time to time at several localities along the west coast, notably the Sloc, Eary Cushlin, Peel Hill and Glen Cam. Inland the Brandywell area has a long history of intermittent occupation and they have also nested in the Sulby Glen area, the Corrany valley and the slopes of South Barrule. Rabbit holes are used particularly in the sandy warren behind Orrisdale Head and on the Ayres from Blue Point eastward, especially in those parts carpeted with Burnet rose. Most nests are in wild country but there are old records from the walls of Peel Castle and they have recently bred in a roadside wall at Derbyhaven.

Very often double-brooded, young may be seen out of the nest from about 3rd June.

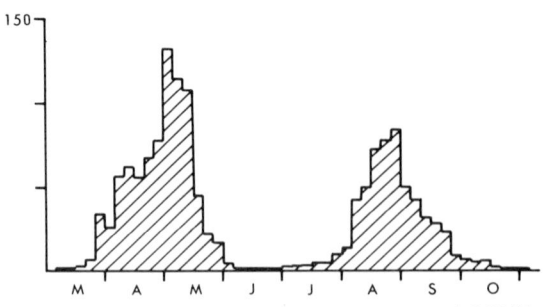

Wheatear. Average passage bird days per five day period (Calf).

As a passage migrant the Wheatear is especially plentiful in spring, but also occurs in good numbers in autumn. Earliest of all was a male at Ramsey on 4th February 1957 and in 1887 several were seen at the Chicken Rock on 17th February. In 7 years since 1928 the first Wheatear has been seen between 1st and 10th March, the mean first date being 18th March. The main passage period is from early April to about 20th May with a notable peak at the beginning of that month. Movement is sometimes very heavy, notably on 29th March 1937 when hundreds passed through the Calf and on 4th April 1980 when 63 were counted on the Ayres. On 13th April 1885 there was a huge movement in which 7 were killed at Langness Lighthouse and 52 were killed or captured at the Bahama light ship. The same movement was also noted off the Antrim coast and the western seaboard of Scotland. Again in 1980, there was an exceptional movement in early May. One hundred passed through the Calf on 2nd and good numbers came in over Bradda on 3rd. On 4th 200 passed through the Calf and on 6th there were 300. Twenty or more birds could be found regularly on the golf course at Sandwick and 40–50 were counted in upper Druidale – a worthy number for such a locality, for as Ralfe wrote they are 'scattered thinly over the mountains, where they fly from post to post along the great drystone walls which cross them or lower down, utter their hand clicking note from the high earthen fences of the pastures.' Often on spring passage Wheatears of the Greenland race will linger several days in their northward progress, visiting likely nest sites, before deserting the area. They set up temporary territories and put on weight for the long flight to Iceland or Greenland. Weight gain is really striking, birds having increased from 25 gm to 35 gm in 10 days and from 29 gm to 42 gm in 17 days on the Calf.

Autumn passage is seen throughout August with a peak during the last fortnight. It continues through September and there are a few October records nearly every year. The mean last date over the last 56 years is 19th October and Wheatears have been seen during the first week of November in 7 of those years. There have been two December records – one at the Raggatt quarry (Patrick) on 8th (1968) and another present from 15th to 17th at Poyll Dhooie, Ramsey in 1947. The highest autumn day counts on the Calf were 130 on 26th August 1979 and 200 on 24th August 1984. The Wheatear is one of *Ny shiaght cadlagyn*, 'the seven sleepers' of Manx folk lore, which were supposed to hibernate.

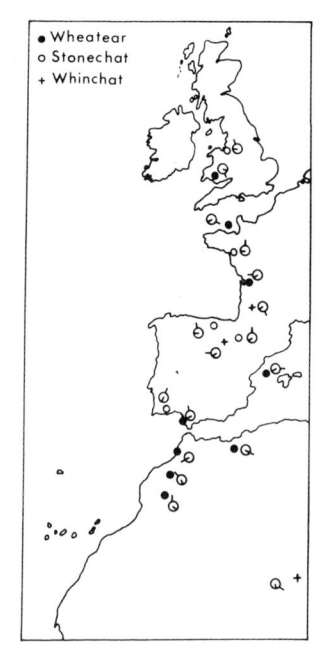

Recoveries of Wheatear, Stonechat and Whinchat.

Between 1959 and 1983 1,442 Wheatears were ringed on the Calf producing nine recoveries – one from Glamorgan, Jersey and Gironde (France), 2 from Spain, 3 from Morocco and one from Algeria.

The Greenland race *O.o. leucorrhoa*, a larger and more brightly coloured bird, occurs commonly on spring and autumn passage. The earliest Calf date for this sub-species is 6th April and it has been estimated that over 90% of migrants in May are of this race – in fact on northward passage it is commoner than the nominate race. In autumn Greenland Wheatears occur until mid October but are now in the minority.

Manx: *Claggan cloaie*

Black-eared Wheatear

Oenanthe hispanica

Vagrant.

A male of the white-throated type was watched for several hours on the Calf on 30th May 1968. At the time this was the 19th British record of this handsome black and white wheatear which winters in Africa and has a Mediterranean breeding distribution (Wright 1973). A female wheatear present from 7th to 11th October 1971 was either this species or a Pied Wheatear. *O. pleschanka.*

Ring Ouzel
Turdus torquatus

Regular passage migrant which formerly bred.

Although never very plentiful the Ring Ouzel has always been a regular passage migrant. There used to be a small breeding population but it is very doubtful if Ring Ouzels have nested on the Isle of Man during the last 50 years.

The Corrany valley was the only known breeding area, birds nesting regularly at Park Llewellyn below North Barrule from about 1875 into the present century. Nesting probably continued infrequently up to 1930 and pairs were seen there, without evidence of breeding, in 1935 and 1937. In late June 1949 a pair was seen at Vaaish (German) and in late May 1973 there was a pair at Creg ny baa, the male finally becoming a road casualty in T.T. week. The Isle of Man is rich in the rocky moorland covered with heather and bilberry, which is so attractive to the Ring Ouzel, but the loss of this bird as a breeding species is in keeping with the drastic decline in Ireland since 1900. There it used to breed in 27 of the 32 counties, but is now reduced to very small populations in the mountains of Leitrim/Sligo, Wicklow and perhaps Donegal and County Down. Suggested explanations have been the climatic amelioration which has permitted the Blackbird to extend into more rugged mountainous country at the expense of the Ring Ouzel and the loss of upland habitat through ploughing and the burning of heather and gorse.

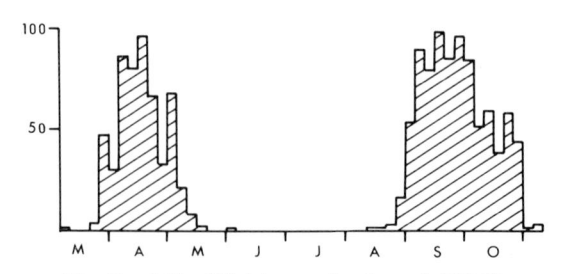

Ring Ouzel. Total bird days per five day period (Calf).

244

Spring passage usually starts about 24th–26th March, continuing until the first few days of May. The earliest date within the usual period of migration was 6th March 1966, but in 1943 one was seen at Keppel Gate on 12th February and there is also a record of one at Traie Dullish quarry on Peel Hill on 6th January 1979 (Moore 1980). Heavier autumn passage occurs throughout September and October. Ralfe described a flock of 20–30 birds on 12th September 1901 on the steep and rough mountain side above Lag ny Keeilly 'which chuckling like Blackbirds and moving wildly and shyly from stone to stone, followed each other over the rock-encumbered slope to the heaths at the summit of the ridge.' Single birds or small groups of 2–4 are usual, but there have been a number of autumn days with Calf counts in excess of 10 with maxima of 30 on 7th September 1967 and 31 on 27th October 1965. There was a notable movement between 20th and 31st October 1976 with day counts of 10, 15, 21 and 22. Although the latest Calf date is 9th November there have been a few other records up to 16th November and one at Injebreck on 4th December 1930. On the main island Ring Ouzels are scarce at such popular migration points as Langness and the Point of Ayre, although occasional lighthouse casualties are recorded, but are seen mostly in the central and southern hills, especially on the Carnanes above Fleshwick. An anomaly, which may be more apparent than real is that autumn migration is decidedly heavier on the Calf while spring records are greatly in the majority on the main island.

Between 1959 and 1983 186 Ring Ouzels were ringed on the Calf producing recoveries from the Massif Centrale and Gironde in France and from the High Atlas of Morocco.

Blackbird

Turdus merula

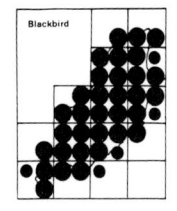

Very common resident, passage migrant and winter visitor.

The Blackbird has always been one of the most abundant Manx landbirds although the origins of the large numbers seen on passage and wintering here have only become apparent through ringing during the last fifty years.

It is a common inhabitant of all varieties of woodland, curraghs, parks and gardens and of the coast where it is overgrown with brambles, ivy and honeysuckle. In spite of the relatively mild winter climate it is very unusual for laying to take place before the beginning of April. Exceptionally early was a nest with eggs at Ramsey on 11th March 1931 and a single egg at Peel on 21st March 1953. April and May are the principal breeding months and a clutch of 4 eggs has been found as late as 16th July in 1941. Four is easily the commonest clutch size, three and five not unusual and 6 eggs decidedly rare. There is an interesting record of a Douglas bird embarking on a second clutch on 10th May 1955 and laying 5 eggs, a further 3 eggs were laid from 23rd May presumably by another bird. As in other parts of Britain there are records of Blackbird's and Song Thrush's eggs in the same nest and of using the same nest for successive broods. There is also one record of a bird laying 4 clutches during the same breeding season (Cowin 1938). It is one of the small number of species which have been found nesting in a palm tree. In the early years of the Calf Observatory only 2–3 pairs bred on the islet, but numbers had increased to 16 pairs in 1969 and 20 pairs in 1973. Although there was then a decline to only 10 pairs in 1976 a peak of 26 pairs was reached in 1980.

Notable passage has been observed from mid January and continues to mid April with a peak in late March/early April. Although overall autumn numbers greatly exceed those passing through in spring the heaviest passage seen on the Calf was on 4th April 1960 when there were over 2,000 birds.

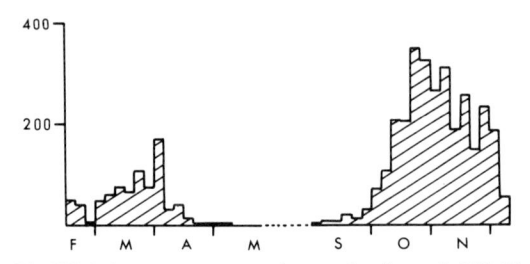

Blackbird. Average passage numbers per five day period (Calf).

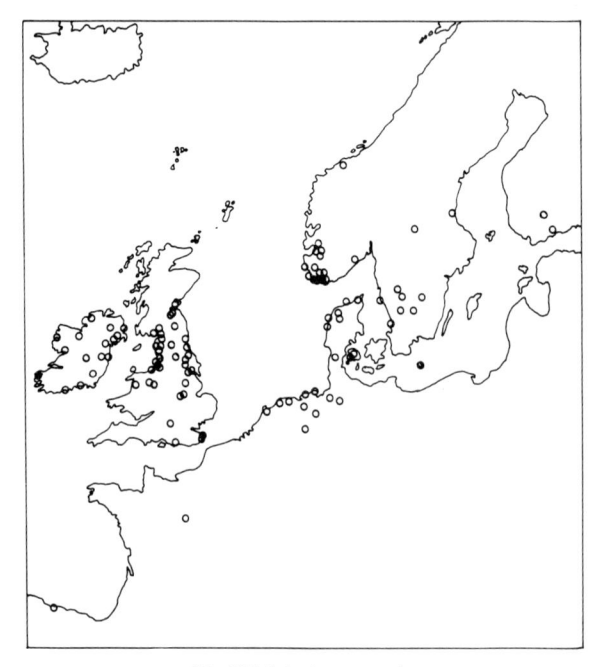

Blackbird ringing recoveries.

Autumn passage builds up steadily during October to a peak at the end of the month, considerable numbers continuing through to early December. Peak counts were 500 on 22nd October 1968 and 17th November 1981. Good numbers are sometimes seen at Lighthouse attractions and Ralfe mentions 63 being killed at the Point of Ayre on 20th February 1890.

Blackbirds are plentiful through December and January and a feeding flock of up to 40 is regular at Kirby during these months.

During the first 25 years of the Calf Observatory 7,176 birds were ringed yielding 94 recoveries. Ringing on the main island has produced an additional 84 recoveries. Only six Blackbirds ringed as nestlings have been recovered – five of these on the Isle of Man within 5 km of ringing, the other in Co. Durham in early August.

Month of distant ringing or recovery of 122 Blackbirds with a connection away from the Isle of Man

	J	F	M	A	M	J	J	A	S	O	N	D
Ireland	6	1	2	1	1	1				1	2	2
Shetland					1							
Scotland S. of Clyde/Tay			2		1		3			2		
England NW	1	1	2			2	2	1		1		
England NE	1		6	2	1	1	2	2				
England S. of Mersey/Humber	1	2		1	1	3				1	2	1
North Wales							1			1		
Finland				1			1	1				
Sweden		1	2	2	2	1	2	1				
Denmark		1	3	3		2						2
Norway	1		3	1			5	2		3	2	
Germany	1		3		1	2						
Holland	1		3	1						1		1
Belgium						1						
France			1									
Spain			1									

Breeding season ringing recoveries away from the Isle of Man come mainly from northern England, southern Scotland, Fenno-Scandia, north Germany and Holland while winter returns have a strong Irish flavour. The Spanish recovery was of a bird ringed as a juvenile on 17th August 1965 and found in Santander on 12th February 1966, an extremely unusual place for a British bird in winter.

The most rapid eastward movement was recorded by 2 Blackbirds ringed on the Calf in March and reaching Hamburg and West Jutland in 6 and 8 days respectively. There have been two sets of very closely related ringing recoveries from Scandinavia, the details of which are as follows:–

ad.M.	8.2.70	Port Erin.
caught	9.10.70	Sira, Flekkefjord, Vest Agder, Norway.
ad.M.	29.11.69	Laxey.
dead	15.10.70	Konsmo, Laudal, Vest Agder, Norway.

juv.M.	5.11.69	Calf of Man.
dead	17.10.70	Ana-Sira, Flekkefjord, Vest Agder, Norway.

Konsmo and Ana-Sira are just 40 and 20 km from Sira.

1st.y.M.	30.3.73	Calf of Man.
contr.	31.3.74	Klitmøller, Thisted, Denmark.
ad.F.	11.10.73	Calf of Man.
contr.	3.4.74	Klitmøller, Thisted, Denmark.
1st.y.M.	9.4.74	Tørvekjær, Thisted, Denmark.
contr.	31.10.74	Calf of Man.

Tørvekjær is less than 10 km from Klitmøller.

A juvenile ringed on the Calf in late October was recovered in Lancashire 8 years and 3 months later, while another bird was retrapped on the Calf 8 years after ringing.

Albinism is more common in Manx Blackbirds than any other species. There have been many records of pure white birds, including a brood of 3 in a nest near Ramsey and pied birds are far from rare.

Manx: *Lhondhoo*

Fieldfare

Turdus pilaris

Common passage migrant and winter visitor.

Although numbers vary hugely from year to year, there seems to have been no long term change in the winter status of the Fieldfare. On the other hand Fieldfares undoubtedly linger longer in spring than formerly and have now been recorded in every month.

Usually the first Fieldfares arrive during the first three weeks of October. Kermode recorded a small flock at Killabregga above Sulby Glen on 28th August 1889 and it was not until 1959 that this was bettered by a single bird on the Calf on 26th August. Since then there has been one further August record (on 19th in 1971) and five between 17th and 30th September. Up to about 25th October flocks are usually small, heralding the main passage period which continues to mid November. On the Calf there have been several autumn day counts in excess of 1,000 with 3,000 flying west on 24th October 1972 and 2,300 on 7th November 1979. On the main island both on passage and through the winter months flocks of 30–100 occasionally up to 300, are typical and 1,000 at Grenaby (Malew) on 27th October 1975 were exceptional. Generally they frequent the uplands, although in cold weather they descend to lower ground and the coast. Substantial flocks sometimes appear briefly in January and February, probably driven westward by severe conditions and continuing to Ireland. Although fields on the lower slopes of the hills in such areas as Druidale, Ballamodha and the Foxdale/Braaid district are perhaps the most typical Fieldfare sites, they are present at many places over the northern plain in mid winter and share with Redwings a liking for the boggy lightly wooded terrain of the Ballaugh and Greeba Curraghs.

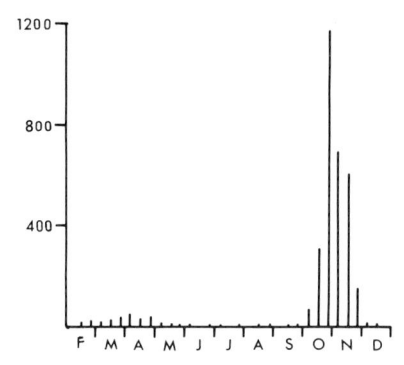

Fieldfare. Average bird days per five day period (Calf).

The small numbers passing through the Calf in spring (best day count 500 on 1st April 1981) are in no way comparable with those passing through the main island. Significant spring flocks occur almost entirely to the north of the central valley with all the greatest numbers occurring on the northern plain in April. In 1966 there were 8–900 at Andreas and over 200 at Laxey on 11th April, in 1974 thousands collected at Ballaskilley, Bride, leaving on 4th April and in 1976 about 10,000 Fieldfares, Redwings and Blackbirds passed over the Point of Ayre, flying at a height of 300 m on 12th April with several thousand on fields near Bride on 27th April. Fieldfares are of course seen in large numbers at the lighthouses but have had a much lower mortality at the Point of Ayre than Redwings. Twenty-two were killed on 19th March 1928 – far and away the heaviest night's toll.

Although once recorded on 29th May, records for that month (up to about 12th) were unusual prior to 1964 when birds were seen on the Calf on 30th May and 4th June. Since then Fieldfares have been recorded nearly every year during May and, on the Calf, on three further occasions during June up to 9th. The occurrence of these late records has coincided with the westward extension of the Fieldfare's breeding range with nests in northern Scotland from 1967 and the Peak District from 1969. July remains the most unlikely month – there were 2 at Traie Vane on 3rd in 1934 and it was recorded on the Calf in 1966.

There have been no recoveries from 94 birds ringed on the Calf.

Manx: *Ushag sniaghtey* = Snow bird

Song Thrush
Turdus philomelos

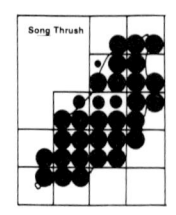

Common resident, summer and winter visitor and passage migrant.

Although in July 1789 Townley was able to write that he knew of nowhere where Blackbirds and Throstles were seen or heard in such numbers as at Douglas, Ralfe considered the Song Thrush to be 'not an abundant bird' rather more than 100 years later. Commonest in suburban gardens it was nevertheless well distributed up to the heads of the cultivated valleys, and so it remains, being notably commoner in autumn and winter than during the breeding season.

First eggs are usually laid in early April although there have been a number of records from 19th March. Three eggs in a Lezayre nest on 11th March 1928 were exceptionally early, but could not match another clutch found in the same parish on 17th January 1890. Eggs have not been recorded after 10th July, but Madoc saw a young bird just out of the nest and still unable to fly on 2nd August. Four is easily the commonest clutch size followed by five and three eggs. There is only one record of a clutch of 6. The same nest may be used more than once during the same year, even if the first clutch has failed, and there is a record of a third brood hatching in the same nest on 16th June. Most nests are in hedgerows especially in ivy and conifers, but ground nesting has been reported on a number of occasions, sometimes in a bank, but also on flat ground – among bluebells as on the Calf in 1970 or even on the open shore as at Scarlett in 1905. Madoc described a nest built in the middle of a potted cactus in a shed. At Cooil Dharry, a typical woodland glen of 14 hectares there were 2–4 territories in 1975, 1976 and 1977 (Cain 1978), while on the Calf it breeds only occasionally with 1 pair in 1964 and 1970 and two in 1965.

Ringing recoveries have shown that while the majority of Manx breeding birds are probably resident some (both adult and juvenile) move west to Ireland in the autumn. Increasing autumn movement is seen during September, but the main passage is in October, especially at the end of the month. On the Calf fair numbers continue until the Observatory closes in December – the highest day count there was 300 on 17th October 1979. During the winter the resident population is augmented by visitors from Scotland and northern England, and cold weather produces further westward movement in mid winter. The relatively light spring passage occurs from late February to the end of March. The Calf maximum was 150 on 6th March 1965.

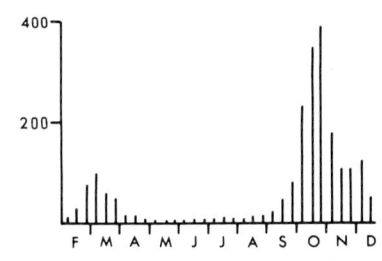

Song Thrush. Average passage numbers per ten day period (Calf).

Three thousand one hundred and fourteen Song Thrushes were ringed on the Calf between 1959 and 1983 producing 27 recoveries – a total increasing to 63 when recoveries of birds ringed on the main island and Manx recoveries from elsewhere are included. Of these 63, 38 had a connection away from the Isle of Man, the months of recoveries in various regions being tabulated below. Movements of ringed birds within the Isle of Man are usually less than 5 km. A striking negative finding is that only 7 Song Thrushes were retrapped (after either one or two years) on the Calf over a 25 year period.

Month of distant ringing or recovery of 38 Song Thrushes with a connection away from the Isle of Man

	J	F	M	A	M	J	J	A	S	O	N	D
Ireland	2	1	1			1		1		1	1	2
Angus/Clackmannan			2		1		1					
Kirkcudbright				1								
England NW			2	1			1	1	1			
England NE	1			2	4	1	3	1		1		
Derby					1							
Oxford												1
Kent				1								
Bergen (Norway)								1				

The majority of recoveries show evidence of westerly or south-westerly movement in autumn or winter. Exceptions included two birds ringed on the Calf as adults in early autumn and recovered in Co. Wexford (in June nearly three years later) and in Co. Wicklow (two years later). The Kent bird had been ringed in the previous November, while the Oxford recovery was of a first year bird ringed on the Calf 7 weeks earlier. Three birds have been recovered between 5 years and 1 month and 5 years and 5 months after ringing.

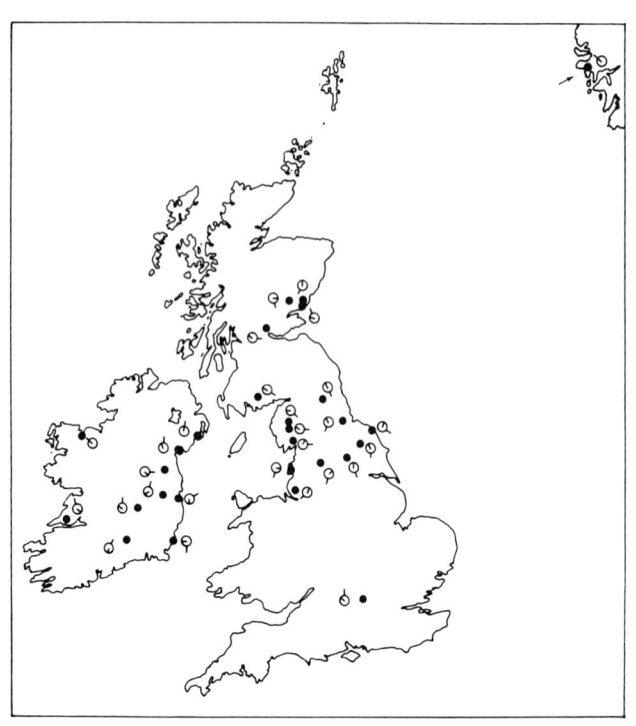

Song Thrush ringing recoveries.

Three subspecies of the Song Thrush have been identified on the Calf of Man. The majority of migrants belong to *T.p. clarkei*, the race breeding throughout most of the British Isles. In the Outer Hebrides and Skye it is replaced by the darker and more heavily spotted *T.p. hebridensis* and birds resembling this race are seen in both spring and autumn, but the situation is complicated by the fact that birds from other parts of the west of Scotland and from Co. Kerry are intermediate between these two races. *T.p. philomelos* is a scarce migrant, usually in late autumn. This is the race of central and eastern Europe and birds from Germany, Denmark and eastern France are intermediate between it and *T.p. clarkei*.

The only report of albinism concerned a bird seen at Ramsey in early October 1931, being almost entirely white except for a few cinnamon coloured markings in one wing.

Manx: *Lhon. Thresh len*

Redwing

Turdus iliacus

Common passage migrant and winter visitor.

There has been no obvious change in the status of the Redwing during the last hundred years. Both on passage and through the winter months numbers vary considerably from year to year due mainly to climatic conditions to the north and east. Although broadly speaking Fieldfares choose higher ground than do Redwings the two species are often seen together in large mixed flocks, typically collecting in roadside ash trees and descending onto neighbouring fields. In autumn Redwings are often seen almost swarming over berry-laden hawthorns. The greatest numbers occur during the second half of October, flocks of 150–300 are quite usual and as many as 1,000 have been seen together. The first Redwings of the autumn usually precede the earliest Fieldfares by several days and occasionally as much as three weeks. The earliest record was of a single bird at Barregarrow on 11th September 1975 and since 1966 advance parties have been seen during September most years. Typical sites are the fields and hedges of the northern plain, the Baldwin valleys and the neighbourhood of the Foxdale Dams. During winter open woodland is a favourite resort, notably at Kirby, where a flock of up to 60 in January and February is regular, the Nunnery and and Ballaugh Curraghs. They are often found on playing fields such as those at Tromode, where a flock is present for several weeks during January and February most years. In the early spring a small party may sometimes be found indulging in a delightful subdued song. In harsh weather conditions they suffer badly and in the search for food lose much of their usual shyness. Ralfe mentions how they searched for food in the crevices along the shore at Ballagyr while in 1947 they ventured into the streets of Peel in early February. The arctic conditions of January and February 1963 caused considerable mortality.

Return passage occurs through March and although Redwings are seen in April every year numbers after about 5th are usually small, a notable exception being 150 on the Calf on 27th April 1966. In that year one was recorded for the first time in May and records for that month are now almost annual with several for the last 3 days and in 1977 one on 4th June. On the Calf the highest spring day count was 2,000 on 7th March 1965, although in autumn the best is only 1,000 on 12th October 1976 when a huge flock was present during a Lighthouse attraction. Redwings are night and day migrants and have consistently been reported at the lighthouses on both spring and autumn passage. The Point of Ayre has been quite notorious for Redwing casualties – examples of the death toll being 17 on 16th October 1925, 52 and 33 on 19th and 20th March 1928 and 32 on 12th October 1928. It is more than likely that most of the 192 'thrushes' killed on 20th February 1890 were Redwings.

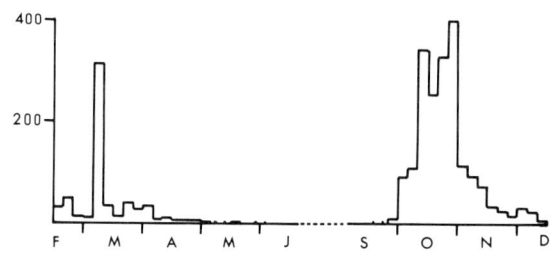

Redwing. Average numbers per five day period (Calf).

Five hundred and seventy-seven Redwings were ringed on the Calf between 1959 and 1983. Two have been recovered: one on the north coast of Algeria in late January 15 months after ringing and the other on the Biscay coast of France 4 years and 3 months after ringing. A nestling ringed in southern Finland was controlled on the Calf 4 years 4 months later. A Redwing ringed at Port Erin on 29th September was retrapped in the same garden 9½ weeks later.

Both *T.i. iliacus* and *T.i. coburni* are regular in spring and autumn, proportions varying from year to year. Generally speaking the larger and darker *T.i. coburni*, which breeds in Iceland and the Faeroes is dominant in spring, while the continental form *T.i. iliacus* is the more abundant in autumn.

Manx: *Lhon Geayee*

Mistle Thrush
Turdus viscivorus

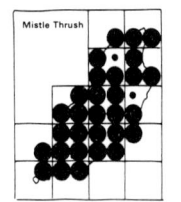

Common resident. Probably also occurs as a passage migrant.

Although by 1782 the Mistle Thrush was a scarce breeding bird in Cumberland, it was not until 1800 that it was recorded in Ireland, breeding in Co. Louth in 1807 and it is more than likely that it's colonisation of the Isle of Man took place around the same time. By 1850 it had spread throughout Ireland and to Ralfe it was, as now, a common resident.

The Mistle Thrush is a bird of farmland, up to the moorland fringes, and of parks and gardens. The traditional nest site is in the fork of a tree, often an ash, or on a horizonal branch. A bulky nest adorned with green moss and often embellished with pieces of fabric, plastic or paper it is conspicuous in the leafless conditions of early spring. More unusual trees include the Monkey Puzzle and the palm, while Ralfe described one nest among the sticks of an old Magpie's nest. Small shrubs such as gorse and blackthorn are also used and in spite of the ready availability of trees there is a fascinating catalogue of other nest sites used. These include rocky ledges, both inland and on the coast, an open gravestone in Kirk Maughold churchyard, the pillar of a railway bridge over the Cornaa River and a pile of railway sleepers. Buildings are sometimes used, nests being built on beams in sheds, in rafter holes of ruins and on the timbers of a disused water wheel. In Port Erin a nest was built in the lettering above a chemist's shop and, in the ruins of St German's Cathedral on St Patrick's Isle, Peel, nests were built in the arches of the north and south transepts. On Snaefell a pair nested on a rocky ledge by the railway at a height of 600 m in 1927.

Ralfe relates a nice story about a Mistle Thrush's nest at Lorne House when, in the period between 1845 and 1860 it was the Governor's residence. Some valuable lace belonging to Lady Isabella Hope went missing when put out to bleach and was eventually traced to the nest into which it had been incorporated. In Malew Churchyard a nest was found with its rim adorned with artificial flowers appropriated from wreaths.

The Mistle Thrush is well known as an early nester. At Lambhill (Bride) a fresh nest had been built by 29th January 1956 and in 1934 a nest in the Mooragh Park, Ramsey held three eggs on 8th February. More usually first eggs are laid during the last few days of March or in early April. Four is the usual clutch size, although often only three eggs are laid and rarely five. Two broods are usual and nesting activity is not seen after the end of June. Mistle Thrushes have occasionally bred on the Calf.

Family parties are seen in early summer and small flocks, typically of 15 to 25 birds are seen from August to November. Larger flocks are rare – 47 near St Johns on 30th August 1973, 56 above Union mills on 19th September 1979 over 100 in the Cornaa Valley on 10th August 1976 and 122 at Close Leece (Patrick) on 22nd August 1985. On the Calf the highest day count was only 28 on 21st October 1974. The earliest date for a flock of any substance is 12th June when there were 20 at Ballacrye (Ballaugh) in 1977. The autumn flocks seem to remain in the same general area for several weeks and are probably made up of local birds. Although not proved through Manx ringing recoveries it is probable that there is a small autumn passage through the Isle of Man as birds ringed in southern Scotland and Northumberland have been recovered in Ireland. Mistle Thrushes have only rarely been reported from the lighthouses.

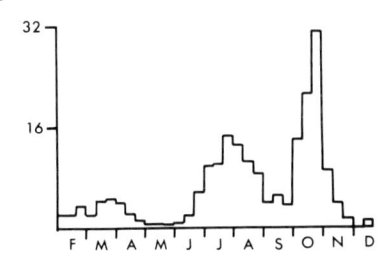

Mistle Thrush. Average passage numbers per ten day period (Calf).

From mid November song is heard and birds are seen mostly in pairs. Rarely flocks have been noted in spring, notably 30 at Maughold in late February 1976, 10 at Ballaugh on 22nd March 1975 and 18 at the Mooragh on 31st March 1961.

White examples have been reported on three occasions – from the north in 1903, Keilthustag (Bride) in 1956 (feeding young) and Ballaughton (Braddan) in 1965.

During 25 years 143 Mistle Thrushes have been ringed on the Calf producing 5 recoveries. A further 4 recoveries have resulted from ringing on the main island but none have shown movement of more than 5 km.

Manx: *Lhon Keylley*

Grasshopper Warbler
Locustella naevia

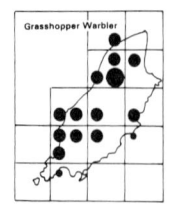

Irregular and locally distributed summer visitor and passage migrant in small numbers.

It was not until 1903 that Ralfe and Graves 'discovered' a number of Grasshopper Warblers singing in Ballaugh Curraghs in late May and subsequently heard the song in the central curraghs. Unknown to Ralfe the song was already familiar to people in the Foxdale area and there seems little doubt that its presence elsewhere had been overlooked.

Long renowned among migrant passerines for its remarkable numerical fluctuations from year to year, the Grasshopper Warbler has from time to time been quite abundant in suitable habitats. During the early part of the present century breeding records were confined to the curraghs of Ballaugh and Greeba and perhaps the Lhen. In 1925 Madoc found a pair feeding a young bird among bracken and brambles on the Calf on 15th August and in several of the next seventeen years, especially in 1930 they appear to have bred in quite large numbers on the Isle of Man. Between 1942 and 1971 they were only recorded in June 1947 (when a nest was found at Ballachurry, Andreas), 1960 and 1961. 1972, 73 and 74 were excellent years with breeding birds at a number of localities to the south of the central valley. Good numbers could often be heard in the damp rough moorland around Glen Rushen and in both 1972 and 1974 (but characteristically not in 1973) there were at least 7 pairs in the rather boggy ground between Stoney Mountain and South Barrule plantation. At Fleshwick up to 4 birds sang through the summer in 1973, but not in 1974 while song was also heard on the other side of Stoney Mountain at Kionslieau in 1974 and further south at Tosaby Garey the following year. 1976 and 77 and 1980 and 81 produced migrant records only but in the remaining years they bred, probably in small numbers at Renshent (a little north of Tosaby) and in the Ballaugh Curraghs, and in 1979 in Union Mills curragh. On the Calf of Man Grasshopper Warblers bred in 1960 and 1971.

The usual clutch of five eggs is laid in late May or early June, and according to Madoc, sometimes well into July.

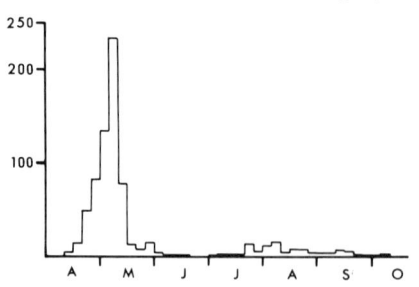

Grasshopper Warbler. Total bird days per five day period (Calf).

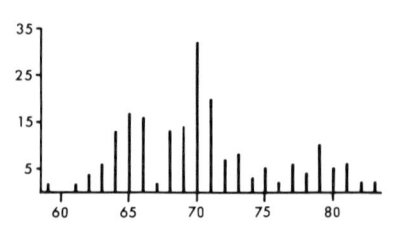

Grasshopper Warbler. Annual ringing totals 1959–83 (Calf).

The mean first arrival date is 25th April, exceptionally early birds being one at Langness on 2nd April 1961 and one at Round Table on 8th April 1963. On the Calf passage is at a peak during the first ten days of May and the highest day count was 75 on 6th May 1970. Light autumn passage is seen from about 20th July to 20th September. Three birds have occurred on the Calf on several August days and late birds were recorded there on 3rd and 9th October 1969 and 10th October 1978.

Two hundred Grasshopper Warblers were ringed on the Calf between 1959 and 1983. After a series of good years between 1964 and 1971, which included the impressive total of 32 birds ringed in 1972, the annual ringing totals since indicate how this species has declined, at least as a passage migrant.

Sedge Warbler

Acrocephalus schoenobaenus

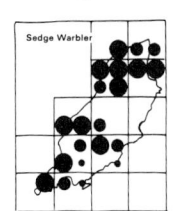

Common summer visitor and passage migrant.

Ralfe believed that prior to 1885 the Sedge Warbler had been overlooked, but it seems much more likely that this noisy and conspicuous little bird was indeed absent, certainly as a breeding bird. Towards the end of the century it became recognised as an abundant visitor to the Ballaugh Curraghs and had also been found at Lough Cranstal, Congary, the dubs at Ballalough (German) and along the Rivers Sulby, Dhoo and Glass. Latterly it had been found in the Castletown area which Ralfe acknowledged as a recent colonisation. Early this century it was found nesting at the Dog Mills, a site which together with the Curraghs of Ballaugh and Greeba and Lough Cranstal remains to this day an important breeding ground. The Isle of Man is of course well endowed with the rather dense overgrown riparian vegetation so favoured by this species and sporadic nesting has taken place at many other places including the Calf in 4 years since 1959 and the bracken covered margins of the Ayres. In 1979 M. Fitzpatrick found 20–30 pairs nesting at the Dog Mills Lough and there were probably more in Ballaugh Curraghs. Recent estimates of numbers singing in late May have been 19 at Lough Cranstal, 9 at Ballacain Dubs and at least 15 at the Guilcagh. Small numbers are also regularly found at the Lhen and Kentraugh.

Five or 6 eggs are laid in late May or early June, although a late clutch was found on 19th July in 1934.

On passage Sedge Warblers are abundant in spring and scarce in autumn. In fact spring numbers at Bardsey and the Calf far outstrip those at any other observatory in Britain (Riddiford and Findley 1981). Movement is seen throughout May with a peak in the middle of that month. The mean first date is 26th April, the earliest record being of one singing near Peel on 2nd April 1945. There have been some recent early records from the Calf – 14th April in 1979 and 12th in both 1980 and 1981. The highest day count on the Calf was 400 on 11th May 1965. In autumn there is a trickle of birds

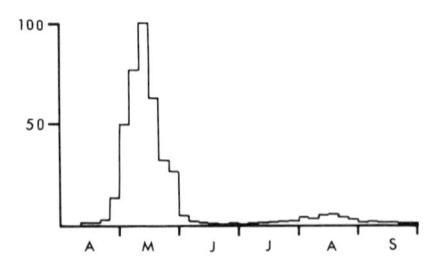

Sedge Warbler. Average bird days per five day period (Calf).

through August (the Calf maximum was only 20 on 17th August 1966) with a few during September. Sedge Warblers have twice been seen in October – the latest being one on the Calf on 7th (1975). On the main island Sedge Warblers may be found in many localities during early May and a few are ringed every year in a Port Erin garden. Numbers ringed on the Calf vary greatly from year to year and seem to bear little relation to the national Common Bird Census Indices. Quite exceptional years for Calf ringing were 1965 (251 birds), 1966 (278) and 1970 (289). The slump to only 26 and 24 birds ringed in 1973 and 1974 reflected the nadir for the C.B.C. following which numbers varied between 116 and 197 until the serious slump to 49 ringed in 1982.

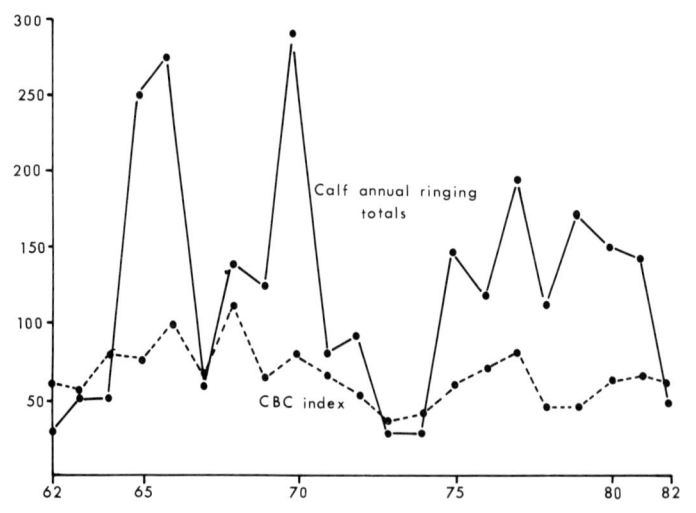

Sedge Warbler. Annual ringing totals (Calf) and national CBC indices (1962–82).

From a total of 2803 Sedge Warblers ringed on the Calf there have been 7 recoveries, while a further 6 controlled on the Calf and 3 on the main island had been ringed elsewhere. Of 8 birds trapped in late July or August on the south coast of England (including 3 from Radipole, Weymouth and 2 from Thurlestone, Devon) 7 passed through the Calf in spring and only one in autumn. Other recoveries and controls have come from Counties Clare and Tyrone, Shropshire and Buckinghamshire, Bardsey Island, Holland, France and southern Spain.

Marsh Warbler
Acrocephalus palustris

Vagrant

The first of two Calf records was of an immature trapped on 13th August 1974 (Wright 1977), the other was on 5th November 1984.

Reed Warbler
Acrocephalus scirpaceus

Scarce but regular passage migrant.

The first Manx record was on 25th August 1970 when one was trapped on the Calf. Since 1973 between one and four Reed Warblers have been recorded annually. The extreme dates of 9 spring birds were 27th April and 26th June, while autumn records (11) have ranged from 11th August to 3rd November. Away from the Calf of Man three have been trapped in a Port Erin garden, two have been heard singing in the Ballaugh Curraghs in late May and two were trapped at the Dog Mills Lough on 2nd and 3rd November 1982. All nine birds ringed on the Calf in the autumn were immatures.

An adult male ringed on the Calf on 14th June was controlled in Warwickshire on 22nd July the same year, while an adult female ringed in Glamorgan on 25th May was controlled at Port Erin on 9th May three years later.

Icterine Warbler
Hippolais icterina

Uncommon passage migrant.

There have been 11 records from the Calf where the Icterine Warbler was first identified on 27th August 1967. The only spring record was of a male in song and later trapped on 24th May 1973. The remaining records were fairly evenly distributed between 13th August and 25th September.

Melodious Warbler
Hippolais polyglotta

Uncommon passage migrant.

The first Manx record was of one ringed on the Calf on 10th August 1964. Since then there have been 13 further records from the Calf – 23rd and

31st May, 14th July (an adult) and between 6th August and 17th September. All but one of eight autumn birds trapped were immatures.

The two Hippolais warblers on the Manx list can be difficult to separate in the field and on three further occasions during the autumn members of this genus have been seen on the Calf but defied specific identification. The Melodious Warbler breeds in North Africa, Iberia, France, Switzerland and Italy but is replaced through most of the remainder of Europe by the Icterine Warbler, the two species overlapping in north-east France and Switzerland. Their pattern of occurrence on the Calf is almost identical.

Subalpine Warbler
Sylvia cantillans

Rare passage migrant.

The Subalpine Warbler was first recorded on the Calf on 8th September 1966 and there have since been six spring records as follows:– one on Langness on 7th May 1974 and on the Calf a second year male on 1st June 1977, a female of the south-eastern race *S.c. albistriata* on 14th May 1980 and another second year male on 24th May 1981. In 1984 males were trapped on 28th April and 17th June. It has a Mediterranean breeding distribution and winters in north Africa.

Barred Warbler
Sylvia nisoria

Scarce but fairly regular autumn passage migrant.

First recorded at Ballamoar, Jurby on 27th October 1931, Barred Warblers were reported in 13 of the years from 1959 to 1982. All but one of the 22 birds seen on the Calf and 3 of the 5 seen on the main island were ringed suggesting that the juveniles which pass through the Isle of Man go largely unnoticed. Records have been fairly evenly spread from 7th August (1966) to 29th September with 4 late birds at the end of October and one on 3rd November (1974).

Although breeding no nearer to Britain than Schleswig (9°E) and wintering well to the east in Arabia and east Africa, the Barred Warbler is a regular autumn visitor throughout the eastern seaboard of Scotland and England.

Lesser Whitethroat
Sylvia curruca

Scarce passage migrant which has bred occasionally.

The Lesser Whitethroat was not added to the Manx list until 1908 when J. Bell found a nest with five eggs at Ballabaragh on the Bride/Andreas boundary. The identity of these eggs was confirmed at the Natural History Museum, South Kensington and a few years later Bell found a second nest with 4 eggs about 400 m away. Between 1926 and 1944 there were further breeding records from Douglas, the Ballaugh Curraghs, Andreas and Ballure near Ramsey but there have been none since. The Isle of Man is at the extreme western limit of the Lesser Whitethroat's breeding range – it has never been found nesting in Ireland.

There have been about 90 records of this species, nearly all of them from the Calf, although it has been recorded twice from the Ballaugh Curraghs and Ramsey, once from Langness and Onchan Harbour and 7 have been ringed at Port Erin since 1975. Spring passage is confined almost totally to May. There have been two records each for June and July and about five for August. Most of the admittedly few autumn records have been in September and October and a notable feature has been the long stay of several autumn birds on the Calf, with one present from 28th October to 7th November 1969, one from 9th to 17th October 1974 and a third from 20th September until 9th November 1976 – the latest Manx record. It does appear to have been rather more common since 1974, 1980 being an exceptional year with 15 records. Lesser Whitethroats occur a little more frequently at Bardsey where there was unprecedented spring passage in 1980.

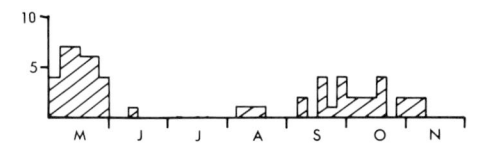

Lesser Whitethroat. Total bird days per five day period (Calf).

An example of the eastern race *S.c. blythi* was seen near the Observatory on the Calf on 2nd October 1978.

Whitethroat
Sylvia communis

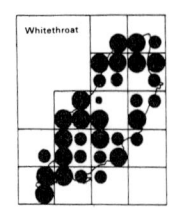

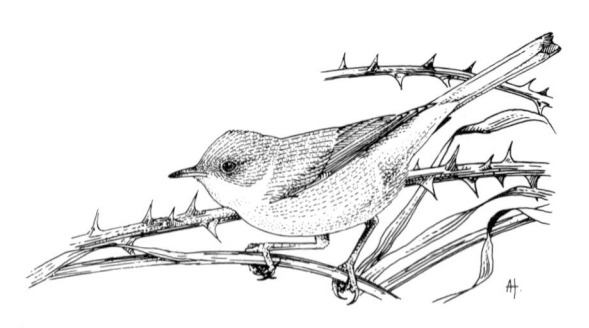

Common summer visitor and passage migrant.

Prior to the establishment of the Calf of Man Bird Observatory in 1959 there was no evidence of any long-term change in the status of the Whitethroat. 1959 was an exceptional year for Whitethroat passage through the Isle of Man with 386 birds ringed on the Calf, a total approached in both 1966 and 1968 but only beaten by the 448 of 1965. The Observatory's first ten years illustrated the fairly marked declines and recoveries typical of many species, but in 1969 there was a profound slump echoing the great crash in the British breeding population which was so clearly demonstrated by the Common Bird Census. This crash was also noted in other parts of western Europe and has been attributed to the severe droughts which have affected the Whitethroat's winter quarters in the Sahel zone of West Africa (Winstanley et al. 1974). Surprisingly over 230 Whitethroats were ringed the following year to be followed by a further decline to the all time low of 35 birds ringed in 1974, the year when the Farmland C.B.C. index was only 18% of the 1966 level. In the years 1975–81 Calf ringing suggested a partial recovery with yearly totals ranging between 90 and 167 but an apparent downward trend is again taking place. Although there are no supporting census figures the Manx *breeding* population crashed in 1969 but recovery started in 1972 and, apart from a poor showing in 1978, has been sustained.

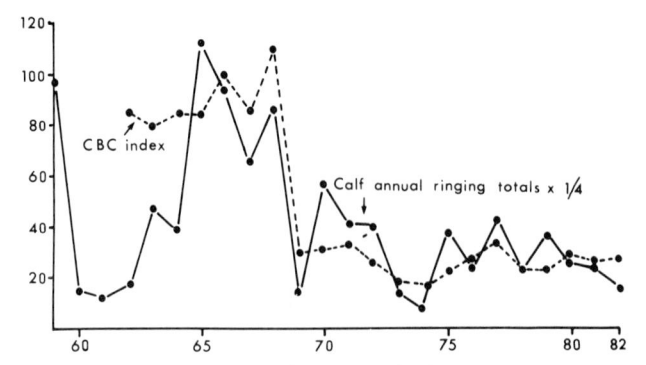

Whitethroat. Annual ringing totals $\times \frac{1}{4}$ (*Calf*) and CBC national indices (1959–82).

Before the 1969 crash the Whitethroat was common as a breeding bird throughout the lowlands of the Isle of Man especially on the coastal brooghs overgrown with bracken and brambles, the overgrown landward margin of the Ayrelands, the drier parts of the curraghs and the untidy hedgerows which are such a feature of the island. Variable numbers have bred on the Calf with a peak of 5 pairs in 1963 and 1964 – they failed to breed between 1970 and 1973 and in recent years 1980 was the best with 4 pairs. After the crash Whitethroats were largely reduced in their breeding range to a 3 km wide coastal strip from Eary Cushlin north, spreading out at Ballaugh to embrace the northern plain. The Whitethroat has yet to regain its former abundance in the southern lowlands where it remains very local and it was not until 1979 that recolonisation of the parishes of Maughold, Lonan and Onchan took place.

Although eggs have been found as early as 3rd May, most clutches are started in the second half of that month and the young from second broods may still be in the nest in early August, with 26th the latest date recorded.

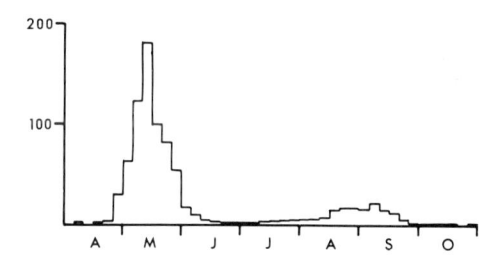

Whitethroat. Average bird days per five day period (Calf).

Whitethroats are very much more abundant on spring passage than in the autumn. The earliest record is of one on the Calf on 5th April 1944 and there have been 4 other records before 10th April, the mean first arrival date being 25th April. Spring passage reaches a peak in mid May and a few birds continue to pass through the Calf during the first few days of June. Prior to 1969 there were some notable periods of Whitethroat passage through the Calf. In 1959 there were 1,100 birds between 6th and 8th May and in each year from 1965 to 1968 day counts of 300 were achieved. The greatest fall occurred on 11th May 1965 when 280 out of about 1,000 were trapped. Three hundred were grounded the next day and a further 85 were trapped. Since 1969 there have been peaks of 150 on 2 days, 100 on two other days but as often as not the maximum count has been 35 or less. Light autumn passage is mostly between mid August and late September with a peak count of 50 on 9th September 1959. October records are very rare, but the latest Calf bird on 27th October 1975 has now surrendered its record to one which was ringed at the Dog Mills on 2nd November 1982.

From 3,854 birds ringed on the Calf between 1959 and 1983 there have been 10 recoveries to which can be added the recovery of one bird ringed on the main island and four Manx recoveries of birds ringed elsewhere. Five

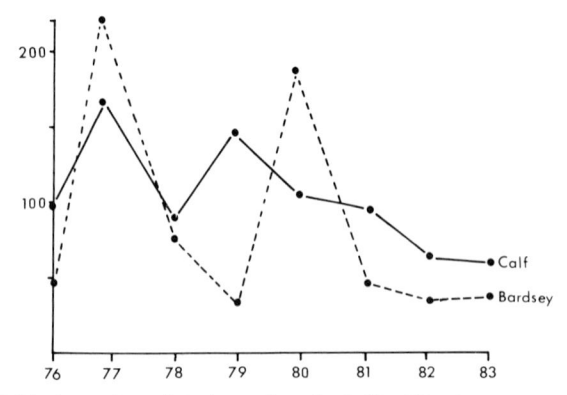

Whitethroat. Annual ringing totals on the Calf and Bardsey (1976–83).

foreign recoveries have come from the Iberian Penninsula – two close to the western end of the Franco-Spanish frontier and one each from north west Spain, north east Portugal and the coast of central Portugal. The last mentioned was recovered in mid January, the remainder in autumn. Manx recoveries in spring of 2 Skokholm birds and 1 from Gt. Saltee, all ringed in previous springs were unremarkable but three others ringed on the Isle of Man in spring had clearly overshot as one was recovered three weeks later to the south west in Co. Leix and the other two were recovered to the south east at Wigan later the same summer. An adult female ringed on the Calf in May was recovered on the Suffolk coast a year later. A breeding male ringed on the Calf in 1977 was retrapped, again breeding, in 1979, but was not present in 1978, while one ringed on the Calf as a pullus in 1978 was retrapped the following spring but did not stay to breed.

Manx: *Fynnag ny Keylley*

Garden Warbler
Sylvia borin

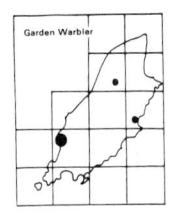

Regular passage migrant in small numbers which has bred occasionally.

It was not until May 1900 that the first Manx Garden Warbler was seen and by 1923 it had occurred several times as a lighthouse casualty at the Point of Ayre. From then until 1962 scarcely a year went by without records of 1–3 birds, since which it has occurred annually.

Since 1921, when the Garden Warbler was heard singing at Lezayre in July, there have been breeding season records in 17 years and actual evidence of nesting in just 8. Between 1931 and 1937 C. F. Butterworth repeatedly found nests in the south of the island, including 1 at the Monk's Bridge (Silverdale) and 2 at Surby in 1932. The only other locality he revealed was

Glenchass. In mid June 1944 a nest containing 2 or 3 young and 2 eggs was found at Ballachurry (Andreas) and in early August 1976 a pair was seen feeding three young at Glen Maye (where there were also frequent observations through the summer of 1978). Other summer records, usually of singing birds have come from Kirby (1943), Greeba Curragh, Ballamoar Reserve and the Silverburn (all in 1974), Claghbane near Ramsey (1975) and Ballaugh Curraghs in 1981.

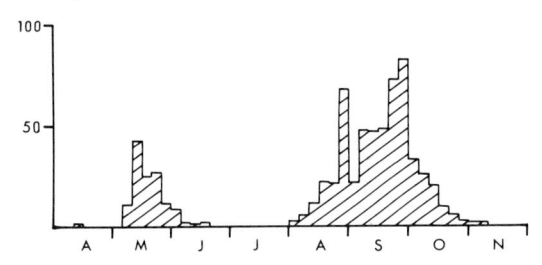

Garden Warbler. Total bird days per five day period (Calf).

On passage the Garden Warbler is quite well represented in spring but much more abundant in autumn. The earliest, and indeed the only Calf record for that month, was one on 13th April 1963. Most of the spring movement is between 5th May and 5th June and return gradually builds up in August, peaks at the end of September and continues to the end of October. There have been 7 November records the latest being one on the Calf on 9th (1976) and at Port Erin where one was ringed on 18th November 1974. On the Calf the spring maximum was 12 on 11th May 1965, while there have been 20 on three occasions in September. Prior to 1959 migrants were seen very predominantly in spring. Of 26 records between 1925 and 1959 10 were surprisingly in April, 10 in May, 4 in August and 1 each in September and October.

Three hundred and eighty birds have been ringed on the Calf producing 2 recoveries from southern England.

Manx: *Kiaulleyder garee*

Blackcap
Sylvia atricapilla

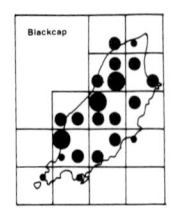

Scare summer visitor and fairly common passage migrant. Small winter population.

A cock Blackcap at Maughold Head Lighthouse in May 1918 was the first Manx record of a species which is becoming increasingly familiar. About the same time there were further reports from Port Mooar (Maughold) and Raby (Patrick) and in 1926 there were suggestions of breeding with a bird carrying food near Douglas and a male singing regularly through the summer in a Ballabeg garden. A nest was built at Glenchass in 1931 but during the next 35 years there were only four records during June or July and none from likely breeding places. A male was seen at Groudle in early July 1966 and since 1973 there seems little doubt that several birds have nested each year. In 1973 a male sang regularly in Ballure Glen (Ramsey) until mid-June and there was another song record in early June from Glen Wyllin. The following year song was heard regularly throughout June at Cronkbourne (Braddan) and Cooil Dharry and breeding was eventually confirmed in Silverdale on 23rd June when adults were seen carrying food and fledglings were located. Birds have been present through the summer at these three sites in several of the last ten years and a female was seen carrying food at Cooil Dharry in late June 1977. Other localities with song records in June or early July are Port Soderick Glen (1975 and 1980), Spooyt Vane (1977), Abbeylands (1977), the nearby junction of the Baldwin Rivers (1979 and 1981), Tromode Dam, Laxey Glen, south Ramsey and Gob y Volley (all in 1979), Curragh Beg and the Raggatt (1980) and Fleshwick Plantation in 1981. At Glenmaye beach a Blackcap was seen carrying food in late June 1979 and song was heard there throughout the following summer while in the Ballaugh Curraghs a juvenile was ringed on 23rd July 1979, song was heard in June 1980 and a pair was seen twice in late June in 1982. It is likely that Blackcaps may be nesting in other wooded glens having plentiful undergrowth and at more localities along the wooded slopes to the west of Ramsey. The recent colonisation of the Isle of Man follows the notable increase and expansion of range in the eastern half of Ireland.

On the Calf of Man passage starts during the second half of April, reaches a peak during the first two weeks of May and is negligible after the end of that month. The earliest record for the islet is 11th April 1981 and the highest spring day total was 15 on 11th May 1965. Autumn movement increases from about 10th September and is heaviest during the second half of October. November records are fairly frequent and the highest day total was 30 on 24th October 1968.

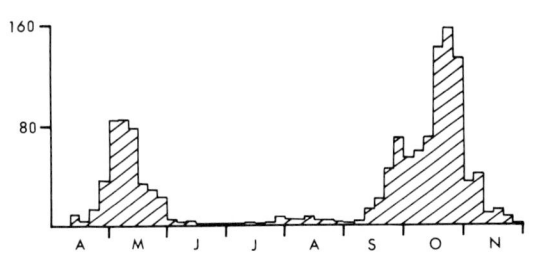

Blackcap. Total bird days per five day period (Calf).

Blackcaps have long been known to overwinter in Ireland, especially in the suburbs of Dublin. A female was present at Ramsey during the winters of 1937 and 1938 and a male frequented a Douglas garden for a few days in January 1943 before being found dead. Further winter records followed from Greeba and St Judes in 1960, Douglas in 1965, Glen Auldyn in 1967, and Laxey in 1969 and since 1973 there have been several records every year. These come mostly from the towns but also from several rural localities. During winter they come readily to bird tables and are often present in the same garden for many weeks. On a number of occasions two have wintered together. There is no evidence to indicate the origin of birds wintering on the Isle of Man – are they in fact residents or are they winter visitors? Two interesting Irish ringing recoveries would suggest the latter – a male ringed in Austria in August 1961 was found dead in Co. Wicklow on 14th December 1961 and another male ringed at Antrim in early January 1979 was killed in south west Germany in July 1981. Do our wintering birds also spend their summers in central Europe?

Seven hundred and twelve Blackcaps have been ringed on the Calf between 1959 and 1984. These together with birds ringed on the main island have yielded 7 recoveries and 1 control of a bird ringed elsewhere. Four of the recoveries relate to ringing and controlling on the Calf and at Port Erin during the same year – the time differences of two spring birds were 2 and 4 days and of juveniles ringed in late July and late November 22 and 13 days respectively. Four Blackcaps ringed in the autumn between 2nd October and 10th November have been recovered abroad – on the north Biscay coast of France in early February, in NW Spain in April, in western Portugal in November and on the Atlantic coast of Morocco at the end of February. There is one control of a bird ringed near the Dee estuary (North Wales) as a juvenile in mid July and trapped on the Calf 9 weeks later and another of a bird ringed 4 days previously on 7th May on Lundy.

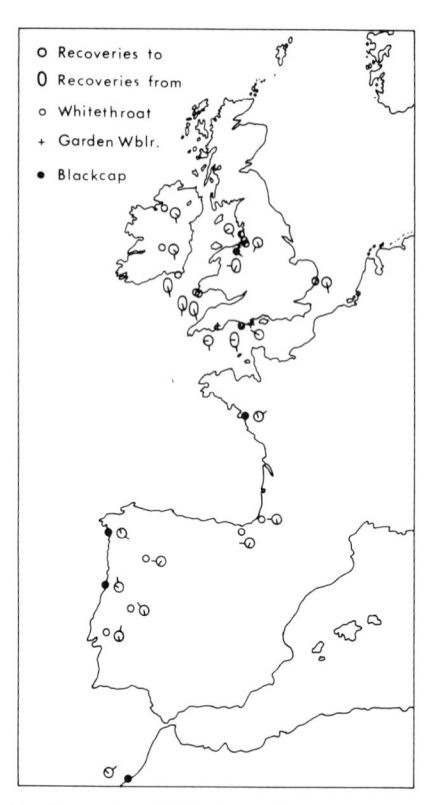

Sylvia Warbler. Recoveries of Whitethroat, Garden Warbler and Blackcap.

Manx: *Bayrn dhoo*

Greenish Warbler
Phylloscopus trochiloides

Uncommon migrant.

The first Manx record was of one seen near the mill-pond on the Calf on 24th July 1962. There have since been five further records between 7th June and 14th July – three males have sung in the Observatory garden and three of the six birds were trapped and belonged to the race *P.t. viridanus*. (Another bird caught and ringed as this species on 30th May 1967 was rejected by the Rarities Committee and the previously accepted 1962 record is now under review).

The Greenish Warbler breeds from southern Asia to the Baltic and has been extending its range westward during the present century. *P.t. viridanus* is the form found in the European part of its range.

Pallas's Warbler

Phylloscopus proregulus

Vagrant.

The trapping of a superbly plumaged example of this minute warbler in the main Heligoland trap on 27th October 1981 was one of the great Calf events. (Jennings 1982). There were only 3 British records of this east Asiatic species prior to 1958 but it has occurred with increasing frequency since and 1981 was a record year with 30 records, later to be overhauled by 1982 which produced at least 116 taking the grand total close to 300.

Yellow-browed Warbler

Phylloscopus inornatus

Scarce but fairly regular passage migrant in late autumn.

There seems little doubt that Yellow-browed Warblers were correctly identified at the Chicken Rock Lighthouse on 19th October 1953 and 15th November 1955. Since 1968 there have been a further 23 records, 5 being of birds ringed at Port Erin, the other 18 from the Calf. The earliest date was 27th September 1972, there has been one other September record, 20 spread fairly evenly through October and three in November, the latest being 20th (1980).

Despite having a breeding range to the east of the Urals and wintering in India and south east Asia, the Yellow-browed Warbler is a regular visitor in small numbers especially to the east coast of Britain.

Dusky Warbler

Phylloscopus fuscatus

Vagrant.

An example of this east Asiatic warbler was trapped on the Calf on 14th May 1970. At the time this was the 11th British record and it remains the only spring record although by 1982 the total had reached 38. It was later found dying in Limerick city on about 5th December 1970 (Wright 1973).

Wood Warbler
Phylloscopus sibilatrix

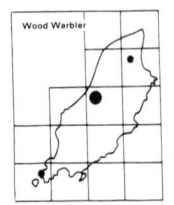

Scarce but regular passage migrant which has bred.

It was on 29th May 1901 that the song of the Wood Warbler was identified for the first time in the Isle of Man in Rhenass Glen by F. S. Graves. Although never again reported from Rhenass, Graves heard it again in the west at Ballamoar (Patrick) in late May 1905. On the same day Ralfe discovered several singing in the Elfin Glen, a site which together with neighbouring Lhergy Frissel and Ballure Glen, was to remain the most important Manx haunt for this species for more than 40 years. At the Elfin Glen where, wrote Ralfe, 'the steep sides of the little ravine, covered with a growth of hyacinth, tall male ferns, and wild raspberry bushes, are wooded with a mixed plantation of oaks and Scotch firs of considerable age and size,' Wood Warblers were without fail heard each summer until the wood was cut down during the First World War. In 1922 there were several pairs in Ballure Glen and they were heard near Lezayre Church; but it was at Lhergy Frissel that breeding was first confirmed when a nest with 5 eggs was found on 11th June 1924. Two nests were found at Ballure in 1927 and song was heard through June there or at Lhergy Frissel almost annually until 1943 when another nest was found at the latter site (Gill 1944). Song was also heard through the summer of 1934 at Glenduff 4 km to the west, and in 1947 and finally in 1953, at Lhergy Frissel. Between 1923 and 1947 there were isolated May records from several parts of the Island and migrants occurred regularly at Garwick up to 1935, while between 1947 and 1967 hardly a year went by without song being heard at Lambhill (Bride). In 1973 2 or 3 were again heard at Ballure one day in early May and song has since been heard during this month at Surby in 1976, Tromode in 1979, Glenmaye in 1980 and in Colby Glen where 3 were heard and seen on 2nd May 1981. There was no suggestion of breeding at any of these sites, but at Cooil Dharry, where one had sung in mid May 1976, song was heard regularly from 12th May to 4th June 1980 and at nearby Glen Mooar a Wood Warbler was heard singing on 13th June the same year.

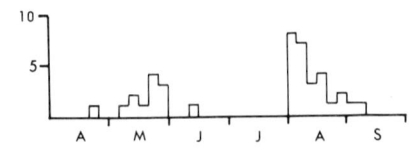

Wood Warbler. Total bird days per five day period (Calf).

On the Calf there have been 50 records (35 ringed) between 1959 and 1983 making it about as common there as the Lesser Whitethroat. Spring passage between 23rd April and 12th June is registered by just 14 birds the remainder having occurred between 1st August and 8th September.

Strangely at Port Erin, where B. Karran has been ringing since 1969, spring records are almost twice as common as autumn, although numbers are perhaps too small to be statistically significant. The latest Manx record was in 1985 when a bird was trapped at Port Erin on 29th October and retrapped on 6th and 8th November. (In 8 days its weight increased from 11.3 to 14.4 g.)

A bird ringed in early May on the Calf was controlled on Great Saltee almost exactly 2 years later and a nestling ringed near Strontian (Argyllshire) in early June was controlled on the Calf 2 months later.

Manx: *Kiaulleyder Keylley*

Chiffchaff

Phylloscopus collybita

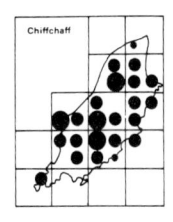

Common summer visitor and passage migrant which sometimes winters in small numbers.

In 1892 Ralfe believed that the Chiffchaff was unknown in the Isle of Man but he later learned that birds had been heard in the Douglas area in 1874 and 1882. The first occurrence therefore took place at a time when the Chiffchaff was greatly expanding its range in Ireland, where in 1850 it only bred in 7 counties while less than 50 years later it was nesting in all. By 1900 it could be described as a regular but local visitor to the Isle of Man and the 1920s saw a marked increase to the point where it could be found in every suitable locality on the Island, a situation which, with fluctuations from year to year, exists to this day.

Its chosen habitat is mixed or deciduous woodland with rough undergrowth so that it is common in the glens such as Silverdale, Port Soderick and Cooil Dharry, along the wooded slopes overlooking the northern plain and in the overgrown parts of such mansions as Kirby, the Nunnery and Milntown as well as the margins of the older plantations like South Barrule and Greeba. In the mid-70s there were up to 6 territories in Cooil Dharry Glen and 5 in Glen Helen. The earliest known laying date for the Island is 4th May and most clutches are started before the middle of that month although a nest at Ballachurry (Andreas) still held young on 21st July 1951. Five or six eggs are usual.

The Chiffchaff is one of the earliest summer visitors to arrive and 1 of the latest to leave although extreme dates are impossible to quote owing to the presence of wintering birds. The earliest Calf record was on 4th March 1978, but movement there does not really start until the last 10 days of March, reaching a peak in mid April. The spring maximum on the Calf was 150 on 4th May 1970. On the main island song has twice been heard on 13th March. The majority of autumn birds pass through the Calf in September, although gradually declining movement continues to the end of November. The highest autumn day total was also 150 on 28th September 1970. Snatches of song are not infrequently heard in autumn up to 17th October.

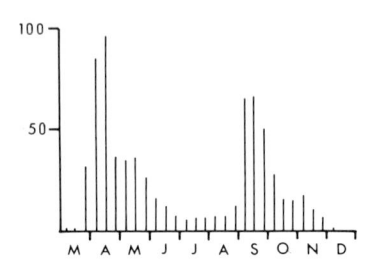

Chiffchaff. Average bird days per ten day period (Calf).

The first suggestion of over-wintering came in 1951 when a leaf warbler was present at Ballachurry (Andreas) for the last two weeks of December. Another bird was present at Ballasalla throughout January 1969 and since 1976 there have been up to 3 separate wintering records most years. Winter reports are commonest from the towns and at Port St Mary they have twice come from close to the shore.

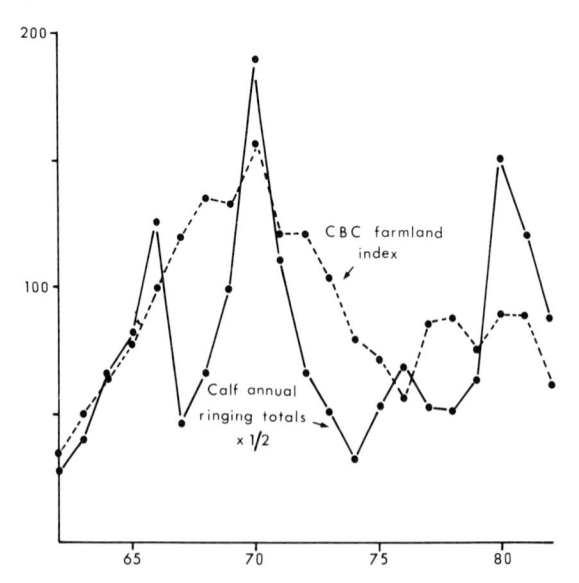

Chiffchaff. Annual ringing totals $\times \frac{1}{2}$ (Calf) and CBC national indices (1962–82).

Three-thousand-five-hundred and eighty-six Chiffchaffs were ringed on the Calf during the Observatory's first 25 years. Although only 10 recoveries have resulted, 14 birds ringed elsewhere have been controlled on the Island. Three Calf controls had been ringed on Bardsey 2 days, 3 days and $7\frac{1}{2}$ months earlier and 5 were either ringed or controlled in Dorset with, in one case, a time differential of 5 days. Two others had been ringed in Surrey and at Beachy Head, Sussex, while a male ringed on the Calf on 24th April was breeding at Gibraltar Point (Lincolnshire) 350 km E.S.E. between 22nd June and 16th August the same year. The most distant wintering of Calf visitors is in Senegal and the Gambia (2) with recoveries over the intervening regions from Casablanca (Morocco), Vizcaya (northern Spain) – 18 days – and Normandy (France). Further east Calf birds have occurred in S.W. Belgium and north Holland. To the north a Galloway ringed juvenile was controlled in autumn on the Calf 7 weeks later while another Chiffchaff ringed on 6th June on the Calf was controlled on Fair Isle 9 days later. A bird ringed at Malahide (Co. Dublin) in early June was controlled 10 months later at Port Erin.

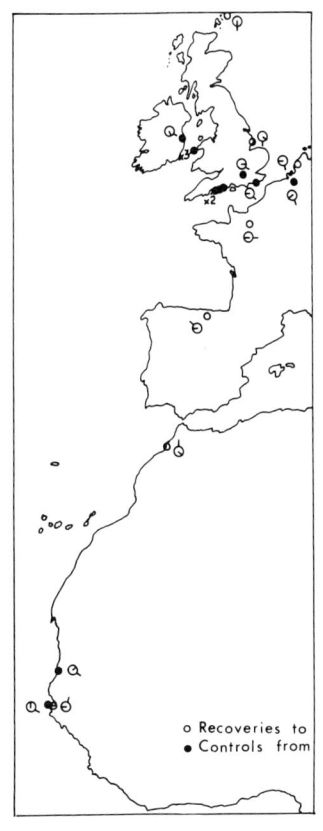

Recovery sites and origins of Chiffchaffs ringed or controlled on the Isle of Man.

Apart from the nominate race *P.c. collybita*, *P.c. abietinus*, which breeds in Scandinavia and eastern Europe, occurs annually in autumn in small numbers, while *P.c. tristis*, the Siberian form occasionally passes through in October and November. Birds showing intermediate characteristics also occur as is to be expected in a clinal species. A bird trapped in late May 1979 was very yellow underneath and bright green/olive above and comparable to examples of the race *P.c. ibericus* which is mainly resident in Iberia and north-west Africa. Such vagrancy is possible, but the very variable nature of the species over much of its range indicates that the bird was more likely to have been an unusually plumaged individual of the nominate race.

Manx: *Beealerey*

Willow Warbler

Phylloscopus trochilus

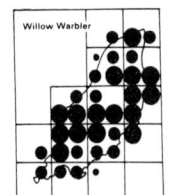

Common summer visitor and passage migrant.

Ralfe described the Willow Warbler as 'one of the few summer visitors which are pretty plentiful in Man'. The somewhat restrained tone of this observation could hardly apply now to a bird whose liquid decrescendo trill is arguably the most characteristic song of the Manx spring and early summer. As they pass through the Island in April and May they are the trout fisherman's companions as they follow the larger watercourses northwards, their oft repeated songs seeming to echo the sound of the shallow stream as it tumbles over its stony bed. Many remain to nest close to the rivers, typical of this population were 44 singing males located along a 3 km stretch of the lower Neb in late June 1975. In the wooded glens and on the slopes overlooking the northern plain they share their habitat with the Chiffchaff, but they are perhaps commonest in lightly wooded wet areas such as the Curraghs of Ballaugh and the central valley, the Lagagh, Lough Cranstal, and the gareys of Tosaby and Ballacorris. In the plantations they are common, favouring particularly the forest clearings, the peripheral areas and the young plantations. The failed plantation, stifled by heather growth as in parts of Glen Rushen and the exposed wind-blown stands such as Sartfell (350 m above sea level) are also well populated. A pair bred on the Calf in 1970.

Six, less commonly 5 or 7, eggs are laid in May – the season being a little later than that of the Chiffchaff. Young in a Lhergy Frissel nest on 19th May 1944 were unusually early.

In four years Willow Warblers have been noted on the Calf on 26th March and there have been occasional records of singing during the last 5 days of the month. Calf movement, like that at Portland and Skokholm, starts earlier than at other more easterly observatories (Riddiford and Findley, 1981), has an early peak in mid April and a larger peak during the first 10 days of May – the spring maximum was 450 on 8th May 1981. Autumn

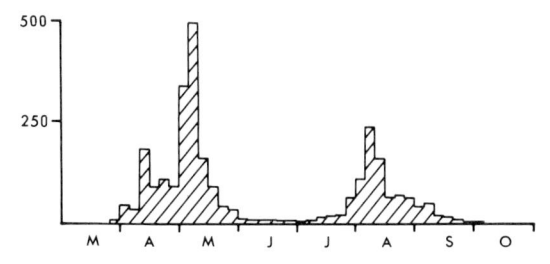

Willow Warbler. Average bird days per five day period (Calf).

passage is lighter; starting in late July it is greatest during the first half of August and quite well sustained until mid September. October records are rare, the latest Calf bird was on 13th October 1976, but song was heard at Ballaugh on 17th October 1930. The highest autumn day count on the Calf was 400 on 9th August 1969.

Fifteen-thousand, three hundred and ninety-six Willow Warblers were ringed on the Calf between 1959 and 1983 making it easily the most frequently ringed species. Overall it has accounted for 16% of all birds ringed and in both 1980 and 1981 over 24%. A comparison of Calf and Bardsey ringing totals between 1976 and 1983 shows extraordinary similarity although the slump of 1979 and the peak of 1981 were both more dramatic at Bardsey. There have been 30 recoveries of Manx-ringed birds and a further 22 birds ringed elsewhere have been controlled on the Isle of Man. Fourteen birds

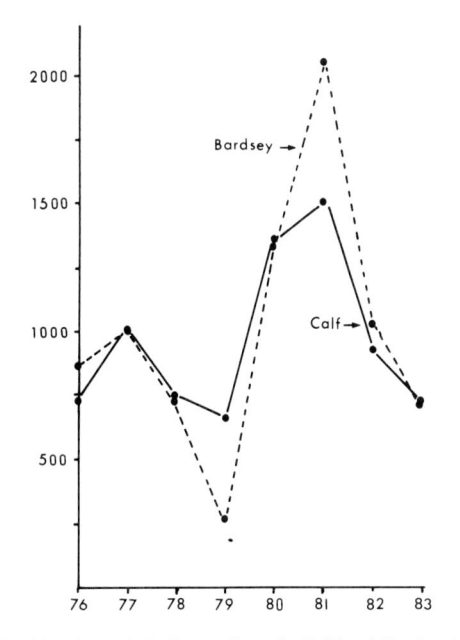

Willow Warbler. Annual ringing totals on the Calf and Bardsey (1976–83).

were trapped in south west Britain in spring – 7 at Portland, 1 on Lundy, 1 in Gloucestershire and 5 in west Wales and all but 3 of the Portland birds were also spring trappings on the Calf. Six birds from S.E. England were evenly divided between spring and autumn as were 8 trapped in Scotland between Islay in the west, the Isle of May in the east and Melvich on the north coast. South of the English Channel Manx birds were trapped in the Channel Islands (2), north and central France, Spain (2) and Portugal. Although a bird ringed in north Kent in May and controlled on the Calf 4 days later provides evidence of some Calf birds crossing the Straits of Dover in spring it seems that the majority cross the channel between the Cherbourg peninsula and Portland and thence through west Wales to the Isle of Man. All the birds trapped in eastern Scotland were trapped on the Isle of Man in spring and they may well return south by a much more easterly route. Birds ringed in Islay and Kintyre in autumn have been controlled on the Isle of Man the same autumn and another autumn ringed bird was controlled at Hilbre to the south east 2 days later suggesting that birds passing through the Calf in autumn make for the short channel crossing from S.E. England, although 1984 saw the autumn recovery of Manx ringed birds on Lundy and in Dorset. Other speed records include Portland to Calf in 48 hours and 4 days, Bardsey to Calf in 2 days, Calf to Kintyre in 3 and 6 days, Calf to Stirling in 12 days and Port St Mary to Orleans in 14 days. On the main island a number of birds have been retrapped in subsequent years probably breeding near the ringing site.

Birds showing the characteristics of the northern form *P.t. acredula* are annual in spring and autumn, but numbers vary greatly from year to year.

Manx: *Drean vane* = White Wren

Goldcrest

Regulus regulus

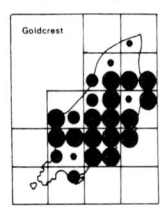

Common breeding bird, present throughout the year and abundant as a passage migrant.

There is nothing to suggest any change in the status of the Goldcrest in the Isle of Man. Sensitive to hard winters, but with a remarkable capacity for rapid recovery, there are however notable fluctuations from year to year and it is only since the establishment of the Calf Observatory that the true magnitude of passage, especially in autumn, has become apparent.

As a breeding bird the Goldcrest is widely distributed through plantations of all ages and is almost the only species found in the ornithologically boring depths of the mature conifer forest. This habitat probably accounts for the majority of nesting Goldcrests, but they are also found in wooded glens, gardens and on ground overgrown by gorse. Manx nest sites have included the fork of a thorn bush, trailing ivy, gorse and also honeysuckle and the witch's broom on a birch – both sites described as exceptional by Bruce Campbell in his *Field Guide to Birds' Nests*. From a very small sample the earliest egg date is on or before 20th April with young fledging from a second brood as late as 2nd August. Eight to ten is the usual clutch size.

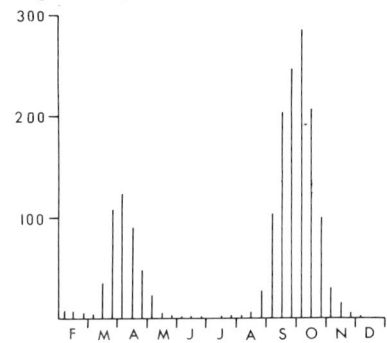

Goldcrest. Average bird days per ten day period (Calf).

Ralfe's view that the Goldcrest is commoner in winter than summer is probably still valid, but no season compares with the autumn, when, during September and October, numbers are considerable. In the plantations and along the hedgerows and the river banks the incessant mouse-like squeaks advertise the progress of a loose party of up to 40 birds. The much lighter spring passage is from mid March to early May. Calf maxima for a single day were both achieved during 1981 400 on 29th March and 500 on 6th October. A comparison of ringing totals for the two observatories over the last 8 years suggests that birds passing through the Calf exceed those at Bardsey by a proportion of 5 : 3.

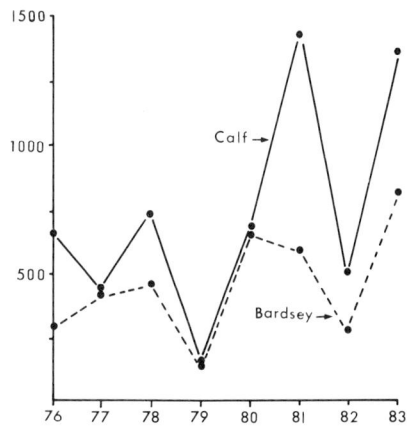

Goldcrest. Annual ringing totals on the Calf and Bardsey (1976–83).

Between 1959 and 1983 11,451 Goldcrests were ringed on the Calf, a total only exceeded by the Willow Warbler. In addition over 2,000 have been ringed at Port Erin since 1969 and this combined effort has produced 14 recoveries away from the Island together with 9 controls of birds ringed elsewhere. There is a definite pattern of south easterly movement in winter with a number of birds trapped in the English midlands, 1 in Surrey and 2 individuals in Holland and Belgium. A Goldcrest ringed on the Calf in mid September was recovered at sea between Southampton and Bremerhaven 3 weeks later. To the south 3 Manx birds were trapped at Bardsey and 1 in S.W. Wales and there have been other individuals from Fermanagh and Down, Kintyre, Tyneside and south Yorkshire (2). The Fermanagh bird was ringed there in late August and controlled on the Calf 5 weeks later while the Tyneside bird was found dead at South Shields just 3 days after being ringed on the Calf on 5th April. Two birds seemed quite disorientated – 1 was ringed at 10.00 hours on the Calf on 6th September and was controlled at Sanda (Kintyre) 145 km NNW at 10.30 hours the following day, its weight having dropped from 5.8 g to 4.5 g, the other was ringed on the Calf on 27th March and controlled at Bardsey 3 days later. Over 30 Goldcrests have been trapped at both Port Erin and the Calf during the same year, usually 1–5 days intervening.

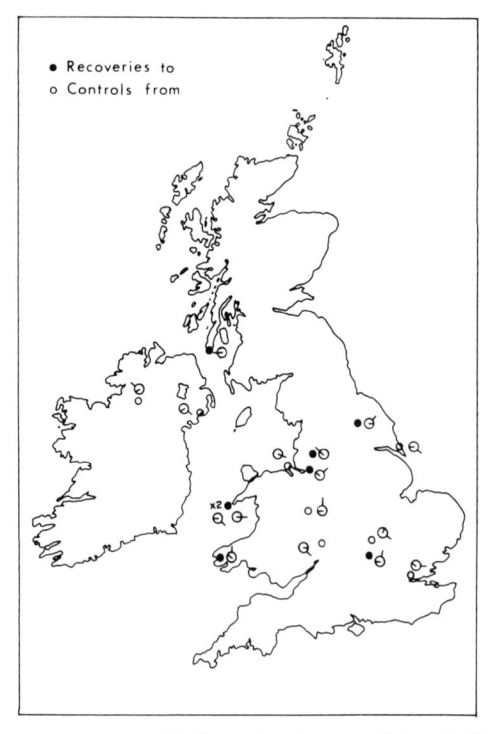

Recovery sites and origins of Goldcrests ringed or controlled on the Isle of Man.

The continental race *R.r. regulus* is of frequent occurrence in small numbers, usually in late autumn.
Manx: *Ushag y fuygh* = Bird of the timber

Firecrest
Regulus ignicapillus

Scarce but regular passage migrant and occasional winter visitor.

The first Manx record was a Lighthouse casualty at Douglas Head on 3rd March 1948, to be followed in 1956 by one with 4 Goldcrests at the Chicken Rock Lighthouse on 9th October.

The Firecrest was recorded on the Calf in 7 of the 11 years from 1962 to 1972 with 6 spring and 2 autumn records during this period. Since 1973 it has been of annual occurrence on the Calf and there have been more than a dozen records for the main island.

Manx records now exceed 50 with 4 autumn records for every bird seen in spring. Over half of the Firecrests seen on the Isle of Man have been ringed and this species is doubtless overlooked among the Goldcrests whose company it usually shares. In spring there have been 3 March records, 8 in April and 2 in May on 1st and 25th. One was present on 4th and 5th June and on 22nd and 23rd June 1981 a male sang by the Calf Observatory. Five birds have been seen in September – 1 on 17th and the others on 30th, but October is easily the best month for Firecrests with records of more than 20 individuals, while 8 of the 9 November records were in the first ten days of that month.

The first December record was in 1974 when a male was caught in Laxey on 14th. Another was ringed at Laxey on 21st December the following year and 1–2 birds probably spent that winter at Surby with records on 3rd December (2), 26th December, 22nd January and 12th February.

The increased frequency of records since 1962 seems to be associated not so much with the operation of the Calf of Man Observatory as with the Firecrest's colonisation of parts of south east England and, perhaps more significantly, Denmark as a breeding bird.

Spotted Flycatcher
Muscicapa striata

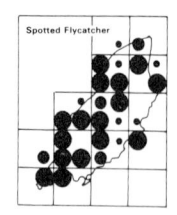

Fairly common but locally distributed summer visitor and common passage migrant.

As he carefully listed all the known records of the Spotted Flycatcher it is assumed that Ralfe considered this a decidedly uncommon species. It is possible that during the latter part of the 19th century breeding was confined to the southern outskirts of Douglas – a nest had been found at Thornton in about 1874 and by 1897 it was fairly numerous in the vicinity of the Nunnery. A few years later a nest was found on the ruins of the old starch mills in Sulby Glen and in 1908 breeding was confirmed at Ballamoar (Jurby). Ralfe quoted a few autumn records probably referring to migrants. By 1934 Madoc was able to write 'Year by year these birds get commoner and have now spread to all parts of the Island', but just 6 years later Williamson stated that it nested rather sparingly in Man and this remains a fair assessment of its status. In Britain the Common Bird Census has shown a decline in the breeding population to only about half the level of the early 1960s, but

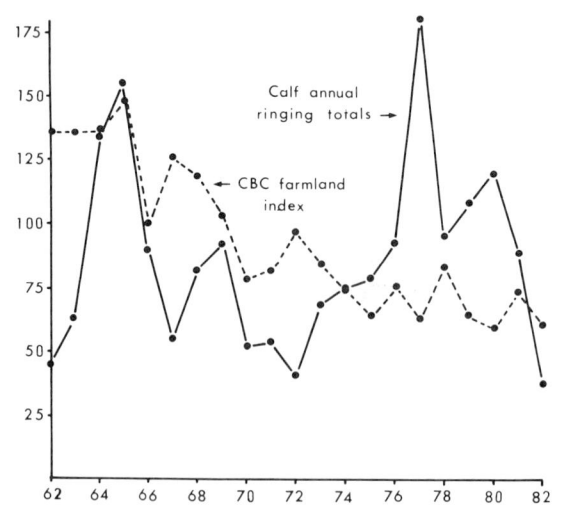

Spotted Flycatcher. Annual ringing totals (Calf) and farmland national CBC indices (1962–82).

while the peak C.B.C. year 1965 coincided with an exceptional Calf ringing tally of 155 birds, this was bettered in 1977 when 180 birds were ringed.

Spotted Flycatchers nest in gardens and open woodland, especially along the watercourses. Small areas such as upper Silverdale, Port Soderick Glen, the Raggatt and Ballaugh Cronk will have 2 or 3 breeding pairs. Nests are built on ledges and recesses on buildings, bridges and walls, on quarry faces and on trees, but perhaps the most unusual site was in $\frac{2}{3}$ of a coconut suspended

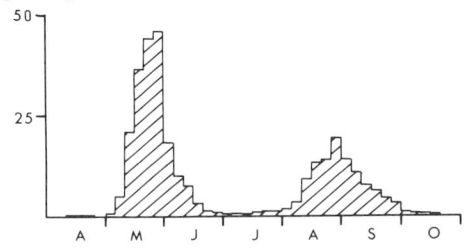

Spotted Flycatcher. Average bird days per five day period (Calf).

for tit feeding at Lezayre. Williamson did not accept Madoc's implication that a pair used to breed annually near the farmhouse on the Calf, but a pair did nest on the islet in 1971 at the bottom of the Mill Giau where it enters the sea. The nest was within 50 m of high water mark and almost 200 m from the nearest trees. The earliest calculated egg date is 20th May and young have rarely been seen in the nest after the first week in July indicating that Manx birds are rarely double brooded. One late brood left the nest about 13th August and a pair was feeding fledged young in the tree tops of Ballaglass Glen on 12th September 1976. Four or five eggs are usual, but one clutch of six has been recorded.

As a passage migrant the Spotted Flycatcher is commoner in spring than autumn. Early birds have included individuals at Ballacross (Andreas) on

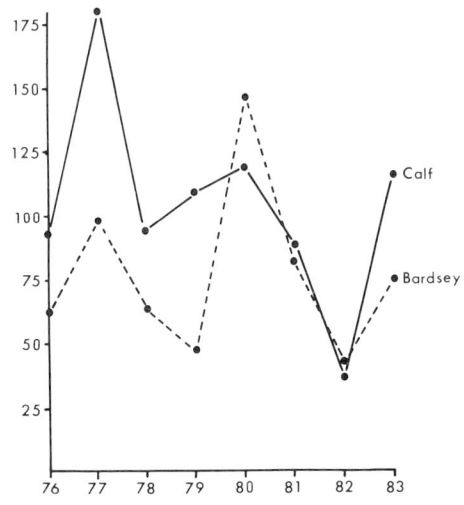

Spotted Flycatcher. Annual ringing totals on the Calf and Bardsey (1976–83).

16th April 1980, at Garwick on 19th April 1953 and two on the Calf on 26th April 1983, but they are rare before 5th May and the main period of passage is during the second half of that month, decreasing numbers continuing to mid June. The best Calf spring day total was 80 on 22nd May 1965. Autumn passage increases during August to a peak at the end of the month and declines through September. October records are rather uncommon, the latest being a bird on the Calf on 20th October 1968. Fifty birds passed through the Calf on 19th August 1966. Judged on ringing totals since 1976 overall passage on the Calf exceeds that at Bardsey by 26%.

Two thousand and forty-four Spotted Flycatchers were ringed on the Calf between 1959 and 1983 – 11 were recovered and there were two controls of birds ringed elsewhere. Three Calf birds have been ringed or recovered on Bardsey and 2 others around the estuary of the Welsh Dee. Foreign recoveries have come from western France (3) north east Spain (2) and the Congo basin (2). A bird ringed at Spurn on the east coast of England in late May was recovered on the Calf exactly a year later.

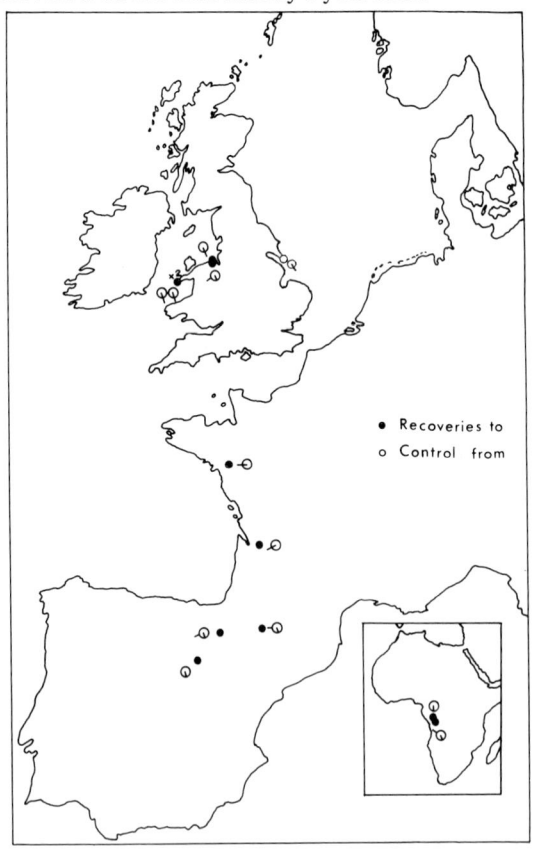

Recovery sites and origin of Spotted Flycatchers ringed or controlled on the Isle of Man.

Manx: *Skybbyltagh breck*

Red-breasted Flycatcher
Ficedula parva

Rare passage migrant.

The first Manx record was of a male at the Lhen on 24th April 1955 (Corlett 1957). This remains the earliest record and there have since been a further six in spring between 10th May and 21st June and ten or eleven in autumn between 2nd September and 22nd November. Apart from the Calf, records have come from Santon Gorge, Langness and Port Erin and have included immature birds and at least three adult males. Red-breasted Flycatchers have now been recorded in 8 of the last 14 years with 3 in the autumn of 1976.

This is a central and eastern European and Asian breeding species, which normally winters in southern and south-eastern Asia with a few in Africa.

Pied Flycatcher
Ficedula hypoleuca

Rather scarce passage migrant.

Unknown in Ireland until 1875, the first Manx record was of a male in Glenmaye village on 25th April 1901. It was not until the spring of 1927 that the Pied Flycatcher was again identified on the Isle of Man and the

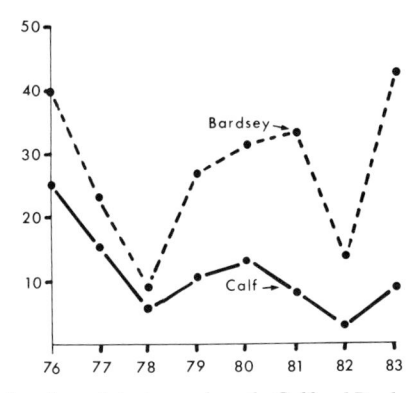

Pied Flycatcher. Annual ringing totals on the Calf and Bardsey (1976–83).

next 32 years produced a further six records. With the establishment of the Observatory on the Calf in 1959 it became apparent that it is a regular passage migrant in small numbers. An average of about ten birds per year have been ringed there and recently a few have been trapped most years at Port Erin. Elsewhere this species is rarely seen and there is no evidence of any significant change in the numbers passing through the Island. The Pied Flycatcher is a common breeding bird in Wales and Lakeland and it is hardly surprising that it occurs much more commonly at Bardsey.

The earliest record is of a pair at Glen Roy on 12th and 13th April 1980 and there have been seven other April records during the last week of that month. Spring movement is extremely light and continues to about 25th May. Autumn passage from early August to early October is much more substantial with a peak day total of 20 on 13th August 1975. The latest Calf record was of one on 12th October 1981, but a bird was seen at Port Erin on 22nd October 1982.

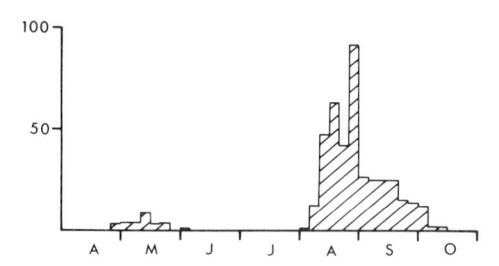

Pied Flycatcher. Total bird days per five day period (Calf).

The ringing of 254 Pied Flycatchers on the Calf has yielded two recoveries – one from Portugal and the other from the Mediterranean coast of Morocco.

Long-tailed Tit
Aegithalos caudatus

Fairly common resident, numbers perhaps augmented by winter visitors.

The first Manx record was of two obtained from a flock of 8 near Douglas in 1877, but although perhaps increasing, at least as a winter visitor, Ralfe considered the Long-tailed Tit to be an uncommon bird. It seems to have been very local in its distribution, records up to about 1925 being confined to the Douglas area (breeding in the Braddan/Quarterbridge district) and Lezayre parish where it was thought to have nested in the 1890s. Kermode, Ralfe and Madoc all believed that migrants visited the Island in winter, but although not improbable, proof of this is still wanting. Long-tailed Tits were found in winter near Patrick in 1928, in the Laxey/Garwick area from 1932, and at Injebreck in October 1938. From 1937, when a pair nested at Glenmaye, breeding was proved nearly every year in the Douglas area and in northern Lezayre and adjacent parts of Andreas parish. From 1942 parties were often found in the Ballaugh Curraghs in winter but they were unknown south of the Nunnery until a pair was found at Crogga in April 1949 and there was a party at Santon in October 1953. In September 1957 two were seen on the Calf, but they were not recorded again there until several parties of up to 15 birds were recorded in the autumn of 1973. By then they could regularly be found in Silverdale and a flock of over 30 was seen in Bradda Glen in November 1974. The last ten years have seen a consolidation of its status as a breeding bird in the long established localities and also along the Glen Wyllin and Glen Mooar streams in Michael, along the central valley, well into the Baldwin valleys and along the Groudle and Cornaa streams.

Nest building starts during the last week of March and newly hatched young have been found as early as 24th April. Long-tailed Tits are single brooded and young are unlikely to be found in the nest after the end of May.

Family parties are seen from June onwards, and although the larger flocks of 20–30 birds are more typical of the autumn there were over 30 in Silverdale on 25th June 1978. Long-tailed Tits are quite sensitive to hard winters and the late summer flocks usually reflect the severity of the previous winter. Since 1973 Long-tailed Tits have occurred on the Calf in 6 out of 11 autumns, records falling between 7th October and 17th November. Although some Calf records have involved individuals, most have been of parties of 7–15 birds – unfortunately although 35 have been ringed there have been no recoveries, but their visits are very brief and all appear to be day-trippers from the main Island. Flocks continue to be seen up to the end of February and

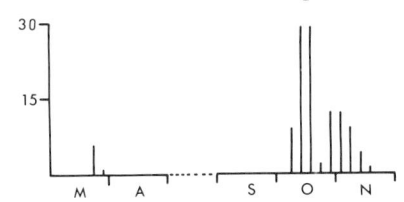

Long-tailed Tit. Total bird days per five day period (Calf).

1–2 birds have twice appeared on the Calf in late March. Flocks of Long-tailed Tits particularly favour the wooded glens and the trees which fringe the lower reaches of the Glass (especially Tromode and the Nunnery) and the Neb. Barnell Reservoir and the Curraghs of Ballaugh and Greeba are also favourite resorts. One bird ringed in the Ballaugh Curraghs in mid July was retrapped 4 years 9 months later.

J. C. Crellin made an unusual observation of two Long-tailed Tits feeding in a midden at Ballachurry (Andreas) in December 1975.

Manx: *Caillagh Veg yn Arbyl*

Marsh Tit

Parus palustris

Vagrant.

Neither the Marsh Tit nor the very similar Willow Tit *P. montanus* occur in Ireland and there are only seven Manx records of small black-capped tits. First was one watched at very close quarters by the highly experienced F. S. Graves at Lezayre in August 1922. He was uncertain as to whether it was *P. palustris* or *P. montanus* and such uncertainty must surely apply duals at Government House on 15th November 1931, at nearby Ashfield on 22nd December 1932, at Tromode on 1st September 1973, at Ballacallin (Patrick) on 8th September 1973 and the two seen at the Raggatt nearby on 7th August 1979. The one unequivocal record of the Marsh Tit was of three birds clearly seen and identified by their call notes as they fed in pines at Baldwin on 14th February 1953.

The Willow Tit is generally more migratory than the Marsh and one cannot ignore the fact that the Willow Tit is a well represented resident in Galloway breeding a mere 35 km from the Island while the nearest nesting place of the Marsh Tit is more than twice that distance away in southern Cumbria.

Coal Tit

Parus ater

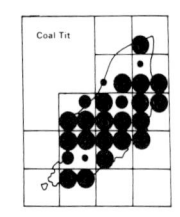

Common resident.

Although common and widely distributed in Ireland, it was not until 1896 that Coal Tits were first seen on the Isle of Man – at Laxey and at Ballachurry (Andreas). By 1903 they were becoming increasingly common in the Douglas area and the first record of nesting came from Ballamoar (Patrick) in 1908 with further records from Lewaigue and Ballamoar (Jurby) the following year. Sadly, the Coal Tit's abundance on the larger adjacent islands has resulted in very little documentation of its spread in the Isle of Man, but by 1970 it could be said that all suitable habitats were occupied. In the coniferous plantations it is second only in abundance to the Goldcrest and it is also a common inhabitant of the wooded glens, the mixed woodland associated with such mansions as Kirby and the Nunnery and of the larger gardens. While new conifer implantations have undoubtedly played an important role in the Coal Tit's increasing prosperity the increases have taken place in all forms of woodland and it is arguably now the commonest Manx tit.

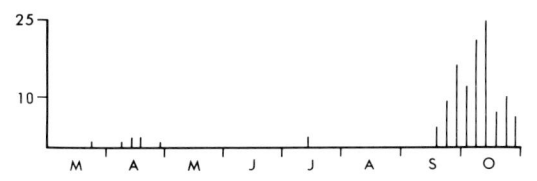

Coal Tit. Total bird days per five day period (Calf).

To the Calf of Man it is a regular visitor between 17th September and 31st October with a maximum of 10 on 7th October 1977. There have also been 6 spring records between 22nd March and 28th April and one in July. Fifty-four Coal Tits have been ringed on the Calf producing two recoveries – one at Port Erin, from where there has also been a Calf control and one at Laxey, a distance of 33 km. Five other birds ringed on the main island have shown movement of less than 1 km.

The local Manx population most resembles *P.a. britannicus*, but birds showing the characteristics of *P.a. hibernicus* which occurs in Ireland and clines into *P.a. britannicus* in west Wales and west Scotland, also occur e.g., 3 on the Calf during westerly winds on 25th October 1979. The continental race *P.a. ater* has not yet been identified.

Blue Tit
Parus caeruleus

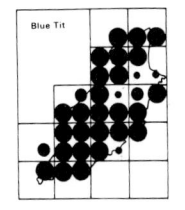

Common resident. Movement away from the Isle of Man has been observed.

The colonisation of the Isle of Man by the Blue Tit is relatively recent. In 1722 Bishop Wilson noted its absence, but by 1872 it was present near Onchan and was found near Peel 4 years later. During the last six years of the 19th century it was quite widely reported and clearly increasing rapidly. The first breeding record came from Sulby parsonage in 1896. From Ralfe's failure to mention the Blue Tit in his supplement of 1923 it must be assumed that its status as a common resident had by then been established for many years.

Blue Tits are best known as garden birds, but they are plentiful in roadside and riparian trees and in the lightly wooded parts of curragh and garey.

They are resident in all the wooded glens and in the Ballaugh Curragh were very easily the most frequently trapped birds during an intensive September ringing programme. At the Dog Mills Lough in late summer Sedge Warblers were the dominant species, after which Wrens and Blue Tits were ringed with almost equal frequency (Fitzpatrick 1980).

Nest building may be seen as early as 4th April, but most clutches are started during the last week of April and the first week of May. Although single brooded, young have been found still in the nest as late as 17th July. In 1957 a pair nested in a nest box in the garden of the Calf farm.

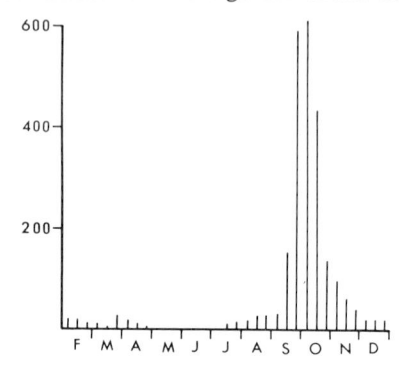

Blue Tit. Total bird days per ten day period (Calf).

In the autumn small flocks gather and move about the island and regularly visit the Calf between mid September and early November. Ringing work suggests that in most years the Calf visitors are Manx birds but in both 1970 and 1980 numbers were considerably greater than usual and were, at least in the former year supplemented by birds from further afield. The maxi-maximum count since the establishment of the Observatory was 130 on 25th September 1980. In 1970 125 birds were ringed, all were in their first year and none were seen to fly south. One bird ringed on 8th October was a traffic casualty in Selkirkshire three months later. In late September and October 1957 there was a phenomenal invasion of tits on the south and east coasts of England from areas around the North Sea. This spread in a north-westerly direction and during the first two weeks of October Blue Tits were spread about all over the Calf (Williamson 1959).

During winter mixed parties of Blue, Great and Coal Tits, Long-tailed Tits, Goldcrests and Treecreepers are quite a common sight as they rove through wooded glens and gardens. Blue Tits are occasional visitors to the Calf in spring from mid March to the end of April.

Between 1959 and 1983 712 Blue Tits were ringed on the Calf from which there were 18 recoveries. From other Manx sources there have been a further 16 recoveries, but all except the Scottish recovery mentioned above have been on the Isle of Man. Movement has been mostly less than 5 km (many have been controlled at Port Erin shortly after ringing on the Calf) but 5 birds have shown movement of between 24 and 33 km. The Manx longevity record is held by a bird ringed in Castletown as a juvenile in late July and found dead there 5 years and 3 months later.

Manx: *Drean Gorrym*

Great Tit
Parus major

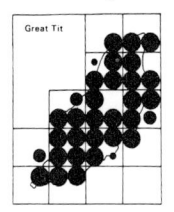

Common resident.

Of the Great Tit Ralfe wrote 'Until recently this was the only Tit that could fairly be called common in the island; it is well distributed, frequenting the neighbourhood of houses, shrubberies, gardens, and hedges, and mixing in plantations with Chaffinches and Goldcrests.' Earlier Dr Crellin of Orrisdale had suggested that the Great Tit was unknown in the Isle of Man prior to about 1830. Certainly the last 80 years have seen no apparent change in its status and the very rare references in the literature relate to its sometimes odd choice of nest site, examples being in a cannon at Ballakeigan (Arbory) and in the top of a hand-operated iron water pump, the birds entering by the handle and departing through the spout.

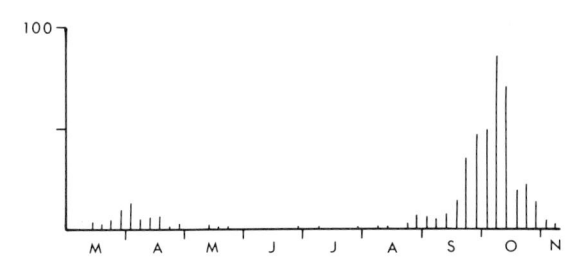

Great Tit. Total bird days per five day period (Calf).

As with the other tits some numbers appear on the Calf between mid-September and the end of October. These in no way compare with the Blue Tit but are appreciably greater than those of the Coal Tit and Long-tailed Tit. The best day count was only 15 on 9th October 1970. In spring the Great Tit is more regular on the Calf than the other tits with records between 14th March and 24th May.

The ringing of 175 birds on the Calf has produced 7 recoveries and there have been a further 4 recoveries of birds ringed elsewhere on the Isle of Man. There have been two movements of 33 km, the others being of 5 km or less.

Manx: *Drean Mooar*

Nuthatch

Sitta europaea

Very rare vagrant.

There are just two published records. One was seen in a residential area of Douglas prior to a snow storm on 8th December 1981 and another was seen and heard near the Groudle Hotel during heavy snow on 2nd January 1984.

Treecreeper

Certhia familiaris

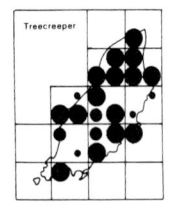

Fairly common resident.

Probably overlooked previously, the Treecreeper was first recorded in the Isle of Man in 1882. Early records came from several localities between Orrisdale (Ballaugh) and Ramsey and from south Douglas, but by 1904 it had been found at Baldwin, Laxey and Ballamoar (Patrick). During the first half of the present century Treecreepers probably occupied most suitable areas north of a line between Patrick village and Douglas and may well have been overlooked in the south. The first record for the Calf was in 1943 when on 1st July one was seen on the farmhouse wall and in 1955 a nest was found at Ballasalla. By 1970 it was plentiful in trees along the Silverburn from Castletown, through Silverdale as far as Grenaby and could also be found at Kentraugh.

A few pairs are probably present in all the wooded glens and in the open woodland associated with such great houses as Milntown, Ballakillingan, Ballamoar, Kirby and the Nunnery. They are present at Montpelier near the headwaters of the Sulby and in the hedgerows of the Ballaugh Curraghs. The earliest of a number of April nests was one which held 4 eggs at Milntown on 20th April 1909 and young have fledged as late as 20th July. The typical nest site is behind loose bark or ivy, but more bizarre sites include the gap between a meat safe and the wall of the house (Ballachurry) and several in the gaps between the timbers of wooden buildings. The widespread habit of roosting in a hole fashioned in the bark of a Wellingtonia has been noted at Ramsey and Glen Helen.

There are one or two records from the Calf between April and October most years – 31 have been ringed there including one on 19th August which was later controlled at Port Erin on 13th September and 19th November the same year. In winter they join parties of tits and Goldcrests on the main island.

Manx: *Snaueyder*

Golden Oriole
Oriolus oriolus

Rare passage migrant.

A Golden Oriole was shot in the Isle of Man in June 1868 and a female caught at Laxey on 25th April 1879. After a gap of 65 years two adult males appeared at Congary south of Peel on 3rd July 1944 and in 1955 one was found dead under wires at Patrick on 25th April. Since 1974 there have been a further nine records between 12th May and 22nd June – 3 from the Calf (including a male in song in June 1978), 2 from Maughold and one each from Port Erin, Kentraugh, Peel and Andreas. Mid May 1979 produced a moribund female at Port Erin and a male at Maughold, both on 14th and a male near Andreas (10 km to the north west) on 19th, records which coincided with 4 at Great Saltee from 13th to 15th, an exhausted bird in Dublin on 14th as well as 4 at Cape Clear on 13th with perhaps 7 birds there up to 21st. At Bardsey two were trapped on 13th and another on 15th.

Red-backed Shrike
Lanius collurio

Rare passage migrant.

The first Manx record was of one trapped daily on the Calf from 1st to 4th September 1961. There have since been 8 further records from the Calf and 3 from the south of the main island. Six spring records have occurred between 26th May and 8th June, there was one on 8th July and five autumn birds have been recorded between 1st September and 24th November. In autumn Red-backed Shrikes have shown a tendency to linger, an immature bird staying on the Calf from 3rd to 14th September 1979 and another first winter bird remaining in a Port Erin garden from 17th to 24th November, making it by 3 days the latest British Red-backed Shrike this century. There was another late juvenile in Castletown on 2nd November 1981.

Great Grey Shrike
Lanius excubitor

Rare passage migrant and occasional winter visitor.

One was shot near Orrisdale (Ballaugh) on 30th October 1865 and another near Ramsey in January 1896. In 1931 two were present at Glenchass on 30th and 31st March, one remaining to 2nd April, and another was seen at Port St Mary from 10th to 13th October. In 1963 a male was present on the Castletown by-pass from 10th April to 2nd May and since 1970 there have been 9 further records – 3 in spring (late March, 8th April and 18th May) and 5 in autumn (all from the Calf from between 14th and 25th October and one on 13th November). The only recent winter record was of one by the old railway line at Ballaugh on 10th January 1975.

Woodchat Shrike
Lanius senator

Vagrant.

There are just two records from the Calf of Man – one was present from 22nd April to 9th May 1966 and another, an adult female on 26th June

1981. The Woodchat Shrike is of almost annual occurrence at Great Saltee and only marginally less frequent at Bardsey.

Jay
Garrulus glandarius

Vagrant.

The Jay had long been the most conspicuous absentee from the Manx bird list, because although virtually absent from Anglesey it is well distributed in all counties bordering the Irish Sea. Eventually in 1982 one was seen at Ballagyr (German) on 16th September and again on 5th November. The great irruption which occurred the following autumn did not penetrate to the Isle of Man, but another record came from Cronk y voddy, just 4 km from Ballagyr, in May 1985.

Magpie
Pica pica

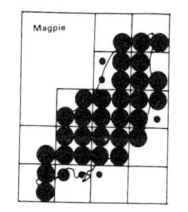

Common resident.

Of this species Bishop Wilson wrote in 1722 'It is not long since a person, more fanciful than prudent or kind to his country, brought in a breed of Magpies, which have increased incredibly, so as to become a nuisance.' Clearly the introduction had taken place well before 1687 when, together with *Kytes, Ravens and Scar Crowes*, they were listed as vermin in the Castle Rushen papers, payment being made for each head. It must have preceded the Magpie's appearance in Ireland at Wexford in about 1676, a colonisation which may have been natural or the result of introduction by the English who settled in south-east Ireland in great numbers in the late 17th century. Ralfe regarded the Magpie as common all over the cultivated parts of the Isle of Man and he gave no hint that numbers at the turn of the century were at the low ebb described in Britain generally (Parslow 1967). About that time flocks of up to 40 were not uncommon, attracted in some cases by the practice of using offal to manure fields. During the present century numbers have steadily increased and in 1937 the first flock in excess of 100 was seen feeding on pig-swill at Ballaugh. On the Calf one or two pairs nested in the early 1900s and in 1943, although not in 1938 or 1939. Since 1959, when 2 pairs nested on the islet, the breeding population had increased with 5–6 pairs in the late sixties to a peak of 14 pairs in 1979, falling away to just 7 pairs in 1982 and 1983. On the main island Magpies are very plentiful along the hedgerows of farmland and penetrate into suburban gardens. They are particularly common on the Ayres and in wooded curragh and garey and occur in very wild and open localities all around the coast and in the hills up to about 250 metres above sea level.

Nest building may begin in mid February and eggs have been found as early as 4th April, but most Manx clutches are started in mid April. In 1929 young did not leave a Peel nest until after 7th July. Five or six eggs are usual and seven eggs have been recorded. Most nests are of the traditional domed type and the upper part of an isolated hedgerow hawthorn is the commonest site. Nests near the top of isolated or small groups of tall trees are also common but the richly varied choice of nest site displayed by Manx Magpies is one of the more interesting features of the island's ornithology. Monkey puzzles have been used and, particularly in the north, low nests in willow are quite common. In treeless areas such as the Ayres nests are built in gorse bushes close to the ground, while on the coastal brooghs nests are found in low brambles and blackthorn thickets. Nests in dead bracken and long heather have also been found and Coward and Madoc found a nest on the ground at Port St Mary. On the Calf, where the majority of nests are in low brambles against stone walls, cliff nesting is not uncommon. In 1979 three of the fourteen pairs which bred on the Calf nested on maritime cliff faces and one such nest was unusually built entirely of dead bracken stems (Jennings 1984). Nests built on the Calf in brambles and on cliff ledges are sometimes of the open type, but there is also a record of Magpies building an open nest in an apple tree on the main island.

Throughout the year Magpies are seen in pairs and small parties. Between late December and the end of February flocks of 20–40 birds are quite often seen and in places where there is a rich and regular food supply such as Litts factory in East Baldwin similar gatherings occur throughout the year. Comparable parties regularly visit the Calf in autumn with 110 in a single flock on 7th November 1975. In 1976, when exceptional numbers of Jackdaws and Rooks also visited the islet, over 90 Magpies were present on 4 days between 25th October and 12th November, with a record 148 on 26th October. In early November 1984 a flock of 30–40 landed on the Chicken Rock Lighthouse.

Two hundred and four Magpies have been ringed on the Calf and these, together with the many nestlings ringed on the main island, have produced 5 recoveries, 2, 6, 15, 32 and 46 km from their place of ringing.

Manx: *Pieanat, Piannad*

Chough
Pyrrhocorax pyrrhocorax

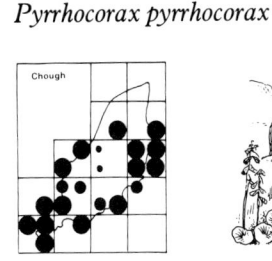

Fairly common resident.

Evidence of the Chough's long standing association with the Isle of Man comes from the Perwick Bay midden deposit dated at approximately AD90 in which skeletal remains of several individuals were identified. Strangely it receives no mention from such writers as Chaloner, Willughby and Townley, and it is Jardine (1838–43) who wrote as follows about his visit to the island in 1827: 'That part where we have seen it most abundant is in the Isle of Man, an island of considerable extent, and having precipitous coasts for at least two-thirds of its circumference. Round these shores it is so common that we once procured nearly thirty specimens in a forenoon ... During the breeding season, when we have chiefly seen these birds, we found them almost constantly on the coast near the caves and fissures where the nests were placed; and they were very seldom seen more than a quarter of a mile inland, but they made excursions so far, alighting among the rocky parts of the upland sheep pasture, and occasionally feeding and walking on the dry pasture itself, where they appeared to procure insects, their stomachs being chiefly at this time filled with coleoptera ... When the situation of the nests was approached, no great restlessness or anxiety was exhibited. They were placed in rents of the rocks, in the entrance of the caves or in overhanging ledges of rock, built much in the same manner as those of the true Crows.' Train (1845) described the Chough as very numerous on the Calf and in his first edition of *British Birds* Yarrell (1843), through J. R. Wallace a Douglas printer, described how they bred in security in the very rocky southern extremity of the Isle of Man.

There is some evidence that in the mid nineteenth century the Chough suffered a very severe decline. Philornis (1867) stated that it was formerly so abundant that its eggs were used as an article of food but had become extinct, and in his fourth edition (1876–82) Yarrell wrote 'It was formerly resident in the Isle of Man, particularly its southern part, and the rock called the Calf of Man, where it used to breed and may perhaps still do so.' While recognising a significant decline since Jardine's visit, Ralfe was aware of no significant diminution in the twenty years up to 1905 – it had disappeared from the Lonan coast and the Douglas area but maintained its stronghold in the south and west and also occurred sporadically along other parts of the rocky coast. He recorded just two flocks of 20, smaller flocks being frequently seen throughout the year. Forty years later Cowin and Megaw (1943) were able to write of an undoubted increase in the species and mentioned a recent flock of 70 on the Calf. Bracegirdle (1964) estimated the population in 1962 at over 100 pairs, yet the following year a survey yielded only 20 pairs, 6 of which were on the Calf (Rolfe 1966), although following a very severe winter Kerruish believed that the breeding population that year was nearer to 50 pairs. A careful review of breeding records during the period 1972–81 suggested a fairly stable population of 58–61 breeding pairs and the very thorough census of 1982 put the population at 49–60 pairs with a further 61–65 non-breeding birds giving a total population of 159–185 birds (Bullock et al. 1983). This survey showed that about 6% of the British and Irish breeding population is found on the Isle of Man. With six pairs in 1 sq km, the Calf had the highest breeding density in the British Isles. In summary, excluding annual fluctuations, the Chough suffered a major decline in the mid nineteenth century, partly recovering and stabilising during the final two decades. The period 1900–1940 saw a fair increase in the population which for the last 40 years has again been stable.

A commonly quoted reason for the loss of the Chough in other parts of Britain is that it has been unable to compete successfully for food and nesting-sites with the Jackdaw. There is little similarity between the surface feeding and highly omnivorous Jackdaw and the digging and probing of the Chough in search of leather-jackets and other grubs. Although their coastal habitats overlap the Chough is essentially a bird of the wilder more remote areas typified by the Calf of Man from which the Jackdaw is absent as a breeding bird. The difference in choice of nest sites of the two species was best expressed by Williamson (1959) when he wrote that the Chough's nest is 'nearly always a place more roomy and open than a Jackdaw would abide ... I cannot

38°F. Isotherm – January.    *Breeding distribution of the Chough.*

say that I have visited a Chough's nest in Man which a Jackdaw would have found it worth-while to steal.' More relevant probably was the succession of cold winters during the 19th century which would have had a much less punishing effect on the Choughs of western Britain. A glance at the January isotherms and the Chough's distribution suggests that 38°F is the minimum mean temperature acceptable to the species within the British Isles. The influence of egg-collecting and shooting must also have been important. The drastic decline of the Chough in the Isle of Man in the 19th century could be totally attributable to indiscriminate shooting of the type which Jardine so enthusiastically described, the bird's extinction only being prevented by the survival of a small population on the relatively inaccessible Calf. Manx farmers now recognise the Chough as a harmless bird with none of the less endearing habits of other corvids, but this has not always been the case – Williamson recorded three being shot when feeding in a turnip field in 1939 and a nest was destroyed by a farmer a few years later. Even now the malicious destruction of nests by vandals occurs occasionally. The Red-Legged King of Crows has long proved a popular pet and many have been removed from Manx nests for this purpose. Often, after years of high-spirited entertainment, pet Choughs have drowned. Best known was a bird hand-reared by a Ramsey fishmonger, which used to fly free in the town readily perching on strangers' shoulders. Manx Choughs have lived for up to 12 years in captivity.

Reviewing Manx breeding records from a variety of sources Bullock found that the mean clutch size was 3.39, the average number of nestlings 2.61 and the number of fledged young 1.88, but one of the present authors assessing data from 26–30 nests found comparable figures of 4.26, 3.06 and 3.15. Certainly clutches of 6 eggs are rare as are broods of 5. Most eggs are laid between mid April and mid May although three eggs which hatched in a Calf nest on 15th April 1959 must have been laid during the last few days of March. There is also a record of three immature birds with an adult on the Sugar Loaf on 7th May 1960 which would give a laying date around 13th March. Choughs are single brooded but if the first clutch is lost a replacement may be laid – sometimes in the same nest. Two young were ringed in a building on the Ayres on the late date of 12th July 1953. In 1980 a two-year old male 'helper' assisted his parents in rearing a brood on the Calf. His activities included allopreening with both pair members, accompanying them while collecting nesting material, accompanying the male during the incubation period and assisting with the feeding of the young throughout the fledging period. The helper found a mate in the autumn of 1980 and they built a nest at a new site the following spring (Jennings 1984). Bullock et al. described co-operative threesomes at 4 nests on Islay, one in Northern Ireland and at two Welsh nests. The majority of nests are coastal and are situated either in large crevices, in the cavernous recesses among elevated boulders or in caves, as so beautifully described by Ralfe: 'One nesting place is in a cave of unusual size and regularity of outline. The green brows above, on which in May the delicate lilac squill is profusely in flower, slope nearly to its roof. On either side of its entrance are cliffs almost sheer; from above it cannot directly be entered, but beyond the crags on one side is a little strand, in whose recesses fronds of maidenhair, tenderly green, are watered by the springs trickling down the fissures. From this strand, by clambering at the foot of the precipice over low rocks and little sandy patches, the cave can be reached at the ebb. At high water the tide fills its mouth and part of its interior, but never reaches the end, its utmost point being marked by the floats and broken timber which lie among the heaped up shingle, green and slippery with mould. A warm, heavy dampness pervades the air of the place; about the entrance Grey Crows build; outside on the cliff crevices afford space for the eggs of the Razorbill and the nests of the Shag; and the high shelves form roosts for the Cormorant. Rock Pipits flit above the tangle cast up on the sand; parties of Black Guillemots swim on the green water just outside the rocks. Behind the brows are cultivated fields, but their edges are waste and rough with long grass, heather and low gorse. On these grassy and earthy slopes the nests of Herring Gulls are abundant, and their clamour fills the air. In this cave the first Chough's nest I saw was placed high on a dark shelf in 1877 and the same site has been used in a later year. Later still in 1895, the cave had a nest in a fissure in the roof, some thirty feet above the water, which at high tide filled the cavern beneath.' There are very few rock arches in the Isle of Man, but the roof of such an arch is particularly favoured as a nest site. Occasionally on the coast mining relics are used. Ralfe has described a nest regularly built on the sill of a half framed window of an old mine-working on the west coast and shafts and tunnels have also been used. Choughs are well distributed along the rocky coast from Peel to Port Erin (about 18 pairs) and round to Perwick Bay, and from Santon north to Maughold. One or two pairs nest on the coast between Glen Wyllin and Peel. Between 5 and 10% of Manx Choughs nest inland, mostly in buildings up to 300 m above sea-level and 7 km from the coast. Again it is the deserted mine-workings which have provided some of the most typical sites, notably the buildings above Glen Rushen and the wheel cases in the Corrany valley and below Beinn y Phott, where in 1938 Ravens and Choughs both nested – the nest would usually be built in a first floor joist hole. In at least two localities Choughs are known to have nested below ground level in recesses in a broad vertical shaft. Elsewhere in the hills they have nested in ruined tholtans and more especially in the less dilapidated outhouses which continue to be used to shelter sheep and cattle, indeed a roof seems to make the building more attractive to the Choughs which gain access through a skylight or window. In such buildings nests have been found in upstairs fireplaces, chimneys, first floor ledges and joist holes and on projecting stones just beneath the roof. On the margin of the Ayres Choughs nested for several years on top of a pillar inside a disused military building, and a bridge on the St John's-Kirkmichael railways was also regularly tenanted. On the Calf the disused lighthouses have long provided sites in upstairs fireplaces and window ledges and they have also nested recently in an artificial nest box put up on the silo near the Observatory (Jennings 1984). There appears to be no record of Choughs nesting inland in natural sites on the Isle of Man the nearest being nests in quarries at such places as Glen Rushen, Stoney Mountain and near Laurel Bank, where Ravens, Choughs and Kestrels all nested in the same small quarry one year. A typical nest is a bulky edifice made of stems of heather and lined with sheeps wool, but if space is limited the nest may be made of wool alone. Wool is an essential constituent and Holyoak (1972) described how a pair repeatedly flew about 2 km from the Calf (where, at that time there were no sheep) to the main island to collect wool, the round trip taking between 7 and 30 minutes. The unchivalrous male, despite accompanying his mate on about a dozen trips, managed to bring back only one small bill-full of wool! The softest wool is usually selected and, at least on the Calf, rabbit fur is very frequently used to produce the warm cup so essential on cold damp cliff sites.

Describing his observations made in the late 1930s, Williamson (1959) wrote of the importance of the flock which '... remains the hub and centre of the social life of the Chough through the summer, and when feeding on the ground or flying from place to place, the members of the summer flock tend to group themselves in pairs. Periodically, on the Calf, pairs would rise together and leave this flock, flying directly towards some point on the coast, and by following up such pairs I was often able to locate their nests, though the majority of course proved inaccessible. Even when hunting alone the pair shows flock-consciousness, rising to join a small group passing overhead, or answering with their high-pitched *chee-ow* call-note the voices of distant birds.' Choughs do not breed in their first spring so it is these young birds, albeit already paired, which make up the lasting nucleus of the flock. Even in such well populated areas as the Calf and the west coast these spring and early summer flocks rarely exceed 20 birds, but with the arrival of family parties after the nesting season they increase considerably in late June and July. As already mentioned there were over 70 over the Calf on 29th July 1939 and a similar number over the Sound on 6th July 1980. Further north along the west coast there were flocks of over 60 in late June 1953 and 1979, while on the less heavily populated east coast there were 24 at Maughold in late June 1955 and 20 at Clay Head at the end of July 1981.

In winter over three quarters of the population is found to the south of a line between Peel and Douglas. Flocks of between 15 and 65 birds may be found all around the coast and more especially over the adjacent fields. Langness in particular has a regular flock which assembles in late September or early October and disperses in March. Maxima in recent years have been between 26 and 42 birds with a record 60 on 22nd October 1983. On Langness their most usual companions as they feed along the great stacks of wrack along high water mark are Rooks, while on farmland they often forage with Hooded Crows.

Shoreline feeding is largely confined to the winter, providing an abundant source of sandhoppers and other insect life when frosty weather makes the ground too hard for the probing bill. Observations on the Calf have shown that the Chough feeds particularly on the most heavily grazed areas of the old pastures and the short maritime turf. Farming on the Calf ceased in 1958 allowing bracken to spread into the old pastures and the remaining grass to grow longer. The Chough population dwindled from 10 pairs, hastened also by the severe winter of 1963, to just 4 pairs in 1967. In 1969

Loaghtan sheep were introduced and there followed a notable increase in breeding population and fledging of young (Bullock and del-Nevo 1983). Perhaps more important has been the constantly high rabbit population in recent years. Rabbits are the selective grazers responsible for the short turf in the old farm pastures. Burnt ground also provides a useful supplementary feeding area where Choughs can easily dig (Haycock and Bullock 1982). They seek a small tipulid larva which feeds on the rhizoids of the moss which is the first plant to recolonise such areas. On Langness the golf course provides a seemingly excellent feeding ground which is rarely used although Williamson mentioned how a pair visited a particular green so often and dug so zealously that the greenkeeper put up a scarecrow to discourage them. Yarrell reported Choughs following the plough in the Isle of Man. While prolonged very cold weather can seriously reduce the Chough population, so drought in May and June can affect food supply by driving the all important leather jackets deeper into the soil and out of reach of the Chough's bill.

Between 1959 and 1983 157 Choughs were ringed on the Calf producing 9 recoveries. One additional bird ringed on the main island has also been recovered. One bird was recovered 27 km from its place of ringing, the others had all moved less than 10 km. Indicative of the drastic effect of the winter of 1962–3 was the recovery of 5 birds, either dead or dying between 28th December and 23rd January.

Manx: *Caaig*

Jackdaw

Corvus monedula

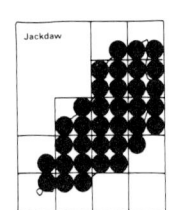

Common resident.

Jackdaw bones have been identified from the Perwick cave midden deposit dated at AD 90, yet Ralfe observed that its lack of a gaelic name might suggest that it was a late introduction to the Isle of Man. The earliest reference in the literature comes from Townley who found Jackdaws breeding on Douglas Head in 1789. Rather more than 100 years later Ralfe described it as common in towns and villages and mentioned colonies at Peel Castle and Castle Rushen. He knew of many colonies around the rocky coast and mentioned nests in the northern sand cliffs. Inland, natural breeding sites existed on the rocky slopes of the Carrick and Mount Karrin, which guard the entrance to Sulby Glen, and also a long way upstream near the headwaters of the river. It seems unlikely that there has been any significant change in numbers during the present century.

In the larger settlements they nest particularly in chimneys and to a lesser extent in holes in buildings. In more rural situations the pigeon holes which are such a feature of Manx farm and mill buildings are widely used and the long deserted farm ruins and mine buildings provide excellent nest sites in their chimneys and joist holes. The highest altitude at which Jackdaws nest on the Isle of Man is at 360 m at Brandy Cottage overlooking Druidale. Although Ralfe commented on the scarcity of nests in holes in trees, such sites are now commonly used. Around the coast they nest plentifully in holes and fissures (though not on the Calf) but they do not share the Chough's liking for caves. On the Santon coast Port Soldrick's possession of a small colony has earned it the alternative name of Jackdaw Bay. First eggs are not usually laid until the last week in April, but there is one remarkable record of two dead nestlings being picked up near Ramsey on 4th April 1929.

Throughout the year flocks of 15–30 birds are common around the coast and during winter they sometimes join other corvids on the great banks of wrack at such places as Sandwich and Port Grenaugh. Inland exclusive flocks of up to 200 Jackdaws may be found feeding in the fields, but the greatest numbers are those accompanying Rooks as they fly to roost at dusk. There is no evidence of migration to or from the Isle of Man, but the Calf witnesses small spring influxes and receives much larger flocks in autumn. Day counts of 250–500 birds are made most years during October, but the greatest numbers were in 1976 when there were 2,100 on 22nd October and 2,200 on 25th; all seem to be day-trippers.

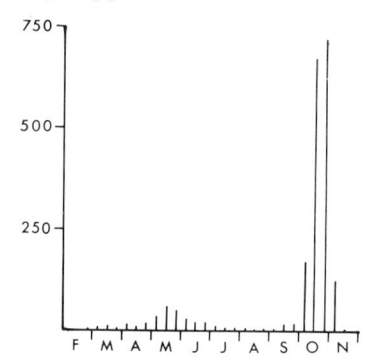

Jackdaw. Average bird days per ten day period (Calf) 1969–81.

Only 15 Jackdaws have been ringed on the Calf with one recovery and 6 other birds ringed elsewhere on the Isle of Man have also been recovered – four showed movement of less than 5 km the others 16, 21 and 23 km.

Pied birds are quite often seen and there are also records of a complete albino and of a bird of Collared Dove colouring in Douglas.

Manx: *Caaig, Juan teayst* = John Dough

Rook

Corvus frugilegus

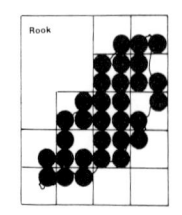

Common resident.

Writing in 1789, Townley commented on the nearly treeless state of the Isle of Man and was tempted to state that there were no Rooks, but was told that there had been a small rookery at the Nunnery which had been 'done away with.' Two years later there was a small rookery at Braddan Church (Robertson 1794), but in 1812 Quayle wrote of the scarcity of Rooks which were virtually confined to one northern estate, in all probability Ballakillingan. During the early 19th century however trees were planted with great enthusiasm and as they reached maturity the Rook population multiplied enormously so that towards the end of that century Ballachurry (Andreas) had 700 nests and 600–1,000 young Rooks were being shot annually at Ballamoar (Patrick). Ralfe listed just over 100 rookeries in 1905 but gives no clue as to the total number of nests. The population was probably declining as a result of a resolution by the Manx Agricultural Society which had debated 'The Plague of Rooks' in 1896 and recommended shooting down the nests. Shooting in Santon parish had led to the extinction of rookeries at Ballavale, Oatlands and Ballaquiggin while (for reasons unknown) the great Ballachurry colony had declined to 120 nests. During the 1914–18 War the Board of Agriculture circularised owners of rookeries urging their destruction so that by 1923 Ralfe (in an admittedly incomplete list) could only name 65 occupied sites. There were now no rookeries in either Santon, Bride or Castletown, Kirby had been deserted and 6 of the 9 rookeries in German had been deserted.

Recovery took place over the next 15 years and in 1938 and in each year between 1940 and 1945 complete (or almost complete) censuses were carried out. There were again just over 100 rookeries and a peak count of 6,526 nests (corrected to 6,696) was made in 1941. The same year a Governor's order made the shooting of Rooks by landowners compulsory and granted right of entry to any land for that purpose. Laying down of poison in the winter of 1942/3 at Ballakillingan apparently compromised a number of rookeries in that area. The anti-Rook campaign reached its peak in 1944 when several colonies were destroyed by the hoses of the fire brigade while the young were still in the nests. Public indignation resulted in the premature abandonment of the project. The 1945 census showed a 14% reduction on the 1941 nest total (Williamson and Cowin 1945).

The census of 1962 (Ladds 1963) revealed a further reduction of 4%, a remarkably small drop compared with the profound declines averaging 50% in a number of English counties over roughly the same period (Sage and Vernon 1978). This census revealed striking changes in various parts of the Island when compared with the 1938 figures. Huge increases were seen in the sheadings of Rushen (115%) and Ayre (31%) while there were notable losses in Middle (28%) and Glenfaba (27%).

The period 1962 to 1975 saw a much greater decline of 14%. The upward trends in Rushen and Ayre were comprehensively reversed and there were notable losses in Michael and Garff. A closer look at counts at individual rookeries in the south showed that the town colonies at Port St Mary, Port Erin (Bradda Glen) and Castletown had maintained their numbers very well almost certainly due to their immunity from shooting. Annual counts at many rookeries between 1976 and 1979 showed a steady overall increase which was confirmed in the full census of 1980 which once more approached the 1962 total – Middle, Glenfaba and Ayre had all prospered, while the other three sheadings showed little change.

Counts of Manx Rooks' nests giving figures corrected to allow for rookeries overlooked in earlier years and comparative index based on the 1938 count being 100

Year	Actual count	Corrected total	Index figure	Nests per sq km
1938	5,736	6,488	100.0	11.32
1940	5,368	6,156	94.8	10.74
1941	6,526	6,696	103.2	11.68
1942	6,430	6,434	99.1	11.22
1943	6,612	6,612	101.9	11.53
1944	6,259	6,259	96.5	10.92
1945	5,785	5,785	89.5	10.09
1962	5,556	5,556	85.6	9.69
1975	4,646	4,646	71.6	8.11
1980	5,229	5,385	83.0	9.39
1985	6,085	6,085	93.8	10.62

Williamson and Cowin suggested that the fluctuations in rookery sizes from year to year were closely related to the amount of late winter sunshine, while in Britain as a whole long term trends have been attributed to increased urbanisation, change in agricultural practices, destruction of nesting sites, the use of pesticides, deliberate poisoning, shooting and climatic changes. In the Isle of Man the use of toxic seed dressings may well have contributed to the losses of the 1960s, the recovery in numbers during the last decade being a result of their withdrawal. Deliberate poisoning, although seen in south Braddan as recently as 1981, must now have a negligible effect, but shooting has certainly resulted in the recent extinction of the Plantation colony at Port St Mary and Ballamillaghyn in Braddan, and has produced major losses at Lhergydhoo (German) and Braust (Andreas). Confined to widely separated individual rookeries the effect seems to be minimal – neighbouring colonies expand proportionately as has been seen in Port St Mary High Street and at Ballamona and The Groves in Braddan parish.

In Britain as a whole during the 30 years up to 1975 the large rookeries have tended to break up so that the numbers of colonies with 1–25 nests have increased at the expense of the larger ones. In the Isle of Man there was an overall increase in number of rookeries, the losses being from the 101–200 size group with increases in all the three smaller size groups. In 1980 there had been a further small increase in the total number with losses in the smallest group, further increases in the 26–100 nest groups and a small but perhaps significant increase in the larger units. With an average of 39 nests per rookery in 1975 the Isle of Man showed a striking similarity to the counties of Cumberland (42.6), Down (40.5), Armagh (39.3) and Antrim (40.1). The Isle of Man averages 8 nests/sq km, the same as Northern Ireland and very similar to Wigtown (8.4) and Dumfries (7.8). No English county except the Isle of Wight (10.3) exceeds the Manx density of nests/sq km.

Size distribution and nesting density in Manx rookeries

Year	1–25	26–50	51–100	101–200	201–300	301–400	Total nests	Total rookeries	Nests per rookery
1938	44	16	19	13	4	2	5,736	98	58.73
1940	51	14	14	20	1	1	5,368	101	53.15
1975	60	25	27	6	1	0	4,640	119	38.99
1980	50	34	30	8	2	0	5,382	124	43.40
1985	48	30	30	12	2	0	6,085	122	49.88

An annotated list of the 271 Manx rookeries known to have been occupied at some time during the last 100 years has been published in *Peregrine* (Cullen 1982). Twelve of these have on occasions held 200 or more nests:

1. *Ballachurry (Andreas)*. In the late 19th century this rookery in the grounds of one of the great farm mansions of the northern plain was credited with 700 nests. Reduced to about 120 by 1903, numbers have since varied between 100 and 173.
2. *Kirby (Braddan)*. Braddan church held a small rookery in 1791 and in 1903 the rookery at Kirby was 'reduced' and the Braddan Church colony was listed separately. Amazingly neither site was occupied in 1923 yet they combined to provide the biggest rookery in the 1938–44 surveys with over 400 nests in each of the war years. There is no longer a rookery at Braddan churchyard, but the Kirby complex is now composed of 3 colonies with an aggregate of about 130 nests.
3. *Christchurch, Laxey*. Present in 1903, this rookery in the centre of the village embracing the churchyard and electric railway station, held 173 nests by 1945, between 234 and 276 from 1975 to 1981 and 337 in 1984. During the last decade it has been comfortably the largest rookery on the island.
4. *The Nunnery (Braddan)*. Possibly the Island's first rookery, it had been in existence prior to 1789. A large rookery in 1903 and 1923 it declined from 317 nests in 1938 to 192 in 1944 and became extinct before 1968.
5. *Ballakillingan (Lezayre)*. One of the Island's oldest rookeries, perhaps the only one in 1812. It held a large rookery in 1903 and was probably the largest Manx colony in 1923. With 310 nests in 1941 Ballakillingan was second only to Kirby, but poisoning probably contributed to the decline to less than half this figure by 1944, a trend which continued to just 22 nests in 1975.

6. *Billown House (Malew)*. Another rookery in the vicinity of one of the Island's manor houses, Billown was occupied in 1903 and 1923 but was not listed in 1938–40. Nevertheless it held a considerable rookery in 1941 and reached a peak of 306 nests in 1944. Although by 1962 there had been a substantial drop to 230 nests, it was at that time the largest Manx colony. It had declined to only 69 nests by 1980.
7. *Injebreck (Braddan)*. Greatest of the hill rookeries beautifully situated in trees around a country house at the head of the West Baldwin valley. When first listed in 1923 there was a considerable colony and between 1938 and 1945 it consistently held over 200 nests with a peak of 250 in 1943. Still prospering with 65–90 nests during the last ten years.
8. *Ballamoar (Patrick)*. In the late 19th century one of the Island's largest rookeries and still held 235 nests in 1941. By 1968 there had been a massive decline and the colony has now moved to Patrick Vicarage with some overflow to Ballacosnahan. This complex is increasing and held 187 nests in 1980.
9. *Bishopscourt (Ballaugh)*. A long-established colony from before 1903 which declined from 213 nests in 1940 to 85 nests two years later. Appears to have shifted to the Bishopscourt Glen during the war, the present colony is thriving with over 100 nests divided between the glen and the house.
10. *Thornhill (Lezayre)*. Present in 1923 and holding just over 200 nests in 1940, Thornhill declined through the war years to 70 nests in 1945 and just 18 by 1968. Most of the present rookery in this residential area of Ramsey is around The Grove.
11. *Eaglehurst and Thornton (Douglas)*. A few nests appeared at Thornton a little before 1923 and during the war years these large town houses with their big gardens in west Douglas held 145–190 nests. In 1975 their combined total was barely 120 nests but has since increased to just over 200.
12. *Glen Moar, St Johns (German)*. This colony was established prior to 1938, but no count up to 1968 was over 100. By 1975 there were 143 nests, and with extension around the field to the north of the house the rookery had increased to 242 nests in 1985.

From this list it can be seen that nearly all the major rookeries have been in the grounds of mansion houses and today most of the dozen colonies with over 100 nests are so sited, but the typical Manx rookery is a collection of up to 50 nests in trees round a farm. Human habitation seems desirable, but remote sites such as Eary ny suie (Marown) and Creg y Cowin in East Baldwin continue to prosper although the farms are long deserted. At the eastern end of Lough Cranstal there is a rookery over marshland and at Port St Mary the colony in the garden of Rocklands is adjacent to High Water Mark. Approximately 82% of nests and rookeries are below 100 m above sea level and of 7 colonies at altitudes over 200 m the highest is at 260 m.

In the census of 1980 the number of nests built in each species of tree

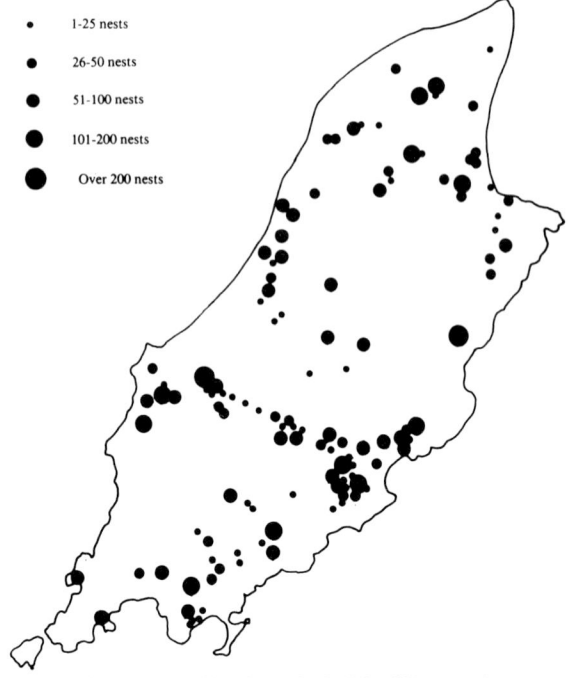

Distribution of Rookeries in the Isle of Man 1985

was counted in over 80% of cases (Cullen 1982). Thirty-three per cent of these nests were built in conifers, mostly pines, but there were also 38 nests in larches, 21 nests in a magnificent Monterey pine at Ballavale (Santon), 7 were in monkey puzzles, 20 were in cypresses and 5 were in a yew at Glen Moar (German). Glen Moar also had two nests in holly. The beech was comfortably the most popular deciduous tree, accounting for almost 28% of nests and the sycamore was also important with over 21%. Surprisingly

Number of rookeries and nests at each altitude in the Isle of Man in 1975

Altitude	No. of rookeries	No. of nests
0–25 m	24	897
26–50 m	41	1,564
51–75 m	17	825
76–100 m	15	520
101–125 m	4	176
126–150 m	6	323
151–175 m	2	11
176–200 m	3	43
201–225 m	2	57
226–250 m	4	163
251–275 m	1	65

less than 5% of nests were in elms. The oak (153 nests – 3.5%) was only of significance in Lezayre parish where it was the commonest nesting tree, accounting for 35% of nests – at Springfield near Douglas there were three nests in a Spanish oak. In spite of its abundance in the Isle of Man the ash only accounted for just over 3% of nests, while only 1.64% were in horse chestnuts. At the unusual marshland rookery at Lough Cranstal 50 nests were built in willows and occasional nests (31 in all) were in limes in various parts of the Island. Scarce nesting trees were alder (most of the 24 nests at Ballacain), silver birch (three nests at Thornton), cherry (two nests at the hill rookery at Lhergyrhenny), black poplar (2 nests at Ballakew), and the sweet chestnut which is utilised at Bishopscourt. Although there are no recent records, Rooks have nested on chimneys in the Island. This was first observed in 1890 when the rookery in the trees around Lorne House (Castletown) extended across the road and two nests were built on the chimney of Bridge House on the edge of the outer harbour. In 1904 Bridge House held 4 nests. At Folieu House (Maughold) a nest was built annually on a chimney from 1937 to 1942. By 1944 the chimney pot had been removed but the persistent birds then nested down the chimney.

The diet of the Rook makes it both a help and a hindrance to the farmer. Animal food is made up principally of the beneficial earthworm and the harmful leather jacket, while the great bulk of vegetable matter taken is grain. While much of the grain will be waste anyway, Rooks are nevertheless guilty of taking grain shortly after it is sown. They do to their credit take a relatively small amount of weed seed but can cause damage to root crops such as potatoes and turnips. They engage in street scavenging and have been seen to take peanuts suspended in red mesh bags for tits. While Rooks feed for the most part on farmland, frequenting grass and ploughed fields, fair numbers also feed along the tide line on the rich insect population of the great rolls of drying wrack.

To the Calf the Rook is a regular visitor mainly in autumn, the most being 785 on 25th October 1976. They usually fly over to the islet on fine mornings returning in the evening although small numbers have been seen flying westward towards Ireland. Ringing gives no evidence of migration but Ralfe gave instances of flocks over the Bahama light vessel in autumn and of birds coming over during the day from Ireland in early November and seeming 'much exhausted' at the Chicken Rock.

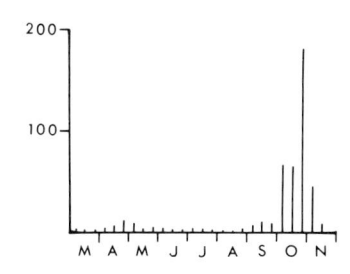

Rook. Average bird days per ten day period (Calf) 1969–81.

Albinism has been seen on a number of occasions and in the parish of Maughold a white Rook was thought to foretell a wedding.

Manx: *Trogh*

Carrion/Hooded Crow
Corvus corone

Carrion Crow
C.c. Corone

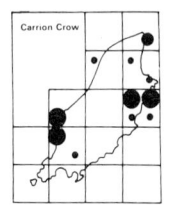

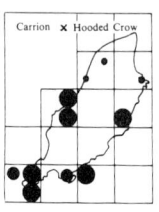

Rather uncommon resident which hybridises with the much more plentiful Hooded Crow *C.c. cornix*. Passage migrant and probable winter visitor in small numbers.

There seems little doubt that the Carrion Crow did occur in the Island during the latter half of the 19th century although by 1923 Ralfe still had no personal experience of the black subspecies. It had been seen at Park Llewellyn on the southern slopes of North Barrule and there was also an apparently reliable record of a female Carrion mated with a Hooded Crow successfully hatching eggs, but it is only since 1923 that the Carrion Crow has been recognised as a consistently resident subspecies. In that year a male Hoodie and a female Carrion nested on Peel Hill and the following year a second pair, the sexes reversed, nested there. In 1926 a mixed pair bred at Gob ny Garvain on the Maughold coast and 1929 saw the establishment of a tenancy by a mixed pair at Clay Head which was to continue for many years. Another mixed pair nested at Santon head in 1931 and Madoc implied that several pairs of Carrion Crows nested on the east coast subsequently. 1939 saw the nesting of a mixed pair in a tree at Glen Camm (German), a site which remains similarly occupied to this day. Mixed pairs have since nested at Lambhill (Bride) during the 1950s, at Langness since at least 1957 and on the Calf since 1961. More recently mixed pairs have bred at Billown Quarries, Lag ny Keeilley, Barnell and Port Soldrick. Very rarely have two Carrions nested – they did so at Ghaw Yiarn on the Calf in 1962 and in a tree near Bulgham Bay in 1981. There are three definite instances of hybrids breeding. In 1974 and 1975 two very dark hybrids nested in a Sitka spruce close to the Calf Observatory, in 1980 a hybrid paired with a Hooded Crow nested on Peel Headland and in 1983 a hybrid was found nesting with a

Carrion Crow at Eary Ween in East Baldwin. Hybrids do represent a complete range of plumage between the two subspecies and at the extremes are very difficult to identify as such. The Carrion Crow breeding population is probably between 10 and 20 individuals – hybrids number between 25 and 50. In Britain the zone of secondary hybridisation passes through Inverness and the Isle of Arran and the Isle of Man is the most southerly point where both subspecies are resident.

The Carrion Crow is most usually seen as one of a mixed pair or in a family group with hybrids, but 1983 saw flocks of 8 on the Ayres and 17 on the German coast on the same day in late December suggesting immigration. On the Calf small passage flocks pass through in autumn with a notable 12 on 10th October 1980, although the largest flock was one of 14 which flew north east on 8th April 1961.

Hooded Crow

C.c. cornix

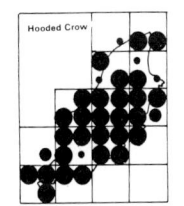

Common resident.

Described as Scarcrows in 1687 Hooded Crows were regarded as vermin and fetched one penny per head, while in 1700 Leigh wrote that Sea Crows were said to breed in the Isle of Man but were not used as food. The impression gained from several 19th century writers is that the Hooded Crow was not particularly common, but to Ralfe the Greyback was one of the Island's most characteristic birds with fair numbers breeding around the rocky coast, although it was sparingly distributed in the highlands and glens. Eighty years later it is probably rather more common and nests commonly in the towns. Ralfe had commented on how little it was persecuted and this remains strangely true in spite of the fact that it is regarded as a villain of comparable status to the Great Black-backed Gull.

The Crow's nest is like a small Raven's nest. Although some nests on the coast are on high inaccessible ledges the more usual site is in a gully and often quite near the top of the craggy rock face and easily accessible. Inland most nests are in trees although a shelf on near-vertical grassy moorland is a not infrequent site. Most clutches are of 4 eggs followed in frequency by 5, while clutches of 3 and 6 are rather rare. A Glen Auldyn nest held 4 eggs on the exceptionally early date of 5th March (1908) but eggs in early April are not common, most clutches being started in the second half of that month. A nest near the Bungalow (Snaefell) still held 4 eggs on 19th June (1942). The Calf population has gradually increased from 3 pairs in 1960 to 10–12 pairs since 1976.

Outside the breeding season flocks of up to 40 birds are quite often seen, sometimes attracted to patches of burnt heather. Larger flocks are uncommon and have tended to occur in March – there were 100 near Dalby in early spring 1964 and west coast movement of 60–80 birds has been noted several times. On the Calf visiting flocks of Hooded Crows are regular in autumn with a maximum of 70 on 13th September 1962.

There have been just 3 recoveries of ringed birds showing movement of up to 7 km. 74 have been ringed on the Calf – one being recovered when 8 years old.

Manx: *Fannag Ghlass*

Raven
Corvus corax

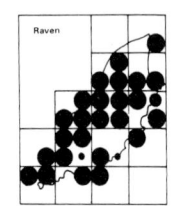

Well distributed resident.

At Andreas church Thorwald's cross-slab shows Odin with a Raven perched on his shoulder while he is devoured by the Fenris wolf at Ragnarök, the ultimate battle of Norse mythology. This remarkable 10th century slate carving is one of the earliest illustrations of a Manx bird. During the same period Ravens left their mark in Manx place names notably between Spanish Head and Black Head where the Norse name for the promontory was Krakanes. By 1511 this had become Croknesse and later Cregneash which now only survives as the name of the village. Declared a noxious bird by the law of 1687, two pence was payable for its head and the Castle Rushen papers list heads for all parishes except Ballaugh during 1689 and 1690.

In 1903 Ralfe knew of about fifteen nesting places of the Raven and possibly one of the oldest of all was on the rocky south facing slopes of Greeba. This site has the Gaelic name Edd feeagh vooar (nest of the great Raven) and is marked as such on a map dated 1870. A photograph taken in 1893, appearing in Ralfe's book, shows the nest on precisely the same ledge as is still occupied today even though it is now surrounded by a mature plantation. Ralfe knew of no other inland nests but coastal sites included the Ladder on Peel Hill, Ooig Vooar on the Patrick coast, Wallberry on the Marine Drive, Skinscoe north of Laxey and Maughold Head. Due very largely to the adoption of inland sites 33 pairs nested in 1941 (Cowin 1941) and a like number in 1977, when inland sites had increased still further at the expense of coastal sites (Cullen 1978). During the six years 1978–83 Ravens nested at 17 localities which were not occupied in 1977 and a realistic assessment of the present population would be approximately 40 pairs, the proportion of coastal to inland sites being about 3:5.

There are about 22 coastal sites which have been used by Ravens during the last ten years with probably 15–18 being used in any one year. The most densely populated stretch of coast in 1977 was between Niarbyl and Spanish Head – taking distances 'as the raven flies' there were 6 nests in a stretch of 12.5 km. Ooig Vooar is probably the only regularly tenanted site between Niarbyl and Peel, but between Peel and Ladyport there are 2–3 nests and on the east coast there are 3–4 between Maughold and Laxey, one at Groudle and up to 3 between Douglas and Santon Gorge. On Langness there is an all too accessible site on the rocks below the Herring Tower. The nest is typically built on a ledge on a slate cliff, often having a somewhat overhanging cliff face above and with a south or south-westerly aspect. Rarely does the cliff face directly out to sea but advantage is taken of indentations of the coast so that the nest overlooks the coast or even, as at Pistol Castle (Santon), looks inland. Nests at Peel Headland, the Marine Drive and Port Soldrick (Santon) are on the landward side of stacks. At Shellag nests are built on the frequently eroded Bride sand cliffs. Cliff nests are usually at a height of 10–30 m, rarely up to 65 m.

Inland the last fifty years have seen an increasing tendency to return to tree nesting. Such nests were unknown until 1932 when a pair nested in the heronry at Ballamoar (Jurby) where they sucked the eggs from seven of the eight herons' nests. Trees were later used at Ballaglass (1934), Glen Helen (1939), in the Montpelier rookery (1943), Creg y Cowin (1946) and Injebreck in 1949. During 1976 and 1977 tree nests were found at Ballamoar, Glen Helen (two pairs), Injebreck, Glen Roy, Cooil Dharry and Bishopscourt Glen and others have since been located in the Cringle Plantation, at Close Mooar (Lonan), Ballavarkish (Bride) and on Lhergy Frissel above Ramsey. In 1977 six out of 17 inland nests were in trees, now there must be nine or ten tree nests each year. Pines, firs and beeches are most often used, but nests in larch, alder and sycamore have been recorded. Nests in trees are between 3 and 15 m high, are found in woodland areas rather than isolated trees and are usually very close to a stream. Other inland nests are located in quarries or gorges almost equally and at Greeba, Ballakerka and Laxey mines are on low cliffs. They are built at heights of between 6 and 15 m. In 1977 one inland nest was at an altitude of 15 m, four were between 51 and 75 m, 11 between 120 and 230 m and one was at 290 m above sea level. Tree nests were distributed through these altitudes and accounted for both the lowest and the highest nest. Generally however there is a growing tendency to use lowland sites inland and such sites are bound to be in trees more often than not. While Ravens do use the same nest year after year, many pairs use any one of several nests close together and may use alternative sites up to 500 m away. They nearly always remain faithful to the same type of site, but in the north an alternative site to the Shellag sand cliff was in a tree just inland at Ballavarkish. Nests on buildings are very rare – the last was probably in the wheel case below Beinn y Phott in 1943. If Ravens lose their eggs a second clutch will often be laid, either in the same nest or another in the vicinity and Graves (1933) has described how Ravens on Peel Hill relined an old nest only to have it occupied by Shags – the same pair built two further nests that spring and both were taken over by Shags resulting in the Ravens' failure to breed that year. There are other instances of Shags using Ravens' nests and in the 1977 survey four former nests were then occupied by Fulmars. In 1984 Peregrines successfully nested in a Ravens' nest of considerable antiquity and Cowin described how a pair of Kestrels bred in a Ravens' nest in both 1939 and 1940. One year Ravens, Kestrels and Choughs all nested in the Vaaish Quarry near Glen Helen and in 1938 Ravens and Choughs both nested in the same wheel-case below Beinn y Phott (F. Wilkinson *pers. comm.*).

In 1976 and 1977 16 out of 25 clutches were started between 23rd February and 8th March but in 1982 14 out of 23 were started between 19th February and 5th March and of these 5 clutches were started before 23rd February (Elliot and Nuttall 1983). The earliest published Manx record is of a brood of 6 in a nest at Ballaugh on 11th March 1956 suggesting that the first egg was laid before 14th February. In recent years Baie 'n Ooig on the Calf has been consistently early, fledging young as early as 15th April in 1977 – this site has also accounted for the latest fledging date in late July 1965. Five eggs is much the commonest clutch size although as many as 7 eggs are sometimes laid.

Numbers of eggs in clutch and young in brood in 177 nests of Manx Ravens

Number of eggs/young	1	2	3	4	5	6	7	Average size	No. of nests in sample
Number of clutches	5	8	15	9	24	5	4	4.00	70
Number of broods	11	30	37	23	4	1	0	2.83	107

The Raven has long been subjected to persecution by man, partly as the target of egg collectors but more because of its reputation for taking lambs, although it is only the sickly and the dead which are at risk. Typical was the attitude of a Glen Auldyn shepherd as related by that indefatigable bird nester James Bell in 1908. '(The nest) was built on a ledge about eighteen inches wide, in a sheer part of the quarry, about fifteen feet from the top and about forty to fifty feet from the bottom. I spoke about the nest to one of the shepherds of the land adjoining, and he intimated his intention of shooting the bird while it was sitting, owing to the havoc made by the ravens during the lambing season. With a little persuasion, however, he agreed to spare them if I would take the eggs. So with the aid of a good stout rope, I secured the eggs at daybreak on 7th March, and, as requested, I threw the nest to the bottom of the quarry. Some fourteen days later the shepherd called at my office to tell me the ravens were building again in precisely the same spot, and exactly four weeks to the day of taking the first, a second clutch of five eggs was taken.' Nearly a quarter of the nests found during the census of 1941 were robbed and in 1955 the two parent birds were shot on the nest at Gob y Volley. Now happily Ravens are rarely destroyed, nor are their eggs taken. Young birds are occasionally taken to be reared as pets and easy coastal nests are a continuing temptation to stone-lobbing vandals but when man does interfere with Ravens' breeding it is usually unwittingly by quarry working or heather burning.

After the breeding season Ravens are seen in family parties and from early September occur in small flocks of up to 30 – recently a flock of 46 was seen on the Ayres heath in early November, probably attracted by the rubbish tip where smaller flocks have previously been noted. There is also a record of 40 roosting in a quarry in Patrick. On the Calf the biggest flock was one of 34 on 23rd September 1966. During winter Ravens do venture much more readily from their typical remote moorland and coastal habitat to the cultivated lowlands where their companions at the carcase of a luckless sheep are often Great Black-backed Gulls. Flocks of non-breeding Ravens are sometimes seen in March and April.

Over 200 nestlings have been ringed on the Isle of Man (but none on the Calf) and twelve have been recovered, the greatest movement being 34 km. Raven ringing demands a considerable effort and G. Elliot and M. Fitzpatrick have achieved a remarkable average of 40 pulli per annum during the period 1982–85. In the late 1940s and early 1950s R. Q. Crellin led a group which ringed up to 20 young birds annually. There is no evidence of movement to or from the adjacent islands although apparent westward passage was observed on the Calf once during April.

Manx: *Feeagh, Feeagh Vooar*

Starling

Sturnus vulgaris

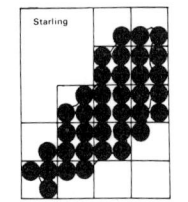

Abundant resident, passage migrant and winter visitor.

Ralfe wrote of a great increase in the Starling's abundance during the final quarter of the last century and thirty years later Madoc described a further steady increase. It is impossible to say whether this increase has continued although it is likely as other parts of western Britain have seen further increases during the last fifty years.

Strangely Ralfe described the nesting of Starlings in the cliffs of the Calf and in holes in trees and within Rooks' nests at Ballamoar as the only breeding in 'unartificial surroundings.' Now they can be found nesting in tree holes very commonly throughout the Island, while they have also colonised numerous localities on the rocky cliffs between the mouths of the Sulby and Santon Rivers and on the coast south of Peel. They also nest in the northern sand cliffs at Ballaugh. From the Calf they were absent for several years, but two pairs returned to nest in 1962 and by 1968 the population had increased to about 30 pairs, with between 15 and 50 pairs each year since. On the Calf they nest only in the cliffs. When bread is put out in the Observatory garden they tread on it as they search for leather jackets – real Starlings as they all were centuries ago! Starlings nest in good numbers in all buildings with suitable cavities whether in town or village, farm or tholtan. Altitude is no bar so long as nest sites are available. In Ramsey harbour a pair nested one year in a rectangular steel box at the end of a dredger.

Flocks form from mid July onwards and are made up predominantly of young birds, while in October and November, and again in February and March huge flocks pass through the Island. On the Calf up to 2,000 in westerly

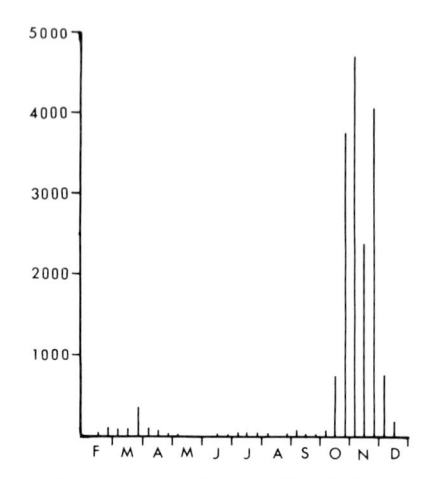

Starling. Average bird days per ten day period (Calf). Passage only 1978–81.

movement are seen each autumn with a maximum of 6,000 on 24th October 1971. The islet has smaller numbers in spring, the most being 1,000 on 22nd March 1976, but later the same year over 30,000 passed the Point of Ayre between 1100 and 1800 hours during an ESE Force 4–5 wind. In the late 1920s fair numbers of night migrants were killed at the Point of Ayre lantern – 7–14 dead were reported several times with 27 casualties on one occasion.

The winter population is considerably augmented by visitors and flocks of several hundred are often seen in low lying coastal areas such as Langness and Strandhall and on farmland at about 150 m above sea level, where their regular associates are Fieldfares and Redwings. Winter roosts which are not constant, may number several thousand.

Eight hundred and eleven Starlings were ringed on the Calf between 1959 and 1983 yielding 10 recoveries, but the main Island has provided a further 40 recoveries. Of 24 birds ringed and recovered on the Isle of Man, 22 showed movement of less than 5 km. Of the remainder one came from Co. Armagh, two from the Mull of Galloway, one from Holyhead, three from Shropshire/Worcestershire and 14 from a band of country bounded by St Bees Head and Teesmouth and by the Mersey and the Humber. The remainder came from Holland (2), Denmark, the Polish coast and southern Finland. While a proportion of Manx bred Starlings are resident others have shown movement north, south, east and west. The eastern origin of our winter visitors is obvious.

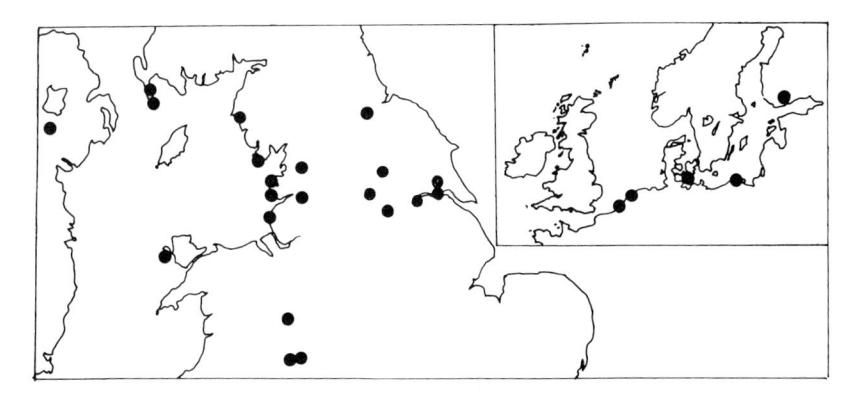

Starling ringing recoveries.

A Starling found at Andreas in late May 1914 had been ringed three months earlier at the Mull of Galloway Lighthouse and is thought to be the first ringed bird to have been recovered on the Isle of Man. Five birds have been recovered when over 6 years old, the oldest being one ringed on Langness in its first autumn and recovered in the same locality 8 years 8 months later.

Manx: *Truitlag*

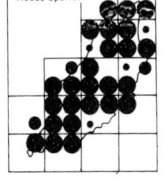

House Sparrow
Passer domesticus

Common resident.

There is no evidence of any change in the status of the House Sparrow in the last 100 years. It is principally associated with human dwellings wherein the vast majority of nests are found, though some are built in ivy, within the basement of Rooks' and Herons' nests and in bird boxes. The close association with man is well illustrated by the desertion of the Calf farm buildings when farming ceased there in 1958 since which the only nesting involved a single pair in 1971.

After the breeding season flocks gather in fields and along the hedgerows, often in association with finches. Rarely does the sparrow component of these flocks exceed fifty, 150 on Langness in late December 1978 being exceptional.

To the Calf the House Sparrow is an increasingly scarce spring and autumn visitor with maxima of 25 on three dates in October and November but not more than 5 in a day in recent years.

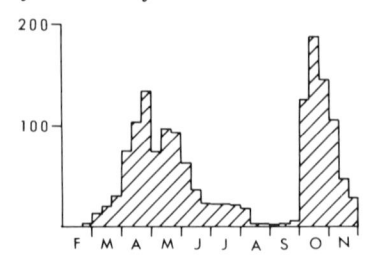

House Sparrow. Total bird days per ten day period (Calf).

Between 1959 and 1983 132 House Sparrows were ringed on the Calf with just one recovery. Ringing on the main island has however produced a further 28 recoveries showing that this is one of our most sedentary birds. Nearly all moved less than 2 km – one travelled 5 km from the Calf to Port St Mary and another 14 km from Laxey to Port Soldrick (Santon). The longest time between ringing and recovery was 5 years 10 months.

There have been a number of white House Sparrows recorded – particularly from the north – and partial albinism is relatively common.

Manx: *Jallyn*

Tree Sparrow

Passer montanus

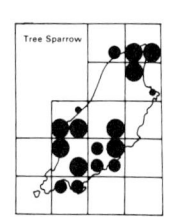

Rather scarce and locally distributed resident which may also occur as a passage migrant and winter visitor.

Either due to under-recording or to genuine scarcity Ralfe was able to give only a handful of records of the Tree Sparrow in the *Birds of the Isle of Man*, but in an addendum he described how in the summer of 1905 he and F. S. Graves located the species breeding at Scarlett quarries and at Billown lime kilns, Castletown, Strandhall, Mount Gawne, Port Grenaugh and the Calf and J. Bell had eggs from the Crossags, Ramsey in 1908 and the Dog Mills in 1910. Madoc comments on the scarcity of the Tree Sparrow in the annual bird reports of 1929, 1932 and 1934, yet in the latter year described it in his book as 'by no means uncommon,' no doubt prompted by the occurrence of a flock of over 100 present near Castletown on 4th March 1934, many staying on for up to three weeks. Tree Sparrows were resident (up to 12 birds) at the Creggans (Malew) from 1936–42 and probably nested regularly, and 2 pairs were known to breed at Sandygate (Jurby) in 1945 and 1946. For many years from 1950 they nested at Great Meadow and by 1968 it was regarded as widespread, but local in the south and centre of the island. During the last ten years probable breeding colonies have been located at Balladoole (Arbory) at several localities in the Billown/Malew Church/Great Meadow area, at Ballasalla and Silverdale and at Ballaquiggin (Santon). In the Douglas area there have been colonies at Middle Farm, Tromode falls and along the hedges at Cronk-ny-Mona, and in the Peel district at Ballelby, Barnell and East Lhergydhoo. In the north they have been found in the Dollagh/Crawyn area (Ballaugh) and in buildings near Lough Cranstal. Often breeding singly, colonies, when they occur are only of 3–5 pairs. Typical nest sites are in holes in buildings, hedges and trees, nest boxes and, at Balladoole, in the basement part of Herons' nests.

Outside the breeding season there had been occasional reports of flocks of up to 15 birds up to 1961 since which flocks have been appreciably larger and much more frequent. 1961 was a momentous year in Ireland where there was a very sudden increase in the breeding range (Ruttledge 1966) and it thus seems likely that there was a coincidental Manx Tree Sparrow explosion. Flocks of between 20 and 40 birds have been reported most winters since 1961, typically in fields of stubble or kale and usually in a specific party within a much larger flock of other seed eaters such as Linnets, Chaffinches, occasionally Bramblings or Skylarks. A flock of 61 Tree Sparrows was seen north of Derbyhaven on 26th December 1984.

On the Calf 10–30 birds are recorded on many days in spring to the end of May; the maximum spring count was 60 on 25th April 1961. Autumn visits are less constant and spread from late August to the end of October with a peak of 65 on 27th August 1981. Birds have sometimes been seen to fly west from the Calf, but the ringing of 71 Tree Sparrows there has

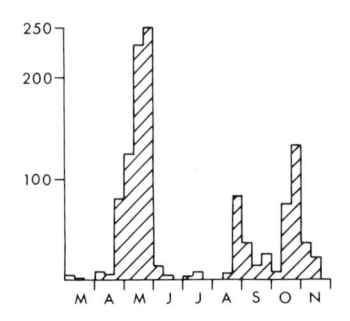

Tree Sparrow. Total bird days per ten day period (Calf).

yielded no returns and so it remains a realistic possibility that the undoubtedly increased numbers of the last twenty or so years merely reflect a much larger Manx breeding population.

Chaffinch

Fringilla coelebs

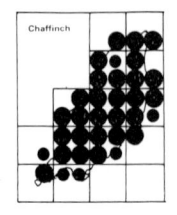

Abundant resident, passage migrant and winter visitor.

Ralfe and Kermode both regarded the Chaffinch as the most abundant of all small birds and in 1943 Williamson believed it was then the commonest Manx bird. Its breeding strength must now be well below that of the Wren and the Robin and the overall impression is one of slight decline over the last 40 years.

Irrespective of altitude, the Chaffinch breeds in all localities where there are trees or well established hedgerows. A few pairs can be found in all the wooded glens, they are abundant in the curraghs of Greeba and Ballaugh and in all the plantations particularly South Barrule, Archallagan and Cringle and are frequent inhabitants of the suburban or rural garden. In her Common Bird Census of Cooil Dharry, a wooded glen of some 14 hectares, Cain (1978) located 12–18 territories in 1975–7, while along a 4 km stretch of the River Glass from the Baldwin confluence to Quarterbridge (farmland and woodland) 20 territories were located in 1975.

Chaffinches have been seen carrying nesting material in mid February and a brood hatched on 23rd April 1883, but such early nesting is quite exceptional, most clutches being completed during the first three weeks of May. Although usually single brooded a pair successfully fledged two families on the Calf in 1982. One or two replacement clutches may be laid and on the Calf young flew from a third nest on the late date of 15th July in 1981. Four eggs are usual, but five not uncommon. Chaffinches have been found nesting on top of a palm branch. On the Calf nesting took place in 1939, 1969 and in each year since 1979, with two pairs in 1982 and 1983.

Flocks begin to form in early August, but passage (predominantly westward) does not start until late September. Large numbers pass through the Island during October and November – peak day counts in excess of 500 birds occurring on the Calf most autumns. Over 3,000 flew north across the Sound in one hour on 29th October 1946 (Dunt 1948), but the highest day total since the opening of the Calf Observatory was 2,500 on 28th October 1972. Recently on the adjacent part of the main island over 1,500 were found roosting in gorse at Cregneash on 4th October 1983.

Winter flocks of 20–150 birds are widely distributed in farmland, feeding in stubble, kale and turnip fields from December to the end of February. The Chaffinch is usually the dominant species in flocks which may include

Greenfinches, Tree Sparrows and Bramblings. Large flocks are seen most winters but the 500 birds present daily in the same stubble field at Tromode for nine weeks from mid January 1983 was unusual both for its size and its enduring loyalty to the same site.

Spring passage, if indeed it occurs at all, is negligible, the best Calf flock being only 40 on 28th March 1960.

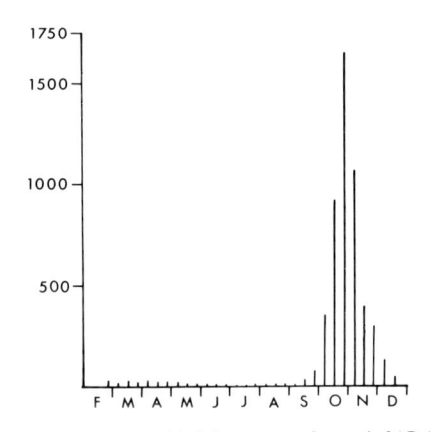

Chaffinch. Average bird days per ten day period (Calf).

One thousand six hundred and twenty-one Chaffinches ringed during the Calf Observatory's first 25 years yielded 17 recoveries and there have been a further six involving the main island. Of 11 birds recovered on the Isle of Man, ten moved less than 8 km, the other ringed on the Calf in October was picked up in Ramsey 40 km away the following March – all had been ringed between 15th April and 13th October. Six birds passing through the Island in late autumn had an association with northern Europe – Holland,

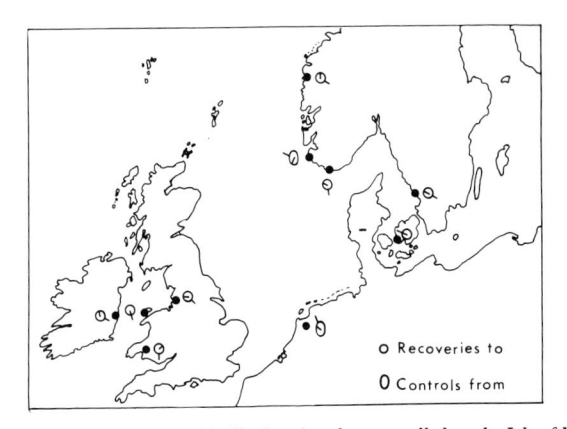

Recovery sites and origins of Chaffinches ringed or controlled on the Isle of Man.

Denmark, Sweden and Norway (3) and four other autumn birds were recovered in the British Isles in April – Dublin, Oban and Cumbria (2). One ringed in February was recovered in mid Wales in June and another present on the Calf in mid May was recovered at Holyhead almost one year later.

In 1904 an albino was included in a brood containing three normal nestlings in Ballasalla.

As well as the British form *F.c. gengleri*, the nominate race occurs in small numbers in spring and in variable numbers in late autumn.

Manx: *Ushag y Choan* = Bird of the valley, *Ushag veg vreck* = Little pied bird

Brambling

Fringilla montifringilla

Regular passage migrant. Rather scarce, but occasionally abundant winter visitor.

The Brambling has long been known as a regular winter visitor to the Island and during the last 25 years observations on the Calf have shown that a few birds also pass through on spring passage. Twice recorded in September, the earliest being two birds on 24th in 1972, the first Bramblings usually reach the Calf between 4th and 13th October. On many days only single birds will be seen, but there will usually be three or four days when 10–40 birds are present, the maximum being 60 on 6th November 1978. Movement falls away markedly after mid November. On the main island winter flocks may be present in the same area for several weeks from December to February and sometimes March. They are most often seen on stubble or ploughed fields with other seed eaters, particularly Chaffinches, and rarely exceed 40, indeed 3–10 are the most usual. There was a notable 200 near the Braaid on 13th January 1967, otherwise the only flocks in excess of 80 were in the early part of 1974 when there were unprecedented numbers on rough ploughed land to the north and west of Douglas. At Hillberry there was a steady build up from 50 on 5th January to 300 on 11th and 800 on 21st with still 100 in mid February, while to the west of Mount Rule there were 100 on the late date of 28th March. Rarely are Bramblings found feeding on beech mast in the Isle of Man, the few records coming from Kirby. The token spring passage occurs mainly in April – there have been a few May records the latest being two on the Calf on 14th May 1978 and two at Andreas on 18th May 1941.

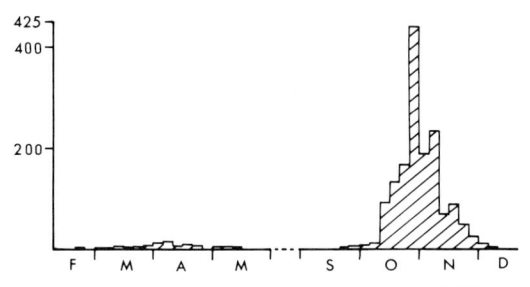

Brambling. Total bird days per five day period (Calf).

A Brambling ringed on Great Saltee (Wexford) on 9th April 1962 was controlled on the Calf two days later and another ringed in Worcestershire in mid February 1979 was found dead at Ballaoates (Braddan) – a regular Brambling site – in early December 1980.

Greenfinch
Carduelis chloris

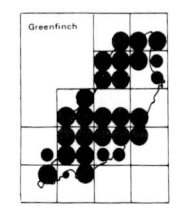

Common resident, which also occurs as a passage migrant and winter visitor.

During the last 80 years there has been no obvious change in the status of the Greenfinch. It is a resident of suburban and rural gardens, the hedgerows of cultivated land and the woodland fringe and parts of the older plantations such as South Barrule and Archallagan. Greenfinches have nested on Langness and in 1974 and 1975 a pair successfully nested in the fuchsia hedge near the Calf Observatory. Laying starts in mid April and young may still be found in the nest in early August.

From early July small flocks of up to 20 birds may be seen and with remarkable regularity a party of about 20 Greenfinches gathers on waste ground near Sandwick, perhaps eventually doubling in size and remaining through the winter until the end of February. Birds visit the Calf in increasing numbers from late September, reaching a peak at the end of October or early November – numbers are not great, the most being 160 on 2nd November 1981. On

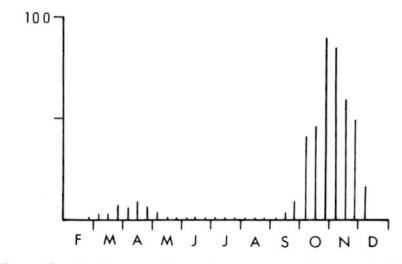

Greenfinch. Average bird days per ten day period (Calf).

the main island the largest gathering was a flock of 350 which frequented fields adjacent to the Marine Drive during the first two weeks of October 1974, and there was a comparable flock in stubble at neighbouring Nunnery Howe in early November 1941, but there is an old record of 7–800 on Langness on 19th November 1884. During the winter flocks rarely exceed 40 and may be found with other seed eaters in farmland, curragh and not infrequently along the shore line.

Five hundred and five Greenfinches were ringed on the Calf between 1959 and 1983 and to 14 recoveries can be added another 31 from the main island. Of these, all but three were recovered on the Isle of Man, most showed minimal movement, just five being recovered between 10 and 21 km from their place of ringing. There has been one recovery from Cheshire, one from Cumbria and one from County Down.

Manx: *Corkan Keylley glass*

Goldfinch

Carduelis carduelis

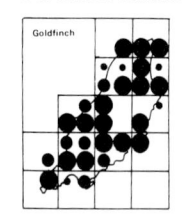

Fairly common resident – a rather variable part of the population emigrating in winter. Regular passage migrant.

About 1860 the Goldfinch was a common Manx bird, but there followed a catastrophic decline such that between 1874 and 1887 it was virtually extinct. No satisfactory explanation has been offered but both in the Isle of Man and throughout Britain (for the decline was nationwide) bird-catchers have often been blamed. There were signs of a recovery during the final decade of the 19th century although Ralfe had to wait until the spring of 1897 when a small flock near Laxey provided him with his first sight of wild Goldfinches in Man. Nesting was being reported from time to time but in his supplement of 1923 Ralfe wrote that neither in summer nor winter was it numerous and suggested that it had suffered as a result of the 'Noxious Weeds Act'. From about 1930 there were signs of increasing numbers and during the next twenty years flocks of up to 30, and occasionally as many as 50, were reported from time to time, usually in autumn. Breeding numbers remained low and although there was a record flock of over 100 at Hillberry on 1st November 1952 it was not until the 1960s that the breeding population started to increase notably, an expansion which is probably still continuing.

Quite well distributed as a breeding bird in rural gardens – especially those with orchards or other trees, lowland wooded glens and town parks, A. S.

Moore found 22–26 pairs holding territory within a 3 km radius of Peel in the summer of 1975. Of nesting trees the horse chestnut is probably the most popular and various conifers are often used. There are also records of Goldfinches nesting in cabbage palms. The breeding season is long – eggs may be found from about 22nd April and young flew from a St Judes nest on 17th September 1946 (Crellin 1947). In 1980 a pair made an unsuccessful nesting attempt near the Observatory on the Calf.

During August and September flocks, probably made up entirely of local birds and numbering as many as 60 may occupy the same area of rough lowland pasture for several weeks. Fields flanking the lower stretches of Silverburn, Glass and Neb and the Langness saltmarsh are favourite resorts. Smaller transient parties are quite widespread through October and November throughout the main island. This is the period of passage on the Calf where peak day totals of 60–70 birds are recorded in late October nearly every year. On 17th October 1975 and 6th October 1978 high counts of 100 were made, but October 1984 brought quite unprecedented Calf passage with a record 245 on 15th, 110 on 30th and again on 2nd November. In some years December flocks are quite plentiful on the main island, but more often than

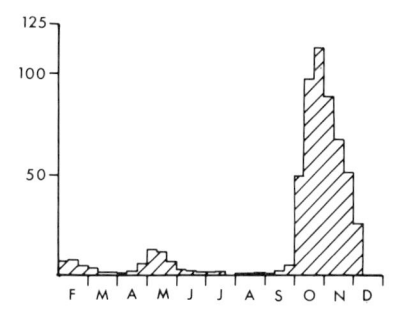

Goldfinch. Average bird days per ten day period (Calf).

not the species is absent or extremely scarce from January to March. The majority of the local population undoubtedly leaves the Isle of Man for the coldest part of the winter, but by late April the breeding localities have been reoccupied and during May minor passage is seen through the Calf although the highest day total was only 15 on 30th May 1979.

During the period 1959–83 335 Goldfinches were ringed on the Calf and these, together with birds ringed on the main island have produced 7 recoveries. One ringed as a nestling in Cumbria was controlled on the Calf in its second autumn and a juvenile ringed on the Calf on 13th October was controlled in Gironde, France 11 weeks later. The remaining five all involved the Calf and Port Erin – four being ringed and controlled during the same spring with date differences of 0, 9, 10 and 20 days.

Manx: *Lossey ny Keylley* = Flame of the woods, *Kiark my Leydee* = My lady's hen

Siskin

Carduelis spinus

Regular passage migrant and winter visitor.

Kermode and Ralfe could only quote three occurrences of the Siskin although the former considered it to be a winter migrant in small numbers. No other published records were to appear until 1928, but from then until the late 1940s there was about one record per annum. Such records were usually of 2–6 birds and parties of 20–30 were decidedly unusual. Strangely the period 1948–56 produced no records at all after which a similar pattern of records was re-established until 1972 since when Siskins have occurred on an entirely different scale. The Siskin is undoubtedly often overlooked, it is very much a bird that needs to be pursued in likely localities where alder or birch are well represented, yet the notable increase since 1972 has been seen not only on the main island, but also on the Calf where a comparable level of observation had been in operation for the previous decade. Numbers vary markedly from year to year, but every year there are reports of several small parties and the good years, with reports of flocks of 30–40 birds from more than one locality, are now quite frequent. Such years were 1972–3, 1975–6, 1980–1 and the quite exceptional autumns of 1981, 1984 and 1985. Prior to 1981 the average number of autumn bird days on the Calf had been 77 with top figures of 206 in 1975 and 299 in 1980. In 1981 there were 442 bird days and in 1984 399. The highest day total for the Calf was 70 on 5th October 1981. The late autumn of 1981 saw a notable influx in many parts of the island, but at its greatest along the River Neb above the Raggatt where there were flocks of 40 and 80 birds on 2nd November and 40 regularly over the next three weeks.

Although Siskins have been reported in all months, records between April and August are very rare and most of the main island occurrences are between October and January. A few localities are particularly favoured and include the Neb valley above and below St Johns, where the alders of Close Leece and Ballig are repeatedly visited, Tromode Dam, Cooil Dharry and Glen

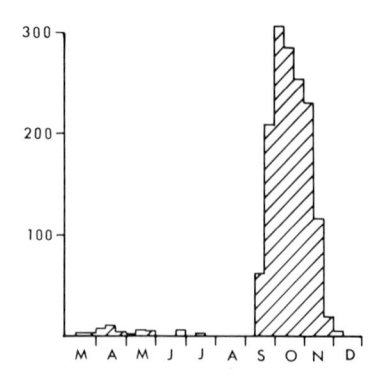

Siskin. Total bird days per ten day period (Calf).

Wyllin and the birches on the southern edge of the Greeba Plantation where they often occur with Redpolls.

Linnet
Carduelis cannabina

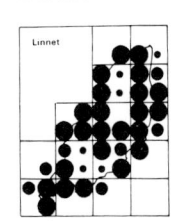

Common, and present throughout the year. Breeding population of residents and summer visitors. Also occurs as passage migrant and perhaps as a winter visitor.

Notably conspicuous to Townley (1791), the Linnet has long been one of the most characteristic birds of the island, nesting, especially near the coast, where rough land is overgrown by gorse. In winter flocks occupy ploughed land, stubble and kale fields. In all seasons it seems no more or less common than it was 80 years ago.

Four to five eggs are usual and clutches may be started as early as 19th April. The breeding season is at its height during May and June but there is a record of a clutch of 4 being started as late as 27th July. In 1940 Williamson assumed that the Linnet was resident in small numbers on the Calf, but when wardening started in 1959 there were only 2 breeding pairs. Subsequently there was a gradual increase, with occasional lean years, to an estimated 50 breeding pairs in 1982. On the Ayres Wallace (1972) found 50 territories in a Common Bird Census of 565 hectares between Blue Point and the Point of Ayre in 1965.

By mid July small parties of up to 20 birds begin to gather and in late August Langness in particular will usually have a flock of about 100 Linnets. On the Calf passage is seen from mid September into December with the highest numbers during October. Peak day counts in excess of 300 occur most years – the highest total being 560 on 13th October 1976. From January to March Linnets can be very scarce in some years, while in others this is the period wherein the biggest flocks, occasionally up to 300, occur. Winter flocks may linger in the same vicinity for several weeks and may not break up until early April. April sees rather light passage on the Calf with up to 50 birds in a day.

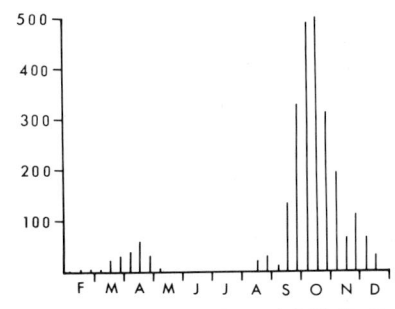

Linnet. Average bird days per ten day period (Calf). Passage only.

From 1,399 Linnets ringed on the Calf between 1959 and 1983 there have been 5 recoveries, while 34 have been retrapped in subsequent years. There have also been 5 recoveries of birds ringed on the main island. Only three Manx-ringed Linnets have been recovered elsewhere – a juvenile ringed in June was found in northern Spain in April, another ringed in July was recovered in Co. Dublin the following February and another ringed in its first October was recovered in Co. Waterford 32 days later. On the Calf one bird was retrapped five years after being ringed.

There has been one record of albinism – a bird in a flock of 20 on Langness in October 1984 was white except for a dark streak on the crown and on either side of the breast.

Manx: *Fillip ny Kempey* = Sparrow of the hemp, *Ushag y lieen* = Bird of the flax

Twite

Carduelis flavirostris

Regular but scarce passage migrant and winter visitor which was formerly resident.

Apart from the Shearwater, the Twite is the only species with the title 'Manx', Manx Linnet being a Lancashire name according to Mitchell (1892). Such a name must surely reflect at least a certain degree of former abundance, although from the two sources quoted by Ralfe it must have only bred in very small numbers in the hills during the second half of the 19th century. J. Bell had a clutch of 4 eggs from heather on the Ballaghennie Ayres in May 1908 and after a gap of almost 20 years Madoc had records of adults feeding young at a mountain location in 1927 and at Spanish Head in 1932 and 1934. A pair was seen in Lonan in mid June 1943 and in some years up to 1968 Twites were reported in July, August or September. Since then

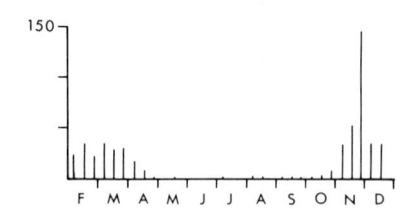

Twite. Average bird days per ten day period (Calf).

first arrivals have nearly always occurred on the Calf during the last three weeks of October and records after the middle of April are very uncommon. In 1982 two were seen on the Calf on 30th September, while in the same year there had been three on the late date of 5th May. Peak numbers are seen on the Calf during November when day counts of over 30 are not uncommon and maxima have been 85 on 22nd November 1972 and 90 on 10th

November 1976. Although the Observatory is unmanned during January and for much of December and February a flock of up to 40 is nearly always present when the warden resumes work, and is presumed to have wintered on the islet. On the main island Langness is the most favoured resort and flocks, sometimes in excess of 40 birds, are seen regularly during November and December. Twites are only very rarely reported from the main island in January, but do occur a little more often in late February and March. As a passage migrant and winter visitor the Twite appears to be entirely confined to the coast in the Isle of Man.

Redpoll
Carduelis flammea

Locally distributed summer resident and regular passage migrant. Small numbers remain through the winter in some years.

Ralfe knew very little about the status of the Redpoll and had second-hand knowledge of 2–3 pairs breeding near the Nunnery in 1892, of a party in Ballaugh Curraghs in early June 1900 and of a number definitely breeding in Barrule Plantation in 1905 – a very scanty catalogue which probably reflected little change since 1879–84 when Kermode had described it as an infrequent resident, whose numbers are increased in winter.

It is likely that the Ballaugh Curraghs, where Bell had a clutch of 5 eggs in 1911 and Madoc saw a number of nests in the 1920s and early 1930s, has annually held a small breeding population throughout this century. Numbers there have increased since about 1972 and the population estimated at 15–30 pairs in 1979. Since 1972 Redpolls have also been present at other sites, the first being the young plantation at Kionslieu which was frequented for several summers. In the summer of 1973 a pair was seen at Doarlish Cashen and a few pairs have bred variously each year since in the plantations of Slieau Mooar and Glen Rushen and in neighbouring Kerrowdhoo and Kella. In 1978 at least two pairs bred in willow scrub at Tosaby and Renshent (between St Marks and the Eairy) and in the Archallagan Plantation. In the central valley, where breeding in Greeba Curraghs was confirmed in 1977, Redpolls bred just north of Glen Vine village in 1978 and to the west may well have nested in the curragh adjoining the lower Neb above the Raggatt in 1979 and 1980. Fresh breeding sites located in 1979 were in the Conrhenny and Ballaugh plantations. Redpolls now breed in greater numbers and in more localities than at any time in the last 100 years, the population in the traditional curragh habitat having expanded notably and small colonies having appeared in the younger coniferous plantations, a trend reflecting the striking increases seen in the Common Bird Census indices in Britain as a whole since the late 1960s.

On the Calf passage occurs from late September to early November, peak day counts are between 25 and 50 most years with 60 on 27th October 1978. Small numbers pass through from mid April to the end of May – up to 1975 day totals never exceeded five, but since then spring numbers have become greater with a peak count of 17 on 24th May 1981. Outside the normal period of spring passage the cold winter produced an unprecedented movement of Mealy Redpolls *C.f. flammea* in 1979 with 28 on 22nd and 31 on 31st March.

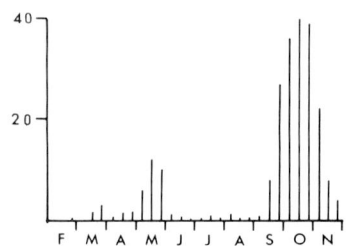

Redpoll. Average bird days per ten day period (Calf).

On the main island parties of up to 6 are sometimes seen in autumn but are rather uncommon in winter. The birchwood on the southern margin of the Greeba Plantation is one of the best places and attracted a flock of 40 Redpolls for several weeks during November 1975. One or two may overwinter in gardens and have sometimes visited bird tables.

One hundred and ninety-nine Redpolls were ringed on the Calf between 1959 and 1983 producing three recoveries – from Suffolk, Belgium (a great source of ringing recoveries from northern Britain) and the Dog Mills (Bride).

The vast majority of birds passing through the Calf belong to the race *C.f. cabaret* which breeds in the British Isles and central Europe, but there is often a good showing of the pale nominate northern European form *C.f. flammea* in autumn. A bird showing the characters of the Greenland race *C.f. rostrata* was seen on the Calf on 1st June 1972.

Manx: *Bytermmyn dhone, Lossan ruy*

Arctic Redpoll

Carduelis hornemanni

Very rare passage migrant.

An example of the Arctic Redpoll showing the characters of *C.h. exilipes* was seen feeding with six Mealy Redpolls on the seeds of stinging nettles outside the Calf of Man Observatory on 14th November 1972 (Madge 1979).

Crossbill

Loxia curvirostra

An irregular visitor in late summer, a few being seen in most irruption years.

The first Manx record was in 1889 when two were shot from a flock at Ballakillingan (Lezayre) on 28th August, and from 1890 to 1892 Crossbills were seen constantly in the Skyhill area. Irruptions to Britain took place in 1887, 1888 and 1889, that of 1888 reaching Ireland on a large scale and resulting in a notable increase in breeding involving no less than 18 counties. Although there is no evidence of breeding in the Isle of Man it is not unlikely that Crossbills did nest at Skyhill in the aftermath of these invasions. Whether a resident population remained after 1892 is not known, but a small flock was present in the same area at Ballacowle Glen from January to April 1898 and further support for breeding here came in 1901 when a supposedly immature female was found with a broken wing in mid July. This bird was kept as a pet until its death 14 years and 4 months later. The 1903 irruption produced a flock of 20 at Glen Helen in mid July and that of 1909 a party of 8–9 at Glenduff, not far from Ballakillingan in the middle of August.

Of all 20th century invasions, that of 1927 had the greatest impact on the Isle of Man. In the north a party of 16 was present at Gob y Volley on 31st July and there were a few at Lewaigue (Maughold) on 22nd August, but numbers on the Calf on 2nd August were quite unprecedented. Walking up from the Sound to the farmhouse Madoc found separate flocks of 40 and 100 along the track and adjacent moor and at the farm itself the only tree was 'full of them.' Small flocks from the irruptions of 1930, 1935 and 1938 reached the island, but coinciding with the decline in breeding population in Ireland there were no further published records of Manx Crossbills until 1952. In that year, following the occurrence of a single male at Howstrake on the unusual date of 2nd January, a party of 12 was present for two weeks at Ballagawne (Rushen) in mid July and exactly four years later the same tree at Ballagawne attracted a flock of 15–20 birds and individuals were seen at Injebreck and Ramsey later that month. Crossbills were reported from Ballagawne and the Calf in July and August 1959 but surprisingly the huge irruption into Ireland which started in June 1962 realised just three Calf records between 17th July and 8th August. 1963 saw the earliest summer record with 6 at Aust (Lezayre) on 9th June and 21 flew west over the Calf on 27th August. Crossbills have since been seen in 1966, 1972 and each year (except 1982) from 1978 to 1985. Best of these years were 1966, when they were recorded from the Calf on eight days between 21st July and 29th September, with 30 birds on the latter date and 1985 when there were 5 on 27th June, 1 on 3rd July, 8 on 26th September and records on 7 days between 7th and 22nd October, with 7 birds on 19th. The last 20 years have produced main island records from Lewaigue, Snaefell Mines, Sky Hill plantation, Cringle plantation (7 in June 1981), Arrasay Plantation and Crosby.

Scarlet Rosefinch

Carpodacus erythrinus

Vagrant.

There have been two records of adult males singing on the Calf. First was one outside the Observatory on 1st June 1969 (Wright 1973), while the other was present in the withy area from 10th to 13th June 1980. A third bird was seen on the Calf on 16th June 1985.

The breeding range of the Scarlet Rosefinch, which embraces more of the Palaearctic than any other finch, is from the shores of the Bering sea to the Baltic and has recently extended into the Scandinavian countries and in 1982 – Scotland (Mullins 1984).

Bullfinch

Pyrrhula pyrrhula

Rare visitor.

It is one of the oddities of Manx ornithology that, like the Jay, the Bullfinch is absent as a resident breeding species. In his earliest list of 1879–84 Kermode wrote that the Bullfinch was formerly not uncommon about Castletown, but during the next 100 years there were barely thirty published records and several of these, including records of nest building in the south of the Island in 1931 and 1934, are of very doubtful authenticity. There was however an exceptional collection of records towards the end of 1985 – at Port Erin a male was ringed on 12th October, followed 3 days later by a female, then on 18th November two males and three females were seen at Ballamenagh (Glen Roy) and the last few days of December saw two at Tynwald Mills, St Johns on 29th and 3 at Glen Vine on 31st. Two were shot near Ramsey in June 1885 and another in February 1899 and Madoc had occasionally seen birds at Glen Helen and near Douglas where, one summer, he watched a male collecting food for, he assumed, an unseen family.

British Bullfinches are remarkably sedentary and the autumn visits of the larger northern form hardly ever extend further south than Shetland and Fair Isle. It is likely that some Manx records refer to birds escaped from captivity, but during the last twenty years the very heavy bias towards late March and early April strongly suggests migration. There have been three Calf records between 29th March and 3rd April.

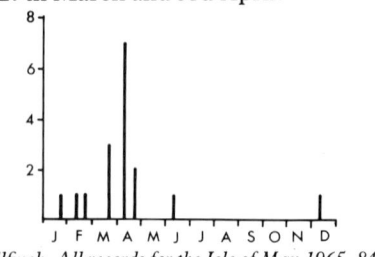

Bullfinch. All records for the Isle of Man 1965–84.

Hawfinch
Coccothraustes coccothraustes

Rare visitor.

Kermode adjudged the Hawfinch a rare and occasional winter visitor. Records for the main island are as follows: one shot near Abbeylands on 7th November 1881, one seen at Spring Valley (Douglas) on 2nd January 1897, a pair at Ballagawne (Rushen) on 23rd November 1931, a pair between Poortown and St John's on 14th February 1937 and a male and two females in the same locality on 16th December 1945 (Clementson 1947). There have since been four records from the Calf – on 14th May 1965, from 24th May to 2nd June 1967, on 6th May 1979 and on 8th November 1978.

Yellow-rumped Warbler
Dendroica coronata

Vagrant.

One was seen near the Observatory on the Calf of Man on 26th October 1976 (Haycock 1978) and another, a male, occurred on the islet on 30th May 1985. These were the sixth and tenth records for Britain and Ireland.

The Yellow-rumped Warbler, probably better known as the Myrtle Warbler, breeds in the coniferous forests of Alaska, Canada and New England and winters in the eastern and southern United States south to Panama and the West Indies.

Song Sparrow
Zonotrichia melodia

Vagrant.

A Song Sparrow was caught in the Mill Giau on the Calf on 13th May 1971 and was seen in the area several times up to 3rd June (Wright 1972). This was the 4th record for Britain and Ireland of this abundant North American species and by 1982 there had been just one further record.

Lapland Bunting

Calcarius lapponicus

Regular autumn passage migrant in very small numbers.

The Lapland Bunting was first recorded at Sandwick, Castletown Bay by Madoc on 14th November 1929 and between 1959 and 1985 there were a further 40 records from the Calf, 12 of them ocurring in 1985. All have been between 16th September and 23rd November with the great majority in the second half of this period. They have occurred in every year except one since 1970 and although single birds are the rule, there were three together on 6th November 1974.

Snow Bunting

Plectrophenax nivalis

Regular passage migrant and winter visitor in small numbers.

There has been no change in the status of the Snow Bunting during the last 100 years. On the Calf birds are regularly seen from mid October to the end of November and there is no more than a token showing in March. Birds are usually seen singly and the biggest party was only 6. On the main island Snow Buntings are seen with equal frequency from October through to the end of March. The earliest record was of 6–7 at Port St Mary on 8th September 1958 followed by a few late September records from 25th. The latest of just five April records concerned a single bird on Langness on 18th April 1957, but a male was found dying at Niarbyl on 26th May 1978.

Although Snow Buntings may occur anywhere around the coast they are commonest by far on the Ayres and at Langness. Inland they are found on the barren mountain sides from Snaefell to Keppel Gate and west as far as Injebreck, but there are no records for the Michael hills and they are scarce on the southern hills too. The greatest flock consisted of 50–60 with thrushes at the Point of Ayre on 1st October 1880, there were more than 30 on the road to the Ayres on 4th December 1974 and 24 at Ballagyr (German) on 7th March 1937. As on the Calf most Snow Buntings are seen singly but parties of 5–10 occasionally occur.

Manx: *Pompee sniaghtee*

Yellowhammer
Emberiza citrinella

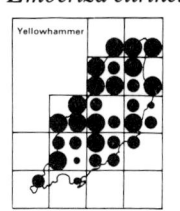

Common resident.

Ralfe considered the Yellowhammer to be the most abundant of all small birds inhabiting the hedgerows of open cultivated land. In winter he found it one of the commonest species congregating in farmyards and on the village margins while more than a century earlier Townley had seen a December flock of over 100. Its abundance continued until the late 1960s since which its range as a common breeding bird has contracted considerably. Previously plentiful over all farmland, and especially in the sheadings of Rushen and Middle it can now only be regarded as truly plentiful on the northern plain. In the parishes of Michael and German it is still well represented along a 3 km broad coastal belt and there are fair numbers along the central valley, particularly towards the west. Elsewhere it is decidedly local with 2–3 pairs at such localities as Maughold village, Agneash, the Clay Head and Begoade roads, parts of Santon parish and at Fleshwick. Its scarcity in Rushen sheading is almost unbelievable to those who recall its former abundance. The Common Bird Census of 565 hectares of the Ayres in 1965 revealed only 8 territories, but this is largely heathland bordered to the south by a thin ribbon of neglected farmland and this figure in no way reflects the population of the cultivated plain. Along the River Neb between Peel and Ballaleece, a distance of about 4 km, there were 16 territories in 1980, while in the central valley between Kerrowgarrow and Greeba there were 11 along a distance of barely 2 km. The breeding areas are occupied from March to late August. First eggs are laid from early May, but while May and June are the main breeding months, the season continues through July and August. Eggs in the latter month are not uncommon and there is even a record of a nest with two fresh eggs at Ballagawne (Rushen) on 1st September 1888. An analysis of 49 nests, mostly from Middle sheading, showed that three is the commonest clutch size, being twice as common as two and four eggs and there was only one instance of five eggs being laid.

During the winter small parties, occasionally up to 20, are sometimes seen, but in a number of years Yellowhammers have apparently been absent from October to February. There is no evidence of emigration but it is hard to find any other explanation for the notable diminution in numbers in winter. They are not common on the Calf where the spring maximum was 10 on 23rd April 1963 and the best autumn counts were only 3 on two dates in September.

Manx: *Ushag vuigh* = Yellow bird

Cirl Bunting
Emberiza cirlus

Vagrant.

The only definite record of the Cirl Bunting is of a male amongst a party of Chaffinches and Yellowhammers at Knock e Dooney (Andreas) on 12th May 1946 (Rogers 1949).

Ortolan Bunting
Emberiza hortulana

Vagrant.

The only record is of an immature bird seen in the lighthouse garden on the Calf on 20th August 1983.

Rustic Bunting
Emberiza rustica

The only Manx record is of a male trapped on the Calf on 17th May 1985.

The Rustic Bunting breeds from northern Sweden, Finland and eastward across Russia to the Bering Sea. It is a rare annual visitor to Britain in both spring and autumn.

Little Bunting
Emberiza pusilla

Vagrant.

A Little Bunting was caught in a mist net near the Observatory on the Calf on 28th October 1976 (Haycock 1978). It was a first year bird and the only Manx record of this rare visitor from north-east Europe and northern Asia which usually winters in an area from northern India to southern China.

Reed Bunting
Emberiza schoeniclus

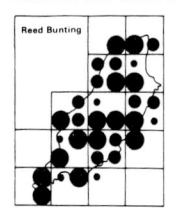

Common resident, summer visitor and passage migrant.

Although hardly abundant the Reed Bunting has increased considerably during the last 80 years. Ralfe considered it a scarce and local bird and only knew of its nesting in the Curraghs of Ballaugh, although more widely distributed in winter. During the first quarter of this century it extended its range appreciably and Madoc was able to write of its presence in all curraghs, reedy pools and marshy ground. It was probably during the 1940s that the spread into drier localities began, nests being found in several years at Howstrake (Onchan). Now, apart from the traditional wetland habitats, Reed Buntings are found all around the coast wherever there are grassy brooghs, overgrown with bracken and brambles and also close to sea level at Langness and Port Moar. In a few places in Onchan parish they share roadside hedgerows with Yellowhammers and they occupy dry habitats in the hills, including cleared areas of conifer plantation, up to about 200 m above sea level. Typical of these more elevated inland sites are Park Llewellyn (Maughold), the western slopes of Colden, the Ronague and Earystane in Arbory and the plantations of Archallagan and Conrhenny. On the Calf, where dry situations are particularly favoured (dead bracken and rank heather), Reed Buntings received no mention from Williamson in 1940 but have bred every year since the opening of the Observatory in 1959. From only 2–5 pairs in the 1960s, the next decade saw a build up to 19 pairs followed by a notable recent decline. Four to five eggs are usual and first clutches are usually laid during the middle fortnight of May.

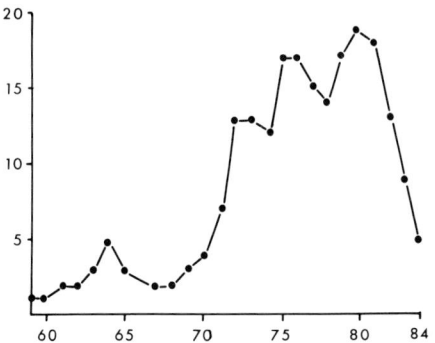

Reed Bunting. Breeding pairs on the Calf. 1959–84.

In some years Reed Buntings are absent from the end of November to mid March, in others flocks may be seen through the winter months, perhaps 10–20 strong but never approaching the 40 mentioned by Madoc. On the Calf, where the full breeding population is usually present from the second half of April, it occurs as a passage migrant in small numbers in March and April and from September to November. The best day count was 20 on 20th September 1980.

Four hundred and ninety-five birds ringed on the Calf between 1959 and 1983 two were recovered from Fleshwick and Port St Mary. In the period 1970–1984 64 out of 424 Reed Buntings ringed were retrapped, one of these being in its 7th year since ringing.

Manx: *Pompee ny Guirtlagh*

Black-headed Bunting

Emberiza melanocephala

Vagrant.

A female was seen near the Observatory on the Calf on 1st June 1978. The species breeds from Italy through Asia Minor to Iran and migrates in a south-easterly direction into India (Jennings 1981).

Corn Bunting

Miliaria calandra

Once a common breeding bird, now a very rare visitor.

The Corn Bunting declined markedly during the last quarter of the 19th century, although to Ralfe it was 'still pretty frequent' in the level northern and southern districts. It was very scarce in the Peel district, while in Lonan, where it had been abundant around 1870 and was commonly killed for the table, it was also much reduced. Early this century it was plentiful along the margins of the coast from Strandhall to Langness up to about 1942 and at Scarlett for a further four years, while in the north tenancy of the Lhen, one of the island's most regular haunts, was probably relinquished in the early 1930s. Corn Buntings were last reported from Ballaugh in 1947 and the last Manx nest was found on Jurby Airfield in 1948. For the next eight years the breeding population was probably confined to the Cranstal area in Bride and 1956 saw the end of the Corn Bunting as a Manx breeding bird. There have since been just seven records, the most recent being one singing at Port Soderick on 14th May 1976, 1 by the Millpond on the Calf on 15th May 1978 (the only record for the islet) and 1 at Fleshwick on 12th June 1983 with another record from nearby Surby 11 days later.

Although there were a few winter records, in many years Corn Buntings were absent from late October to early March. Small flocks were sometimes seen, especially in spring.

The decline of the Corn Bunting has been a feature of western Britain. In the east, where farming methods are generally more sophisticated, numbers have been well maintained and it has been suggested that the decline is associated with increased rainfall being a feature of climatic amelioration rather than any changes in agricultural practices.

A white example was shot at Orrisdale in the 19th century.

Manx: *Pompee ny Hoarn* = Bunting of the barley, *Ushag rouayr ny Hoarn* = Fat bird of the barley

Northern Oriole

Icterus galbula

Vagrant.

A first year male was trapped on the Calf on 10th October 1963 and was seen up to 15th October. At the time this was the third British record of this North American species and there have since been eleven more.

Appendix 1

Category D Species

Certain species have been placed in Category D by the British Ornithologists' Union, as there is reasonable doubt that they have ever occurred in a truly wild state in Britain.

Red-headed Bunting

Emberiza bruniceps

Escape.

At least 15 birds have been recorded on the Calf between 23rd April and 24th September. All have been males and some often lingered for a few days, one remaining there for 13 days. A Red-headed Bunting present on the Calf from 31st May to 3rd June 1978 was in all probability the same bird as was seen at Port Erin on 4th June.

Breeding in south-west and central Asia, Red-headed Buntings winter in southern India, where huge numbers are caught and exported as cage birds to Britain and the Low Countries (Ferguson-Lees 1967 and Dennis 1968). They often appear in fine anticyclonic weather which has previously been put forward in arguments over natural vagrancy, but really means there has been favourable weather to cross from Holland or Belgium where the greatest numbers are imported. They have become decidedly rare in Britain during the last few years due no doubt to more restricted importing over much of Europe.

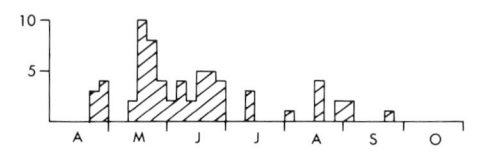

Red-headed Bunting. Total bird days per five day period (Calf).

Appendix 2

Plant species mentioned in the text

Alder *Alnus glutinosa*
Apple *Malus* spp.
Ash *Fraxinus excelsior*
Beech *Fagus sylvaticus*
Bell heather *Erica cinerea*
Bilberry *Vaccinium myrtillus*
Black poplar *Populus nigra*
Blackthorn *Prunus spinosa*
Bluebell, Wild hyacinth *Endymion non-scriptus*
Bogbean *Menyanthes trifoliata*
Bog myrtle *Myrica gale*
Bracken *Pteridium aquilinum*
Bramble *Rubus fruticosus*
Burnet rose *Rosa pimpinellifolia*
Cabbage palm *Cordyline australis*
Cherry *Prunus avium*
Chile pine, Monkey puzzle *Araucaria araucana*
Corsican pine *Pinus nigra*
Creeping willow *Salix repens*
Downy birch *Betula pubescens*
Dwarf gorse *Ulex minor*
Elm *Ulmus* spp.
Escallonia *Escallonia macrantha*
Eucalyptus *Eucalyptus gunnii*
European larch *Larix decidua*
Fir *Abies* spp.
Fuchsia *Fuchsia magellanica*
Gorse *Ulex europaeus*
Hawthorn *Crataegus monogyna*
Hazel *Corylus avellana*
Holly *Ilex aquifolium*
Honeysuckle *Lonicera periclymenum*
Horse chestnut *Aesculus hippocastanum*
Ivy *Hederea helix*
Japanese larch *Larix Kaempferi*
Khasia berry *Cotoneaster simonsii*
Lawson's cypress *Chamaecyparis lawsoniana*
Lime *Tilia* spp.
Ling, Heather *Calluna vulgaris*

Lodgepole pine *Pinus contorta*
Maidenhair fern *Adiantum capillus-veneris*
Male fern *Dryopteris filix-mas*
Marram grass *Ammophila arenaria*
Monterey pine *Pinus radiata*
Oak *Quercus robur*
Privet *Ligustrum vulgare*
Raspberry *Rubus idaeus*
Reed *Phragmites australis*
Rowan *Sorbus aucuparia*
Rush *Juncus* spp.
Scots pine *Pinus sylvestris*
Sea campion *Silene maritima*
Silver birch *Betula pendula*
Sitka spruce *Picea sitchensis*
Spanish oak *Quercus x hispanica*
Spring squill *Scilla verna*
Sweet chestnut *Castanea sativa*
Sycamore *Acer pseudoplatanus*
Thrift, Sea pink *Armeria maritima*
Water horsetail *Equisetum limosum*
Wellingtonia *Sequoiadendron giganteum*
Wild thyme *Thymus serpyllum*
Willow *Salix* spp.
Yew *Taxus baccata*
Yorkshire fog *Holcus lanatus*

Appendix 3

Complete list of Manx mammals (excluding cetaceans)

Hedgehog *Erinaceus europaeus*
Pygmy shrew *Sorex minutus*
Natterer's bat *Myotis nattereri*
Pipistrelle *Pipistrellus pipistrellus*
Common long-eared bat *Plecotus auritus*
Rabbit *Oryctolagus cuniculus*
Brown hare *Lepus capensis*
Mountain hare *Lepus timidus*
*Short-tailed vole *Microtus agrestis*
Wood mouse *Apodemus sylvaticus*
House mouse *Mus musculus*
Brown rat *Rattus norvegicus*
Stoat (*Manx* = Weasel) *Mustela erminea*
Ferret *Mustela furo*
Common Seal *Phoca vitulina*
Grey Seal *Halichoerus grypus*
Feral goat *Capra* (domestic)

*Skeletal remains found in owl pellets.

Appendix 4

Fishes mentioned in the text

Salmon *Salmo salar*
Brown Trout *Salmo trutta*
Sea Trout *Salmo trutta*
Minnow *Phoxinus phoxinus*
Eel *Anguila anguila*
Three-spined Stickleback *Gasterosteus aculeatus*
Herring *Clupea harengus*
Whiting *Merlangius merlangus*
Sand-eel *Ammodytes* spp.

Gazetteer

Place name	Grid Reference	Place name	Grid Reference
Abbeylands	370797	Ballaharra	264824
Agneash	431860	Ballajora	478905
Aldrick	176675	Ballakeigan	255685
Amulty	196716	Ballakerka, *Pl.*	387924
Andreas	413996	Ballakermeen School	372761
Anvil, The	197662	Ballakesh Ayre	433035
Archallagan, *Pl.*	302787	Ballakew	303738
Arrasy *Pl.*	250789	Ballakillingan	424945
Ashfield	389778	Ballakilmartin	405793
Aust	434968	Ballaleece	272821
Ayres	430032	Ballalough (Castletown)	260681
		Ballalough (German)	263834
Baie 'n Ooig	150660	Ballamenagh	425805
Baldrine	428814	Ballamillaghyn	356791
Baldwin, *Res.*	360835	Ballamoar (Jurby)	368979
Ballacain Dubs	359968	Ballamoar (Patrick)	250821
Ballacallin	239811	Ballamoar Reserve	251811
Ballacarrooin	405829	Ballamodha	276738
Ballachrink	312716	Ballamona Hospital	363782
Ballachurry (Andreas)	404966	Ballamona Moar	347962
Ballachurry (Rushen)	208698	Ballanard	375781
Ballacoar	420828	Ballanayre Strand	276867
Ballacoine	323885	Ballaoates	363794
Ballacorris	312741	Ballaquiggin	325717
Ballacosnahan	252818	Ballaquine	296884
Ballacreetch	376795	Ballasalla	280701
Ballacross (Andreas)	410975	Ballasteen Dub	407991
Ballacross (German)	262838	Ballaugh	348935
Ballacutchal	327751	Ballaugh Cronk	340958
Balladoole	248680	Ballaugh Curragh	365948
Ballafesson	205702	Ballaugh *Pl.*	357914
Ballafletcher	368776	Ballaughton	361761
Ballagarraghyn	292815	Ballavale	315724
Ballagarrett	429019	Ballavarkish	460007
Ballagawne	214695	Ballavarrey	406985
Ballaghaue	419994	Ballavarvane	300747
Ballaghennie Ayre	436039	Ballawhane	398012
Ballaglass Glen	465898	Ballelby	220787
Ballagyr	261848	Ballig	285824

345

Place name	Grid Reference	Place name	Grid Reference
Ballure, *Res.*	453929	Carrick Bay	226687
Ballyra	313914	Cashtal Mooar	231832
Barnell, *Res.*	251811	Cas ny Hawin	303694
Barony	468876	Castletown	264675
Barregarrow	321880	Chapel Bay	211682
Bay Fine	181679	Chasms	193663
Bay ny Carricky	226687	Chicken Rock	142639
Bay Stacka	188663	Claghbane	445933
Beary	286832	Clagh Ouyr	414889
Beary Mountain	313832	Clay Head	444804
Beckwith's Mine	253779	Clett Elby	149654
Begoade	418801	Close Lake	415958
Beinn y Phott	381860	Close Leece	266818
Billown Farm	262698	Close Moar	410855
Billown Moar/House	260696	Cluggid	393922
Billown Quarries	269701	Clypse, *Res.*	403808
Bishopscourt	328924	Coan Shellagh	216750
Bishopscourt Farm	330924	Colby	231701
Bishop's Dub	335933	Colby Glen	231709
Blaber River	318840	Colby, *R.*	231710
Black Head	187658	Colden	343843
Block Eary	390900	Colden *Pl.*	356840
Blue Point	392026	Congary	248829
Braaid	320762	Conister	388755
Bradda	192707	Conrhenny, *Pl.*	413828
Bradda Glen	193697	Contrary Head	227828
Bradda Head	182699	Cooil Dharry	319898
Braddan Church	363769	Cooilrio	417810
Brandy Cottage	345866	Cornaa	473878
Brandywell	390858	Cornaa, *R.*	450898
Braust	421003	Corrany	453898
Bride	449012	Corvalley	324771
Bride Hills	443009	Cow Harbour	166664
Bridge House	266674	Cranstal, Lough	455025
Brookdale *Pl.*	438923	Crawyn	342965
Bulgham Bay	457858	Creggans	277689
Bungalow	396867	Cregneish	189673
Burroo	158645	Creg ny baa	392819
		Creg y Cowin	378843
Caigher Point	151647	Cringle, *Pl.*	251749
Calf	158656	Crogga	335727
Calf Stack	147657	Croit e Caley	222694
Carn	192715	Cronkbourne	371775
Carnanes	207714	Cronk Fedjag (Arbory)	237750
Carraghan	368849	Cronk ny iree laa	225747
Carrick	388930	Cronk ny Mona	385792

Place name	Grid Reference	Place name	Grid Reference
Cronk y Voddy	301859	Gansey	215687
Crossags	439934	Garey	424951
Cross's Mine	261780	Garth	317774
Culbery	150651	Garwick	434815
Curragh Beg	446977	Gat y Wing	402016
		Ghaw Jeeragh	183682
Dalby	219784	Ghaw Lang	151651
Dalby Mountain	240779	Ghaw Yiarn	167655
Derby Castle	396773	Gibdale	159663
Derbyhaven	284676	Glascoe Dub	446989
Dhoo, Lough	361962	Glass, *R.*	368800
Dhoo, *R.*	350777	Glen, The	155654
Dhoon	461863	Glen Auldyn	433931
Doarlish Cashen	233784	Glen Cam	291876
Dog Mills	452978	Glenchass	199676
Dollagh Dub	348947	Glen Crammag	371875
Douglas Bay	385766	Glencrutchery	387781
Dowse	301827	Glen Drink	434862
Dreemskerry	476911	Glenduff	410942
Druidale	363883	Glenfaba	240830
Druidale Farm	368888	Glen Foss	421870
		Glen Helen	302844
Eaglehurst	372758	Glen Maye	236798
Eairnerey	206727	Glenmaye *R.*	230799
Eairy Dam	297778	Glen Mooar	302894
Eary Beg, *Pl.*	296837	Glen Roy	415838
Eary Cushlin	224757	Glen Rushen, *Pl.*	240762
Eary ny suie	339822	Glen Rushen Waterworks	247778
Earystane	230726	Glentramman	420940
Eary Ween	373837	Glen Vine	333786
East Baldwin	369825	Glen Wyllin	314902
East Lhergydhoo	272846	Gob Lhiack	347719
Elfin Glen	448932	Gob ny Creggan Glassey	297889
Ellanbane	409946	Gob ny Garvain	489899
Ellerslie	323786	Gob ny Strona	499913
Eyreton Castle	329794	Gob y Deigan	284874
		Gob y Volley	372938
Fern Glen	436927	Golf Links Hotel	292671
Fistard	200675	Government House	391781
Fleshwick	201714	Great Meadow	265688
Fold Point	167673	Greeba Curragh	305804
Folieu	466928	Greeba Mountain	317815
Fort Island	296673	Greeba *Pl.*	320812
Foxdale	278779	Groudle	420782
Foxdale Dams	294782	Grove, The	444956
Foxdale, *R.*	277800	Groves, The	351785

Place name	Grid Reference	Place name	Grid Reference
Guilcagh	395981	Lag ny Keeilley	216746
		Lambhill	453008
Harcroft	360759	Langness	287665
Harstal	216765	Laurel Bank	284835
Haunted House	285665	Laxey	433845
Herring Tower	285656	Laxey Mines	407875
Hillberry	385797	Laxey, *R.*	426855
Honey Hill	402819	Lewaigue	469921
Howstrake	405781	Lezayre	423941
		Lhen	377016
Injebreck	355849	Lhen, *R.*	396996
		Lhergydhoo	275852
Jurby Airfield	361983	Lhergy Frissel	453935
Jurby Church	349984	Lhergyrhenny	378883
Jurby East	383993	Lhiattee ny Beinnee	211728
Jurby Head	343983	Lingague	222722
		Little London	321861
Kallow Point	212671	Loch Promenade	382756
Kate's Cottage	385823	Lorne House	266676
Keilthustag	424019	Lynague	281861
Kentraugh	225691		
Keppel Gate	385823	Malew Church	268695
Kerrowdhoo, *Res.*	400803	Marine Drive	372735
Kerrowdhoo & Kella, *Pl.*	226765	Maughold Head	499913
Kerrowgarrow	293808	Middle Farm	356748
Kerrowmoar	399945	Middle, *R.*	353742
Killabregga	375908	Mill Giau	154650
Killane, *R.*	366966	Milntown	437942
King William's College	276680	Monk's Bridge	280704
Kione ny Garee	187689	Montpelier	354881
Kione ny Halbey	163651	Mooragh Lake	449952
Kione Roauyr	167656	Mount Gawne	214687
Kione y Ghoggan	199664	Mount Karrin	377919
Kionslieu Dam	289782	Mount Rule	354792
Kirby	364766		
Kirkmichael	317908	Narradale	401937
Kitterland	171665	Neb, *R.*	273820
Knockaloe	236822	Niarbyl	209775
Knock e Dooney	405023	North Barrule	442909
Knockrushen	260671	Nunnery	371753
Knocksharry	275858		
		Oatlands	325725
Ladder	233834	Oirr Vooar	151659
Ladyport	288879	Onchan	399782
Lagagh	409015	Onchan Harbour	404776
Laggan Agneash	417868	Onchan Head	402772

Place name	Grid Reference	Place name	Grid Reference
Ooig Vooar	227810	Richmond Hill	340746
Ormly Hall	447959	Rocklands	209680
Orrisdale	325930	Ronague	245725
Orrisdale Head	318928	Ronaldsway Airport	282684
		Round Table	247758
Park Llewellyn	438900	Rue Point	408034
Park ny Eairkan	414927	Rushen Abbey	278701
Patrick Vicarage	250818		
Peel	245840	St Johns	277818
Peel Castle	241846	St Judes	395967
Peel Headland	253850	St Marks	296741
Peel Hill	237839	St Maughold's Well	496919
Perwick	203673	St Michael's Isle	296673
Pistol Castle	339714	Sandwick	283673
Point of Ayre	467051	Sandygate	374974
Poortown	268831	Santon, *R.*	308734
Port Cornaa	473878	Santon Gorge	297695
Port Cranstal	468026	Santon Head	333703
Port e Chee	371769	Sartfell	333871
Port Erin	196690	Sartfield	354993
Port e Vullen	473928	Scarlett	256661
Port Grenaugh	315704	Shellag	460999
Port Jack	399773	Sharragh Vane	370897
Port Lewaigue	468930	Shenvalla	244817
Port Mooar	488910	Silverburn, *R.*	271690
Port St Mary	209675	Skerrip	454842
Port Soderick	347727	Skinscoe	450843
Port Soldrick	303696	Sky Hill	431939
Poyll Breinn	285666	Slea ny bery	184658
Poyll Dhooie	443951	Slegaby	184658
Poyllvaaish	245675	Slieau Curn	342906
Pulpit	197662	Slieau Dhoo	352894
Pulrose	365754	Slieau Earystane	236732
		Slieau Freoghane	341883
Quarterbridge	367762	Slieau Lhean	426877
		Slieau Moar, *Pl.*	233762
Raby	236802	Slieau Ouyr	437879
Raclay	204718	Slieau Ree	379824
Raggatt	244829	Slieau Ruy	328824
Ramsey	452943	Slieau Whallian	264804
Ravensdale	351919	Sloc	214734
Regaby	431975	Smeale	419021
Renshent	296770	Snaefell	398881
Rheast	358868	Snaefell Mines	407875
Rhenab	465889	Sound	172664
Rhenass	313857	South Barrule	257759

Place name	Grid Reference	Place name	Grid Reference
South Barrule, *Pl.*	274763	Tholt y Will	378897
South Harbour	159648	Tholt y Will *Pl.*	370897
Spaldrick	194696	Thornhill	443957
Spanish Head	179659	Thornton	372756
Spooyt Vane	308886	Tosaby	295761
Springfield	358758	Traie Dullish	236840
Snuff-the-Wind	261780	Traie Lagagh	227811
Staward	386943	Traie Vane	215771
Stoney Mountain	283764	Tromode	372777
Strandhall	238687	Tromode Dam	372783
Strang	361782		
Stroin Vuigh	212741	Union Mills	353778
Strooan Calmane	381742		
Sugar Loaf	194662	Vaaish	292840
Sulby	388947		
Sulby Glen	382915	Wallberry	370734
Sulby *Res.*	372888	Wart's Bank	182638
Sulby, *R.*	384920	West Baldwin	353812
Surby	206704	Whing	360731
		White Strand	267856
Thalloo Queen	457881	Wigeon Pool	291683
Thistle Head	233838	Will's Strand	269860

Pl. = *Plantation*
R. = *River*
Res. = *Reservoir*

Bibliography

The most important sources of records, without which the Systematic List could not have been prepared, are the Manx Bird Reports (under a variety of titles) and the Calf of Man Bird Observatory Annual Reports. No acknowledgement is made in the text, but details are as follows.

Manx Ornithological Notes
1905–08 in *British Birds*, P. G. Ralfe
1909–12 in *British Birds*, P. G. Ralfe and F. S. Graves
1912–28 in *British Birds*, P. G. Ralfe

Report of Bird Migration
1925–27 as Manx Museum Pamphlets, P. G. Ralfe

Ornithology of the Isle of Man
1928–34 in *North Western Naturalist*, P. G. Ralfe
1935 in *North Western Naturalist*, H. W. Madoc
1936 in *North Western Naturalist*, H. M. Rogers
1937 in *North Western Naturalist*, F. A. Craine
1938 as Manx Museum Pamphlet, F. A. Craine
1939–45 in *North Western Naturalist*, H. M. Rogers
1946–47 as Manx Museum Pamphlet, H. M. Rogers

Manx Ornithological Notes
1948 in *Peregrine*, H. M. Rogers
1949–56 in *Peregrine*, W. S. Cowin
1957–63 in *Peregrine*, P. R. Foulkes-Roberts
1964–67 in *Peregrine*, E. D. Kerruish
1972 in *Peregrine*, J. P. Cullen

The Manx Bird Report
1973–81 in *Peregrine*, J. P. Cullen
1982 in *Peregrine*, J. P. Cullen and A. S. Moore
1983 in *Peregrine*, A. S. Moore
1984 in *Peregrine*, A. S. Moore and J. P. Cullen

Calf of Man Report
1959–60 in *Proc. I.O.M.N.H. and A.S.*, E. Brun
1961 in *Proc. I.O.M.N.H. and A. S.*, P. R. Evans and G. D. Craine
1962–63 in *Proc. I.O.M.N.H. and A.S.*, A. H. Morley

The Calf of Man Bird Observatory Annual Report
1964 (Wardens: A. H. Morley & R. Rayment), G. D. Craine
1965, P. Bennett
1966–67 (1966 Warden: P. Bennett), M. Alexander
1968–74, R. M. Wright
1975–77, R. J. Haycock
1978–81, P. P. Jennings
1982–83, A. del-Nevo
1984–85, D. Walker

Statistical data have also been extracted from the following reports without acknowledgement.

Bird population changes for the years 1962–82 (providing the Common Birds Census indices) produced by L. A. Batten and J. H. Marchant with P. A. Hyde and K. Taylor and published in *Bird Study*.

Bardsey Ringing Reports for the years 1976–82 produced by P. Roberts and 1983 by J. Phillips and V. Wood, published in the *Bardsey Observatory Reports*.

References to Ralfe and Madoc without qualification relate to the following important works:

Madoc, H. W. (1934) *Bird-life in the Isle of Man*, London.
Ralfe, P. G. (1905) *The Birds of the Isle of Man*, Edinburgh.
Ralfe, P. G. (1924) *Supplementary notes to 'The Birds of the Isle of Man'*, Edinburgh.

Other references

Alexander, W. B. (1945–7) The Woodcock in the British Isles. *Ibis* 87: 512–550; 88: 1–24, 159–179, 271–286, 427–444; 89: 1–2.
Bell, J. (1908) Bird-nesting in the Isle of Man. *Proc. I.O.M. Nat. Hist. Ant. Soc.* 1: 455–461.
Bell, T. H. (1962) *The Birds of Cheshire*, Altrincham.
Birch, J. W. (1964) *The Isle of Man. A Study in economic geography*. Cambridge.
Blundell, W. (1648–56) *A History of the Isle of Man*. Manuscript. Manx Society 25 (Pub. 1876).
Bourne, A. G. (1956) The Breeding distribution and population of the Alcidae in the south-west of the Isle of Man. *Peregrine* 2.4: 2–5.
Bourne, A. G. (1957) Further observations on the distribution of the Alcidae in the south-west of the Isle of Man. *Peregrine* 2.5: 29–36.
Bracegirdle, R. C. (1963) The Greater Spotted Woodpecker in Man. *Peregrine* 3.4: 123–126.
Bracegirdle, R. C. (1964) The Chough. *J. Manx Mus.* 6.80: 194–196.
Bullock, I. D. and del-Nevo, A. (1983) The Choughs of the Calf. *Peregrine* 5.5: 226–229.
Bullock, I. D., Drewett, D. R. and Mickleburgh, S. P. (1983) The Chough in Britain and Ireland. *Brit. Birds* 76: 377–401.
Bullock, I. D., Drewett, D. R. and Mickleburgh, S. P. (1983) The Chough on the Isle of Man. *Peregrine* 5.5: 229–237.

Bunn, D. S., Warburton, A. B. and Wilson, R. D. S. (1982) *The Barn Owl*, Calton.
Butler, L. (1978) *A Guide to Rushen Abbey*.
Cadman, H. (1898) *Harry Druidale. Fisherman from Manxland to England*. London.
Cain, F. J. (1978) Common Bird Census in Cooil Dharry. *Peregrine* 4.6: 281–282.
Camden, W. (1586) *Britannia*. London.
Chaloner, J. (1656) *A Short Treatise of the Isle of Man*. London.
Clementson, G. (1941) Wild Geese in Man. *Yn Shirragh ny Ree (Peregrine)* 1: 7–8.
Clementson, G. (1947) The Hawfinch in the Isle of Man. *Peregrine* 1.4: 24–25.
Clementson, G. (1948) The Little Auk. *Peregrine* 1.5: 23–24.
Corlett, T. E. (1957) Red-breasted Flycatcher in the Isle of Man. *Peregrine* 2.5: 3.
Cornwallis, R. K. and Townsend, A. D. (1968) Waxwings in Britain and Europe during 1965/66. *Brit. Birds*. 61: 97–118.
Cowin, W. S. (1935–56) Diaries – unpublished.
Cowin, W. S. (1938) Blackbird laying four times in year and feeding young while laying again. *Brit. Birds*.
Cowin, W. S. (1941) A census of Breeding Ravens. *Peregrine* 1: 3–6.
Cowin, W. S. (1948) The Waxwing Invasion during the winter of 1946–47. *Peregrine* 1.5: 16–17.
Cowin, W. S. (1956) Roseate Terns in the Isle of Man. *Peregrine* 2.4: 1.
Cowin, W. S. and Megaw, B. R. S. (1943) The Red-legged 'King of Crows' *J. Manx Mus.* 5.69: 121–122.
Cowin, W. S. and Rogers, H. M. (1945). Ravens nesting in a Rookery. *Brit. Birds* 38: 53.
Craine, G. D. (1962) Tawny Owl and Red-backed Shrike on the Calf. *Peregrine* 3.3: 98.
Cramp, S., Bourne, W. R. P. and Saunders, D. (1974) *The Seabirds of Britain and Ireland*. London.
Creer, M. (1952) Unusual site of Swallow's nest. *Peregrine* 2.1: 23.
Crellin, J. C. (1952) Kittiwakes at Maughold Head. *Peregrine* 2.1: 18–19
Crellin, J. C. (1960) Kite (*Milvus milvus*) – a new Manx bird. *Peregrine* 3.2: 39.
Crellin, R. Q. and G. F. (1944) The Barn Owl as a Resident in the Isle of Man. *Peregrine* 1.2: 17–18.
Crellin, R. Q. and G. F. (1947) Sparrowhawk capturing bat. *Peregrine* 1.4: 25.
Crellin, R. Q. and G. F. (1947) Cave-nesting Swallows. *Peregrine* 1.4: 25.
Crellin, R. Q. and G. F. (1947) Late nest of a Goldfinch. *Peregrine* 1.4: 28.
Crellin, R. Q. and G. F. (1948) Some Birds of Maughold Head. *Peregrine* 1.5: 2–5.
Cullen, J. P. (1977) First record of Temminck's Stint in the Isle of Man. *Peregrine* 4.5: 236.
Cullen, J. P. (1978) A Census of Breeding Ravens in the Isle of Man. *Peregrine* 4.6: 264–273.
Cullen, J. P. (1979). Alpine Swifts at Maughold Head. *Peregrine* 5.1: 31–32.
Cullen, J. P. (1980) A Review of the Status of Terns in the Isle of Man. *Peregrine* 5.2: 68–73.
Cullen, J. P. (1981) A Long-billed Dowitcher on Langness. *Peregrine* 5.3: 120–122.
Cullen, J. P. (1982) Tree Selection in Manx Rookeries. *Peregrine* 5.4: 165–166.
Cullen, J. P. (1982) The Rookeries of the Isle of Man. *Peregrine* 5.4: 168–193.
Cullen, J. P. (1984) Nesting of the Common Gull in a Manx gravel pit. *Peregrine* 5.6: 284.
Cullen, J. P. (1985) Manx Rookeries in 1985. *Peregrine* 6.1: 36–41.
Cullen, J. P. (1985) The Little Egret – a new Manx bird. *Peregrine* 6.1: 60.
Cullen, J. P. (1985) The first Manx nest of the Red-breasted Merganser. *Peregrine* 6.1: 35.

del-Nevo, (1983) White-throated Robin. *Calf of Man Bird Observatory Annual Report for 1983* 75–77.

Dennis, R. H. (1968) Red-headed Buntings on Fair Isle during 1950–67. *Brit. Birds* 61: 41–43.

Dennis, R. H. (1979) *Scottish Bird Report 1978* 13.

Denton, T. (1681) Description of the Isle of Man and its Customs. Manuscript. *Yn Lioar Manninagh.* 3: 435–444.

Dunt, R. H. (1948) North-west movement of Chaffinches in Autumn. *Peregrine* 1.5: 11.

Elliot, G. and Nuttall, J. (1983) A Survey of Ravens in the Isle of Man. *Peregrine* 5.5: 238–239.

Feltham, J. (1798) A Tour through the Isle of Man in 1797–98.

Ferguson-Lees, I. J. (1967) Red-headed Buntings in Britain and Ireland. *Brit. Birds* 60: 345–346.

Fisher, J. (1952) A history of the Fulmar *Fulmarus* and its population problems. *Ibis* 94: 334–354.

Fisher, J. (1966) The Fulmar population of Britain and Ireland, 1959. *Bird Study* 13: 5–76.

Fisher, J. (1966) *The Shell Bird Book*. London.

Fitzpatrick, M. (1980) Bird Ringing in the Dog Mills Lough and Ballaugh Curraghs. *Peregrine* 5.2: 66–67.

Fitzpatrick, M. (1980) First breeding of the Tufted Duck in the Isle of Man. *Peregrine* 5.2: 73.

Foulkes-Roberts, P. R. (1949) Late breeding of Barn Owls. *Peregrine* 1.6: 16.

Foulkes-Roberts, P. R. and Williamson, K. (1963). The Great Spotted Cuckoo, a new Manx bird. *Peregrine* 3.4: 132.

Garrad, L. S. (1972) *The Naturalist in the Isle of Man*. Newton Abbot.

Garrad, L. S. et al. (1972) *Industrial Archaeology of the Isle of Man*. Newton Abbot.

Garrad, L. S. (1972) Bird remains, including those of a Great Auk *Alca impennis*, from a midden deposit in a cave at Perwick Bay, Isle of Man. *Ibis* 114.2: 258–259.

Gawne, J. (1944) A Memory of the Great Auk? *Peregrine* 1.2: 4.

Gill, J. J. (1944) The Breeding of the Wood Warbler in Man. *Peregrine* 1.2: 9–11.

Glasman, M. C. (1945) Notes on the Swallow. *Peregrine* 1.3: 9–11.

Glasman, M. C and M. (1944) The Failure of the Terneries, 1943. *Peregrine* 1.2: 15–16.

Graves, F. S. (1933). An unfortunate pair of Ravens. *N.W. Nat.* 9.2: 152.

Haycock, R. J. (1974) Prey taken by Short-eared Owls on the Calf of Man. *Calf of Man Bird Observatory Annual Report for 1974*. 68–79.

Haycock, R. J. (1977) Recoveries of Shags ringed on the Calf of Man. *Calf of Man Bird Observatory Annual Report for 1977*. 26–32.

Haycock, R. J. (1978) Recent additions to the Manx Bird List from the Calf of Man. *Peregrine* 4.6: 275–280.

Haycock, R. J. and Bullock, I. D. (1982) The Chough attracted to burnt areas for food. *Brit. Birds.* 75: 91–92.

Holyoak, D. (1972) Behaviour and ecology of the Chough and the Alpine Chough. *Bird Study*. 19: 215–227.

Hudson, R. (1973) *Early and late dates of Summer migrants*. B.T.O. Guide No. 15.

Isle of Man Board of Agriculture and Fisheries. *Reports on the Agricultural Returns*.

Jardine, Sir W. (1838–43). *Birds of Great Britain and Ireland*.

Jennings, P. P. (1981). Recent additions to the Manx Bird List from the Calf of Man and Further Records of some Scarce Migrants. *Peregrine*. 5.3: 114–119.

Jennings, P. P. (1983). Peregrine prey on the Calf of Man. *Peregrine* 5.5: 240.

Jennings, P. P. (1984). An instance of co-operative breeding in the Chough. *Peregrine* 5.6: 282.
Jennings, P. P. (1984). Unusual nest of Magpie. *Peregrine* 5.6: 283.
Kalchreuter, H. (1982). *The Woodcock.* Mainz.
Kermode, P. M. C. (1888). List of Birds of the Isle of Man. *Trans. I.O.M. Nat. Hist. and Antiq. Soc.* 1: 15–23
Kermode, P. M. C. (1901) List of Birds of the Isle of Man, with notes. *Yn Lioar Manninagh.* 3: 516–543.
Kinvig, R. H. (1975) *The Isle of Man. A social, cultural and political history.* Liverpool.
Kneen, J. J. (1925) *The Place-names of the Isle of Man.* Douglas.
Ladds, E. F. (1948) The First Nesting of the Black-headed Gull. *Peregrine* 1.5: 22–23.
Ladds, E. F. (1963) A Rookery Census in 1962. *Peregrine* 3.4: 127–128.
Leigh, C. (1700) *The natural history of Lancashire, Cheshire and the Peak, in Derbyshire.* Oxford.
McIntyre, J. et al. (1978) Nesting of the Hen Harrier in the Isle of Man. *Peregrine* 4.6: 283–284.
Macpherson, H. A. and Duckworth, W. (1886) *The Birds of Cumberland.* Carlisle.
Madge, S. C. (1979). Arctic Redpoll on the Calf of Man: First Manx Record. *Peregrine* 5.1: 33–34.
Magee, J. D. (1965). The breeding distribution of the Stonechat in Britain and the causes of its decline. *Bird Study* 12: 83–89.
Mainland, J. W. (1955). Green Woodpecker on the Chicken's Rock. *Peregrine* 2.3: 1.
Marshall, P. R. (1979). A Crane at Scarlett. *Peregrine* 5.1: 33.
Marstrander, C. J. S. (1932). Det Norske landnåm på Man. *Norske Tidsskrift for Sprogvidenskap.* 6 (English summary 333–355). Oslo.
Megaw, B. R. S. (1941). New Facts about the Manx 'Puffins'. *J. Manx Mus.* 5.65: 50.
Mitchell, F. S. (1892). The Birds of Lancashire.
Moore, A. S. (1985). The Fulmar in the Isle of Man 1927–84. *Peregrine* 6.1: 47–59.
Moore, A. S. (1985). The Chough in the Isle of Man in 1984. *Peregrine* 6.1: 43–45.
Moreau, R. E. (1951) The British status of the Quail and some problems of its biology. *Brit. Birds* 44: 257–276.
Morgan, R. A. and Glue D. E. (1977) Breeding, Mortality and Movements of Kingfishers. *Bird Study.* 24: 15–24.
Moss, R. J. (1949) An Unrecorded Kittiwake Colony. *Peregrine* 1.6: 23.
Moss R. J. (1953) Sabine's Gull in the Isle of Man. *Peregrine* 2.2: 2.
Mullins, J. R. (1984) Scarlet Rosefinch breeding in Scotland. *Brit. Birds* 77: 133–135.
Nuttall, J. (1981) An Analysis of Long-eared Owl pellets. *Peregrine* 5.3: 122.
Preston, K. (1979) Twenty-sixth Irish Bird Report 1978. *Irish Birds* 1: 417.
Preston, K. (1980) Twenty-seventh Irish Bird Report 1979. *Irish Birds* 1: 556.
Preston, K. (1982) Twenty-ninth Irish Bird Report 1981. *Irish Birds* 2: 223.
Quayle, T. (1812) *A General View of the Agriculture of the Isle of Man.* London.
Ralfe, P. G. (1934) Notes on the Bird Life of the Calf of Man. *Proc. I.O.M. Nat. Hist. Antiq. Soc.* 3: 514–519.
Ray, J. (1678) *The Ornithology of Francis Willughby.* London.
Riddiford, N. and Findley, P. (1981) *Seasonal Movements of Summer Migrants.* Tring.
Robertson, D. (1794) *A Tour through the Isle of Man.* London.
Rogers, H. M. (1949) The Cirl Bunting. *Peregrine* 1.6: 6.
Rolfe, R. (1966) Status of the Chough in the British Isles. *Bird Study* 13: 221–226.
Ruttledge, R. F. (1966) *Ireland's Birds.* London.
Sacheverell, W. (1702) *An Account of the Isle of Man.* London.

Sage, B. L. and Vernon, J. D. R. (1978) The 1975 National Survey of Rookeries. *Bird Study*. 25: 64–86.

Sayle, A. J. (1980) Wren feeding juvenile Blue Tit. *Peregrine* 5.2: 74.

Sharrock, J. T. R. (1976) *The Atlas of Breeding Birds in Britain and Ireland*. Berkhamstead.

Slinn, D. J. (1957) The Breeding Status of the Great Black-backed Gull in the Isle of Man. *Peregrine* 2.5: 4–13.

Slinn, D. J. (1959) Breeding Population of the Great Black-backed Gull in Man in 1957. *Peregrine* 3.1: 3–7.

Slinn, D. J. (1960) The Kittiwake in the Isle of Man. *Peregrine* 3.2: 58–62.

Slinn, D. J. (1962) The Fulmar in the Isle of Man. *Peregrine* 3.3: 81–92.

Slinn, D. J. (1969) Sea Birds in the Isle of Man. *J. Manx Mus*. 7: 108–112.

Slinn, D. J. (1971) The Numbers of Seabirds Breeding in the Isle of Man during 1969–70. *Proc. I.O.M. Nat. Hist. and Antiq. Soc*. 7: 419–439.

Smith, R. E. (1974) Autumn Territories of Robins on the Calf of Man. *The Calf of Man Bird Observatory Annual Report for 1973*. 58–67.

Smith, R. E. (1976) Robin Territories on the Calf of Man in Autumn 1974. *The Calf of Man Bird Observatory Annual Report for 1975*. 89–97.

Smith, R. E. (1977) Robin Territories on the Calf of Man in Autumn 1975. *The Calf of Man Bird Observatory Annual Report for 1976*. 97–101.

Snow, D. W. (1968) Movement and mortality among British Kestrels. *Falco tinnunculus. Bird Study* 15.2: 65–83.

Southern, H. N. (1939) The status and problem of the bridled Guillemot. *Proc. Zool. Soc. Lond*. 109: 31–41.

Stevenson, J. M. (1941) An old record of the Roller. *Yn Shirragh ny Ree*. 1.1: 28.

Townley, R. (1792) *A Journal kept in the Isle of Man*. Whitehaven.

Train, J. (1845) *An Historical and Statistical Account of the Isle of Man*. Douglas.

Ussher, R. J. and Warren, R. (1900) *The Birds of Ireland*. London.

Waldron, G. (1744) *A Description of the Isle of Man*. London.

Watson, P. S. (1981) Seabird observations from commercial trawlers in the Irish Sea. *Brit. Birds*. 74: 82–90.

Williamson, K. (1938) Suspected polygamy in the Redshank. *Brit. Birds*. 32: 120–121.

Williamson, K. (1939) The Birds of the Ayrelands. *J. Manx Mus*. 4: 74–76.

Williamson, K. (1939) A Manx Record of the extinct Great Auk. *J. Manx Mus*. 4:168–172.

Williamson, K. (1940) Numbers of Black Redstarts on passage in Man. *Brit. Birds* 33: 252–254.

Williamson, K. (1940) The Puffins of the Calf Isle. *J. Manx Mus*. 4.63: 203–205.

Williamson, K. (1941) The Barnacles and Claiks of the Calf. *J. Manx Mus*. 5.64: 19–20.

Williamson, K. (1941) Ornithology of the Calf of Man. *Proc. I.O.M. Nat. Hist. Antiq. Soc*. 7: 419–439.

Williamson, K. (1944) Historical Records of the Peregrine Falcon. *Peregrine* 1.2: 1–4.

Williamson, K. (1944) Peregrines feeding on rabbits. *Peregrine* 1.2: 28.

Williamson, K. (1947) The West Coast Movements of the Black Redstart. *Peregrine* 1.4: 1–6.

Williamson, K. (1948) Lapwing Habitats in the Isle of Man. *Peregrine*. 1.5: 7–10.

Williamson, K. (1959) Observations on the Chough. *Peregrine* 3.1: 8–14.

Williamson, K. (1959) An invasion of tits on the Calf of Man. *Peregrine* 3.1: 22.

Williamson, K. (1960) Taxonomic notes on some birds in the Manx Museum. *Peregrine* 3.2: 55.

Williamson, K. (1962) Long-tailed Skua at Douglas. *Peregrine* 3.3: 97.
Williamson, K. (1973) The antiquity of the Calf of Man Manx Shearwater colony. *Bird Study* 20: 310–311.
Williamson, K. and Cowin W. S. (1945) The Nature of the Rookery. *Peregrine* 1.3: 12–19.
Wilson, Bishop Thomas (1722) History of the Isle of Man Camden's *Britannia* 2nd Ed.
Winstanley, D., Spencer, R. and Williamson, K. (1974) Where have all the Whitethroats gone? *Bird Study* 21: 1–14.
Wood, G. W. (1917) Manx Falcons at the Coronation. *Mannin* 9: 525–529.
Wright, M. (1972) Song Sparrow on the Calf of Man. *The Calf of Man Bird Observatory Annual Report for 1971.* 74–76.
Wright, M. (1973) Island. *Birdwatchers' Year.* Berkhamstead.
Wright, M. (1975) Buff-breasted Sandpiper on the Calf of Man. *Peregrine* 4.3: 236.
Wright, M. (1977) Marsh Warbler on the Calf of Man. *Peregrine* 4.5: 233–235.
Yarrell, W. (1871) *British Birds.* 4th Ed. London.

Index of English and scientific names of birds

Accipiter gentilis 99
  nisus 100
Acrocephalus palustris 259
  schoenobaenus 257
  scirpaceus 259
Actitis hypoleucos 149
Aegithalos caudatus 284
Alauda arvensis 211
Alca torda 180
Alcedo atthis 206
Alectorix rufa 111
Alle alle 187
Alopochen aegyptiacus 78
Anas acuta 85
  clypeata 86
  crecca 82
  penelope 80
  platyrhynchos 83
  querquedula 86
  strepera 81
Anser albifrons 75
  anser 75
  brachyrhynchus 75
  fabalis 75
Anthus campestris 218
  novaeseelandiae 217
  pratensis 219
  spinoletta 221
  trivialis 218
Apus apus 205
  melba 206
Aquila chrysaetos 102
Ardea cinerea 70
Arenaria interpres 151
Asio flammeus 202
  otus 201
Athene noctua 200
Auk, Great 183
  Little 187
Aythya ferina 88
  fuligula 89
  marila 89
  nyroca 88

Bittern 69
  Little 69
Blackbird 245
Blackcap 266
Bluethroat 233
Bombycilla garrulus 226
Botaurus stellaris 69
Brambling 320
Branta bernicla 77
  canadensis 76
  leucopsis 77
Bucephala clangula 93
Bullfinch 330
Bunting
  Black-headed 336
  Cirl 334
  Corn 336
  Lapland 332
  Little 334
  Ortolan 334
  Red-headed 339
  Reed 335
  Rustic 334
  Snow 332
Buteo buteo 101
  lagopus 102
Buzzard 101
  Honey 96
  Rough-legged 102

Calcarius lapponicus 332
Calidris alba 129
  alpina 133
  canutus 128
  ferruginea 130
  maritima 131
  minuta 130
  temminckii 130
Calonectris diomedea 57
Caprimulgus europaeus 204
Carduelis cannabina 325
  carduelis 322
  chloris 321

flammea 327
flavirostris 326
hornemanni 328
spinus 324
Carpodacus erythrinus 330
Cepphus grylle 184
Certhia familiaris 290
Chaffinch 318
Charadrius alexandrinus 124
  dubius 122
  hiaticula 123
  morinellus 124
Chiffchaff 271
Chlidonias niger 177
Chough 295
Cinclus cinclus 227
Circus aeruginosus 97
  cyaneus 98
Clamator glandarius 197
Clangula hyemalis 91
Coccothraustes coccothraustes 331
Columba livia 190
  oenas 192
  palumbus 193
Coot 119
Coracias garrulus 207
Cormorant 64
Corncrake 116
Corvus corax 310
  corone 308
  frugilegus 302
  monedula 300
Coturnix coturnix 113
Crake, Baillon's 116
  Spotted 115
Crane 120
Crex crex 116
Crossbill 329
Crow, Carrion 308
  Hooded 309
Cuckoo 197
  Great Spotted 197
Cuculus canorus 197
Curlew 143
Cygnus columbianus 73
  cygnus 74
  olor 72

Delichon urbica 216
Dendrocopos major 209
Dendroica coronata 331

Dipper 227
Diver, Black-throated 52
  Great Northern 52
  Red-throated 51
Dotterel 124
Dove, Collared 195
  Rock 190
  Stock 192
  Turtle 196
Dowitcher, Long-billed 138
Duck, Ferruginous 88
  Long-tailed 91
  Tufted 89
Dunlin 133
Dunnock 230

Eagle, Golden 102
  White-tailed 96
Egret, Little 69
Egretta garzetta 69
Eider 90
Emberiza bruniceps 339
  cirlus 334
  citrinella 333
  hortulana 334
  melanocephala 336
  pusilla 334
  rustica 334
  schoeniclus 335
Eremophila alpestris 212
Erithacus rubecula 231

Falco columbarius 106
  peregrinus 108
  rusticolus 108
  subbuteo 107
  tinnunculus 104
  vespertinus 106
Falcon, Gyr, *see* Gyrfalcon
  Red-footed 106
Ficedula hypoleuca 283
  parva 283
Fieldfare 248
Firecrest 279
Flycatcher, Pied 283
  Red-breasted 283
  Spotted 280
Fratercula arctica 188
Fringilla coelebs 318
  montifringilla 320
Fulica atra 119
Fulmar 55

Fulmarus glacialis 55

Gadwall 81
Gallinago gallinago 136
  media 138
Gallinula chloropus 118
Gannet 63
Garganey 86
Garrulus glandarius 293
Gavia arctica 52
  immer 52
  stellata 51
Godwit, Bar-tailed 141
  Black-tailed 140
Goldcrest 276
Goldeneye 93
Goldfinch 322
Goosander 95
Goose, Barnacle 77
  Bean 75
  Brent 77
  Canada 76
  Egyptian 78
  Greylag 75
  Pink-footed 75
  White-fronted 75
Goshawk 99
Grebe, Black-necked 55
  Great Crested 54
  Little 53
  Red-necked 54
  Slavonian 54
Greenfinch 321
Greenshank 147
Grouse, Black 111
  Red 110
Grus grus 120
Guillemot 177
  Black 184
Gull
  Black-headed 156
  Common 158
  Glaucous 164
  Great Black-backed 165
  Herring 161
  Iceland 164
  Lesser Black-backed 159
  Little 155
  Mediterranean 155
  Sabine's 156
Gyrfalcon 108

Haematopus ostralegus 120
Haliaeetus albicilla 96
Harrier, Hen 98
  Marsh 97
Hawfinch 331
Hawk, Sparrow, *see* Sparrowhawk
Heron, Grey 70
Hippolais icterina 259
  polyglotta 259
Hirundo rustica 214
Hobby 107
Hoopoe 208
Hydrobates pelagicus 61

Icterus galbula 337
Irania gutturalis 233
Ixobrychus minutus 69

Jackdaw 300
Jay 293
Jynx torquilla 208

Kestrel 104
Kingfisher 206
Kite, Black 96
  Red 96
Kittiwake 167
Knot 128

Lagopus lagopus 110
Lanius collurio 292
  excubitor 292
  senator 292
Lapwing 127
Lark, Shore 211
  Sky, *see* Skylark
  Wood, *see* Woodlark
Larus argentatus 161
  canus 158
  fuscus 159
  glaucoides 164
  hyperboreus 164
  marinus 165
  melanocephalus 155
  minutus 155
  ridibundus 156
  sabini 156
Limnodromus scolopaceus 138
Limosa lapponica 141
  limosa 140
Linnet 325
Locustella naevia 256

Loxia curvirostra 329
Lullula arborea 210
Luscinia megarhynchos 232
   svecica 233
Lymnocryptes minimus 136

Magpie 293
Mallard 83
Martin, House 216
  Sand 212
Melanitta fusca 92
   nigra 91
Merganser, Red-breasted 94
Mergus albellus 94
   merganser 95
   serrator 94
Merlin 106
Miliaria calandra 336
Milvus migrans 96
   milvus 96
Moorhen 118
Motacilla alba 224
   cinerea 223
   flava 222
Muscicapa striata 280

Nightingale 232
Nightjar 204
Numenius arquata 143
   phaeopus 142
Nuthatch 290
Nyctea scandiaca 200

Oceanodroma leucorhoa 62
Oenanthe hispanica 243
   oenanthe 241
Oriole, Golden 291
  Northern 337
Oriolus oriolus 291
Osprey 103
Otus scops 200
Ouzel, Ring 244
Owl, Barn 198
  Little 200
  Long-eared 201
  Scops 200
  Short-eared 202
  Snowy 200
  Tawny 200
Oystercatcher 120

Pandion haliaetus 103

Parakeet, Rose-ringed 197
Partridge, Grey 112
  Red-legged 111
Parus ater 286
   caeruleus 287
   major 289
   palustris 286
Passer domesticus 315
   montanus 316
Perdix perdix 112
Peregrine 108
Pernis apivorus 96
Petrel, Leach's 62
  Storm 61
Phalacrocorax aristotelis 66
   carbo 64
Phalarope, Grey 152
  Red-necked 152
Phalaropus fulicarius 152
   lobatus 152
Phasianus colchicus 114
Pheasant 114
Philomachus pugnax 135
Phoenicurus ochruros 233
   phoenicurus 235
Phylloscopus collybita 271
   fuscatus 269
   inornatus 269
   proregulus 269
   sibilatrix 270
   trochiloides 268
   trochilus 274
Pica pica 293
Picus viridis 209
Pigeon, Feral 190
Pinguinus impennis 183
Pintail 85
Pipit, Meadow 219
  Richard's 217
  Rock 221
  Tawny 218
  Tree 218
  Water 221
Platalea leucorodia 72
Plectrophenax nivalis 332
Plover, Golden 124
  Grey 126
  Kentish 124
  Little Ringed 122
  Ringed 123
Pluvialis apricaria 124
   squatarola 126

Pochard 88
Podiceps auritus 54
  cristatus 54
  grisegena 54
  nigricollis 55
Porzana porzana 115
  pusilla 116
Prunella modularis 230
Psittacula krameri 197
Puffin 188
Puffinus gravis 57
  griseus 58
  puffinus 58
Pyrrhocorax pyrrhocorax 295
Pyrrhula pyrrhula 330

Quail 113

Rail, Water 114
Rallus aquaticus 114
Raven 310
Razorbill 180
Redpoll 327
  Arctic 328
Redshank 145
  Spotted 145
Redstart 235
  Black 233
Redwing 252
Regulus ignicapillus 279
  regulus 276
Riparia riparia 212
Rissa tridactyla 167
Robin 231
  White-throated 233
Roller 207
Rook 302
Rosefinch, Scarlet 330
Ruff 135

Sanderling 129
Sandgrouse, Pallas's 190
Sandpiper, Buff-breasted 135
  Common 149
  Curlew 130
  Green 148
  Purple 131
  Wood 148
Saxicola rubetra 237
  torquata 239
Scaup 89
Scolopax rusticola 139

Scoter, Common 91
  Velvet 92
Shag 66
Shearwater, Cory's 57
  Great 57
  Manx 58
  Sooty 58
Shelduck 78
Shoveler 86
Shrike, Great Grey 292
  Red-backed 292
  Woodchat 292
Siskin 324
Sitta europaea 290
Skua, Arctic 153
  Great 154
  Long-tailed 154
  Pomarine 152
Skylark 211
Smew 94
Snipe 136
  Great 138
  Jack 136
Somateria mollissima 90
Sparrow, House 315
  Song 331
  Tree 316
Sparrowhawk 100
Spoonbill 72
Starling 313
Stercorarius longicaudus 154
  parasiticus 153
  pomarinus 152
  skua 154
Sterna albifrons 176
  anaethetus 175
  dougallii 173
  hirundo 173
  paradisaea 174
  sandvicensis 171
Stint, Little 130
  Temminck's 130
Stonechat 239
Streptopelia decaocto 194
  turtur 196
Strix aluco 200
Sturnus vulgaris 313
Sula bassana 63
Swallow 214
Swan, Bewick's 73
  Mute 72
  Whooper 74

Swift 205
  Alpine 206
Sylvia atricapilla 266
  borin 264
  cantillans 260
  communis 262
  curruca 261
  nisoria 260
Syrrhaptes paradoxus 190

Tachybaptus ruficollis 53
Tadorna tadorna 78
Teal 82
Tern, Arctic 174
  Black 177
  Bridled 175
  Common 173
  Little 176
  Roseate 173
  Sandwich 171
Tetrao tetrix 111
Thrush, Mistle 254
  Song 250
Tit, Blue 287
  Coal 286
  Great 289
  Long-tailed 284
  Marsh 286
Treecreeper 290
Tringa erythropus 145
  flavipes 148
  glareola 148
  nebularia 147
  ochropus 148
  totanus 145
Troglodytes troglodytes 228
Tryngites subruficollis 135
Turdus iliacus 252
  merula 245
  philomelos 250
  pilaris 248
  torquatus 244
  viscivorus 254
Turnstone 151
Twite 326
Tyto alba 198

Upupa epops 208
Uria aalge 177

Vanellus vanellus 127

Wagtail, Grey 223
  Pied 224
  Yellow 222
Warbler
  Barred 260
  Dusky 269
  Garden 264
  Grasshopper 256
  Greenish 268
  Icterine 259
  Marsh 259
  Melodious 259
  Pallas's 269
  Reed 259
  Sedge 257
  Subalpine 260
  Willow 274
  Wood 270
  Yellow-browed 269
  Yellow-rumped 331
Waxwing 226
Wheatear 241
  Black-eared 243
Whimbrel 142
Whinchat 237
Whitethroat 262
  Lesser 261
Wigeon 80
Woodcock 139
Woodlark 210
Woodpecker, Great Spotted 209
  Green 209
Woodpigeon 193
Wren 228
Wryneck 208

Yellowhammer 333
Yellowlegs, Lesser 148

Zonotrichia melodia 331